POETRY FOCUS

2011 LEAVING CERTIFICATE POEMS AND NOTES FOR ENGLISH HIGHER LEVEL

Martin Kieran and Frances Rocks

GILL & MACMILLAN

Gill & Macmillan Ltd
Hume Avenue
Park West
Dublin 12
with associated companies throughout the world
www.gillmacmillan.ie

© Martin Kieran and Frances Rocks, 2009
978 07171 4562 1

Design by Liz White Designs
Print origination in Ireland by O'K Graphic Design, Dublin

The paper used in this book is made from the wood pulp of managed forests. For every tree felled, at least one tree is planted, thereby renewing natural resources.

All rights reserved.
No part of this publication may be copied, reproduced or transmitted in any form or by any means without written permission of the publishers or else under the terms of any licence permitting limited copying issued by the Irish Copyright Licensing Agency.

PICTURE CREDITS

For permission to reproduce photographs the author and publisher gratefully acknowledge the following:

ALAMY: 5, 32, 26, 36, 41, 64, 94, 98, 113, 118, 123, 127, 133, 137, 145, 150, 172, 181, 186, 195, 203, 207, 220, 224, 237, 243, 252, 256, 305, 309, 313, 321, 331, 336, 344, 368, 383, 399, 411; THE ART ARCHIVE: 356; BRIDGEMAN: 46, 68, 217, 317, 326; COLLINS PHOTOS: 1; CORBIS: 14; GETTY: 60, 199, 231, 363, 378, 394; IMAGEFILE: 9, 23, 73, 77, 81, 86, 90, 142, 168, 177, 190, 260, 358, 389, 414; KOBAL: 248; MARY EVANS PICTURE LIBRARY: 58; PA PHOTOS: 276; PD SMITH: 406; SCOTT HAYES/ ST PATRICK'S CATHEDRAL: 403; TOPFOTO: 18, 109, 154, 165, 301, 372.

ACKNOWLEDGMENTS

The author and publisher are grateful to the following for permission to reproduce copyrighted material:

The poems by Eavan Boland are reproduced by kind permission of Carcanet Press Limited; 'The Tuft of Flowers', 'Mending Wall', 'After Apple-Picking', 'The Road Not Taken', 'Birches', 'Out-Out-', 'Spring Pools', 'Acquainted with the Night', 'Design' and 'Provide, Provide' from *The Poetry of Robert Frost* edited by Edward Connery Lathem. Copyright 1916, 1928, 1930, 1934, 1939, 1969 by Henry Holt and Company, copyright 1936, 1944, 1951, 1956, 1958 by Robert Frost, copyright 1964, 1967 by Lesley Frost Ballantine; The poems by Patrick Kavanagh are reprinted from *Collected Poems*, edited by Antoinette Quinn (Allen Lane, 2004), by kind permission of the Trustees of the Estate of the late Katherine B. Kavanagh, through the Jonathan Williams Literary Agency; 'The Uncle Speaks in the Drawing Room', 'Our Whole Life', from *Collected Early Poems 1950-1980* by Adrienne Rich. Copyright © 1993 by Adrienne Rich. Copyright © 1967, 1963, 1962, 1961, 1960, 1959, 1958, 1957, 1956, 1955, 1954, 1953, 1952, 1951 by Adrienne Rich. Copyright © 1984, 1975, 1971, 1969. 1966 by W.W. Norton & Company, Inc. Used by permission of the author and W.W. Norton & Company, Inc. 'Aunt Jennifer's Tigers', 'Storm Warnings', 'Living in Sin', 'The Roofwalker', 'Trying to Talk with a Man', 'Diving into the Wreck', 'From a Survivor', 'Power', from *The Fact of a Doorframe: Selected Poems 1950-2001* by Adrienne Rich. Copyright © 2002 by Adrienne Rich. Copyright © 2001, 1999, 1995, 1991, 1989, 1986, 1984, 1981, 1967, 1963, 1962, 1961, 1960, 1959, 1958, 1957, 1956, 1955, 1954, 1953, 1952, 1951 by Adrienne Rich. Copyright © 1978, 1975, 1973, 1971, 1969, 1966 by W.W. Norton & Company, Inc. Used by permission of author and W.W. Norton & Company, Inc.; The poems by W.B. Yeats are reproduced by kind permission of A P Watt on behalf of Gráinne Yeats.

The author and publisher have made every effort to trace all copyright holders, but if any has been inadvertently overlooked we would be pleased to make the necessary arrangement at the first opportunity.

CONTENTS

INTRODUCTION — vi

Eavan Boland

The War Horse	4
Child of Our Time	9
The Famine Road	13
The Shadow Doll	18
White Hawthorn in the West of Ireland	22
Outside History	26
The Black Lace Fan my Mother Gave me	31
This Moment	36
The Pomegranate	40
Love	45
Leaving Cert Sample Essay	51

Emily Dickinson

'Hope' is the thing with feathers	60
There's a certain Slant of light	64
I felt a Funeral, in my Brain	68
A Bird came down the Walk	73
I Heard a Fly buzz—when I died	77
The Soul has Bandaged moments	81
I could bring You Jewels—had I a mind to	86
A narrow Fellow in the Grass	90
I taste a liquor never brewed	94
After great pain, a formal feeling comes	98
Leaving Cert Sample Essay	102

Robert Frost

The Tuft of Flowers	112
Mending Wall	117
After Apple-Picking	122
The Road Not Taken	127
Birches	132
'Out, Out—'	137

Contents

Spring Pools	142
Acquainted with the Night	145
Design	150
Provide, Provide	154
Leaving Cert Sample Essay	159

Gerard Manley Hopkins

God's Grandeur	168
Spring	172
As kingfishers catch fire, dragonflies draw flame	177
The Windhover	181
Pied Beauty	186
Felix Randal	190
Inversnaid	195
I wake and feel the fell of dark, not day	199
No worst, there is none	203
Thou art indeed just, Lord, if I contend	207
Leaving Cert Sample Essay	211

Patrick Kavanagh

Inniskeen Road: July Evening	220
Shancoduff	224
from The Great Hunger	229
Advent	237
A Christmas Childhood	242
Epic	248
Canal Bank Walk	252
Lines Written on a Seat on the Grand Canal, Dublin	256
The Hospital	260
On Raglan Road	264
Leaving Cert Sample Essay	269

Adrienne Rich

Aunt Jennifer's Tigers	277
The Uncle Speaks in the Drawing Room	279
Power	281
Storm Warnings	283
Living in Sin	285

The Roofwalker	287
Our Whole Life	289
Trying to Talk with a Man	291
Diving into the Wreck	293
From a Survivor	297
Sample Leaving Cert Questions on Rich's Poetry	299

William Wordsworth

To My Sister	304
A slumber did my spirit seal	309
She dwelt among the untrodden ways	313
Composed Upon Westminster Bridge	317
It is a beauteous evening, calm and free	321
The Solitary Reaper	325
from The Prelude: The Stolen Boat	330
from The Prelude: Skating	335
Tintern Abbey	340
Leaving Cert Sample Essay	349

William Butler Yeats

The Lake Isle of Innisfree	358
September 1913	362
The Wild Swans at Coole	367
An Irish Airman Foresees his Death	372
Easter, 1916	376
The Second Coming	383
Sailing to Byzantium	388
from Meditations in Time of Civil War VI: The Stare's Nest by my Window	394
In Memory of Eva Gore-Booth and Con Markiewicz	398
Swift's Epitaph	403
An Acre of Grass	406
from Under Ben Bulben	410
Politics	414
Leaving Cert Sample Essay	417

GLOSSARY OF COMMON LITERARY TERMS	423

Introduction

Poetry Focus is a new, modern poetry textbook for Leaving Certificate Higher Level English. It includes all the prescribed poems for 2011 as well as succinct commentaries on each one. In addition, there are sample student paragraphs on each poem, sample question plans and full graded sample essays. Well-organised and easily accessible study notes provide all the necessary information to allow students to explore the poems and to develop their own individual responses.

- **Explorations** (a series of short questions) follow the text of each poem. These allow students to make initial responses before any in-depth study or analysis. Exploration questions provide a good opportunity for written and/or oral exercises.
- **Study notes** highlight the main features of the poet's subject matter and style. These discussion notes will enhance the student's own critical appreciation through focused group work and/or written exercises. Analytical skills are developed in a coherent, practical way to give students confidence in articulating their own personal responses to the poems and poets.
- **Graded sample paragraphs** aid students in fluently structuring and developing valid points and in using relevant quotations and reference in support.
- **Key quotes** encourage students to select their own individual combination of references from a poem and to write brief commentaries on specific quotations.
- **Sample essay plans** on each poet's work illustrate how to interpret a question and recognise the particular nuances of key words in examination questions. Evaluation of these essay plans increases student confidence in working out clear responses for themselves.
- **There is no single 'correct' approach** to answering the poetry question. Candidates are free to respond in any appropriate way that shows good knowledge of and engagement with the prescribed poems.
- **Full sample Leaving Certificate essays**, graded and accompanied by experienced examiners' comments, show the student exactly what is required to achieve a successful A grade in the Leaving Cert exam and to develop a real enthusiasm for English poetry. This is essential in identifying the task as required by the PCLM marking scheme.

HOW IS THE PRESCRIBED POETRY QUESTION MARKED?

Marking is done (50 marks) by reference to the PCLM criteria for assessment:
- Clarity of purpose (P): 30% of the total (i.e. 15 marks).
- Coherence of delivery (C): 30% of the total (i.e. 15 marks).
- Efficiency of language use (L): 30% of the total (i.e. 15 marks).
- Accuracy of mechanics (M): 10% of the total (i.e. 5 marks).

Each answer will be in the form of a response to a specific task requiring candidates to:
- Display a clear and purposeful engagement with the set task. (P)
- Sustain the response in an appropriate manner over the entire answer. (C)
- Manage and control language appropriate to the task. (L)
- Display levels of accuracy in spelling and grammar appropriate to the required/chosen register. (M)

GENERAL

'Students at Higher Level will be required to study a representative selection from the work of eight poets: a representative selection would seek to reflect the range of a poet's themes and interests and exhibit his/her characteristic style and viewpoint. Normally the study of at least six poems by each poet would be expected.' (DES English Syllabus, 6.3)

The marking scheme guidelines from the State Examinations Commission state that in the case of each poet, the candidates have **freedom of choice** in relation to the poems studied. In addition, there is **not a finite list of any 'poet's themes and interests'**.

Note that in responding to the question set on any given poet, the candidates must refer to the poem(s) they have studied but **are not required to refer to any *specific* poem(s), nor are they expected to discuss or refer to all the poems they have chosen to study**.

In each of the questions in **Prescribed Poetry**, the underlying nature of the task is the invitation to the candidates to **engage with the poems themselves**.

EXAM ADVICE

- You are not expected to write about any **set number of poems** in the examination. You might decide to focus in detail on a small number of poems, or you could choose to write in a more general way on several poems.

- Most candidates write one or two well-developed **paragraphs** on each of the poems they have chosen for discussion. In other cases, a paragraph will focus on one specific aspect of the poet's work. When discussing recurring themes or features of style, appropriate cross-references to other poems may also be useful.
- Reflect on central **themes** and viewpoints in the poems you discuss. Comment also on the use of language and the poet's distinctive **style**. Examine imagery, tone, structure, rhythm and rhyme. Be careful not to simply list aspects of style, such as alliteration or repetition. There's little point in mentioning that a poet uses sound effects or metaphors without discussing the effectiveness of such characteristics.
- Focus on **the task** you have been given in the poetry question. An awareness of audience is important. Are you meant to be writing a letter to the poet? Perhaps you are giving a talk about the poet or writing an article, a review or an introduction to a new collection of the poet's work. If your poetry answer has the appropriate tone and register, it will have an authentic feel and be more convincing.
- Always root your answers in the text of the poems. Support the points you make with **relevant reference and quotation**. Make sure your own expression is fresh and lively. Avoid awkward expressions, such as 'It says in the poem that...'. Look for alternatives: 'There is a sense of...', 'The tone seems to suggest...', 'It's evident that...', etc.
- Neat, **legible handwriting** will help to make a positive impression on examiners. Corrections should be made by simply drawing a line through the mistake. Scored-out words distract attention from the content of your work.
- Keep the emphasis on why particular poets **appeal to you**. Consider the continuing relevance or significance of a poet's work. Perhaps you have shared some of the feelings or experiences expressed in the poems. Avoid starting answers with prepared biographical sketches. Details of a poet's life are better used when discussing how the poems themselves were shaped by such experiences.
- Remember that the examination encourages **individual engagement** with the prescribed poems. Poetry can make us think and feel and imagine. It opens our minds to the wonderful possibilities of language and ideas. Your interaction with the poems is what matters most. Study notes and critical interpretations are all there to be challenged. Read the poems carefully and have confidence in expressing your own personal response.

'Poetry begins – as all art does – where certainties end.'

Eavan Boland (1944–)

Eavan Boland has been one of the most prominent voices in Irish poetry. Born in Dublin but raised in London, she had early experiences with anti-Irish racism that gave her a strong sense of heritage and a keen awareness of her identity. She later returned to attend school and university in Dublin, where she published a pamphlet of poetry after her graduation. Boland received her BA from Trinity College in 1966. Since then she has held numerous teaching positions and has published poetry, books of criticism and articles. She married in 1969 and has two children. Her experiences as a wife and mother have influenced her to explore the beauty and significance of everyday living. Boland writes plainly and eloquently about her experiences as a woman, mother and exile. The author of many highly acclaimed poetry collections, Eavan Boland is Professor of English at Stanford University, California, where she directs a creative writing course.

PRESCRIBED POEMS (HIGHER LEVEL)

1 'The War Horse' (p. 4)

A runaway horse in a quiet suburban estate is the starting point for Boland's explorations of attitudes to warfare and violence throughout Irish history.

2 'Child of Our Time' (p. 9)

Written in response to a newspaper photograph of a child killed in the 1974 Dublin bombings, the poem tries to draw some kind of meaning from the tragedy.

3 'The Famine Road' (p. 13)

The poet dramatically recreates a tragic period in Irish history. Boland also links the Famine with another traumatic experience, the story of a woman diagnosed as infertile by her doctor.

4 'The Shadow Doll' (p. 18)

Boland considers the changing nature of marriage since Victorian times. The silence and submission of women are signified by the porcelain doll in its airless glass dome.

5 'White Hawthorn in the West of Ireland' (p. 22)

The poet's journey into the West brings her into contact with a wildly beautiful landscape where she can explore Irish superstitions and a strange, unspoken language.

6 'Outside History' (p. 26)

Another poem addressing the experience of the marginalised ('outsiders') and reflecting Boland's own humanity as a female Irish poet.

7 'The Black Lace Fan My Mother Gave me' (p. 31)

This poem was inspired by the first gift given by Boland's father to her mother back in 1930s Paris. The souvenir is a symbol of young love and the mystery of changing relationships.

8 'This Moment' (p. 36)

In this short lyric, Boland unobtrusively captures the mystery and magic of the natural world and the beauty of loving relationships.

9 **'The Pomegranate'** (p. 40)

Another personal poem in which Boland uses mythical references to examine the complexity of feelings experienced in mother–daughter relationships.

10 **'Love'** (p. 45)

This reflective poem is addressed to the poet's husband and considers the changing nature of romantic love. In developing her themes, Boland draws on Greek mythology.

• Poetry Focus •

The War Horse

Eavan Boland

This dry night, nothing unusual
About the clip, clop, casual

Iron of his shoes as he stamps death
Like a mint on the innocent coinage of earth.

I lift the window, watch the ambling feather   5
Of hock and fetlock, loosed from its daily tether

In the tinker camp on the Enniskerry Road,
Pass, his breath hissing, his snuffling head

Down. He is gone. No great harm is done.
Only a leaf of our laurel hedge is torn –   10

Of distant interest like a maimed limb,
Only a rose which now will never climb

The stone of our house, expendable, a mere
Line of defence against him, a volunteer

You might say, only a crocus, its bulbous head   15
Blown from growth, one of the screamless dead.

But we, we are safe, our unformed fear
Of fierce commitment gone; why should we care

If a rose, a hedge, a crocus are uprooted
Like corpses, remote, crushed, mutilated?   20

He stumbles on like a rumour of war, huge
Threatening. Neighbours use the subterfuge

Of curtains. He stumbles down our short street
Thankfully passing us, I pause, wait,

Then to breathe relief lean on the sill   25
And for a second only my blood is still

With atavism. That rose he smashed frays
Ribboned across our hedge, recalling days

Of burned countryside, illicit braid:
A cause ruined before, a world betrayed.   30

'his breath hissing, his snuffling head'

GLOSSARY

The War Horse: a powerful horse ridden in war by a knight or cavalry soldier.
4 *mint*: a place where money is made; a machine for making money.
4 *coinage*: collection of coins. Here it refers to imprints the horse makes on the suburban gardens.
5 *ambling*: walking at a leisurely pace.
6 *hock*: joint in the back of a horse's leg.
6 *fetlock*: tuft of hair that grows above and behind the hoof.
6 *tether*: rope for tying an animal.
8 *snuffling*: breathing noisily.
13 *expendable*: can be done without, can be sacrificed to achieve an object.
20 *mutilated*: prevented from having a limb.
22 *subterfuge*: trick used to avoid an argument or an awkward situation.
27 *atavism*: the recurrence of a trait present in distant ancestors.
27 *frays*: noisy quarrel or fight, or cloth that is ragged or strained.
29 *illicit braid*: illegal ribbon, a reference to an Irish secret society, the Ribbonmen, who wore a green ribbon in opposition to the Orangemen and carried out illegal acts such as burning.

EXPLORATIONS

1. Boland felt that 'the daily things I did ... were not fit material for poetry'. Discuss this statement in relation to the poem, with reference to the text.
2. Write your own personal response to the poem, highlighting the impact it made on you.
3. 'I wrote the poem slowly, adding each couplet with care.' Consider how the structure and style of the poem emphasise its message.

• Poetry Focus •

STUDY NOTES

> 'The War Horse' was written in 1972 by a newly married Eavan Boland after she had moved to the suburbs at the foothills of the Dublin Mountains. It was an icy winter, and the 'sounds of death from the televisions were heard almost nightly' as the news about the Northern Ireland Troubles was broadcast. In this poem, Boland questions ambivalent attitudes towards war.

This poem is based on a **real event**, the **appearance** of a 'loosed' **Traveller horse**, described in **lines 1–9**. Boland has said, 'It encompassed a real event. It entered a place in my heart and moved beyond it.' An aural description of the innocuous noise, 'nothing unusual', heralds the arrival of the horse. The horse, a menacing intruder that suggests the opposition between force and formality, wreaked havoc on the neat order of **suburban gardens**. The rigid control of the rhyming couplets mirrors the desire for order in the suburbs.

Onomatopoeia and the alliteration of the hard 'c' vividly describe the horse's walk, like something out of a young child's story: 'clip, clop, casual'. The second couplet counteracts this sense of ordinariness as it describes the damage the horse inflicts. The brutal verb 'stamps' jolts the reader as the garden, 'the innocent coinage of earth', is being destroyed. The metaphor of a mint, which puts an indelible mark on metal to make coins, is used to describe the destruction. The **consequences of war** are also permanent – people are wounded or killed ('stamps death').

The **poet is an observer**: 'I lift the window, watch'. A detailed description of the horse's leg, 'ambling feather/Of hock and fetlock', belies its capacity for violence. There then follows an explanation of where the horse came from, the 'tinker camp on the Enniskerry Road'. The **random nature of violence** is aptly contained in the verbs 'ambling', 'loosed' and also in the long run-on line 'loosed ... Road'. The sounds the horse makes are vividly conveyed using onomatopoeia: 'hissing', 'snuffling'. The moment of danger passes. 'He is gone.' We can feel the palpable relief: 'No great harm is done'. The colloquial language reduces the event to a trivial disruption.

Lines 10–16 show that the poet has adopted a **sensible approach** as she surveys the **damage**, minimising it with an emphasis on the word 'only': 'only a leaf is torn', 'only a crocus', 'only a rose'. These are all 'expendable'; they can be done without. The language becomes more unsettling as violent descriptions are used to show the mangled blooms: 'like a maimed limb ... which now will never climb', 'Blown from growth'. All describe a world that will never be the same again, potential that will never be realised and life that is cut short. From Boland's perspective, 'the screamless dead' can no longer command attention. And who cares anyway? It is of 'distant interest'. This **apathetic view** can be taken by people as they watch atrocities in other countries. The **language of war** is prominent: 'a mere/Line of defence', 'a volunteer', the head is 'Blown'. The poet's focus has now shifted away from the horse and is **concentrated** on war, its **consequences** and the vulnerability of victims.

In lines 17–21, Boland realises that 'we are safe'. War calls for commitment; people must choose to take sides, to fight. This is frightening: 'our unformed fear'. It is there but not expressed, nor given substance or form. Here in this domestic incident is war in miniature, the entry of an intruder who perpetrates damage. The poet asks why the community should care about something so insignificant as a damaged rose or a crushed crocus. She is challenging people who are blasé and examining their **insularity**: 'Why should we care ... corpses, remote, crushed, mutilated?' Are there consequences if people do not care?

Boland criticises her own community in lines 22–30, with the neighbours described as hiding behind curtains ('subterfuge'). This 'I don't want to know' attitude reflects the **ambivalence** about the Troubles in the Irish Republic during the 1970s. The tension, 'I pause, wait', is followed by release: 'breathe relief'. At the conclusion, there are two views at the moment of insight. One is the suburban woman's; the other is an Irish person's awareness of connecting with past history. There is an ancestral memory, 'atavism', which associates the smashed rose with the destruction of the Irish. The ribbon trails back to the violence of English colonialism. Boland and her neighbours chose not to confront the horse, just like the Irish did not confront the invaders. The intruder (the horse, the British) destroyed something beautiful and precious (the rose, Irish culture). The mood here is one of loss and regret. Should both intruders have been challenged? How right is it to live so indifferently? The poem **ends on a bleak note**, a lament for 'a world betrayed'.

ANALYSIS

'We are collectively involved in violence which occurs in our land.' Discuss how this poem reflects this statement. Illustrate your response with reference to the poem.

SAMPLE PARAGRAPH

Boland uses an ordinary, domestic incident, the arrival of a tinker's horse into a suburban garden, to explore the ambivalent attitude often prevalent to wars that seem distant. The colloquial phrase 'No great harm is done' and the neighbours who use 'the subterfuge/Of curtains' both illustrate this insular approach. Everything is all right so long as 'we' are safe. The consequences of war are listed as Boland itemizes them: 'maimed limb', 'now will never climb', 'expendable', 'screamless dead'. The vulnerability of the innocent victims is laid bare. Can we afford to be so indifferent? The implicit statement is that we should care. She then conveys the ancestral memory of how Ireland was invaded by the British. The word 'Ribboned' recalls the Ribbonmen, a secret society that was active against the invaders for a while. We are left feeling that perhaps due to the majority of Irish people's indifference and through a lack of commitment, 'A cause' was lost. The poem ends with a lament, 'a world betrayed', with its long echoing 'ay' sound. I think Boland is upset at people's lack of commitment in a time of trouble.

EXAMINER'S COMMENT

Close reading of the poem is evident in the response. Quotations are very well used here to highlight Boland's attitude to people's commitment to war. Expression is also very good. Grade A standard.

CLASS/HOMEWORK EXERCISES

1. Is this poem a private poem, or does it have a wider significance? Use reference to the poem in your answer.
2. Copy the table below into your own notes and use the blank spaces to fill in the missing critical comments about the last two quotations.

Key Quotes

But we, we are safe	Boland explores a detached, insular attitude towards violence.
why should we care/ If a rose, a hedge, a crocus are uprooted/ Like corpses, crushed, mutilated?	A commonplace incident causes the poet to reflect on our cynical remote, attitude towards war. Assonance emphasises the loss of potential as a consequence of war.
No great harm is done	
recalling days/ Of burned countryside, illicit braid	

Child of Our Time

(for Aengus)

Yesterday I knew no lullaby
But you have taught me overnight to order
This song, which takes from your final cry
Its tune, from your unreasoned end its reason;
Its rhythm from the discord of your murder   5
Its motive from the fact you cannot listen.

We who should have known how to instruct
With rhymes for your waking, rhythms for your sleep,
Names for the animals you took to bed,
Tales to distract, legends to protect   10
Later an idiom for you to keep
And living, learn, must learn from you dead,

To make our broken images, rebuild
Themselves around your limbs, your broken
Image, find for your sake whose life our idle   15
Talk has cost, a new language. Child
Of our time, our times have robbed your cradle.
Sleep in a world your final sleep has woken.

'our times have robbed your cradle'

GLOSSARY

5 *discord*: lack of harmony among people; harsh, confused sounds; conflict.

11 *idiom*: turn of phrase; words which when used together have a different meaning from when used singly.

EXPLORATIONS

1. Boland believes that the 'murder of the innocent' is one of the greatest obscenities. How is this explored in the poem? Write a paragraph in response.
2. Where are the two feelings, tenderness and outrage, evident in the poem? Use reference to the text in your response.
3. What is Boland implying about 'our times'? Is she satisfied or dissatisfied with what is happening? Refer closely to the text in your answer.

STUDY NOTES

'Child of Our Time' was written in 1974 at the height of the Troubles. It was prompted by a harrowing newspaper picture of a fireman tenderly carrying a dead child from the rubble of a bomb explosion in Dublin. It is dedicated to Aengus, the infant son of the poet's friend, who had suffered cot death. This lyric is a response to the sudden and unexpected death of all young children. It also puts an onus on adults to change their ways.

The title of this poem places the little child in a wider context than that of family and town – he is a child of 'our time'. He is our responsibility; he belongs to us. A child should be a **symbol of innocence**, growth, love, potential and the future, but this has been savagely and tragically cut short by 'our time'. Boland did not have children when she wrote this poem ('Yesterday I knew no lullaby'), but in the first stanza she describes how she has been taught to sing a lullaby which is different: 'you have taught me overnight to order/This song'. The child's violent and tragic death demands a response, so she will form and order and 'reason' a poem from the child's 'unreasoned end'. It is a song made of harsh sounds, 'discord'. The tone moves from tender compassion ('lullaby') to indignation ('the fact you cannot listen'). There is no escaping the finality of death, yet the poet is a balanced, reasonable person trying to make **order out of disorder** in a poem that is carefully arranged in three stanzas.

The poem is charged with both **sadness and awareness**. The compassionate voice of the poet is heard in 'rhythms for your sleep,/Names for the animals you took to bed'. However, she is aware of the awfulness of the event: 'final cry', 'end', 'murder'. The language is formal, as befits such a solemn occasion: 'We who should have known', 'Child/Of our time'. This poem has elements of an **elegy** (a poem for the dead): it laments, praises and consoles. The poem's many half rhymes mimic this discordant time: 'idle'/'cradle', 'order'/'murder'.

The collective 'we' in the second stanza is used to show the true context of the little child as a member of the human family. **It is 'we' who are responsible** for not making society safer so that childhood could consist of 'Tales to distract, legends to protect'. The repetitive sound of 'rhymes' and 'rhythms' imitates the rocking sound of a mother nursing her child. Boland's aim is clear: we must learn from our mistakes and reconstruct a better world out of 'our broken images'.

In the third stanza, the poet is insistent that **society takes on this responsibility**, that we 'find ... a new language'. We have to engage in dialogue, not 'idle/Talk', so that we can deliver a safer society for our children. Ironically, it is the little child, who 'our time' has 'robbed' from his cradle, who will form the scaffold around which we can build a new and better society: 'rebuild/Themselves around your limbs'. The final line of the poem is a **prayer and a hope**: 'Sleep in a world your final sleep has woken.' It is a wish that the little child be at rest now and that the world may be woken to its senses by his death.

ANALYSIS

Boland is a 'sensitive poet' who is 'rarely thrown off balance by anger'. Discuss this view of the poet in relation to the poem 'Child of Our Time'. Use references from the poem in your response.

SAMPLE PARAGRAPH

'Child of Our Time' is an example of Boland's control in the face of what must be the most horrific event that humanity can witness: the brutal and senseless murder of an innocent child. The poem is carefully ordered into three stanzas that act as balanced paragraphs in an argument. The first stanza emphasises the meaningless atrocity of 'your unreasoned end'. The second stanza places responsibility where it belongs, on the adult society that should have known how to provide a safe environment for the young: 'We who should have known'. The third stanza urges the adults to do something now, to 'find for your sake whose life our idle/Talk has cost, a new language'. The language is formal and controlled, as befits an elegy. When I listen to Ravel's 'Pavane for a Dead Infant', I hear the same stately rhythm. There are just four sentences in this lyric. The child has taught the poet a lullaby with his death. The adults must learn from this tragedy – they have to learn to talk. May the child awake the world to a new time on account of his tragic death. The balance is impressive, as the poet makes order out of disorder rather than letting her anger explode. The poem lacks sentimentality or even spiritual consolation. Instead, the quiet, insistent voice states that 'we' 'must learn'. Sometimes a soft voice delivers a more powerful message. Boland sensitively deals with a tragic event with an absence of anger and with an insistence that, as a result, lessons must be learned. The poet has learned well from the dead child 'to order/This song'.

EXAMINER'S COMMENT

Boland's careful patterning is explored in this answer to advance the argument that the poet explores the tragic event in a sensitive and controlled way. The comment relating to music shows good personal engagement. Effective use of accurate quotation enhances the response. An A grade.

CLASS/HOMEWORK EXERCISES

1. There is a 'difficult sort of comfort' in literature. Discuss this statement in relation to the poem. Support the point you make with reference to the text.
2. Copy the table below into your own notes and use the blank spaces to fill in the missing critical comments about the last two quotations.

Key Quotes

But you have taught me overnight to order/ This song	The dead child's tragic end has given the poet the inspiration to create this poem.
Tales to distract, legends to protect	These are the appropriate nursery elements of childhood: rhymes, fairytales and myths. The poet sees language as a form of protection against danger.
find for your sake whose life our idle/ Talk has cost, a new language	The adults must learn to engage in dialogue, as the child has paid the price for their useless words.
rebuild/ Themselves around your limbs	
Sleep in a world your final sleep has woken	

The Famine Road

'Idle as trout in light Colonel Jones
these Irish, give them no coins at all; their bones
need toil, their characters no less.' Trevelyan's
seal blooded the deal table. The Relief
Committee deliberated: 'Might it be safe,
Colonel, to give them roads, roads to force
from nowhere, going nowhere of course?'

    one out of every ten and then
    another third of those again
    women – in a case like yours.

Sick, directionless they worked fork, stick
were iron years away; after all could
they not blood their knuckles on rock, suck
April hailstones for water and for food?
Why for that, cunning as housewives, each eyed –
as if at a corner butcher – the other's buttock.

    anything may have caused it, spores,
    a childhood accident; one sees
    day after day these mysteries.

Dusk: they will work tomorrow without him.
They know it and walk clear. He has become
a typhoid pariah, his blood tainted, although
he shares it with some there. No more than snow
attends its own flakes where they settle
and melt, will they pray by his death rattle.

    You never will, never you know
    but take it well woman, grow
    your garden, keep house, good-bye.

'It has gone better than we expected, Lord
Trevelyan, sedition, idleness, cured
in one; from parish to parish, field to field;
the wretches work till they are quite worn,

then fester by their work; we march the corn
to the ships in peace. This Tuesday I saw bones
out of my carriage window. Your servant Jones.'   35

Barren, never to know the load
of his child in you, what is your body
now if not a famine road?

'the wretches work till they are quite worn'

GLOSSARY

During the Irish Famine of 1945–48, the British authorities organised various relief schemes. The hungry were given a small wage to buy food for participating in road building and other community projects. Many of the new roads were constructed in remote areas and served little purpose other than controlling the starving population.

1 *Colonel Jones*: army officer and Chairman of the Board of Works.
3 *Trevelyan*: Charles Trevelyan, a senior civil servant in overall charge of famine relief.
4 *Relief Committee*: groups usually consisting of landlords, the clergy and influential people were set up to distribute food.
5 *deliberated*: considered, discussed.
17 *spores*: germs.
22 *typhoid pariah*: someone shunned because of this deadly blood disease.
25 *death rattle*: last sound of the dying.
30 *sedition*: subversion, treachery.
33 *corn/to the ships*: throughout the famine years, corn was exported from Ireland.

EXPLORATIONS

1 Describe the tone of voice in the opening stanza, using close reference to the text.
2 The poet links the abuse of famine victims with the mistreatment of women in modern society. Is this convincing? Explain your answer.
3 In your view, how chillingly pessimistic are the last three lines of the poem? Give reasons for your answer.

STUDY NOTES

The poem raises interesting questions about marginalised people, a favourite theme in Boland's work. Here she makes a connection between a famine road in the 1840s and an infertile woman in modern times. Boland presents the poem as a series of dramatic moments featuring a variety of characters.

Stanza one begins with the voice of Colonel Jones, a British official, reading from a letter written by Lord Trevelyan, who had overall responsibility for famine relief. The boorish tone of the opening comments about 'these Irish' is explicitly offensive. Trevelyan's generalised insults reflect the **depth of prejudice and suspicion** felt towards an entire population who are 'Idle as trout in light'. Such ruthless disregard is further underlined by the image of the official blood-red seal. The proposed solutions – 'toil' or hard labour building roads 'going nowhere' – could hardly be more cynical and are all the more ironic coming from the 'Relief Committee'.

Stanza two (like **stanzas four** and **six**) is italicised and introduces another speaker, the authoritative voice of a consultant doctor. The unidentified voice quoting statistics to an unnamed woman is casually impersonal. The situation becomes clearer as the poem continues: the medical expert is discussing the woman's failure to have children. Boland portrays him as insensitive and patronising: 'anything may have caused it'. His tone becomes increasingly **unsympathetic as he dismisses her disappointment**: 'You never will, never you know'. He almost seems to take delight in repeating the word 'never'. The doctor's final comments are as severe as some of the remarks made by any of the British officials: 'take it well woman, grow/your garden, keep house'.

In **stanza three**, the poet herself imagines the terrible experiences of the famine victims. The language used to describe their struggle is disturbing: 'Sick, directionless they worked fork'. Prominent **harsh-sounding consonants**, especially 'c' and 'k' in such phrases as 'blood their knuckles on rock', emphasise the suffering. The alarming suggestion of cannibalism ('each eyed –/as if at a corner butcher – the other's buttock') is a reminder of how people were driven beyond normal standards of human behaviour.

Stanza five focuses on the prevalence of death throughout the long famine years. Attitudes harden as widespread disease becomes commonplace. The poet's direct description, steady rhythm and resigned tone combine to reflect the awful reality of the times: 'they will work tomorrow without him'. Boland illustrates the **breakdown of communities** with the tragic example of one 'typhoid pariah' abandoned to die a lonely death without anyone to 'pray by his death rattle'.

This great human catastrophe is made all the more pathetic in stanza seven, which begins with an excerpt from Colonel Jones's response to Trevelyan: 'It has gone better than we expected'. **The offhand tone is self-satisfied** as he reports that the road-building schemes have succeeded in their real purpose of controlling the peasant population ('the wretches'). The horrifyingly detached admission – without the slightest sense of irony – of allowing the starving to 'fester' while 'we march the corn/to the ships' is almost beyond comprehension. The colonel's matter-of-fact comment about seeing 'bones/out of my carriage window' is a final reminder of the colossal gulf between the powerful and the powerless.

In the final stanza, **Boland's own feelings of revulsion** bring her back to the present when she sums up the 'Barren' reality of the childless woman 'never to know the load/of his child'. The famine road is reintroduced as a common symbol for the shared tragedies of both the victims of mass starvation and infertility. The final rhetorical question leaves us to consider important issues of authority and the abuse of power, whatever the circumstances.

ANALYSIS

How effective is the central symbol of the famine road in this poem? Support your points with reference or quotation.

SAMPLE PARAGRAPH

Eavan Boland's famine road represents the terrible futility of all the poor, unfortunate people who perished from starvation. The English government cruelly forced Irish peasants to build roads for no reason other than to keep them from rebelling. In their own words, these roads were 'going nowhere'. In a way, the roads are also a giveaway sign of the colonial administration in Ireland. Their policies had caused the famine to some extent in the first place. But the poet also uses the same symbol to stand for the infertile woman: 'What is your own body now if it's not a famine road?' She also suffers terrible frustration and must consider her life to be pointless. This symbol is very dramatic. It links the two themes of the poem together and makes us think about how the woman listening to the consultant is like a powerless modern day version of the famine sufferer.

EXAMINER'S COMMENT

There are a number of strong points here, with the answer remaining focused on symbolism throughout both strands of the poem. The dramatic significance is not developed. Overall, the language is reasonably well controlled, except for the slightly inaccurate quotation. A solid C grade.

CLASS/HOMEWORK EXERCISES

1. To what extent does 'The Famine Road' show Eavan Boland's sympathies for the outsiders and the marginalised in society? Refer to the text in your answer.
2. Copy the table below into your own notes and use the blank spaces to fill in the missing critical comments about the last two quotations.

Key Quotes

Idle as trout in light Colonel Jones/ these Irish, give them no coins at all	Boland highlights the callous view of the British administration towards the suffering of famine victims.
Trevelyan's/seal blooded the deal table	Vivid imagery indicates the suffering of the people and the brutality of the administration.
but take it well woman, grow/your garden, keep house, goodbye	The arrogance of the doctor's tone emphasises a dismissive attitude to his female patient.
It has gone better than we expected	
What is your body/now if not a famine road?	

• Poetry Focus •

The Shadow Doll

Eavan Boland

They stitched blooms from the ivory tulle
to hem the oyster gleam of the veil.
They made hoops for the crinoline.

Now, in summary and neatly sewn –
a porcelain bride in an airless glamour –   5
the shadow doll survives its occasion.

Under glass, under wraps, it stays
even now, after all, discreet about
visits, fevers, quickenings and lusts

and just how, when she looked at   10
the shell-tone spray of seed pearls,
the bisque features, she could see herself

inside it all, holding less than real
stephanotis, rose petals, never feeling
satin rise and fall with the vows   15

I kept repeating on the night before –
astray among the cards and wedding gifts –
the coffee pots and the clocks and

the battered tan case full of cotton
lace and tissue-paper, pressing down, then   20
pressing down again. And then, locks.

*'They stitched blooms from the ivory tulle/
to hem the oyster gleam of the veil'*

GLOSSARY

A shadow doll was sent to the bride-to-be in Victorian times by her dressmaker. It consisted of a Victorian figurine under a dome of glass modelling the proposed wedding dress.
1 *tulle*: fine net fabric.
2 *oyster*: off-white colour.
3 *crinoline*: hooped petticoat.
8 *discreet*: careful to avoid embarrassment by keeping confidences secret; unobtrusive.
9 *quickenings*: sensations; a woman's awareness of the first movements of the child in the womb.
12 *bisque*: unglazed white porcelain.
14 *stephanotis*: scented white flowers used for displays at both weddings and funerals.

EXPLORATIONS

1 What type of language is used to describe the doll? Do you consider it beautiful or stifling, or both? Illustrate your response with reference to the poem.
2 Do you think marriage has changed for the modern bride? Refer to the last two stanzas in your answer.
3 Choose two phrases from the poem that you found particularly interesting. Explain the reasons for your choice.

STUDY NOTES

'The Shadow Doll' is from the 1990 collection of poems, *Outside History*. The shadow doll wore a model of the wedding dress for the bride-to-be. Boland uses the doll as a symbol to explore the submission and silence surrounding women and women's issues by placing the late twentieth century and Victorian times side by side.

The **first two stanzas** describe the doll vividly, with her 'ivory tulle' and 'oyster gleam'. The 'porcelain doll' is a **beautiful, fragile object**, but the 'ivory' and 'oyster' colours are lifeless. Passivity and restriction are being shown in the phrase 'neatly sewn'. The **pronoun 'it'** is used – the woman is seen as an object, not a real flesh-and-blood human being. The community is described in the preparations: 'They stitched', 'They made'. Are they colluding in the constraint? The phrase 'airless glamour' conveys an allure that has been deprived of life-giving oxygen. The occasion of the marriage is long gone, but the doll remains as a reminder, a shadow of what was.

The **language of containment** and imprisonment is continued in **stanza three**: 'Under glass, under wraps'. The doll is silent and 'discreet'; it knows but does not tell. The bride would have kept the doll throughout her life, so the doll would have been present at all major events such as marriage, childbirth, sickness, longings, 'visits, fevers, quickenings and lusts'. These experiences are not explored in poetry, which is why women and their issues are 'outside history'. They are neither recorded nor commented on.

Stanza four sees the **pronoun change to 'she'** as the poet imagines the Victorian bride considering her own wedding: 'she could see herself/inside it all'. It is as if she becomes like the doll, assuming a mask of 'bisque features' and unable to feel real life: 'holding less than real/stephanotis', 'never feeling/satin rise and fall with the vows'. The only remnant of her life is the silent doll. **Stanza five** ends with the word **'vows'**, and this is the link into the next stanza, which is a view from the twentieth-century bride where the pronoun changes to 'I'.

The poet is 'repeating' the same vows as the Victorian bride. Are these entrapping and imprisoning women? Like the Victorian bride, the modern bride is surrounded by things ('cards and wedding gifts'), yet she is 'astray' (**stanza six**), with the same **sense of disorientation** coming over her. Is she feeling this because she is losing her individual identity as she agrees to become part of a couple?

Stanza seven increases the **feelings of restriction** when the suitcase is described as 'battered', and there is the added emphatic repetition of 'pressing down'. Finally, the single monosyllable **'locks'** clicks the poem to an end. The **onomatopoeic sound** echoes through the years as Boland voices the silence in the depressing ending. Little has changed from Victorian times for women.

ANALYSIS

'Boland's poems often end on a bleak note.' Discuss how 'The Shadow Doll' reflects this statement. Illustrate your response with reference to the text.

SAMPLE PARAGRAPH

The onomatopoeia of the monosyllabic word 'locks' echoes with frightening intensity at the end of the poem 'The Shadow Doll'. It suggests to me the clang of a prison door as the prisoner is locked in and denied freedom. This poem explores the nature and meaning of marriage for women. It starts with the description of the Victorian doll with its wedding dress, which seems to become a stifling mask fitted on a living, breathing woman, 'airless glamour', 'Under glass', 'under wraps'. The modern bride is 'astray'. Marriage is shown as confining and silencing, 'discreet'. The repetition of the phrase 'pressing down' has an almost nightmarish sense of claustrophobia. Both the Victorian bride and the modern bride are surrounded by objects, 'seed pearls', 'stephanotis', 'the cards and wedding gifts'. I find it strange that there is no mention of the prospective groom, or friends or families. Instead there is a growing sense of isolation and intimidation culminating in the echoing phrase 'And then, locks'. What is locked in? What is locked out?

EXAMINER'S COMMENT

The response carefully considers the effect of the ending and Boland's exploration of the theme of marriage as a repressive and restricting force on women. The candidate also touches on interesting questions about the narrow views expressed in the poem. A real sense of individual engagement is evident. Grade A standard.

CLASS/HOMEWORK EXERCISES

1. 'In her poetry, Boland examines concrete images to explore themes.' In your opinion, how valid is this statement? Use reference to 'The Shadow Doll' in your answer.
2. Copy the table below into your own notes and use the blank spaces to fill in the missing critical comments about the last two quotations.

Key Quotes

a porcelain bride in an airless glamour	The Victorian doll is beautiful but stifled. This is used as a symbol for women in marriage.
discreet about/visits, fevers, quickenings and lusts	The doll is a silent witness to the life of the Victorian bride.
The vows/I kept repeating on the night before	The same promises are made by both brides. For Boland, marriage can still trap women.
astray among the cards and wedding gifts	
And then, locks	

White Hawthorn in the West of Ireland

I drove West
in the season between seasons.
I left behind suburban gardens.
Lawnmowers. Small talk.

Under low skies, past splashes of coltsfoot   5
I assumed
the hard shyness of Atlantic light
and the superstitious aura of hawthorn.

All I wanted then was to fill my arms with
sharp flowers,   10
to seem, from a distance, to be part of
that ivory, downhill rush. But I knew,

I had always known
the custom was
not to touch hawthorn.   15
Not to bring it indoors for the sake of

the luck
such constraint would forfeit –
a child might die, perhaps, or an unexplained
fever speckle heifers. So I left it   20

stirring on those hills
with a fluency
only water has. And, like water, able
to re-define land. And free to seem to be –

for anglers,   25
and for travellers astray in
the unmarked lights of a May dusk –
the only language spoken in those parts.

'the custom was/not to touch hawthorn'

GLOSSARY

Hawthorn is a flowering shrub that blossoms in springtime. It is associated with fairytales and superstitions in Irish folklore. People believed that it was unlucky to cut hawthorn or to keep it indoors.

2 *the season*: between spring and summer.

5 *coltsfoot*: wild plant with yellow flowers.
6 *assumed*: became part of.
7 *Atlantic light*: unsettled weather causes the light to vary.
8 *superstitious aura*: disquiet associated with hawthorn stories.
20 *heifers*: cows which have not yet had calves.

EXPLORATIONS

1 Describe the poet's changing mood as she travels from her suburban home to the West. Refer to the text in your answer.
2 There are many beautiful images in the poem. Choose two that you find interesting and briefly explain their appeal.
3 What is the significance of the white hawthorn? What might it symbolise? Refer closely to the poem in your answer.

STUDY NOTES

> In this poem, the folklore associated with hawthorn in rural Ireland is seen as symbolic of an ancient 'language' that has almost disappeared. Boland structures her themes around the image of a journey into the West. It seems as though she is hoping to return to her roots in the traditional landscape of the West of Ireland.

The poem opens on a conversational note. Boland's clear intention is to leave the city behind: 'I drove West/in the season between seasons'. Her tone is determined, dismissing the **artificial life of suburbia** ('Lawnmowers. Small talk.') in favour of the freedom awaiting her. **Stanza one** emphasises the poet's strong desire to get away from her cultivated suburban confines, which seem colourless and overly regulated. The **broken rhythm** of line 4 adds to the abrupt sense of rigidity.

This orderly landscape is in stark contrast with the world of 'Atlantic light' she discovers on her journey. Stanzas two and three contain **striking images of energy and growth**. The 'splashes of coltsfoot' suggest a fresh enthusiasm for the wide open spaces as Boland becomes one with this changing environment. The prominent sibilant 's' underpins the rich stillness of the remote countryside.

She seems both fearful and fascinated by the hawthorn's 'superstitious aura'. The experience is similar to an artist becoming increasingly absorbed in the joy of painting. Run-on lines and the frequent use of the pronoun 'I' accentuate our appreciation of the **poet's own delight** in 'that ivory, downhill rush'.

Stanzas four and five focus on the mystery and superstition associated with hawthorn in Irish folk tradition. Boland's awareness of the **possible dangers** check her eagerness as she considers the stories: 'a child might die, perhaps'. The poet is momentarily caught between a desire to fill her arms with these wild flowers and her own disquieting belief in the superstitions. Eventually, she decides to follow her intuition and respect the customs of the West: 'So I left it'.

The **personification** ('stirring') of the hawthorn in stanza six reinforces Boland's regard for this unfamiliar landscape as a living place. The poet's imagination has also been stirred by her journey. In comparing the hawthorn to water, she suggests its elemental power. Both share a natural 'fluency' which can shape and 're-define land'.

The poet links the twin forces of superstition and landscape even more forcibly in stanza seven. They defy time and transcend recorded history. The hawthorn trees give the poet a **glimpse of Ireland's ancient culture**. Although nature remains elusive, Boland believes that for outsiders like herself – visiting 'anglers' and tourists – it is 'the only language spoken in these parts'. The poet's final tone is one of resignation as she accepts that she can never fully understand Ireland's unique landscape or the past.

ANALYSIS

How well does Boland contrast suburban life with the natural primitiveness of the country in this poem? Refer to the text in your answer.

SAMPLE PARAGRAPH

Eavan Boland uses contrasts very effectively. The poem begins out in the suburbs – 'suburban gardens'. The image she gives is of a neat, stifling show-house. It is stifling. The small talk between neighbours is just being polite. Everything changes when she drives to the West coast. The images are much more vivid – 'hard shyness of Atlantic light'. This suggests the mystery of the West coast of Ireland. Unlike the false lawns and neatly trimmed gardens, the West has sharp weeds and coltsfoot. Nature is untamed. Even the punctuation in the poem distinguishes the two different places. There are fewer breaks when Boland is describing the areas where the hawthorn grows wild. She uses breaks at the start – 'I left behind suburban gardens./Lawnmowers. Small talk'.

EXAMINER'S COMMENT

This is a solid C grade response to the question. Suitable reference is used to highlight the two 'worlds' within the poem. The point about punctuation is also relevant. However, the expression wavers at the start and the language lacks fluency at times.

CLASS/HOMEWORK EXERCISES

1. What do you think Eavan Boland has learned from her journey to the West of Ireland? Refer to the poem in your answer.
2. Copy the table below into your own notes and use the blank spaces to fill in the missing critical comments about the last two quotations.

Key Quotes

I assumed/the hard shyness of Atlantic light	Boland celebrates the natural beauty and ancient culture in the West of Ireland.
I left behind suburban gardens./ Lawnmowers. Small talk	The poet contrasts the confining urban lifestyle with nature's unrestricted wildness.
Under low skies, past splashes of coltsfoot	Lively visual and aural images suggest the mystery and freedom of the countryside.
that ivory, downhill rush	
the only language spoken in those parts	

• Poetry Focus •

Outside History

Eavan Boland

There are outsiders, always. These stars –
these iron inklings of an Irish January,
whose light happened

thousands of years before
our pain did: they are, they have always been   5
outside history.

They keep their distance. Under them remains
a place where you found
you were human, and

a landscape in which you know you are mortal.   10
And a time to choose between them.
I have chosen:

out of myth into history I move to be
part of that ordeal
whose darkness is   15

only now reaching me from those fields,
those rivers, those roads clotted as
firmaments with the dead.

How slowly they die
As we kneel beside them, whisper in their ear.   20
And we are too late. We are always too late.

'whose light happened/ thousands of years before/ our pain did'

GLOSSARY

2 *inklings*: slight idea or suspicion; clues.
6 *history*: record or account of past events and developments; the study of these.
13 *myth*: tale with supernatural characters; untrue idea or explanation; imaginary person; story with a germ of truth in it.
17 *clotted*: soft, thick lumps formed.
18 *firmaments*: sky or heavens.

EXPLORATIONS

1 How are the stars 'outsiders'? Do you think they are an effective symbol for those who are marginalised and regarded as of no importance? Discuss, using reference from the poem.
2 Has the poet succeeded in moving 'to be/part of that ordeal'? Look carefully at the imagery and language in the poem.
3 Explain the significance of the last stanza of the poem: 'How slowly they die/As we kneel beside them, whisper in their ear./And we are too late. We are always too late'. In your opinion, has the poet's dilemma been resolved?

STUDY NOTES

'Outside History' was written in 1990 as part of a collection of poems that were arranged to reflect the changing seasons. This poem is set in January. Boland believes that it is important to remember the experiences of those who have not been recorded in history. These are the outsiders, 'the lost, the voiceless, the silent' to whom she gives a hauntingly beautiful voice.

Lines 1–6

The poem opens with an **impersonal statement**: 'There are **outsiders, always**'. The poet is referring to those who have not been recorded in history. The stars are also outsiders, standing outside and above human history. At their great distance, they are shown as cold and distant ('iron', 'Irish January'). They have a permanence and longevity that are in contrast to human life: 'whose light happened/thousands of years before/our pain did'. The run-on line imitates the light that travels thousands of years to reach us. The phrase 'outside history' is placed on its own to emphasise how the stars do not belong to human history.

Lines 7–10

The poet stresses **the aloneness of the stars**: 'They keep their distance'. They don't want to be involved. Now she turns to 'you', a member of the human race, and places 'you' in context with the words 'place' and 'landscape'. This is where 'you found/you were human' and 'mortal'. 'You' are not like the permanent, icy, aloof stars; 'you' are a suffering member of the human race who is subject to ageing and death. The line 'And a time to choose between them' could refer to choosing between the perspective of the stars, i.e. remaining at an uninvolved distance, or the perspective of a member of the human race, i.e. involved and anguished.

Lines 11–18

The phrase 'I have chosen' marks a **turning point** in the poem. Boland has made a deliberate decision, **moving away from 'myth'** and tradition. She felt that myth obscures history. She regarded figures like Caitlin Ni Houlihan and Dark Rosaleen, female symbols for Ireland, as 'passive', 'simplified' and 'decorative' emblems in male poems. She felt that history was laced with myths, which, in her opinion, were as unreal, cold and distant as the stars are from reality. She regarded these mythic emblems as false and limiting, 'a corruption'. Boland is trying to achieve a sense of belonging and wholeness by unwinding the myth and the stereotype. She wanted reality rather than the glittering image of the stars: 'out of myth into history I move to be/part of that ordeal'.

Just as the stars' light travelled vast distances to reach us, so the darkness of unwritten history is travelling to reach her 'only now'. The run-on stanza again suggests great distances that had to be covered for the poet to connect with past history. There follows a description that suggests the **Irish famine**: 'those fields', 'those rivers', 'those roads' which were covered with 'the dead'. The paradoxical phrase 'clotted as/firmaments' uses the language of the stars to describe the numberless bodies strewn everywhere as a result of the famine. This condensed image evokes a poignant sense of the soft mounds of victims lying as numberless as the stars. The full stop after 'the dead' reinforces the finality of death.

Lines 19–21

The final stanza changes to the collective 'we'. Is this referring to the Irish people accepting responsibility for **honouring the dead** and connecting and being part of history? The rite of contrition is being said: 'as we kneel beside them, whisper in their ear'. It was believed that the person's soul would go to rest in heaven as they had made their peace with God, but the repetition of the last line stresses that the words of comfort have come 'too late'. The people don't know they are being honoured by the poet. However, the poem stands as a testament to them and their unrecorded history. Has she changed her attitude from the beginning of the poem: 'There are outsiders, always'? Has she brought them in from the cold sidelines, including them into history? Or has she and 'we' left it too late?

ANALYSIS

Imagine you have invited Eavan Boland to give a reading of her poems to your class or group. What poems would you ask her to read and why do you think they would appeal to your fellow students?

SAMPLE PARAGRAPH

Fellow students, on behalf of our school, St Dominic's, I would like to welcome the poet Eavan Boland to our assembly. Eavan is going to start this workshop with one of my favourite poems, 'Outside History'. In our modern world with all its affluence and prosperity, there are many marginalised people. This poem starts with 'There are outsiders, always'. It is rather like the statement Christ makes when he states that the poor will always be with us. I found the symbol of the stars very effective as it brought home to me how cold and distant people must feel when they are on the sidelines looking in. It reminded me of the film *In the Shadow of the Moon* which we saw last week. The astronaut was speaking from the perspective of the stars. As he stood on the moon he was able to obliterate the earth with his thumb. From the stars' perspective, human history does not exist. Boland however starts to move 'into history', to be 'part of the ordeal'. She makes a conscious decision to do so, 'I have chosen'. The phrase rings with conviction. She does give a voice to those who have not been recorded in history, the poor, the weak, the women. And even though the poem seems to end on a bleak note, 'We are always too late', the poem has honoured those who died in their thousands, on 'those roads clotted as/firmaments'. The human compassion of the poet is there in the lines 'as we kneel beside them, whisper in their ear'. What a stark contrast to the iron passivity of the stars! I feel Boland has brought the outsider in and given them their proper place in history. We now look forward to hearing from the poet herself, a big round of applause for Eavan Boland.

EXAMINER'S COMMENT

As part of a full essay, this response is imaginative, and it is also well rooted in the text. The student's lively sense of individual engagement is evident in the format of a speech to fellow students. Grade A standard.

• Poetry Focus •

Eavan Boland

CLASS/HOMEWORK EXERCISES

1 Write a letter to Eavan Boland telling her how you responded to some of her poems on your course. Support the points you make by detailed reference to the poems you have chosen.
2 Copy the table below into your own notes and use the blank spaces to fill in the missing critical comments about the last two quotations.

Key Quotes

There are outsiders, always	Boland's aim is to give a voice to those who are on the margins of society.
They keep their distance	The stars are above and impervious to human history.
out of myth into history I move to be/ part of that ordeal	The poet distrusts myth, with its stereotypical images and wishes to be part of the reality of history, which is the story of the human race with all its suffering.
Those roads clotted as/firmaments with the dead	
We are always too late	

The Black Lace Fan my Mother Gave me

Eavan Boland

It was the first gift he ever gave her,
buying it for five francs in the Galeries
in pre-war Paris. It was stifling.
A starless drought made the nights stormy.

They stayed in the city for the summer.   5
They met in cafés. She was always early.
He was late. That evening he was later.
They wrapped the fan. He looked at his watch.

She looked down the Boulevard des Capucines.
She ordered more coffee. She stood up.   10
The streets were emptying. The heat was killing.
She thought the distance smelled of rain and lightning.

These are wild roses, appliquéd on silk by hand,
darkly picked, stitched boldly, quickly.
The rest is tortoiseshell and has the reticent, 15
clear patience of its element. It is

a worn-out, underwater bullion and it keeps,
even now, an inference of its violation.
The lace is overcast as if the weather
it opened for and offset had entered it.   20

The past is an empty café terrace.
An airless dusk before thunder. A man running.
And no way now to know what happened then –
none at all – unless, of course, you improvise:

The blackbird on this first sultry morning,   25
in summer, finding buds, worms, fruit,
feels the heat. Suddenly she puts out her wing –
the whole, full, flirtatious span of it.

• Poetry Focus •

Eavan Boland

'And no way now to know what happened'

GLOSSARY

2 *Galeries*: Paris store.
13 *appliquéd*: trimming.
15 *tortoiseshell*: clear decorative material.
15 *reticent*: reserved, restrained.
17 *bullion*: treasure.
24 *improvise*: make up, imagine.
28 *flirtatious*: enticing, playful.
28 *span*: extent, measure.

EXPLORATIONS

1 The setting is important in this poem. Briefly explain what it contributes to the atmosphere, referring to the text in your answer.
2 Comment on the effect of the short sentences and irregular rhythms in the first three stanzas.
3 Did you like this poem? Give reasons for your response, referring to the text of the poem in your answer.

STUDY NOTES

Set in pre-war Paris in the 1930s, the incident that occurs is the giving of a gift, a black lace fan that the poet's father gave to her mother. A fan was usually seen as a sign of romantic love and desire. However, its significance here is never entirely explained to us. Maybe this is in recognition of our inability to fully understand other people's relationships or to recall the past and the effect it has on us, although we may attempt to. Boland's poem is one of those attempts.

Stanza one begins on a narrative note as the poet recreates a pivotal moment in her parents' lives back in the 1930s. **The fan was a special symbol of young love** and was important because it was 'the first gift' from her father to her mother. Other details of the precise cost and the 'stifling' weather add to the importance of the occasion. Although the Parisian setting is romantic, the mood is tense. Their courtship is framed in a series of captured moments, as though Boland is flicking through an old photo album.

In stanzas two and three, short sentences and the growing unevenness of the rhythm add to this cinematic quality: 'They met in cafés. She was always early'. The hesitant relationship between the lovers is conveyed repeatedly through their nervous gestures: 'He looked at his watch', 'She stood up'. Boland builds up the tension through references to the heat wave: 'the distance smelled of rain and lightning'. The image might also suggest the **stormy nature of what lay ahead** for the couple.

Stanzas four and five focus on the elegant lace fan in **vivid detail**. Boland notes its decorative qualities, carefully embroidered with the most romantic 'wild roses' and fine 'tortoiseshell'. She seems fascinated by the painstaking craft ('stitched boldly') involved in creating this beautiful token of love. But the **poet's appreciation for the fan becomes diminished** with guilt. The tortoiseshell has suffered 'violation' at the expense of the gift. In Boland's mind, the delicate colours decorating the fan came from 'a worn-out, underwater bullion'. The tone is suddenly downbeat as the thought casts a shadow ('the lace is overcast') on her parents' relationship.

In stanza six, the poet returns to the romantic Parisian drama of 'the empty café terrace', but admits that she can never know what really happened that fateful evening in the 'airless dusk before thunder'. Instead, she must 'improvise' it. But at least the romantic moment is preserved in her imagination. Not for the first time, however, there is an underlying suggestion of the reality of relationships over time, and the balance of joy and disappointment that is likely. For Boland, the fan is only a small part of her parents' story. Perhaps she realises that **the past can never be completely understood**.

The striking image of a blackbird dominates the final stanza. The poet returns to the present as she observes the bird 'in summer, finding buds'. The movement of the blackbird's wing is an unexpected link with the black lace fan all those years ago. While the souvenir is old, its significance as a symbol of youthful romance can still be found elsewhere. For the first time, **Boland now seems to understand the beauty of her parents' love** for each other. The last lines are daring and appear to describe both the blackbird and her mother as a young girl holding her new gift: 'Suddenly she puts out her wing –/the whole, full, flirtatious span of it'. The energetic pace of the lines combine with the alliterative sounds and sibilant music to produce a real sense of celebration at the end.

ANALYSIS

It has been said that this is a very unusual love poem. Do you agree with this view? Give reasons for your answer by referring to the text.

SAMPLE PARAGRAPH

'The Black Lace Fan my Mother Gave me' is not a typical love poem. It is out of the ordinary in ways, e.g. Eavan Boland does not try to glorify the relationship between her parents when they first met. Indeed, they seem unsure of each other. The poet tries to work out the story behind their courtship from looking at the lace fan. She imagines the intense heat of that summer in Paris. 'It was stifling.' References to the weather hint at an uncomfortable relationship, 'The heat was killing.' Boland might be referring indirectly to the future problems in the couple's marriage over the years. The fact that the Second World War was about to break out is also a bad sign. Having said that, the gift of the fan is a symbol of the attraction the couple felt. It is a traditional image of true romance. Unlike other love poems, this is a balanced, unsentimental view of how her parents behaved. There was nervousness and excitement when they were first infatuated with each other, but their love was to change over time. She also compares the fan to a blackbird's wing which excites the poet. This gives us a final impression that Boland is happy to imagine the excited love between her parents back in the 1930s. In a way, the poem is more about the love Boland herself feels for her parents as much as about their love.

EXAMINER'S COMMENT

This paragraph focuses well on the way love is presented in the poem. Suitable quotations support the discussion on the way Boland takes a realistic view of her parents. The final point is very interesting and would have been worth developing. A good B grade standard.

CLASS/HOMEWORK EXERCISES

1. Comment on Eavan Boland's use of symbolism in this poem, referring to the text in your answer.
2. Copy the table below into your own notes and use the blank spaces to fill in the missing critical comments about the last two quotations.

Key Quotes	
They stayed in the city for the summer./ They met in cafés	The poet focuses on the nature of the relationship between her mother and father.
A starless drought made the nights stormy	The sultry summer in pre-war Paris is conveyed through sensuous imagery.
These are wild roses, appliquéd on silk by hand,/ darkly picked	The fan symbolises the early courtship and love between the poet's parents.
The past is an empty café terrace	
the whole, full, flirtatious span of it	

• Poetry Focus •

This Moment

Eavan Boland

A neighbourhood.
At dusk.

Things are getting ready
to happen
out of sight.   5

Stars and moths.
And rinds slanting around fruit.

But not yet.

One tree is black.
One window is yellow as butter.   10

A woman leans down to catch a child
who has run into her arms
this moment.

Stars rise.
Moths flutter.   15
Apples sweeten in the dark.

'this moment'

GLOSSARY

7 *rinds*: peels.

EXPLORATIONS

1. What senses does the poet appeal to in her description of the scene? Support your answer by referring to the text.
2. Comment on how Boland manages to create drama within the poem.
3. What do you think is the central theme in the poem? Refer closely to the text in your answer.

STUDY NOTES

> In this short lyric poem, Boland captures the experience of a passing moment in time. It is clear that Boland is moved by the ordinariness of suburban life, where she glimpses the immeasurable beauty of nature and human nature. The occasion is another reminder of the mystery and wonder of all creation, as expressed by the American poet Walt Whitman, who wrote, 'I know of nothing else but miracles'.

The poem's **opening lines** introduce a suburban area in any part of the world. Boland pares the scene down to its essentials. All we learn is that it is dusk, a time of transition. The atmosphere is one of quiet intensity. Full stops break the rhythm and force us to evaluate what is happening. Although we are presented with an **anonymous setting**, it seems strangely familiar. The late evening – especially as darkness falls – can be a time for reflecting about the natural world.

The stillness and dramatic anticipation intensify further in **lines 3–8**. Something important is about to happen 'out of sight'. Boland then considers some of nature's wonders: 'Stars and moths'. In the twilight, everything seems mysterious, even 'rinds slanting around fruit'. The poet's eye for detail is like that of an artist. The rich, sensory image of the cut fruit is exact and tactile. She uses simple language precisely to create a **mood of natural calmness** that is delayed for a split second ('But not yet').

There is time for two more **vivid images** in **lines 9–10**. The startling colour contrast between the 'black' tree and the window that is 'yellow as butter' has a cinematic effect. The simile is homely, in keeping with the domestic setting. The repetition of 'One' focuses our attention as the build-up continues. Again, Boland presents the sequence of events in a series of brief glimpses. It is as if she is marking time, preparing us for the key moment of revelation.

This occurs in **lines 11–13**. The central image of the mother and child intuitively reaching out for each other is a powerful symbol of unprompted love. It is every bit as wonderful as any of life's greatest mysteries. The three lines become progressively condensed as the child reaches her mother. The syntax suggests their eagerness to show their love for each other. Boland's decision to generalise ('A woman' and 'a child') emphasises the **universal significance** of 'this moment'. The crucial importance of people's feelings transcends time and place.

There is a slight tone of anti-climax about the last three lines. However, Boland rounds off her description of the moment by placing it within a wider context. The constant expression of family love is in harmony with everything else that is beautiful in nature. This feeling is suggested by the recurring sibilant 's' sounds and the carefully chosen verbs ('rise', 'flutter' and 'sweeten'), all of which celebrate the excitement and **joy of everyday human relationships**.

ANALYSIS

What features of Boland's writing style are most evident in this poem? Refer closely to the text in your answer.

SAMPLE PARAGRAPH

Some people have described Eavan Boland's poetry as painterly. Her mother was a famous artist. The images she uses to help readers imagine the Dublin suburb are very colourful:

> One tree is black.
> One window is as yellow as butter.

This reminds me of a still life painting. Or of a child's simple artwork. Vivid imagery is typical of her writing. It is more dramatic in that it attracts our attention. I can visualise the suburb at dusk very clearly. Clear expression is another feature of Boland's writing that I love. There is nothing difficult about the poem. Again, it suits all ages, even a young child. This is what is best about 'This Moment'. It is just a simple poem about the happiness of a mother and child. Other great mysteries, such as the way 'Stars are rising' are beyond our understanding. But love between two people is also beautiful. I like the way she makes this point in the poem.

EXAMINER'S COMMENT

This paragraph includes two worthwhile points about imagery and clarity in the poem. These are reasonably well supported with reference (although the quotations are not accurate and the expression is stilted). There is also some personal engagement. An average C grade standard.

CLASS/HOMEWORK EXERCISES

1. Comment on the poet's tone in 'This Moment'. Refer to the text in your discussion.
2. Copy the table below into your own notes and use the blank spaces to fill in the missing critical comments about the last two quotations.

Key Quotes

A woman is leaning down to catch a child	The central thought in the poem is the wonder and beauty of ordinary, natural experiences.
One window is yellow as butter	This colourful, sensuous image intensifies our understanding of the moment Boland is describing.
Apples sweeten in the dark	The use of the sibilant 's' appeals to the senses and has a bittersweet effect.
Things are getting ready/to happen	
And rinds slanting around fruit	

• Poetry Focus •

The Pomegranate

Eavan Boland

The only legend I have ever loved is
the story of a daughter lost in hell.
And found and rescued there.
Love and blackmail are the gist of it.
Ceres and Persephone the names.   5
And the best thing about the legend is
I can enter it anywhere. And have.
As a child in exile in
a city of fogs and strange consonants,
I read it first and at first I was   10
an exiled child in the crackling dusk of
the underworld, the stars blighted. Later
I walked out in a summer twilight
searching for my daughter at bed-time.
When she came running I was ready   15
to make any bargain to keep her.
I carried her back past whitebeams
and wasps and honey-scented buddleias.
But I was Ceres then and I knew
winter was in store for every leaf   20
on every tree on that road.
Was inescapable for each one we passed.
And for me.
              It is winter
and the stars are hidden.   25
I climb the stairs and stand where I can see
my child asleep beside her teen magazines,
her can of Coke, her plate of uncut fruit.
The pomegranate! How did I forget it?
She could have come home and been safe   30
and ended the story and all
our heart-broken searching but she reached
out a hand and plucked a pomegranate.
She put out her hand and pulled down
the French sound for apple and   35
the noise of stone and the proof
that even in the place of death,
at the heart of legend, in the midst

of rocks full of unshed tears
ready to be diamonds by the time   40
the story was told, a child can be
hungry. I could warn her. There is still a chance.
The rain is cold. The road is flint-coloured.
The suburb has cars and cable television.
The veiled stars are above ground.   45
It is another world. But what else
can a mother give her daughter but such
beautiful rifts in time?
If I defer the grief I will diminish the gift.
The legend will be hers as well as mine.   50
She will enter it. As I have.
She will wake up. She will hold
the papery flushed skin in her hand.
And to her lips. I will say nothing.

'my child asleep'

GLOSSARY

The pomegranate (from a French word meaning an apple with many seeds) is a pulpy oriental fruit.

5 *Ceres and Persephone*: mythological figures. Ceres was the goddess of earth and motherhood. Persephone was her beautiful daughter who was forced by Pluto to become his wife and was imprisoned in Hades, the underworld. Ceres was determined to find Persephone and threatened to prevent anything from growing on the earth until she was allowed to rescue her daughter. But because Persephone had eaten sacred pomegranate seeds in Hades, she was condemned forever to spend part of every year there.

9 *city of fogs*: London, where the poet once lived.

18 *buddleias*: ornamental bushes with small purple flowers.

48 *rifts*: gaps, cracks.

49 *defer*: delay.

EXPLORATIONS

1. Boland conveys a clear sense of the city of London in this poem. How does she succeed in doing this? Refer closely to the text in your answer.
2. From your reading of this poem, what do you learn about the relationship between the poet and her own daughter? Refer to the text in your answer.
3. Comment on the poet's mood in the last five lines of the poem.

STUDY NOTES

> In the poem, narrated as one unrhymed stanza, Boland explores the theme of parental loss by comparing her own experiences as a mother and daughter with the myth of Ceres and Persephone. Although it is a personal poem, it has a much wider relevance for families everywhere.

Boland presents this exploration of the mother–child relationship as a dramatic narrative. In the **opening lines**, the poet tells us that she has always related to 'the story of a daughter lost in hell'. This goes back to her early experience as 'a child in exile' living in London. Her **sense of displacement** is evident in the detailed description of that 'city of fogs and strange consonants'. Like Persephone trapped in Hades, Boland yearned for home. But the myth has a broader relevance to the poet's life – she 'can enter it anywhere'. Years later, she recalls a time when, as a mother, she could also identify with Ceres, 'searching for my daughter'.

Lines 13–18 express the intensity of Boland's feeling for her child: she was quite prepared 'to make any bargain to keep her'. The **anxious tone** reflects the poet's awareness of the importance of appreciating the closeness between herself and her teenage daughter while time allows. She expresses her maternal feelings through rich natural images: 'I carried her back past whitebeams'. But she is also increasingly aware that both she and her daughter are ageing. This is particularly evident in **line 20**, as she anticipates an 'inescapable' change in their relationship: 'winter was in store for every leaf'.

Line 24 marks a defining moment ('It is winter') for them both. Observing her daughter asleep in her bedroom, Boland now sees herself as Ceres and the 'plate of uncut fruit' as the pomegranate. This marks the realisation that **her child has become an adult**. The poet imagines how different it might have been had Persephone not eaten the fruit – 'She could have come home' and ended all the 'heart-broken searching'. But Persephone deliberately made her choice, a decision that is emphasised by the repeated mention of her gesture ('she reached/out a hand', 'She put out her hand'). Significantly, Boland is sympathetic: 'a child can be/hungry'.

In **line 42**, the poet considers alerting her daughter ('I could warn her') about the dangers and disappointments that lie ahead. **Harsh imagery** suggests the difficulties of modern life: 'The rain is cold. The road is flint-coloured'. Boland wonders if 'beautiful rifts in time' are the most a mother can offer. Such delaying tactics may only postpone natural development into adulthood.

In the end, she decides to 'say nothing'. There is a clear sense of resignation in the **final lines**. The poet accepts the reality of change. Boland's daughter will experience the same stages of childhood and motherhood as the poet herself: 'The legend will be hers as well as mine'. This truth is underlined by the recurring use of 'She will', a recognition that her daughter's destiny is in her own hands. The poem ends on a quietly reflective note as Boland respectfully acknowledges the right of her daughter to mature naturally and make her own way in life.

ANALYSIS

The poet makes many comparisons between the legend of Ceres and Persephone and her own experiences. How effective are these comparisons? Refer to the text in your answer.

SAMPLE PARAGRAPH

In my view, Eavan Boland has been very successful in blending her own life as a child and mother with Persephone and Ceres. The fact that she uses an ancient legend adds a touch of mystery to the theme of mother-daughter relationships. This gives the poem a universal quality. First, she compares herself to Persephone, the exiled child in London where the stars were 'blighted'. This links the grimy city life to the underworld of Hades. But Boland is more concerned with the present and her fears of losing her own daughter who is growing up fast. By describing her fears through the old story of Ceres, she increases our understanding of how anxious she was feeling. Both parents were 'searching' desperately. Together, the legend and the true-life story of the poet and her reluctance to come to terms with her daughter growing up really show how parents have to let go of their children and give them the freedom to make their own mistakes and learn for themselves. Most parents find it hard to give their children freedom. They can't help it.

EXAMINER'S COMMENT

There are some very good points here in response to a challenging question. Although the response shows personal engagement, the answer could be rooted more thoroughly in the text. The expression is repetitive in places and one or two sentences are overlong. C grade.

CLASS/HOMEWORK EXERCISES

1. What image of Eavan Boland herself emerges from this poem? Refer closely to the text in your answer.
2. Copy the table below into your own notes and use the blank spaces to fill in the missing critical comments about the last two quotations.

Key Quotes

an exiled child in the crackling dusk	Boland emphasises the sense of loss throughout the poem; it affects individuals at various stages of life.
If I defer the grief I will diminish the gift	The poet cannot shield her daughter from reality. Separation and loss are an unavoidable part of ageing.
The rain is cold. The road is flint-coloured	Bleak imagery and sharp sounds suggest the severity of modern life.
Love and blackmail are the gist of it	
The legend will be hers as well as mine	

Love

Eavan Boland

Dark falls on this mid-western town
where we once lived when myths collided.
Dusk has hidden the bridge in the river
which slides and deepens
to become the water   5
the hero crossed on his way to hell.

Not far from here is our old apartment.
We had a kitchen and an Amish table.
We had a view. And we discovered there
love had the feather and muscle of wings   10
and had come to live with us,
a brother of fire and air.

We had two infant children one of whom
was touched by death in this town
and spared: and when the hero   15
was hailed by his comrades in hell
their mouths opened and their voices failed and
there is no knowing what they would have asked
about a life they had shared and lost.

I am your wife.   20
It was years ago.
Our child was healed. We love each other still.
Across our day-to-day and ordinary distances
we speak plainly. We hear each other clearly.

And yet I want to return to you   25
on the bridge of the Iowa river as you were,
with snow on the shoulders of your coat
and a car passing with its headlights on:

I see you as a hero in a text –
the image blazing and the edges gilded –   30
and I long to cry out the epic question
my dear companion:

• Poetry Focus •

Eavan Boland

Will we ever live so intensely again?
Will love come to us again and be
so formidable at rest it offered us ascension   35
even to look at him?

But the words are shadows and you cannot hear me.
You walk away and I cannot follow.

'and when the hero/was hailed by his comrades in hell/their mouths opened and their voices failed'

GLOSSARY

1 *mid-western town*: Iowa, a state in the US. Boland attended the prestigious Iowa Writers' Workshop in 1979 and lived there for a while with her family.
2 *myths*: fictitious tales with supernatural characters and events.
6 *hero*: Aeneas was a hero in the *Aeneid*. He visited the underworld by crossing the River Styx where he saw his dead companions, but they could not communicate with him.
8 *Amish*: strict American religious sect that makes functional, practical furniture without decoration.
31 *epic*: great, ambitious.
35 *formidable*: very impressive.

EXPLORATIONS

1. This poem is an open and honest meditation on the nature of love. Write your own personal response to it, referring to the text in your answer.
2. Do you think the use of the Aeneas myth is effective? Give reasons, using the poem as evidence for your point of view.
3. Explain the significance of the last section of the poem: 'But the words are shadows and you cannot hear me./You walk away and I cannot follow'. In your opinion, is this a positive or negative ending?

STUDY NOTES

'Love' is part of a sequence of poems called 'Legends' in which Boland explores parallels between myths and modern life. She records her personal experience of young love in Iowa at a time when tragedy touched the family, when her youngest daughter was seriously ill and came close to death. This is interwoven with the myth of Aeneas returning to the underworld. The narrative poem explores the nature of human relationships and how they change over time. It also shows the similarity of human experience down through the ages.

Lines 1–6

The poem opens in darkness, **remembering the past**. Her personal experience was in 'this mid-western town' in Iowa, and the poem connects this with the myth of Aeneas visiting the underworld. Aeneas crosses the bridge on the River Styx to reach Hades, the land of the Shades ('the hero crossed on his way to hell'). Boland and her husband were also experiencing their own hell as they visited their very sick little girl in hospital.

Lines 7–12

These lines give us a **clear, detailed picture of their external ordinary life**: 'a kitchen', 'an Amish table', 'a view'. The poem is written in loose, non-rhyming stanzas, which suits reminiscences. Their internal emotional life is shown in the **striking metaphor** 'love had the feather and muscle of wings'. Love was beating, alive, vibrant. 'Feather' suggests it could soar to great heights, while 'muscle' suggests it was a powerful emotion. This natural, graceful love was palpable, substantial, elemental, 'a brother of fire and air'.

Lines 13–19

The **personal drama** of the sick daughter who 'was touched by death' is recalled. But Boland did not lose her child. The word 'spared' links us with the myth again. Aeneas is in the underworld, but because his comrades are shadows, they cannot ask the questions they are longing to ask about the life they once shared. The moment of communication is lost: 'there is no knowing what they would have asked'.

Lines 20–36
Now the poet meditates on the **changing nature of love**. The 'we' becomes 'I' – 'I am your wife'. Do they, as husband and wife, communicate as deeply as they did before? 'We speak plainly' suggests they do not. Her tone is crisp and matter of fact, almost **businesslike**. She wants to recapture the intensity of their love and shared times, when she saw her husband as 'a hero in a text'. In her memory of him, he is outlined by the cars' lights as they pass on the bridge. Described as 'blazing' and 'gilded', he is contrasted to the darkness of the night, as Aeneas is contrasted with the darkness of the underworld. She is longing to experience that special time, that transcendence, again.

Rhetorical questions are posed at the end: 'Will we ever live so intensely again?' The inference is no. She can imagine asking these questions about the life they shared together, but she cannot actually articulate them. This is **similar to Aeneas' dilemma** – his comrades long to ask questions about the life they shared with him, but 'their voices failed'. Neither Boland nor the 'comrades' could express their strong feelings; neither can ask the questions they want to ask. The words of the questions remain unformed, unspoken, 'shadows'.

Lines 37–38
The poem ends with a two-line stanza in which she accepts that the **gap cannot be bridged**: 'You walk away and I cannot follow'. There is a real sense of loss and resignation in Boland's final tone.

ANALYSIS

This poem is about memory. How does the poet explore the theme? Refer either to the content or style in your answer. Illustrate your response with reference to the poem.

SAMPLE PARAGRAPH

By blending myth and personal experience, Boland gives her poems a true sense of universality. But she also blends timelines, the past and the present tenses to give a quality of timelessness to her work. In 'Love', the immediacy and freshness of a potent memory is captured by her use of the present tense: 'Dark falls', 'the bridge ... slides and deepens/to become the water', 'here is our old apartment'. The recent past is shown in the past tense as she recalls what they had: 'We had a kitchen and an Amish table./We had a view', 'love ... had come to live with us', 'We had two infant children'. In the past they had a life together which was lived very intensely. Are they missing any of this now? The tense then changes to the present as Boland states her identity: 'I am your wife'. I notice that it is the partnership she is referring to, not her role as mother. Here she honestly and openly explores her concerns about the changing nature of love. Their moment of crisis is over: 'Our child was healed'. She itemises a list: 'We speak', 'we hear'. They 'love each other still'. But a note of longing is heard in 'I want' and the future tense 'Will we?' Realistically she appraises the current situation and notes 'words are shadows', 'you cannot hear me', 'You walk away', 'I cannot follow'. The intense personal nature of their love has changed. Like Aeneas' comrades, she cannot voice her question ('voices failed'), and her husband, like Aeneas, cannot hear. The changing tenses add a timeless quality to the experience of memory, as time shared is recalled. The poem ends with the never-changing realisation that time cannot be relived.

EXAMINER'S COMMENT

An unusual approach is taken as the response features on the use of tenses as a stylistic feature to communicate theme. There is evidence of close reading of the poem and effective use of accurate quotation throughout. Grade A standard.

CLASS/HOMEWORK EXERCISES

1. 'When myths collided.' Do you consider Boland's use of myths in her work effective in exploring her themes? Discuss, referring to the poems on your course.
2. Copy the table below into your own notes and use the blank spaces to fill in the missing critical comments about the last two quotations.

Key Quotes

But the words are shadows and you cannot hear me./You walk away and I cannot follow	Both the comrades of Aeneas and Boland herself cannot connect with their respective 'heroes'. They shared life and dangers with these heroes, but they cannot ask them a question.
love had the feather and muscle of wings	This metaphor suggests the dynamic and vibrant love between the young wife and husband. It was both uplifting and strong.
across our day-to-day and ordinary distances/we speak plainly	Now in later life they converse in an ordinary way, but Boland seems to be longing to return to a time when they communicated in an extraordinary way.
it offered us ascension/even to look at him	
and I long to cry out the epic question	

LEAVING CERT SAMPLE ESSAY

Q 'The appeal of Eavan Boland's poetry.'

Using the above title, write an essay outlining what you consider to be the appeal of Boland's poetry. Support your points by reference to the poetry of Eavan Boland on your course.

MARKING SCHEME GUIDELINES

Answers to the question must contain clear evidence of engagement with the poetry on the course. Allow that candidates might focus, in part at least, on reasons why the poetry does not appeal to readers. Expect a wide variety of approaches in the candidates' answering.

Some of the following areas might be addressed:

- Her perspective on Irishness, history and myth.
- Her sense of national identity.
- Her siding with victims and the downtrodden.
- Striking love poetry.
- Treatment of the suburbs as a suitable locale for poetry.
- Delicate use of language and imagery, etc.

SAMPLE ESSAY
(The Appeal of Boland's Poetry)

1 *When reading Eavan Boland's poetry, an appealing aspect is that a genuine concern for the past is obvious. There is a sense that women are outside history. She has an attractive, sympathetic response to suffering. Her mixture of public and private events and public and private attitudes are also interesting. I also enjoyed her use of language.*

2 *In 'Outside History', Boland recognises the great women of the past who were ignored: 'There are outsiders, always.' She calls them 'stars', 'iron inklings of an Irish January'. I was delighted that our first woman President, Mary Robinson, quoted this in her inauguration speech. Just as the sky is cluttered with stars that are above and outside man's history, so history is full of these women 'whose darkness is/only now reaching me from those fields'. The contrast between the vastness of the cosmos and the self-importance of the world is striking. Boland's* decision to highlight these women is stated strongly in the phrase 'I have chosen'. The use of 'we' shows that Boland has assumed the role of speaking for the Irish people 'As we kneel beside them', almost trying to hear what they have to say. The poem ends bleakly with the realisation that 'We are always too late'.

3 Boland gives a very interesting woman's perspective in her poems. This is often missing in literature, just as Irish women are missing from recorded history. In 'The Famine Road', Boland has absented herself from the poem. She doesn't personalise the poem, but her presence is felt everywhere in her sympathetic response to the suffering: 'after all could/they not blood their knuckles on rock, suck/April hailstones for water and for food?' The wandering lines portray the wandering roads that were 'going nowhere'. The poem begins with a letter being read by Colonel Jones from Trevalyan to a relief committee. The dismissive tone of the letter comes across vividly in the phrases 'Idle as trout' and 'their bones/need toil'. The terrible death sentence is dramatically shown: 'Trevalyan's/seal blooded the deal table'. The wax seal has become a death warrant.

4 Against this public and political world, the world of the nineteenth-century Irish famine is intertwined with another woman's private sorrow. The italicised verse is given no introduction as a doctor coldly judges what is best for another. Cold statistics are quoted: 'one out of every ten'. What consolation is that to the poor woman who will never know 'the load/of his child' in her? Her body will produce nothing, just as the famine road works result in death: 'This Tuesday I saw bones/out of my carriage window'. This poem works on many levels – the private and personal, the public and historical, the male and female, the master and subordinate – but overseeing it all is the compassionate poet who makes us see the pity of it. This is an appealing aspect for readers.

5 This double private–public aspect of Boland's poetry is interestingly shown in 'Child of Our Time'. A child has died in an explosion in Dublin city. This infant has become a 'child of our time', a victim because we, the adults, did not do enough to protect the vulnerable: 'our times have robbed your cradle'. The dedication, 'for Aengus', refers to a friend's baby who had died a cot death. Here again, Boland is intertwining a public tragedy with a personal grief. Is she telling us that we have to realise that all grief is personal? The conclusion hints at the peaceful world the child will sleep in now that our world has done its worst: 'Sleep in a world your final sleep has woken'. It also suggests that we have woken up to what we have both done ('our idle/Talk') and not done ('We who should have known') and hopefully will mend our ways ('find for your sake ... a new language').

6. The parent–child relationship is also given another perspective in 'This Moment'. This poem has a mysterious quality to it. The description of the 'rinds slanting around fruit' conveys the silent, strange world of Nature. Things are happening, but 'out of sight'. The disjointed line pattern echoes this. The domestic atmosphere is increased by the image of the woman leaning down 'to catch a child/who has run into her arms/this moment'. For a mother and child, this is indeed a golden moment. But again, we have the double perspective on an event. 'This Moment' has two very different sides: the child returning after a day's play into the safety of the home, and the changing, growing world of Nature, working to its own rhythm.

7. I found the poetry of Eavan Boland appealing because of her subject matter and the perspectives she gives us as well as the questions she raises. I found her poetic techniques very powerful in conveying her message, either in the italicised doctor's words in 'The Famine Road' or in the disjointed line structure in 'This Moment'. But I found her compassionate voice most appealing of all, as she quietly shows us that we must remember the Irish women who are not recorded in history; we must find 'a new language' to discuss rather than distrust; and we should appreciate the wonder of our beautiful, ordinary yet extraordinary world: 'A neighbourhood./At dusk'. The appeal of Eavan Boland is both as a woman and a poet.

(approx. 900 words)

GRADE: A2		
P	=	13/15
C	=	13/15
L	=	13/15
M	=	5/5
Total	=	44/50

EXAMINER'S COMMENT

The candidate has concentrated her response to an exploration of Boland's double perspective and her compassionate quality. The appeal of the poems is implicitly stated throughout much of the essay. A solid performance, very well illustrated with apt reference and quotation.

• Poetry Focus •

Eavan Boland

SAMPLE LEAVING CERT QUESTIONS ON BOLAND'S POETRY
(45–50 MINUTES)

1. 'Eavan Boland deals with issues which are both private and personal, but which also have a universal appeal.' Discuss this statement, supporting your answer with reference to the poems by Boland on your course.
2. Write the text of a talk you would give your class on the merits of Eavan Boland's poetry, referring both to the themes explored and the style of her communication. Illustrate your answer by reference to the poems by Eavan Boland on your course.
3. 'Boland, a modern poet dealing with contemporary issues.' How relevant do you think this view of Eavan Boland is? Discuss, using reference to the poetry of hers on your course.

SAMPLE ESSAY PLAN (Q1)

'Eavan Boland deals with issues which are both private and personal, but which also have a universal appeal.' Discuss this statement, supporting your answer with reference to the poems by Boland on your course.

- *Intro:* A personal response is required; mention both content and style. Both the private and public as well as universal dimensions of her poetry are to be explored.

- *Point 1:* 'Child of Our Time' – personal response to newspaper picture of the dead child given resonance by saying all of us need to a new language. Tone both compassionate and admonishing.

- *Point 2:* 'The Pomegranate' – deals with the relationship between mother and daughter, particularly the moment of separation when the child has to go, despite the mother's worry of then being unable to protect her. This personal situation is linked to the myth of Persephone and Ceres, giving it a timeless dimension.

- *Point 3:* 'The War Horse' – metaphorical poem about the attitudes to war. Rigid, controlled couplets show

	the suburban desire for order, while the epic title widens the appeal of the poem. Contemplates history in a unique fashion; the blending of past and present blurs the boundaries of time.
• Point 4:	'This Moment' – a moment in suburbia, at dusk. Emphasis on 'a' suggests it can apply to any child, any neighbourhood. The collective experience is shown.
• Point 5:	'Love' – again, a link with a myth gives a unanimous appeal to the poem. Aeneas and the underworld illustrate the frustration of the poet grappling with the changing aspects of love. A treatment of emotion in an honest way.
• Conclusion:	Boland refers to specific personal moments or events and gives them a widespread interest by linking them with mythology, by changing tones and by her striking visual descriptions. Her poetry transcends the particular to become general.

EXERCISE

Develop one of the above points into a paragraph.

POINT 5 – SAMPLE PARAGRAPH

By interweaving myth with a personal story, Boland creates poetry that becomes universally appealing. She uses this technique in 'The Pomegranate' and also in the poem 'Love'. Here, the story of the hero Aeneas, who goes to the underworld where his dead comrades are, is interwoven with a story of Boland's, when her daughter was seriously ill. In each there is a hero, Aeneas and Boland's husband ('the hero crossed on his way to hell'). Each has their own trauma to deal with. Aeneas cannot hear what 'his comrades in hell' want to ask, as their 'voices failed'. The questions they wanted to ask 'about a life they had shared and lost' will never be known. Similarly, Boland is unable to ask about a life she and her husband had known, as she feels unable to ask the question 'Will we ever live so intensely again?' They had lived in this way when one of their children was 'touched by death in this town/and spared'. Often in times of tragedy people are capable of great things. To Boland, her husband was 'a hero in a text'. Although both are still in love ('We love each other still'), she longs for the love they once shared ('ascension'). It was an almost ecstatic, spiritual experience. But just as Aeneas is never asked questions by his comrades, so her husband is never asked her question. Instead, the 'words are shadows', without substance, silent. He 'cannot hear' her. Yet again, a domestic event is transformed into a wider arena by enmeshing it with a myth, the story of Aeneas crossing the River Styx.

EXAMINER'S COMMENT

As part of a full essay answer, the student has written an impressive A grade paragraph and gives a personal response firmly rooted in the text. The paragraph centres on the use of myth by Boland to explore the wider dimensions of domestic situations. Well supported by quotes.

Last Words

'Eavan Boland's work continues to deepen in both humanity and complexity.'
Fiona Sampson

'Memory, change, loss, the irrecoverable past – such are the shared condition of humankind, with which she scrupulously engages.'
Anne Stevenson

'Poets are those who ransack their perishing mind and find pattern and form.'
Eavan Boland

'Forever is composed of nows.'

Emily Dickinson (1830–86)

Emily Dickinson was born on 10 December 1830 in Amherst, Massachusetts. Widely regarded as one of America's greatest poets, she is also known for her unusual life of self-imposed social seclusion. An enigmatic figure with a fondness for the macabre, Dickinson never married. She was a prolific letter-writer and private poet, though fewer than a dozen of her poems were published during her lifetime. It was only after her death in 1886 that her work was discovered. It is estimated that she wrote about 1,770 poems, many of which explored the nature of immortality and death, with an almost mantric quality at times. Ultimately, however, she is remembered for her distinctive style, which was unique for the era in which she wrote. Her poems contain short lines, typically lack titles and often ignore the rules of grammar, syntax and punctuation, yet she expressed far-reaching ideas within compact phrases. Amidst paradox and uncertainty, her poetry has an undeniable capacity to move and provoke.

• Poetry Focus •

PRESCRIBED POEMS (HIGHER LEVEL)

Emily Dickinson

1 **'"Hope" is the thing with feathers'** (p. 60)

In this upbeat poem, Dickinson addresses the experience of hope and imagines it as having some of the characteristics of a small bird.

2 **'There's a certain Slant of light'** (p. 64)

A particular beam of winter light puts the poet into a depressed mood in which she reflects on human mortality and our relationship with God.

3 **'I felt a Funeral, in my Brain'** (p. 68)

Dickinson imagines the experience of death from the perspective of a person who is about to be buried.

4 **'A Bird came down the Walk'** (p. 73)

The poet observes a bird and tries to establish contact with it, revealing both the beauty and danger of nature.

5 **'I Heard a Fly buzz—when I died'** (p. 77)

Another illustration of Dickinson's obsession with the transition of the soul from life into eternity.

6 **'The Soul had Bandaged moments'** (p. 81)

This intricate poem explores the soul's changing moods, from terrified depression to delirious joy.

7 **'I could bring You Jewels—had I a mind to'** (p. 86)

In this short love poem, Dickinson celebrates nature's simple delights and contrasts the beauty of an everyday flower with more exotic precious gifts.

8 **'A narrow Fellow in the Grass'** (p. 90)

Using a male perspective, the poet details the fascination and terror experienced in confronting a snake.

9 **'I taste a liquor never brewed'** (p. 94)

Dickinson uses an extended metaphor of intoxication in this exuberant celebration of nature in summertime.

10 **'After great pain, a formal feeling comes'** (p. 98)

A disturbing examination of the after-effects of suffering and anguish on the individual. Dickinson's comparisons highlight the experience of deadly numbness.

• Poetry Focus •

'Hope' is the thing with feathers

Emily Dickinson

'Hope' is the thing with feathers—
That perches in the soul—
And sings the tune without the words—
And never stops—at all—

And sweetest—in the Gale—is heard— 5
And sore must be the storm—
That could abash the little Bird
That kept so many warm—

I've heard it in the chillest land—
And on the strangest Sea— 10
Yet, never, in Extremity,
It asked a crumb—of Me.

'And sweetest—in the Gale—is heard—'

GLOSSARY

5 *And sweetest—in the Gale—is heard*: hope is most comforting in times of trouble.
7 *abash*: embarrass; defeat.
11 *in Extremity*: in terrible times.

EXPLORATIONS

1 What are the main characteristics of the bird admired by Dickinson? Does the image contribute to or hinder your understanding of the meaning of hope? Refer to the poem in support of your opinions.

2 Would you consider Dickinson to be an optimist or pessimist? How does the poem contribute to your view?

3 In your view, what is the purpose of the poem – to instruct, to explain, to express a feeling? Support your response by reference to the text.

STUDY NOTES

> Few of Emily Dickinson's poems were published during her lifetime and it was not until 1955, sixty-nine years after her death, that an accurate edition of her poems was published, with the original punctuation and words. This didactic poem explores the abstraction, hope. It is one of her 'definition' poems, wherein she likens hope to a little bird, offering comfort to all.

The dictionary definition of hope is an expectation of something desired. The Bible refers to hope, saying, 'Hope deferred maketh the heart sick', while the poet Alexander Pope (1688–1744) declares that 'Hope springs eternal in the human breast'. In **stanza one**, Dickinson explores hope by using the **metaphor of a little bird** whose qualities are similar to those of hope: non-threatening, calm and powerful. Just like the bird, hope can rise above the earth with all its troubles and desperate times. Raised in the Puritan tradition, Dickinson, although rejecting formal religion, would have been aware of the religious symbolism of the dove and its connection with divine inspiration and the Spirit or Holy Ghost, as well as the reference to doves in the story of Noah's Ark and the Flood. Hope appears against all odds and 'perches in the soul'. But this hope is not easily defined, so she refers to it as 'the thing', an inanimate object. This silent presence is able to **communicate** beyond reason and logic and far **beyond the limitations of language**: 'sings the tune without the words'. Hope's permanence is highlighted by the unusual use of dashes in the punctuation: 'never stops—at all—'. This effective use of punctuation suggests the ongoing process of hope.

Stanza two focuses on the tangible qualities of hope (sweetness and warmth) and shows the spiritual, emotional and psychological **comfort found in hope**. The 'Gale' could refer to the inner state of confusion felt in the agony of despair. The little bird that comforts and shelters its young offers protection to 'so many'. The vigour of the word 'abash' suggests the buffeting wind of the storm against which the little bird survives. The last two lines, which run on, convey the welcoming, protective circle of the little bird's wing.

A **personal experience of hope in times of anguish** ('I've heard') is referred to in **stanza three**. Extreme circumstances are deftly sketched in the phrases 'chillest land' and 'strangest Sea'. This reclusive poet, who spent most of her life indoors in her father's house, deftly catches an alien, foreign element. She then explains that hope is not demanding in bad times; it is generous, giving rather than taking: 'Yet, never, in Extremity,/It asked a crumb—of Me'. The central paradox of hope is expressed in the metaphor of the bird, delicate and fragile, yet strong and indomitable. The tiny bird is an effective image for the first stirring of hope in a time of despair. In the solemn ending, the poet gives hope the dignified celebration it deserves.

Dickinson is a unique and original talent. She used the metre of hymns. She also uses their form of the four-line verse. Yet this is not conventional poetry, due to Dickinson's use of the dash to slow the line and make the reader pause and consider. Ordinary words like 'at all' and 'is heard' assume a tremendous importance and their position is to be considered and savoured. Her unusual punctuation has the same effect as it highlights the dangers ('Gale', 'Sea'). The alliteration of 's' in 'strangest Sea' and the run-on line to suggest the circling comfort of the little bird all add to the curious music of Dickinson's poems. The buoyant, self-confident tone of the poem is in direct contrast to the strict Puritanical tradition of a severe, righteous God, with which she would have been familiar in her youth and which she rejected, preferring to keep her Sabbath 'staying at home'.

ANALYSIS

'Emily Dickinson's poetry contains an intense awareness of the private, inner self.' Discuss how Dickinson gives expression to this interior world in her poetry. Support your exploration with quotations from her prescribed poems.

SAMPLE PARAGRAPH

Everyone has experienced the 'dark night of the soul' when it seems nothing is ever going to go right again. Dickinson, with her simple image of the bird singing in the soul, derived from psalms, provides the perfect optimistic antidote to this dark interior state of mind, 'Hope is the thing with feathers'. She then develops this metaphor throughout the poem, comforting us with the thought that the bird/hope can communicate with us without the need for the restrictions of language, 'sings the tune without words'. There is no end to hope 'And never stops at all'. She understands the darkness of despair, 'in the Gale', 'the strangest Sea'. The use of capitalisation by the poet seems to me to point out the terror of the individual struggling to survive. But the bird of hope provides comfort and warmth, 'And sweetest'. I like the poet's use of enjambment in the lines 'That could abash the little Bird/That kept so many warm'. It is as if the protection of hope encircles the individual, just as the wing of the little bird protects her young in the nest. This is an optimistic, buoyant poem in which Dickinson appears to be instructing the reader that one should never despair. The phrase 'perches in the soul' suggests to me that the poet regards hope as coming of its own volition, it just appears, there is a sense of otherworldliness about it. Hope, she tells us, is generous, never demanding, always giving, 'Yet, never, in Extremity,/It asked a crumb—of Me'. I think the use of the capital for 'Me' shows the heightened concern of someone for him/herself when the feeling of despair envelops.

EXAMINER'S COMMENT

This response shows an awareness of the poet's style and content. It is a solid B grade response. However, it lacks the in-depth analysis required for an A grade answer.

CLASS/HOMEWORK EXERCISES

1. 'Dickinson is a wholly new and original poetic genius.' Do you agree or disagree with this statement? Support your response with reference to the poems on your course.
2. Copy the table below into your own notes and fill in critical comments about the last two quotations.

Key Quotes

'Hope' is the thing with feathers	The image of the bird is used to represent hope.
And sweetest—in the Gale	Hope is needed most in times of trouble.
And sore must be the storm	The danger must be very great.
I've heard it in the chillest land	
Yet, never, in Extremity,/It asked a crumb—of Me	

• Poetry Focus •

There's a certain Slant of light

Emily Dickinson

There's a certain Slant of light,
Winter Afternoons—
That oppresses, like the Heft
Of Cathedral Tunes—

Heavenly Hurt, it gives us—   5
We can find no scar,
But internal difference,
Where the Meanings, are—

None may teach it—Any—
'Tis the Seal Despair—   10
An imperial affliction
Sent us of the Air—

When it comes, the Landscape listens—
Shadows—hold their breath—
When it goes, 'tis like the Distance   15
On the look of Death—

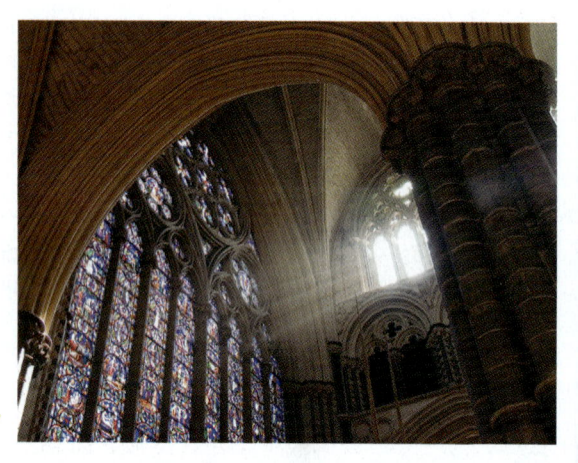

'Heavenly Hurt, it gives us'

GLOSSARY
1 *Slant*: incline; fall; interpretation.
3 *oppresses*: feels heavy; overwhelms.
3 *Heft*: strength, weight.
9 *Any*: anything.
10 *Seal Despair*: sign or symbol of hopelessness.
11 *imperial affliction*: God's will for mortal human beings.

EXPLORATIONS

1. Describe the mood and atmosphere created by the poet in the opening stanza.
2. Comment on Dickinson's use of personification within the poem.
3. Write your own personal response to the poem, supporting your views with reference or quotation.

STUDY NOTES

> Dickinson was a keen observer of her environment, often dramatising her observations in poems. In this case, a particular beam of winter light puts the poet into a mood of depression as the slanting sunlight communicates a sense of despair. The poem typifies her creeping fascination with mortality. But although the poet's subject matter is intricate and disturbing, her own views are more difficult to determine. Ironically, this exploration of light and its effects seems to suggest a great deal about Dickinson's own dark consciousness.

From the outset, Dickinson creates an uneasy atmosphere. The setting ('Winter Afternoons') is dreary and desultory. Throughout stanza one, there is an underlying sense of time weighing heavily, especially when the light is compared to solemn cathedral music ('Cathedral Tunes'). We usually expect church music to be inspirational and uplifting, but in this case, its 'Heft' has a burdensome effect which simply 'oppresses' and adds to the **downcast mood**.

In stanza two, the poet considers the significance of the sunlight. For her, its effects are negative, causing pain to the world: 'Heavenly Hurt, it gives us'. The paradoxical language appears to reflect Dickinson's ironic attitude that **human beings live in great fear of God's power**. Is there a sense that deep down in their souls ('Where the Meanings, are'), people struggle under the weight of God's will, fearing death and judgement?

This feeling of humanity's helplessness is highlighted in stanza three: 'None may teach it' sums up the predicament of our limitations. Life and death can never be fully understood. Perhaps this is our tragic fate – our 'Seal Despair'. Dickinson presents **God as an all-powerful royal figure** associated with suffering and punishment ('An imperial affliction'). Is the poet's tone critical and accusatory? Or is she simply expressing the reality of human experience?

Stanza four is highly dramatic. **Dickinson personifies a terrified world** where 'the Landscape listens'. The earlier sombre light is now replaced by 'Shadows' that 'hold their breath' in the silence. The poet imagines the shocking moment of death and the mystery of time ('the Distance'). While the poem's ending is open to speculation, it seems clear that Dickinson is exploring the transition from life into eternity, a subject that is central to her writing. The only certain conclusion is an obvious one – that death is an inescapable reality beyond human understanding, as mysterious as it is natural. The poet's final tone is resigned, almost relieved. The 'Slant of light' offers no definitive answers to life's questions and the human condition is as inexplicable as death itself.

Throughout the poem, Dickinson's fragmented style is characterised by her **erratic punctuation and repeated use of capital letters**. She uses the dash at every opportunity to create suspense and drama. For the poet, the winter light is seen as an important sign from God, disturbing the inner 'Landscape' of her soul. In the end, the light (a likely metaphor for truth) causes Dickinson to experience an inner sadness and a deep sense of spiritual longing.

ANALYSIS

In your view, what is the central theme in this poem? Support the points you make with suitable reference to the text.

SAMPLE PARAGRAPH

I think that death is the main theme in all of Emily Dickinson's poems, including this one. The poem is very atmospheric, but the light coming through the church window can be interpreted as a symbol of God, hope for the world. However, Dickinson's language is quite negative and it could be argued that our human lives are under pressure and that fear of eternal damnation is also part of life. The phrases 'Heavenly Hurt' and 'imperial affliction' suggest that we are God's subjects, trying to avoid sin in this life in order to find salvation after death. One of the central points in the poem is the fear of dying that people have. It is outside of our control. All humans can do is 'hold their breath'. I believe that the central message of Dickinson's poem is that death comes to us all and we must accept it. The mood throughout the poem is oppressive, just like the sunlight coming in through the church window and the depressing 'Cathedral Tunes' the poet hears. The poet's distinctive punctuation, using dashes and abrupt stops and starts, is part of the tense mood of the poem. Dickinson's theme is quite distressing and the broken rhythms and disturbing images such as 'scar', 'Seal Despair' and 'Shadows' add to the uneasiness of the theme that death is unavoidable.

EXAMINER'S COMMENT

A well-sustained response which attempted to stay focused throughout. In the main, references and quotations were used effectively, and there were some worthwhile attempts to show how features of the poet's style enhanced the presentation of her central theme. Grade A.

CLASS/HOMEWORK EXERCISES

1. How would you describe the dominant mood of the poem? Is it positive in any way? Explain your response, supporting the points you make with suitable reference to the text.
2. Copy the table below into your own notes and fill in critical comments about the last two quotations.

Key Quotes

Winter Afternoons	The oppressive mood is reinforced through the setting itself and suggested by the use of this assonant phrase.
But internal difference	Dickinson believes that the pain of being mortal is an inner one, both psychological and spiritual.
'Tis the Seal Despair	This rich metaphor suggests that because people are subject to God's will, their spiritual fate is sealed.
Heavenly Hurt	
Shadows—hold their breath	

• Poetry Focus •

I felt a Funeral, in my Brain

I felt a Funeral, in my Brain,
And Mourners to and fro
Kept treading—treading—till it seemed
That Sense was breaking through—

And when they all were seated, 5
A Service, like a Drum—
Kept beating—beating—till I thought
My Mind was going numb—

And then I heard them lift a Box
And creak across my Soul 10
With those same Boots of Lead, again,
Then Space—began to toll,

As all the Heavens were a Bell,
And Being, but an Ear,
And I, and Silence, some strange Race 15
Wrecked, solitary, here—

And then a Plank in Reason, broke,
And I dropped down, and down—
And hit a World, at every plunge,
And Finished knowing—then— 20

'And then a Plank in Reason, broke'

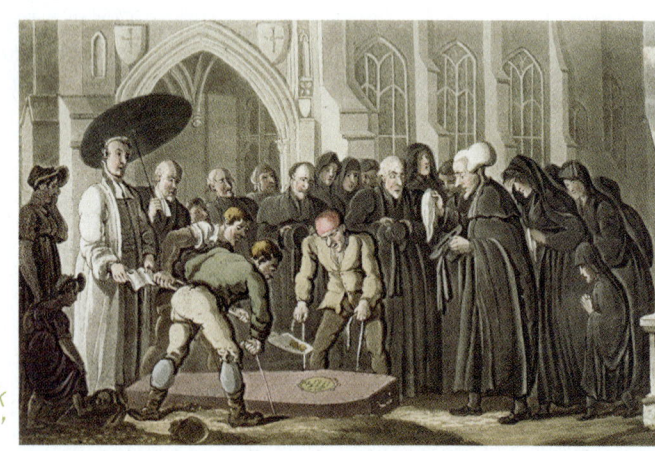

GLOSSARY

3   *treading*: crush by walking on.
4   *Sense*: faculty of perception; the senses (seeing, hearing, touching, tasting, smelling); sound, practical judgement.
12 *toll*: ring slowly and steadily, especially to announce a death.
13 *As all*: as if all.
14 *And Being, but an Ear*: all senses, except hearing, are now useless.

EXPLORATIONS

1. Do you find the pictures in this poem frightening, macabre or coldly realistic? Give reasons for your answer, supported by textual reference.
2. What is the dominant tone in the poem? Where is the climax of the poem, in your opinion? Refer to the text in your answer.
3. Consider the rhyme scheme of the poem. In your view, why does the poet rhyme words like 'Drum'/'numb' and 'Soul'/'toll'? In your opinion, why does the rhyme scheme break down in the last stanza?

STUDY NOTES

This poem is thought to have been written in 1861 at a time of turbulence in Dickinson's life. She was having religious and artistic doubts and had experienced an unhappy time in a personal relationship. This interior landscape paints a dark picture of something falling apart. It is for the reader to decide whether it is a fainting spell, a mental breakdown or a funeral. That is the enigma of Dickinson.

The startling perspective of this poem in **stanza one** can be seen as the view experienced by a person in a coffin, if the poem is read as an **account of the poet imagining her death**. Alternatively, it could refer to the suffocating feeling of the breakdown of consciousness, either through fainting or a mental breakdown. Perhaps it is the dearth of artistic activity. Whichever reading is chosen, and maybe all co-exist, the **interior landscape of awareness is being explored**. The use of the personal pronoun 'I' shows that this is a unique experience, although it has relevance for all. The relentless pounding of the mourners walking is reminiscent of a blinding migraine headache. The repetition of the hard-sounding 't' in the verb 'treading—treading' evocatively describes this terrible experience. The 'I' is undergoing an intense trauma beyond understanding: 'Sense was breaking through'. This repetition and disorientation are synonymous with psychological breakdown.

Stanza two gives a **first-person account of a funeral**. The mourners are seated and the service has begun. Hearing ('an Ear') is the only sense able to perceive the surroundings. All the verbs refer to sound: 'tread', 'beat', 'heard', 'creak', 'toll'. The passive 'I' receives the experience, hearing, not listening, which is an active process. The experience is so overwhelming that 'I' thought the 'Mind was going numb', unable to endure any more. The use of the past tense reminds the reader that the experience is over, so is the first-person narrative told from beyond the grave? Is this the voice of someone who has died? Or is it the voice of someone in the throes of a desperate personal experience? The reader must decide.

The reference to 'Soul' in **stanza three** suggests a **spiritual dimension** to the experience. The 'I' has begun to become disoriented as the line dividing an external experience and an internal one is breaking. The mourners 'creak across my Soul'. The oppressive, almost suffocating experience is captured in the onomatopoeic phrase 'Boots of Lead' and space becomes filled with the tolling bell. Existence in **stanza four** is reduced totally to hearing. The fearful transitory experience of crossing from awareness to unconsciousness, from life to death, is being imagined. The 'I' in stanza four is now stranded, 'Wrecked', cut off from life. The person is in a comatose state, able to comprehend but unable to communicate: 'solitary, here'. The word 'here' makes the reader feel present at this awful drama.

Finally, in **stanza five**, a new sensation takes over, the **sense of falling uncontrollably**. The 'I' has finished knowing and is now no longer aware of surroundings. Is this the descent into the hell of the angels in *Paradise Lost*? Is it the descent of the coffin into the grave? Or is it the descent into madness or oblivion? The 'I' has learned something, but it is not revealed. The repetition of 'And' advances the movement of the poem in an almost uncontrollable way, mimicking the final descent. The 'I' is powerless under the repetitive verbs and the incessant rhythm punctuated by the ever-present dash. This poem is extraordinary, because before the study of psychology had defined it, it is a step-by-step description of mental collapse. Here is 'the drama of process'.

ANALYSIS

'This poem is a detailed exploration of the experience of death.' Discuss this statement, using references from the text to support your views.

SAMPLE PARAGRAPH

When I first read Emily Dickinson's poem 'I felt A Funeral, in my Brain', I was reminded of the macabre pictures of Salvador Dali, where everything is real, but not quite right. It also reminded me of the films of Tim Burton, such as *The Nightmare Before Christmas*. All the elements are there, but nothing is totally right, it is surreal. This imagined funeral in the poem suggests to me the losing of the grip on life by the individual 'I'. The incessant noise, 'treading', 'beating', induces an almost trance-like state as the brain cannot function any more, and so becomes numb. In death, the senses are supposed to shut down, sight is one of the first to go, so I think it is very clever of the poet to suggest that being is just reduced to the one sense hearing – 'an Ear'. I also find the perspective of the poem chilling, the idea that this is the view of someone lying in the coffin observing their funeral is macabre in the extreme. But the most compelling line in the poem is 'And then a Plank in Reason, broke'. This graphically conveys the snap of reason as the 'I' finally loses a grip on consciousness and slips away, hurtling uncontrollably into another dimension. Even the punctuation, with the use of the two commas, conveys this divided reality. But the most unnerving word is yet to come, 'then'. Does the poet know now? What does the poet know, is it about the existence or non-existence of an afterlife? Where is the poet standing now – here or there, alive or dead?

EXAMINER'S COMMENT

An unusual, individual reading of the poem, and generally well supported by reference to the text. There are some weaknesses in expression and the paragraph is not fully focused on the question. Overall, a B grade response.

CLASS/HOMEWORK EXERCISES

1. 'She seems as close to touching bottom here as she ever got.' Discuss this view of Emily Dickinson with reference to the poem 'I felt a Funeral, in my Brain'.
2. Copy the table below into your own notes and fill in critical comments about the last two quotations.

• Poetry Focus •

Emily Dickinson

Key Quotes	
That Sense was breaking through	This enigmatic line could refer to the breakdown of the five senses, or that reason was collapsing or coming.
My Mind was going numb	The narrator in the poem is presented as a passive recipient who can no longer endure this traumatic experience. This is enhanced by assonance.
As all the heavens were a Bell	All the universe had turned into this great pealing of the bell; nothing else existed for the narrator.
And creak across my Soul	
And then a Plank in Reason, broke	

A Bird came down the Walk

Emily Dickinson

A Bird came down the Walk—
He did not know I saw—
He bit an Angleworm in halves
And ate the fellow, raw,

And then he drank a Dew   5
From a convenient Grass—
And then hopped sidewise to the Wall
To let a Beetle pass—

He glanced with rapid eyes
That hurried all around—   10
They looked like frightened Beads, I thought—
He stirred his Velvet Head

Like one in danger, Cautious,
I offered him a Crumb
And he unrolled his feathers   15
And rowed him softer home—

Than Oars divide the Ocean,
Too silver for a seam—
Or Butterflies, off Banks of Noon
Leap, plashless as they swim.   20

'He glanced with rapid eyes'

GLOSSARY

3 *Angleworm*: small worm used as fish bait by anglers.
17 *the Ocean*: Dickinson compares the blue sky to the sea.
18 *silver*: the sea's surface looks like solid silver.
18 *a seam*: opening; division.
20 *plashless*: splashless; undisturbed.

EXPLORATIONS

1 In your view, what does the poem suggest about the relationship between human beings and nature?
2 What effect does Dickinson's use of humour in the poem have? Does it let you see nature in a different way? Support the points you make with reference to the text.
3 From your reading of the poem, what impression of Emily Dickinson herself is conveyed? Refer to the text in your answer.

STUDY NOTES

In this short descriptive poem, Dickinson celebrates the beauty and wonder of animals. While the bird is seen as a wild creature at times, other details present its behaviour and appearance in human terms. The poem also illustrates Dickinson's quirky sense of humour as well as offering interesting insights into nature and the exclusion of human beings from that world.

The poem begins with an everyday scene. Because the bird is unaware of the poet's presence, it behaves naturally. **Stanza one** demonstrates the **competition and danger of nature**: 'He bit an Angleworm in halves'. Although Dickinson imagines the bird within a human context, casually coming 'down the Walk' and suddenly eating 'the fellow, raw', she is amused by the uncivilised reality of the animal kingdom. The word 'raw' echoes her self-deprecating sense of shock. Despite its initial elegance, the predatory bird could hardly have been expected to cook the worm.

The poet's comic portrayal continues in **stanza two**. She gives the bird certain social qualities, drinking from a 'Grass' and politely allowing a hurrying beetle to pass. The tone is relaxed and playful. The slender vowel sounds ('convenient') and soft sibilance ('sidewise', 'pass') add to the seemingly refined atmosphere. However, the mood changes in **stanza three**, reflecting the bird's cautious fear. Dickinson observes the rapid eye movement, 'like frightened Beads'. Such **precise detail increases the drama** of the moment. The details of the bird's prim movement and beautiful texture are wonderfully accurate: 'He stirred his Velvet Head'. The simile is highly effective, suggesting the animal's natural grace.

The danger becomes more explicit in **stanza four**. Both the spectator and the observed bird are 'Cautious'. The crumb offered to the bird by the poet is rejected, highlighting the **gulf between their two separate worlds**. The description of the bird taking flight evokes the delicacy and fluidity of its movement: 'And he unrolled his feathers/And rowed him softer home'. The confident rhythm and emphatic alliteration enrich our understanding of the harmony between the creature and its natural environment. The sensual imagery captures the magnificence of the bird, compared to a rower moving with ease across placid water.

Stanza five develops the metaphorical description further, conveying the bird's poise and mystery: 'Too silver for a seam'. Not only was its flying seamless, it was smoother than that of butterflies leaping 'off Banks of Noon' and splashlessly swimming through the sky. The **breathtaking image and onomatopoeic language** remind us of Dickinson's admiration for nature in all its impressive beauty and is one of the most memorable descriptions in all of Dickinson's writing.

ANALYSIS

In your view, does Dickinson have a sense of empathy with the bird? Support your response with reference to the poem.

SAMPLE PARAGRAPH

It is clear from the start of the poem that Emily Dickinson is both fascinated and amused by the appearance of a small bird in her garden. She seems surprised and almost honoured that out of nowhere 'A Bird came down the Walk'. When it suddenly swallows a worm 'raw', she becomes even more interested. The fact that she admits 'He did not know I saw' tells me that she really has empathy for the bird. Her tone suggests that she feels privileged to watch and she certainly doesn't want to disturb it in its own world. The poet also finds the bird's antics funny. Although it devours the snail, it still behaves very mannerly towards the beetle. Towards the end, Dickinson shows her feelings for the bird when it becomes frightened and she notices its 'rapid eyes'. She sees that it is 'in danger'. The fact that she offered it a crumb also shows her empathy. At the very end, she shows her admiration for the beauty and agility of the bird as it flies off to freedom – to its 'softer home'. The descriptions of it like a rower or a butterfly also suggest that she admires its grace.

Emily Dickinson

EXAMINER'S COMMENT

Apt references and short quotations are used very well to illustrate the poet's regard for the bird. The answer ranges well over much of the poem. Some further discussion on the poet's tone would have been welcome. A good grade B.

CLASS/HOMEWORK EXERCISES

1. Comment on Dickinson's use of imagery in 'A Bird came down the Walk'. Support the points you make with the aid of suitable reference.
2. Copy the table below into your own notes and fill in critical comments about the last two quotations.

Key Quotes

He did not know I saw	Dickinson is excited at the opportunity to view the bird in its natural element.
And then he drank a Dew	The poet's comic observation recognises signs of social etiquette in the bird's behaviour.
He stirred his Velvet Head	While the image conveys the bird's beauty and grandeur, 'stirred' suggests its hidden fear.
And rowed him softer home	
plashless as they swim	

I heard a Fly buzz—when I died

I heard a Fly buzz—when I died—
The Stillness in the Room
Was like the Stillness in the Air—
Between the Heaves of Storm—

The Eyes around—had wrung them dry— 5
And Breaths were gathering firm
For that last Onset—when the King
Be witnessed—in the Room—

I willed my Keepsakes—Signed away
What portion of me be 10
Assignable—and then it was
There interposed a Fly—

With Blue—uncertain stumbling Buzz—
Between the light—and me—
And then the Windows failed—and then 15
I could not see to see—

'The Stillness in the Room/Was like the Stillness in the Air—'

GLOSSARY

4	*Heaves*: lift with effort.	9	*Keepsakes*: gifts treasured for the sake of the giver.
7	*Onset*: beginning.		
7	*the King*: God.	12	*interposed*: inserted between or among things.

EXPLORATIONS

1. How would you describe the atmosphere in the poem? Pick out two phrases which, in your opinion, are especially descriptive and explain why you chose them.
2. Do you think Dickinson uses contrast effectively in this poem? Discuss one contrast you found particularly striking.
3. Look at the last line of the poem. What, in your view, is the poet suggesting to us about a person's fate after death?

STUDY NOTES

> **Dickinson was fascinated with death. This poem examines the moment between life and death. At that time, it was common for family and friends to be present at deathbed vigils. It was thought that the way a person behaved or looked at the moment of death gave an indication of the soul's fate.**

The last moment of a person's life is a solemn and often sad occasion. The perspective of the poem is that of the person dying and this significant moment is dominated by the buzzing of a fly in the room in the **first stanza**. This is **absurdly comic and strangely distorts** this moment into something grotesque. Surely the person dying should be concerned with more important matters than an insignificant fly: 'I heard a Fly buzz—when I died'. The room is still and expectant as the last breaths are drawn, a stillness like the moments before a storm. All are braced for what is to come. The word 'Heaves' suggests the force of the storm that is about to break.

The **second stanza** shows us that the mourners had now stopped crying and were holding their breath as they awaited the coming of the 'King' (God) into the room at the moment of death. The phrase 'Be witnessed' refers to the dying person and the mourners who are witnessing their faith, and it conjures up all the solemnity of a court. The word 'firm' also suggests these people's steadfast religious beliefs. The **third stanza** is concerned with putting matters right. The dying person has made a will – 'What portion of me be/Assignable' – and what is not assignable belongs to God. The person is awaiting the coming of his/her Maker, 'and then it was/There interposed a Fly' – the symbol of decay and corruption appeared. Human affairs cannot be managed; real life intervenes. The **fly comes between ('interposed') the dying person and the moment of death**, which **trivialises** the event.

The fractured syntax of the last stanza shows the **breakdown of the senses** at the moment of death: 'Between the light—and me'. Sight and sound are blurring. The presence of the fly is completely inappropriate, like a drunken person at a solemn ceremony, disturbing and embarrassing and interrupting proceedings. The fly is now between the dying person and the source of light. Does this suggest that the person has lost concentration on higher things, distracted by the buzzing fly? The sense of sight then fails: 'And then the Windows failed'. The moment of death had come and gone, dominated by the noisy fly. Has the fly prevented the person from reaching another dimension? Is death emptiness, just human decay, as signified by the presence of the fly, or is there something more? Do we need comic relief at overwhelming occasions? Is the poet signalling her own lack of belief in an afterlife with God? Dickinson, as usual, intrigues, **leaving the reader with more questions than answers**, so that the reader, like the dying person, is struggling to 'see to see'.

ANALYSIS

Dickinson's poems on mortality often lead to uncertainty or despair. Would you agree or disagree with this statement after reading the poem 'I heard a Fly buzz—when I died'? Discuss this statement, using references from the poem to support your views.

SAMPLE PARAGRAPH

This first-person, reminiscent narrative takes us through a series of images, inside and outside the head, showing us confused feelings and insurmountable problems, leading to an inconclusive ending. The view of this deathbed scene is from the dying person's perspective. The problem is that when all should be focused on the last drawing of breath, all are distracted by the inappropriate arrival of a noisy fly! Life won't be managed, nor death – both are lived and experienced. Life and death are not a play, a work of art; they are messy and disorganised, which goes against the human desire for order and control: 'Signed away/What portion of me be/Assignable'. I feel that the poet may be suggesting that the dying person, distracted by the silly fly, does not reach the understanding and knowledge appropriate at this great moment, and is therefore cheated in some way. The momentous moment has passed, dominated by a buzzing fly. This was no dress rehearsal; you can only die once. Life and death happen. Are we being told that we often lose concentration at important moments, for absurd reasons, and so lose valuable insight? Dickinson is not a reassuring poet in this poem. Instead, she coldly and dispassionately draws a deathbed scene and lets us 'see to see'. Can we? Or are we, like the dying person, distracted and unable to still ourselves at the appropriate time to achieve greater wisdom? The divided voice, that of the person dying and that of the person after death, leaves us with mysteries, and so this poem of Dickinson's on mortality leaves me with bleak uncertainties about the human condition and its ability to control and order.

EXAMINER'S COMMENT

This response is considered and shows a very good discursive treatment of the question. Expression is varied and fluent, and apt quotations are used effectively throughout the answer. Grade A.

CLASS/HOMEWORK EXERCISES

1. Comment on how Dickinson's style contributes to the theme or message in this poem. Quote from your prescribed poems to support your opinions.
2. Copy the table below into your own notes and fill in critical comments about the last two quotations.

Key Quotes

I heard a Fly buzz	The dying person is distracted from this significant moment by the noise made by a fly.
And Breaths were gathering firm/ For that last Onset	The narrator is aware that those present are bracing themselves for the important moment of death, which for believers is associated with the coming of God.
And then it was/ There interposed a Fly	All were disturbed by the dramatic arrival of the fly, disrupting the solemnity of the moment.
And then the Windows failed	
and then/ I could not see to see	

The Soul has Bandaged moments

The Soul has Bandaged moments—
When too appalled to stir—
She feels some ghastly Fright come up
And stop to look at her—

Salute her—with long fingers— 5
Caress her freezing hair—
Sip, Goblin, from the very lips
The Lover—hovered—o'er—
Unworthy, that a thought so mean
Accost a Theme—so—fair— 10

The soul has moments of Escape—
When bursting all the doors—
She dances like a Bomb, abroad,
And swings upon the Hours,

As do the Bee—delirious borne— 15
Long Dungeoned from his Rose—
Touch Liberty—then know no more,
But Noon, and Paradise—

The Soul's retaken moments—
When, Felon led along, 20
With shackles on the plumed feet,
And staples, in the Song,

The Horror welcomes her, again,
These, are not brayed of Tongue—

'As do the Bee—delirious borne'

GLOSSARY

1 *Bandaged moments*: painful experiences.
2 *appalled*: shocked, horrified.
2 *stir*: act; retaliate.
10 *Accost*: address.
11 *Escape*: freedom.
13 *like a Bomb*: dramatically.
13 *abroad*: in unusual directions.
16 *Dungeoned*: imprisoned in the hive.
20 *Felon*: criminal.
21 *shackles*: chains, ropes.
21 *plumed*: decorated.
22 *staples*: fastenings.
24 *brayed*: inarticulate.

EXPLORATIONS

1 What details in the poem evoke the feelings of 'ghastly Fright' experienced by the soul? Support your answer with quotation or reference.
2 Choose one comparison from the poem that you find particularly effective. Explain your choice.
3 Comment on Dickinson's use of dashes in this poem, briefly explaining their effectiveness.

STUDY NOTES

Throughout much of her poetry, Dickinson focuses on the nature of consciousness and the experience of being alive. She was constantly searching for meaning, particularly of transient moments or changing moods. This search is central to 'The Soul has Bandaged moments', where the poet takes us through a series of dramatic images contrasting the extremes of the spirit and the conscious self.

Stanza one introduces the soul as being fearful and vulnerable, personified as a terrified female who 'feels some ghastly Fright', with the poem's stark opening line suggesting restriction and pain. Dickinson's language is extreme: 'Bandaged', 'appalled'. The **tone is one of helpless desperation and introspection**. Yet while the dominant mood reflects suffering and fear, the phrase 'Bandaged moments' indicates the resilient soul's ability to recover despite being wounded repeatedly.

Stanza two is unnervingly dramatic. The poet creates a mock-romantic scene between the victimised soul and the 'ghastly Fright' figure, now portrayed as a hideous goblin and her would-be lover, their encounter depicted in terms of gothic horror. The soul experiences terrifying fantasies as **the surreal sequence becomes increasingly menacing** and the goblin's long fingers 'Caress her freezing hair'. The appearance of an unidentified shadowy 'Lover' is unexpected. There is a sense of the indecisive soul being caught between two states, represented by the malevolent goblin and the deserving lover. It is unclear whether Dickinson is writing about the choices involved in romantic love or the relationship between herself and God.

The stanza ends inconclusively, juxtaposing two opposites: the 'Unworthy' or undeserving 'thought' and the 'fair' (worthy) 'Theme'. The latter might well refer to the ideal of romantic love. If so, it is confronted by erotic desire (the 'thought'). Dickinson's disjointed style, especially her frequent use of dashes within stanzas, isolates key words and intensifies the overwhelmingly **nightmarish atmosphere**.

The feeling of confused terror is replaced with ecstatic 'moments of Escape' in stanzas three and four. The soul recovers in triumph, 'bursting all the doors'. This **explosion of energy** ('She dances like a Bomb') evokes a rising mood of riotous freedom. Explosive verbs ('bursting', 'dances', 'swings') and robust rhythms add to the sense of uncontrollable excitement. Dickinson compares the soul to a 'Bee—delirious borne'. After being 'Long Dungeoned' in its hive, this bee can now enjoy the sensuous delights of 'his Rose'.

The mood is short lived, however, and in stanzas five and six, 'The Horror' returns. The soul becomes depressed again, feeling bound and shackled, like a 'Felon led along'. **Dickinson develops this criminal metaphor** – 'With shackles on the plumed feet' – leaving us with an ultimate sense of loss as 'The Horror welcomes her, again'. Is this the soul's inevitable fate? The final line is unsettling. Whatever horrible experiences confront the soul, they are simply unspeakable: 'not brayed of Tongue'.

As always, Dickinson's poem is **open to many interpretations**. Critics have suggested that the poet is dramatising the turmoil of dealing with the loss of creativity. Some view the poem's central conflict as the tension between romantic love and sexual desire. Others believe that the poet was exploring the theme of depression and mental instability. In the end, readers must find their own meaning and decide for themselves.

ANALYSIS

Comment on the dramatic elements that are present in the poem, supporting the points you make with reference to the text.

SAMPLE PARAGRAPH

'The Soul has Bandaged moments' is built around a central conflict between two opposing forces, the 'Soul', or spirit, and its great enemy, 'Fright'. Emily Dickinson sets the dramatic scene with the Soul still recovering – presumably from the last battle. It is 'Bandaged' after the fight with its arch enemy. The descriptions of the soul's opponent are startling. Fright is 'ghastly', a 'Horror' and a sleazy 'Goblin' who is trying to seduce the innocent soul. Some of Dickinson's images add to the dramatic tension. In the seduction scene, the goblin is described as having 'long fingers'. His intended victim is seen as helpless, petrified with fear. The goblin uses its bony claws to 'Caress her freezing hair'. Both characters seem to have come out of an old black-and-white horror movie. I find the whole situation disturbing. The drama continues right to the end of the poem. The soul is compared to a 'Felon' who has just been recaptured and is being led away in 'shackles'. Such images have a distressing impact in explaining the pressures on the soul to be free. Finally, Dickinson's stop-and-start style is also unsettling. Broken rhythms and her condensed use of language increase the edgy atmosphere throughout this highly dramatic poem.

EXAMINER'S COMMENT

An assured and focused A-grade response, showing a clear understanding of the poem's dramatic elements. The answer addressed both subject matter and style, using back-up illustration very effectively. Expression throughout was also impressive.

CLASS/HOMEWORK EXERCISES

1. How would you describe the dominant tone of 'The Soul has Bandaged moments'? Use reference to the text to show how the tone is effectively conveyed.
2. Copy the table below into your own notes and fill in critical comments about the last two quotations.

Key Quotes

Bandaged moments	While the adjective suggests hurt and weakness, there is also a sense of healing and recovery.
The Lover—hovered—o'er	The verb suggests menace, typical of a poem where almost every image is tinged with fear and uncertainty.
She dances like a Bomb	Another of Dickinson's characteristics is her innovative and highly dramatic comparisons.
Caress her freezing hair	
The Horror welcomes her, again	

• Poetry Focus •

I could bring You Jewels—had I a mind to

Emily Dickinson

I could bring You Jewels—had I a mind to—
But You have enough—of those—
I could bring You Odors from St. Domingo—
Colors—from Vera Cruz—

Berries of the Bahamas—have I—   5
But this little Blaze
Flickering to itself—in the Meadow—
Suits Me—more than those—

Never a fellow matched this Topaz—
And his Emerald Swing—   10
Dower itself—for Bobadilo—
Better—Could I bring?

'Never a fellow matched this Topaz—'

GLOSSARY

3 *Odors*: fragrances, perfumes.
3 *St. Domingo*: Santo Domingo in the Caribbean.
4 *Vera Cruz*: city on the east coast of Mexico.
5 *Bahamas*: group of islands southeast of Florida.
6 *Blaze*: strong fire or flame; very bright light.
11 *Dower*: part of her husband's estate allotted to a widow by law.
11 *Bobadilo*: braggart; someone who speaks arrogantly or boastfully.

EXPLORATIONS

1. Does the poet value exotic or homely gifts? In your opinion, which phrases suggest this contrast most effectively?
2. Slant rhyme is when words almost rhyme, as in 'those' and 'Cruz'. Identify another example of slant rhyme in the poem and suggest why, in your opinion, the poet chooses to rhyme the words in this way. (Consider emphasis, order and music.)
3. What is the tone in this poem: arrogant, humble, gentle, strident, confident? Quote in support of your opinion.

STUDY NOTES

> Although described as a recluse, Dickinson had a wide circle of friends. She wrote letter-poems to them, often representing them as flowers, 'things of nature which had come with no practice at all'. This poem is one without shadows, celebratory and happy, focusing out rather than in as she concentrates on a relationship.

In the **first stanza,** the poem opens with the speaker **considering the gift she will give** her beloved, 'You'. The 'You' is very much admired, and is wealthy ('You have enough'), so the gift of jewels is dismissed. The phrase 'had I a mind to' playfully suggests that maybe the 'I' doesn't necessarily wish to present anything. There is a certain coquettish air evident here. A world of privilege and plenty is shown as, one after another, expensively exotic gifts are considered and dismissed. These include perfumes and vibrant colours from faraway locations, conjuring up images of romance and adventure: 'Odors from St. Domingo'.

The **second stanza** continues the list, with 'Berries of the Bahamas' being considered as an option for this special gift, but they are not quite right either. The tense changes to 'have I' and the laconic listing and dismissing stops. A small wildflower 'in the Meadow', 'this little Blaze', is chosen instead. This 'Suits Me'. Notice that it is not that this suits the other person. **This gift is a reflection of her own unshowy personality**. The long lines of considering exotic gifts have now given way to shorter, more decisive lines.

In the **third stanza,** the speaker has a definite note of conviction, as she confidently states that 'Never a fellow matched' this shining gift of hers. No alluring, foreign gemstone, be it a brilliant topaz or emerald, shines as this 'little Blaze' in the meadow. The gift glows with colour; it is natural, inexpensive and accessible. The reference to a dower might suggest a gift given by a woman to a prospective husband. This **gift is suitable** for a Spanish adventurer, a 'Bobadilo'. The assured tone is clear in the word 'Never' and the jaunty rhyme 'Swing' and 'bring'. The final rhetorical question suggests that this is the best gift she could give. The poem shows that **the true value of a present cannot be measured in a material way**.

ANALYSIS

'Dickinson is fascinated by moments of change.' Discuss this statement using the poem 'I could bring Jewels—had I a mind to' as reference.

SAMPLE PARAGRAPH

Unlike many of Dickinson's poems on our course, this poem turns outwards, as the speaker considers what present would be suitable to give to her 'Bobadilo'. The happy, celebratory tone continues right through the poem. This is a confident, assured woman listing and dismissing exotic gifts in a world of privilege and wealth. The 'Odors' from St Domingo, the 'Colors' from Vera Cruz, the 'Berries' from the Bahamas are looked at and discarded by this knowing woman, 'had I a mind to'. The moment of change here is when the speaker chooses a gift that is natural and unassuming and, more importantly, which is to her liking: 'Suits Me'. It will convey something of her personality to the recipient, the swaggering 'Bobadilo'. This 'little Blaze/Flickering to itself' reflects the hidden qualities of the woman. Although it is not directly stated what this little shining gift is exactly, I think it is likely a meadow flower. It is free and easily picked, but how it shines! This is brighter than any precious stone of 'Topaz' or 'Emerald'. As the decision is reached, the long lines in which the speaker is considering her choice of gift change with her decision. Now short, crisp lines ring out with the self-belief of a woman who knows best. Even the rhyme changes from the slant rhyme where she is considering her options ('those'/'Cruz') in the first stanza to the more definite jaunty full rhyme of 'Swing' and 'bring' in the final stanza. I read that Dickinson's favourite chapter in the Book of Revelations was the description of Jerusalem as a jewel. In this poem, jewels are rejected for something more precious than material worth: beauty. I really enjoyed how Dickinson explored the very feminine trait of considering everything, and then finally deciding after humorous vacillating. This is the moment of change in the poem.

EXAMINER'S COMMENT

A lucid, fluent response to the question, backed up with a convincing use of quotation, ensures a grade A. The point about the change in line length was interesting. Varied vocabulary is impressive throughout.

CLASS/HOMEWORK EXERCISES

1. 'Dickinson disrupts and transforms our accepted view of things.' What is your opinion of this statement? Refer to 'I could bring you Jewels—had I a mind to' in support of your response.
2. Copy the table below into your own notes and fill in critical comments about the last two quotations.

Key Quotes

I could bring You Jewels—had I a mind to	The speaker is confidently considering her options.
But this little Blaze/Flickering to itself	The gift chosen is simple and natural, but it is warm, vivid and beautiful, as conveyed by the lively onomatopoeia.
Suits Me	The gift is appropriate for the speaker to give, as it reflects her confident personality, as shown by the capital 'M'.
Dower itself	
Better—Could I bring?	

• Poetry Focus •

A narrow Fellow in the Grass

A narrow Fellow in the Grass
Occasionally rides—
You may have met Him—did you not
His notice sudden is—

The Grass divides as with a Comb— 5
A spotted shaft is seen—
And then it closes at your feet
And opens further on—

He likes a Boggy Acre
A Floor too cool for Corn— 10
Yet when a Boy, and Barefoot—
I more than once at Noon
Have passed, I thought, a Whip lash
Unbraiding in the Sun
When stooping to secure it 15
It wrinkled, and was gone—

Several of Nature's People
I know, and they know me—
I feel for them a transport
Of cordiality— 20

But never met this Fellow
Attended, or alone
Without a tighter breathing
And Zero at the Bone—

'His notice sudden is—'

GLOSSARY

6 *a spotted shaft*: patterned skin of the darting snake.
13 *Whip lash*: sudden, violent movement.
14 *Unbraiding*: straightening out, uncoiling.
19 *transport*: heightened emotion.
20 *cordiality*: civility, welcome.
24 *Zero at the Bone*: cold terror.

EXPLORATIONS

1. Select two images from the poem that suggest evil or menace. Comment briefly on the effectiveness of each.
2. How successful is the poet in conveying the snake's erratic sense of movement? Refer to the text in your answer.
3. Outline your own feelings in response to the poem.

STUDY NOTES

In this poem, one of the few published during her lifetime, Dickinson adopts a male persona remembering an incident from his boyhood. Snakes have traditionally been seen as symbols of evil. We still use the expression 'snake in the grass' to describe someone who cannot be trusted. Central to this poem is Dickinson's own portrayal of nature – beautiful, brutal and lyrical. She seems fascinated by the endless mystery, danger and unpredictability of the natural world.

The opening lines of **stanza one** casually introduce a 'Fellow in the Grass' (Dickinson never refers explicitly to the snake). **The conversational tone immediately involves readers** who may already 'have met Him'. However, there is more than a hint of warning in the postscript: 'His notice sudden is'. This underlying wariness now appears foreshadowed by the menacing adjective 'narrow' and by the disjointed rhythm and slightly awkward word order within the opening lines.

Dickinson focuses on the volatile snake's dramatic movements in **stanza two**. The verbs 'divide', 'closes' and 'opens' emphasise its dynamic energy. The snake suddenly emerges like a 'spotted shaft'. The poet's **comparisons are particularly effective**, suggesting a lightning bolt or a camouflaged weapon. Run-on lines, a forceful rhythm and the repetition of 'And' contribute to the vivid image of the snake as a powerful presence to be treated with caution.

Stanza three reveals even more about the snake's natural habitat: 'He likes a Boggy Acre'. It also divulges the speaker's identity – an adult male remembering his failed boyhood efforts to capture snakes. The memory conveys something of the intensity of childhood experiences, especially of dangerous encounters with nature. The boy's innocence and vulnerability ('Barefoot') contrasts with the 'Whip lash' violence of the wild snake. **Dickinson's attitude to nature is open to interpretation.** Does the threat come from the animal or the boy? Did the adult speaker regard the snake differently when he was young? The poet herself clearly appreciates the complexities found within the natural world and her precisely observed descriptions ('Unbraiding', 'It wrinkled') provide ample evidence of her interest.

From the speaker's viewpoint in stanza four, nature is generally benign. This positive image is conveyed by the affectionate tribute to 'Nature's People'. The familiar personification and personal tone underline the mutual 'cordiality' that exists between nature and human nature. Despite this, **divisions between the two worlds cannot be ignored.** Indeed, the focus in stanza five is on the sheer horror people experience when confronted by 'this Fellow'. The poet's sparse and chilling descriptions – 'tighter breathing', 'Zero at the Bone' – are startling expressions of stunned terror.

As in other poems, Dickinson attributes human characteristics to nature – the snake 'Occasionally rides', 'The Grass divides' and the bogland has a 'Floor'. One effect of this is to highlight the **variety and mystery of the natural environment**, which can only ever be glimpsed within limited human terms. The snake remains unknowable to the end, dependent on a chance encounter, a fleeting glance or a trick of light.

ANALYSIS

Comment on the effectiveness of Dickinson's use of the male persona voice in 'A Narrow Fellow in the Grass'. Support the points you make with reference to the poem.

SAMPLE PARAGRAPH

In some of her poems, Emily Dickinson chose to substitute her own voice with that of a persona, a fictional narrator. This is the case in 'A Narrow Fellow in the Grass', where she uses a country boy to tell the story of his experiences trying to catch snakes when he was young. It is obvious that he has a great love for nature, but neither is he blind to the cold fear he felt when he came face to face with the 'spotted shaft'. Dickinson's use of language emphasises his youthful terror. She lets him remember his encounter exactly as it happened. The images she uses are powerful and disturbing: 'a tighter breathing'. The boy remembers shuddering with uncontrollable fright, 'Zero at the Bone'. The description is dramatic and I found I could relate to the boy's sense of horror. The poem is all the more effective for being centred around one terrified character, the young boy. I can visualise the child in his bare feet trying to catch a frightened snake in the grass. It is only later that he realises the great danger he was in and this has taught him a lifelong lesson about nature. By using another speaker's persona, Dickinson explores the excitement and danger of nature in a wider way that allows readers to imagine it more clearly.

EXAMINER'S COMMENT

Although the answer drifts at times from the central question, there is good personal engagement and a great deal of insightful discussion. Quotations are well used throughout the answer to provide a very interesting response. Grade A.

CLASS/HOMEWORK EXERCISES

1. In your opinion, how does Dickinson portray nature in 'A Narrow Fellow in the Grass'? Support your points with reference to the poem.
2. Copy the table below into your own notes and fill in critical comments about the last two quotations.

Key Quotes

His notice sudden is	The awkward syntax used to describe the snake's jerky movements adds to our sense of unease.
And then it closes at your feet	Dickinson highlights the lethal unpredictability of the snake.
A Floor too cool for Corn	The cool sensation of the snake's boggy habitat is enhanced by the broad assonant sounds.
Nature's People	
And Zero at the Bone	

Poetry Focus

Emily Dickinson

I taste a liquor never brewed

I taste a liquor never brewed—
From Tankards scooped in Pearl—
Not all the Vats upon the Rhine
Yield such an Alcohol!

Inebriate of Air—am I—   5
And Debauchee of Dew—
Reeling—thro endless summer days—
From inns of Molten Blue—

When 'Landlords' turn the drunken Bee
Out of the Foxglove's door—   10
When Butterflies—renounce their 'drams'—
I shall but drink the more!

Till Seraphs swing their snowy Hats—
And Saints—to windows run—
To see the little Tippler   15
Leaning against the—Sun—

*'Not all the Vats upon the Rhine/
Yield such an Alcohol!'*

GLOSSARY

2   *Tankards*: one-handled mugs, usually made of pewter, used for drinking beer.
3   *Vats*: large vessels used for making alcohol.
6   *Debauchee*: someone who has overindulged and neglected duty.
13 *Seraphs*: angels who are of the highest spiritual level.
15 *Tippler*: a person who drinks often, but does not get drunk.

EXPLORATIONS

1   What is the mood in this poem? Does it intensify or change? Use references from the text in your response.
2   Which stanza appeals to you? Discuss both the poet's style and content in your answer, using quotations from the poem as evidence for your views.
3   Look at the final dash in the poem. Why do you think the poet ended the poem with this punctuation? What is it suggesting about the little tippler? Does it add a sense of fun?

STUDY NOTES

This 'rapturous poem about summer' uses the metaphor of intoxication to capture the essence of this wonderful season. Dickinson's family were strict Calvinists, a religion that emphasised damnation as the consequence of sin. Her father supported an organisation that warned against the dangers of drink, the Temperance League.

This poem is written as **a joyful appreciation of this wonderful life**. The tone is playful and exaggerated from the beginning, as the poet declares this drink was never 'brewed'. The reference to 'scooped in Pearl' could refer to the great, white frothing heads of beer in the 'Tankards'. The poet certainly conveys the merriment of intoxication, as the poem reels along its happy way. The explanation for all this drunkenness is that the poet is drunk on life ('Inebriate', 'Debauchee'). The pubs are the inns of 'Molten Blue', i.e. the sky (stanza two). It is like a cartoon, with little drunken bees being shown the door by the pub owners as they lurch about in delirious ecstasy. The drinkers of the natural world are the bees and butterflies, but she can drink more than these: 'I shall but drink the more!' This roots the poem in reality, as drunken people always feel they can manage more.

But this has caused uproar in the heavens, as the angels and saints run to look out at this little drunk, 'the little Tippler'. She stands drunkenly leaning against the 'Sun', a celestial lamppost. The final dash suggests the crooked stance of the

Poetry Focus

Emily Dickinson

little drunken one. There is no heavy moral at the end of this poem. In fact, there seems to be a slight note of envy for the freedom and happiness being experienced by the intoxicated poet. Are the angels swinging their hats to cheer her on in her drunken rebellion? Is this poem celebrating the reckless indulgence of excess? Or is the final metaphor of the sun referring to Christ or to the poet's own arrival in heaven after she indulgently enjoys the beauty of the natural world?

Nature is seen as the spur for high jinks and good humour. The riddle of the first line starts it off: how was the alcohol 'never brewed'? The exaggerated imagery, such as the metaphor of the flower as a pub and the bee as the drunk, all add to the **fantasy-land atmosphere**. The words 'Inebriate', 'Debauchee' and 'renounce' are reminiscent of the language which those disapproving of the consumption of alcohol might use for those who do indulge. Is the poet having a sly laugh at the serious Temperance League to which her father belonged? The ridiculous costumes, 'snowy hats', and the uproar in heaven ('swing' and 'run') all add to the impression of this land of merriment. The juxtaposition of the sacred ('Seraphs') and the profane ('Tippler') in **stanza four** also adds to the comic effect. However, it is the verbs that carry the sense of mad fun most effectively: 'scooped', 'Reeling', 'drink', 'swing', 'run' and 'Leaning'. The poem lurches and flows in an almost uncontrollable way as the ecstasy of overindulging in the delirious pleasure of nature is vividly conveyed.

There are two different types of humour present in this irrepressible poem – the broad humour of farce and the more **subversive humour of irony**. She even uses the steady metre of a hymn, with eight syllables in lines one and three and six syllables in lines two and four. Dickinson seems to be standing at a distance, smiling wryly, as she gently deflates.

ANALYSIS

'Dickinson was always wary of excess, even of joy.' Discuss this statement in relation to the above poem, using references from the text to support your answer.

SAMPLE PARAGRAPH

I don't agree. I think this is a funny poem and the poet is enjoying herself getting very drunk. But she is not drunk on beer. She is drunk on nature. I think it is very funny when the angels are waving their white caps, egging her on. I think this is a good poem, the best poem I ever red, as it makes me want to red more of Dickinson's poems. There is a good metaphor for drinking all through. Some of it is definately full of joy EG the bee. The part on the tippler leaning against the paling post is also joyful. I think everyone should enjoy Emily's absolutely brilliant poem as it has many good joyful images such as the drinking bee and little tippler.

EXAMINER'S COMMENT

This short answer shows very little knowledge or engagement with the poem. There is no substantial referencing. The language used is repetitive, expression is flawed and there are mechanical mistakes. The over-enthusiastic ending is not convincing. A basic D grade standard.

CLASS/HOMEWORK EXERCISES

1. 'Hypersensitivity to natural beauty produced Dickinson's poetry.' Do you agree or disagree with this statement? Refer to the poem 'I taste a liquor never brewed' in your response.
2. Copy the table below into your own notes and fill in critical comments about the last two quotations.

Key Quotes

From tankards scooped in Pearl	This line, with its use of the descriptive verb, suggests the outlining of the tankard in white, foaming beer.
Inebriate of Air—am I	The narrator in the poem is confessing to drunkenness due to an excessive indulgence in the beauty of nature.
I shall but drink the more!	A reference to the narrator herself. Unlike the butterflies, who are going to stop drinking, she intends to continue.
Till Seraphs swing their snowy hats	
Leaning against the—Sun	

• Poetry Focus •

After great pain, a formal feeling comes

After great pain, a formal feeling comes—
The Nerves sit ceremonious, like Tombs—
The stiff Heart questions was it He, that bore,
And Yesterday, or Centuries before?

The Feet, mechanical, go round— 5
Of Ground, or Air, or Ought—
A Wooden way
Regardless grown,
A Quartz contentment, like a stone—

This is the Hour of Lead— 10
Remembered, if outlived,
As Freezing persons, recollect the Snow—
First—Chill—then Stupor—then the letting go—

'First—Chill—then Stupor'

GLOSSARY

1 *formal*: serious; exact.
2 *ceremonious*: on show.
3 *He*: the stiff Heart, or possibly Christ.
3 *bore*: endure; intrude.
6 *Ought*: anything.
9 *Quartz*: basic rock mineral.
10 *Hour of Lead*: traumatic experience.
13 *Stupor*: numbness; disorientation.

EXPLORATIONS

1. Comment on the poet's use of personification in the opening stanza.
2. How does the language used in the second stanza convey the condition of the victim in pain?
3. Write your own short personal response to the poem.

STUDY NOTES

> Dickinson wrote 'After great pain' in 1862, at a time when she was thought to have been experiencing severe psychological difficulties. The poet addresses the effects of isolation and anguish on the individual. Ironically, the absence of the personal pronoun 'I' gives the poem a universal significance. The 'great pain' itself is never fully explained and the final lines are ambiguous. Like so much of Dickinson's work, this dramatic poem raises many questions for consideration.

From the outset, Dickinson is concerned with the emotional numbness ('a formal feeling') that follows the experience of 'great pain'. The poet's authoritative tone in **stanza one** reflects a first-hand knowledge of trauma, with the adjective 'formal' suggesting self-conscious recovery from some earlier distress. Dickinson personifies the physical response as order returns to body and mind: 'The Nerves sit ceremonious, like Tombs'. The severe pain has also shocked the 'stiff Heart' which has become confused by the experience. Is the poet also drawing a parallel with the life and death of Jesus Christ (the Sacred Heart), crucified 'Centuries before'? The images certainly suggest timeless suffering and endurance. This **sombre sense of loss** is further enhanced by the broad vowel assonance of the opening lines.

The feeling of stunned inertia continues into **stanza two.** In reacting to intense pain, 'The Feet, mechanical, go round'. It is as if the response is unfocused and indifferent, lacking any real purpose. Dickinson uses two **analogies to emphasise the sense of pointless alienation**. The reference to the 'Wooden way' might be interpreted as a fragile bridge between reason and insanity, or this metaphor could be associated with Christ's suffering as he carried his cross to Calvary. The level of consciousness at such times is described as 'Regardless grown', or beyond caring. Dickinson's second comparison is equally innovative: 'A Quartz contentment' underpins the feeling of complete apathy that makes the victims of pain behave 'like a stone'. Is she being ironic by suggesting that the post-traumatic state is an escape, a 'contentment' of sorts?

There is a disturbing sense of resignation at the start of **stanza three**: 'This is the Hour of Lead'. The dull weight of depression is reinforced by the insistent monosyllables and solemn rhythm, but the devastating experience is not 'outlived' by everyone. Dickinson outlines the aftermath of suffering by using one final comparison: 'As Freezing persons'. This shocking simile evokes the unimaginable hopelessness of the victim stranded in a vast wasteland of snow. The poem's last line traces the tragic stages leading to oblivion: 'First—Chill—then Stupor—then the letting go—'. The inclusion of the dash at the end might indicate a possibility of relief, though whether it is through rescue or death is not revealed. In either case, **readers are left with an acute awareness of an extremely distraught voice.**

ANALYSIS

One of Dickinson's great achievements is her ability to explore the experience of deep depression. To what extent is this true of her poem 'After great pain, a formal feeling comes'? Refer closely to the text in your answer.

SAMPLE PARAGRAPH

'After great pain' is a very good example of Emily Dickinson's skill in addressing controversial and distressing subjects, such as mental breakdown. Although she never really explains what she means by the 'pain' referred to in the first line, she deals with the after-effects of suffering throughout the poem. The loss of a loved one can cause very great anguish. What Dickinson does very well is to explain how depression can lead to people becoming numb, beyond all emotion. I believe this is what she means by 'a formal feeling'. She uses an interesting image of a sufferer's nerves sitting quietly in a church at a funeral service. They 'sit ceremonious'. This same idea is used to describe the mourners following the hearse – 'Feet mechanical'. I get the impression that grief and mourning can destroy people's confidence and make them numb. They go beyond grief. Dickinson's images are compelling and suggest the coldness experienced by patients who have suffered depression. They are 'like a stone'. The best description is at the end, when she compares sufferers to being lost in the snow. They will slowly fade into a 'stupor' or death wish. I think Dickinson is very good at using images and moods to explore depression. She is very good at suggesting shock in this poem.

EXAMINER'S COMMENT

Although the expression is awkward in places, there are a number of worthwhile points in the paragraph. There is some good personal engagement with the poem and references are used well in support. A basic B grade standard.

CLASS/HOMEWORK EXERCISES

1. In your opinion, what is the dominant mood in 'After great pain, a formal feeling comes'? Is it one of depression, sadness or acceptance? Refer closely to the text in your answer.
2. Copy the table below into your own notes and fill in critical comments about the last two quotations.

Key Quotes

a formal feeling comes	Dickinson states that the reaction to the experience of intense suffering is stiff and self-conscious.
A Quartz contentment, like a stone	After experiencing trauma, sufferers retreat within themselves, feeling lifeless and inhuman.
This is the Hour of Lead	The metaphor sums up Dickinson's stark acknowledgement of the reality of depression. Broad vowel sounds add further depth to the feeling.
A Wooden way/Regardless grown	
First—Chill—then Stupor—then the letting go	

Emily Dickinson

• Poetry Focus •

LEAVING CERT SAMPLE ESSAY

> **Q** Has the poetry of Emily Dickinson any relevance for young people today? Support the points you make in your answer by reference to the poems by Dickinson on your course.

MARKING SCHEME GUIDELINES

Some of the following areas might be addressed:
- Interesting personal themes.
- Engaging confessional style.
- Oblique imagery is appealing.
- Unusual/eccentric punctuation.
- Experimental use of language.
- Challenging/passionate voice.

SAMPLE ESSAY
(Dickinson's Relevance for Today's Youth)

1 *I feel the poetry of Emily Dickinson would recieve a very positive response from a young person today. I will discuss this with reference to the four poems:*

Hope is a thing with Feathers
There's a certain Slant of Light
I Felt a Funeral in my brain
A narrow Fellow in the Grass

Dickinson's appeal lies not only in the content of these poems – depression, altered consciousness and death. But also in her style, how she conveys her themes.

2 *The oddness of Dickinson's poetry would, I feel, appeal to young people. It has a different slant on things, it is odd. Young people like different, eccentric things. Look at the clothes we wear, we like to be different. In the poem Slant of Light Dickinson takes an odd slant. When one thinks of light, you think of bright, warm happiness. But in this poem, Dickinson is describing light which is cold, oppressive, dying. It is the end of the year so light is dying and it is the end of the afternoon so light is fading.*

Emily Dickinson

3. In this poem she expresses religious doubts which in my opinion young people can relate to. When we were younger we looked at the concept of Heaven and God through 'rose-tinted glasses'. Anyone who dies belonging to us went to live with God in Heaven and everything was happy ever after. But in this poem, a portrayl of a merciless, vengeful God comes across. This is how many young people feel. 'Heavenly hurt' any young person who has lost someone close to them has felt this hurt. But there is no scar to prove this anguish.

4. Emily uses short four line stanza's in her poems which I feel young peple can definately relate to. In this fast, cosmopolitan world everyone enjoys reading a short poem. Her omission of words, articles and verbs is like a text message. Young people shorten words, leave them out in order to write a text. They therefor can relate to Emily's poetry as it is like one of the hundreds of texts they send.

5. She also has little regard for syntex, punctuation and formal grammer like young people in text messages. She uses capital letters for emphasis. 'I felt a Funeral in my Brain'. In text messages young people use capitals to emphasis something for example 'I saw JAMIE at the bus stop!'

6. Emily has two themes – Death and Nature. In her poem, 'I Felt a Funeral' she is describing the opression of her mental disorder. I feel young people can relate to this – not the mental disorder but the oppression Young people have tough lives. In Sixth year there are pre's, Leaving Cert, CAO points, the list is endless. We feel trapped, opressed like Emily. She describes the mourners as 'thuding – thuding'. This is like a bad headache. A headache students get from study and from CAO forms. The poet is lying in a coffin, she is powerless.

   'And then they lifted the box
   And walked across my soul'.

7. Metaphorically speaking Sixth year and all the traumas that go with it is like being powerless in a coffin. Apparently prior to writing this poem, Emily was rejected by a man. All young girls can relate to this – being rejected by the love of your life.

8. In 'Hope is a thing with Feathers' she celebrates human resillance in the face of difficulty. Students can also relate to this poem with all that is going on in

their lives. She praises the power of hope to overcome the worst catastrophies, 'And hard must be the storm.' Hope lifts the human will to survive, hope is indomnitable. Students can relate to this, they have to take what life throws at them. 'Yet never in extremnity, it asked a Crumb of Me'. The worst disaster imaginable leaves hope undaunted. Every young person needs hope and can relate to this poem.

9 Emily's other nature poem is 'A Narrow Fellow in the grass'. Dickinson is wary of nature in this poem. Instead of man and nature living in harmony she feels they have an acquaintance. She describes a snake 'a spotted shaft'. She is afraid of it but is curious to go after it. In my opinion, young people can relate to the curiosity in this poem. Young people are afraid to take drugs but take them out of curiosity. They would be feeling 'Zero at the bone' if they were caught but nevertheless human curiosity takes over. Like Emily going searching for the snake. She is afraid of it but intrigued by it.

10 Young people can respond to Emily Dickinson's poetry in a number of ways. The oddness of her poems entice young people to read them. They are unique. When she expresses religious doubts in her poem 'Slant of Light', in my opinion young people can relate to this. They too can harbour doubts. The compactness of her poems, her omission of words and use of capitals is like a text message which young people can definitaly relate to. Finally her themes suggesting opression relate to young people's student lives. The hardship, the studying. Her final theme of nature and curiosity can relate to young people also. The curiosity to dabble in drugs even with the fear of getting caught.

(approx. 880 words)

SPELLCHECKER

receive	extremity
therefore	syntax
portrayal	grammar
resilience	oppression
definitely	emphasis

GRADE: C1	
P	= 11/15
C	= 10/15
L	= 9/15
M	= 3/5
Total	= 33/50

EXAMINERS COMMENT

This is a reasonable response that tries hard to keep focused on the question. However, there is little detailed analysis of the poems themselves. For instance, although paragraph four makes a valid point about the poet's text-like style, no examples are given. The expression is awkward at times. Other distractions include spelling errors, careless punctuation and inaccurate quotations. As a convention of literary criticism, it is not usual to refer to authors by their first names.

SAMPLE LEAVING CERT QUESTIONS ON DICKINSON'S POETRY (45–50 MINUTES)

1. What impact did the poetry of Emily Dickinson make on you as a reader? Your answer should deal with the following:
   - Your overall sense of the personality of the poet.
   - The poet's use of language/imagery.

   Refer to the poems by Emily Dickinson you have studied.

2. Write about the feelings Emily Dickinson's poetry creates in you and the aspects of her poetry (content or style) that help to create those feelings. Support your points by reference to the poetry of Dickinson on your course.

3. 'Speaking of Emily Dickinson…'
   Write out the text of a public talk you might give on the poetry of Emily Dickinson. Your talk should make reference to the poetry on your course.

SAMPLE ESSAY PLAN (Q3)

'Speaking of Emily Dickinson…'

Write out the text of a talk you might give on the poetry of Emily Dickinson. Your talk should make reference to the poetry on your course.

•	*Intro:*	Original voice and expression of the poet has a broad appeal. Deals with the great themes.
•	*Point 1:*	'I heard a Fly buzz' – fascination with death shown by recreation of deathbed scene.
•	*Point 2:*	'Hope' is the thing with feathers' – a celebration of human resilience in the face of constant difficulty.

- *Point 4*: Style – Dickinson's fondness for capitals and dashes.
- *Point 5*: Impact of reclusive life on themes and style of poetry.
- *Conclusion*: A poet who has much to say to the anxious modern reader coping with an ever-faster world.

EXERCISE

Develop one of the above points into a paragraph.

POINT 1 – SAMPLE PARAGRAPH

Dickinson's fascination with death is seen graphically in the poem 'I heard a Fly buzz'. She introduces a fly buzzing to the deathbed scene. She trivialises the solemn occasion as well as making it more realistic. In stanza one the 'Stillness' magnifies the sound of the buzzing fly. It is like the stillness at the centre of the storm. The storm is death, which is both powerful and destructive, just like the storm. The poet then startles us in stanza two. The reference to 'Eyes' shows the mourners who stand around the deathbed. They have stopped crying. They are waiting for the moment Death, 'King', appears. Then in stanza three we return to the narrator. She has made her last bequests and is ready to face her Maker when the fly makes its presence known. The word 'interposed' is deliberately used to show the fly interfering with the deathbed drama. The last stanza shows us the final moments of the narrator's life. Her sight goes. There is only darkness. 'And then the Windows failed'. Without the eyes and the other senses there can be no reality, as the person then has no means to perceive her surroundings. Here Dickinson is imagining her own death. She is passing comment on one of life's great moments which we must all face, yet succeeds through the introduction of the fly to show that even in the most solemn occasions there is always the trivial and unpredictable. This is what makes her poetry interesting to study.

EXAMINER'S COMMENT

The paragraph includes a number of interesting observations about the chosen poem and the discussion remains well focused on the question. The absence of the register of a talk prevents the student from attaining a higher grade, as the task is not fully completed. Otherwise, a solid B grade.

Last Words

'The Dickinson dashes are an integral part of her method and style ... and cannot be translated ... without deadening the wonderful naked voltage of the poems.'

Ted Hughes

'The Brain—is wider than the Sky—
The Brain is deeper than the sea–'

Emily Dickinson

(On her determination to hide secrets) 'The price she paid was that of appearing to posterity as perpetually unfinished and wilfully eccentric.'

Philip Larkin

'A poem begins in delight and ends in wisdom.'

Robert Frost (1874–1963)

One of the great twentieth-century poets, **Robert Frost** is highly regarded for his realistic depictions of rural life and his command of American colloquial speech. His work frequently explored themes from early 1900s country life in New England, often using the setting to examine complex social and philosophical ideas. Nature is central to his writing. While his poems seem simple at first, they often transcend the boundaries of time and place with metaphysical significance and a deeper appreciation of human nature in all its beauty and contradictions. Despite many personal tragedies, he had a very successful public life. It is ironic that such a calm, stoical voice emerged from his difficult background. At times bittersweet, sometimes ironic, or often marvelling at his surroundings, Frost continues to be a popular and often-quoted poet. He was honoured frequently during his lifetime, receiving four Pulitzer Prizes.

• Poetry Focus •

PRESCRIBED POEMS (HIGHER LEVEL)

Note that Frost uses American spellings in his work.

1 'The Tuft of Flowers' (p. 112)

One of Frost's best-loved works, this poem describes how a simple clump of wild flowers succeeds in uniting two separate people. The poem illustrates Frost's technique of bringing readers through an everyday rustic experience to reveal a universal truth.

2 'Mending Wall (p. 117)

Repairing a damaged wall between his neighbour and himself, Frost considers the theme of community and fellowship and wonders if 'Good fences make good neighbors'.

3 'After Apple-Picking' (p. 122)

Set on his New England farm at the end of the apple harvest, Frost meditates on the nature of work, creativity and of what makes a fulfilled life. Characteristically, the poem is thought-provoking and open to many interpretations.

4 'The Road Not Taken' (p. 127)

Another of Frost's most popular poems. Using the symbol of a remote country crossroads, the poet dramatises the decisions people face in life – and the consequences of their choices.

5 'Birches' (p. 132)

The sight of some forest birches excites Frost's imagination to associate childhood games of swinging on the trees with the process of writing poetry. The poem has been seen as an expression of Frost's own philosophical outlook on life.

6 'Out, Out—' (p. 137)

This affecting poem is based on an actual story of a serious chainsaw accident. Despite the tragedy, Frost leaves readers in no doubt of life's grim reality: 'It goes on'.

7 **'Spring Pools'** (p. 142)

In this beautiful lyric poem, the fragile beauty and transience of the pools give Frost an acute awareness of the natural cycle of growth, decay and renewal.

8 **'Acquainted with the Night'** (p. 145)

This short lyric depicts the dark, alienating side of urban life. Familiar themes include the passing of time and lack of communication. In metaphorical terms, Frost also explores 'the dark night of the soul'.

9 **'Design'** (p. 150)

Frost's sonnet, depicting nature as volatile and terrifying, addresses the possibility of an underlying plan or design for the universe.

10 **'Provide, Provide'** (p. 154)

Another poem that deals with some of Frost's favourite themes – time, old age and independence. For Frost, however, the only certainty or constant in life is change.

• Poetry Focus •

The Tuft of Flowers

Robert Frost

I went to turn the grass once after one
Who mowed it in the dew before the sun.

The dew was gone that made his blade so keen
Before I came to view the leveled scene.

I looked for him behind an isle of trees;   5
I listened for his whetstone on the breeze.

But he had gone his way, the grass all mown,
And I must be, as he had been—alone,

'As all must be,' I said within my heart,
'Whether they work together or apart.'   10

But as I said it, swift there passed me by
On noiseless wing a bewildered butterfly,

Seeking with memories grown dim o'er night
Some resting flower of yesterday's delight.

And once I marked his flight go round and round,   15
As where some flower lay withering on the ground.

And then he flew as far as eye could see,
And then on tremulous wing came back to me.

I thought of questions that have no reply,
And would have turned to toss the grass to dry;   20

But he turned first, and led my eye to look
At a tall tuft of flowers beside a brook,

A leaping tongue of bloom the scythe had spared
Beside a reedy brook the scythe had bared.

The mower in the dew had loved them thus,   25
By leaving them to flourish, not for us,

Nor yet to draw one thought of ours to him,
But from sheer morning gladness at the brim.

The butterfly and I had lit upon,
Nevertheless, a message from the dawn, 30

That made me hear the wakening birds around,
And hear his long scythe whispering to the ground,

And feel a spirit kindred to my own;
So that henceforth I worked no more alone;

But glad with him, I worked as with his aid, 35
And weary, sought at noon with him the shade;

And dreaming, as it were, held brotherly speech
With one whose thought I had not hoped to reach.

'Men work together,' I told him from the heart,
'Whether they work together or apart.' 40

'his long scythe whispering'

GLOSSARY

	Tuft: cluster, bunch.	18	*tremulous*: trembling.
1	*turn*: upturn; toss grass to dry it out.	22	*brook*: stream.
		23	*scythe*: implement used for cutting grass or hay.
3	*keen*: sharp; effective.		
6	*whetstone*: stone used for sharpening scythes.	29	*lit upon*: discovered.
		33	*kindred*: closely related to.

EXPLORATIONS

1. Describe the dominant mood in lines 1–10 of the poem.
2. Choose two images from the poem that you found particularly interesting and effective. Briefly explain your choice in both cases.
3. Would you describe the poem as uplifting? Give reasons for your answer.

STUDY NOTES

> The poem describes how a simple, uncut clump of wild flowers can unite two separate people. It is one of Frost's best-loved works and typifies his technique of bringing readers through an everyday rustic experience to reveal a universal truth – in this case about alienation, friendship and communication. The poem consists of twenty rhymed couplets written in strict verse. Frost once remarked that 'writing without structure is like playing tennis without a net'.

The narrative voice in the **opening section** of the poem is relaxed, in keeping with the unhurried rhythm. Frost's initial tone is low key and noncommittal. The speaker has gone out to turn the grass so that it can dry. Someone else had mowed it earlier 'in the dew before the sun'. **Lines 5–6** reveal the speaker's sense of solitude and isolation; the unnamed mower has 'gone his way'. This leads him to consider **the loneliness of the scene and of human experience**. The introspective mood becomes more depressed as the poet searches for his fellow worker. Figurative descriptions of the 'leveled scene' and 'an isle of trees' add to the atmosphere of pessimism as the speaker implies that he must also be 'alone'. For Frost, this is the essential human experience for all, "Whether they work together or apart".

The poem's **second section** is marked by the sudden appearance of a 'bewildered butterfly'. After fluttering 'round and round' looking for the 'resting flower' that gave it such delight the day before, it then flies close to the speaker: 'on tremulous wing came back to me'. The adjective 'tremulous' suggests fragility and a **new sense of excited anticipation in the air**. The butterfly seems to reflect the speaker's 'questions that have no reply'. Perhaps they have both enjoyed great happiness in the past. The butterfly eventually turns and leads the speaker to a 'tall tuft of flowers beside a brook' that have escaped the mower's scythe – not by accident, but because 'he had loved them' and left them to flourish out of 'sheer morning gladness'.

The significance of the meadow flowers and the brook cannot be overlooked, because here the mood suddenly changes to optimism. The presence of the mysterious butterfly establishes communication between the early-morning mower and the narrator. Frost suggests this connection with his vivid description of the spared flowers as 'a leaping tongue of bloom'. In the **final section**, the speaker and the butterfly 'lit upon,/Nevertheless, a message from the dawn'. With images such as the 'wakening birds around' and a 'spirit kindred to my own', we might assume that this 'message' could indeed be one of human friendship and communal love.

The ending is paradoxical: 'Men work together … Whether they work together or apart'. However, **Frost believed in spiritual presence and was inspired by an overwhelming sense of fellowship**. Although apart, the speaker and the absent mower are working with a shared appreciation of nature's beauty and a common commitment to a better world. The poem could also be interpreted biographically, since Frost had lost several of his loved ones and may well have written it as an emotional outlet. Even though his family members were deceased, he remains close to them in spirit. Whatever the poet's intention, readers should draw their own conclusions from the poem.

ANALYSIS

In your view, is 'The Tuft of Flowers' a dramatic poem? Refer closely to the text in your answer.

SAMPLE PARAGRAPH

I liked Frost's poem 'The Tuft of Flowers' for many reasons – one of which was its dramatic storyline. It has been described as a lyrical soliloquy. The narrative element is there from the start. The first mower mentioned seems a mysterious character who got me wondering. The central character (poet) is obviously close to nature as he goes about his work turning the grass. His inner drama interests me most, as his attitude changes from loneliness at the beginning to happiness and companionship. The two moods contrast dramatically. First, the sadness of 'I looked for him', 'I listened for his whetstone' and 'brotherly speech' and then the more sociable 'Men work together'. The clear, vivid imagery is also dramatic, especially the butterfly's flight – 'On noiseless wing' – and the description of the small outcrop of flowers – 'a leaping tongue of bloom'. Frost sets his poems in the secluded New England landscape and this provides a beautiful setting for what are deep meditations about the important questions in life – 'questions that have no reply'. The rhythm or movement of the poem quickens in the final lines as the poet expresses his positive view of life – 'Men work together'. I thought this was the ideal way to end and rounded off this quietly dramatic poem perfectly.

EXAMINER'S COMMENT

A very well controlled answer, focusing on some key elements of drama and demonstrating a close understanding of the poem. Good personal interaction and commentary also. References were handled effectively and points were clearly presented throughout. Grade A.

CLASS/HOMEWORK EXERCISES

1. In your opinion, what is Frost's main theme or message in 'The Tuft of Flowers'? Refer closely to the text of the poem in your answer.
2. Copy the table below into your own notes and fill in critical comments about the last two quotations.

Key Quotes

I went to turn the grass once	Frost's personal narrative voice uses the language of ordinary day-to-day speech.
And I must be, as he had been—alone	Solitude (leading to a revelation or epiphany) is one of the poem's central themes.
sheer morning gladness	The sibilant 's' effect suggests the movement of the scythe as well as the positive mood.
I thought of questions that have no reply	
a message from the dawn	

Mending Wall

Robert Frost

Something there is that doesn't love a wall,
That sends the frozen-ground-swell under it
And spills the upper boulders in the sun,
And makes gaps even two can pass abreast.
The work of hunters is another thing: 5
I have come after them and made repair
Where they have left not one stone on a stone,
But they would have the rabbit out of hiding,
To please the yelping dogs. The gaps I mean,
No one has seen them made or heard them made, 10
But at spring mending-time we find them there.
I let my neighbor know beyond the hill;
And on a day we meet to walk the line
And set the wall between us once again.
We keep the wall between us as we go. 15
To each the boulders that have fallen to each.
And some are loaves and some so nearly balls
We have to use a spell to make them balance:
'Stay where you are until our backs are turned!'
We wear our fingers rough with handling them. 20
Oh, just another kind of outdoor game,
One on a side. It comes to little more:
There where it is we do not need the wall:
He is all pine and I am apple orchard.
My apple trees will never get across 25
And eat the cones under his pines, I tell him.
He only says, 'Good fences make good neighbors.'
Spring is the mischief in me, and I wonder
If I could put a notion in his head:
'*Why* do they make good neighbors? Isn't it 30
Where there are cows? But here there are no cows.
Before I built a wall I'd ask to know
What I was walling in or walling out,
And to whom I was like to give offense.
Something there is that doesn't love a wall, 35
That wants it down.' I could say 'Elves' to him,
But it's not elves exactly, and I'd rather
He said it for himself. I see him there,

• Poetry Focus •

Bringing a stone grasped firmly by the top
In each hand, like an old-stone savage armed.   40
He moves in darkness as it seems to me,
Not of woods only and the shade of trees.
He will not go behind his father's saying,
And he likes having thought of it so well
He says again, 'Good fences make good neighbors.'   45

'Something there is that doesn't love a wall'

GLOSSARY

1 *Something there is that doesn't love a wall*: ice and frost dislocate walls (also a pun on the poet's name).
4 *abreast*: side by side.
27 *Good fences make good neighbors*: one reading is that a strong fence protects by keeping people apart.
36 *Elves*: small supernatural beings, often malevolent.

EXPLORATIONS

1 In your opinion, what is it that doesn't love a wall? Support your answer with reference to the poem.
2 There are two speakers in the poem. Which one is the wiser, in your view? Refer to the text in your answer.
3 Point out two examples of humour in the poem and comment on how effective they are in adding to the message of the 'Mending Wall'.

STUDY NOTES

This popular poem of Robert Frost's was written in 1913 and appears first in his second collection, **North of Boston**. When the land was being cleared for agriculture, the stones gathered were made into walls. Frost said this poem 'contrasts two types of people'. President John F. Kennedy asked Frost to read this poem to Khrushchev, Russia's leader at the time of the Cuban Missile Crisis, when there was a possibility of another world war. The Berlin Wall was a symbol of the cold relations between Russia and the US. Imagine the leaders listening to the line 'I'd ask to know/What I was walling in or walling out'.

'Mending Wall' was responsible for building a picture of Frost as an ordinary New England farmer who wrote about normal events and recognisable settings in simple language. **Line 1** is mysterious: 'Something there is that doesn't love a wall'. **A force is at work to pull down the barriers** people insist on erecting. The speaker repairs the holes in the wall left by hunters: 'I have come after them and made repair'. But there are other holes in the wall, though 'No one has seen them made or heard them made'. In a yearly ritual, 'at spring mending-time', the poet and his neighbour meet to carry out repairs. Each looks after his own property as they walk along: 'To each the boulders that have fallen to each'. But a tone of coldness creeps into the poem amid this neighbourly task, with the repetition of how the wall has separated them at all times: 'set the wall between us', 'keep the wall between us'.

It is a difficult task, as the stones fall off as quickly as they are placed: 'Stay where you are until our backs are turned!' The **good-humoured banter** of the workers comes alive in the humorous remark, and readers feel as if they are there in New England watching the wall being repaired. The light-hearted mood is continued in **line 21** as the poet describes the activity as an 'outdoor game'. Then he comments that they don't even really need the wall where it is: 'He is all pine and I am apple orchard'. The poet jokes that his apple trees cannot go over and eat his neighbour's pine cones. His neighbour then speaks: 'Good fences make good neighbors'. He comes across as a serious type, quoting old sayings, in **contrast** to the mischievous poet: 'Spring is the mischief in me'. Frost is allying himself with the turbulent force that is pushing through the land, creating growth and pulling down walls. The neighbour is shown as one who has accepted what has been said without question, one who upholds the status quo.

In **line 31**, the poet poses questions to himself and wishes he could say to his neighbour, '*Why* do they make good neighbors?' **He then wonders what a wall is keeping in and keeping out**. He also wonders what is pulling down the wall. He mockingly suggests 'Elves', then discounts that. Frost presents his rather uncommunicative neighbour in a series of unflattering images: 'an old-stone savage armed', 'He moves in darkness'. Is the poet saying that we must question received wisdom and not blindly follow what we are told? The neighbor, who accepts, is presented as a figure of repression who 'moves in darkness'. He just repeats 'Good fences make good neighbors' like a mantra. Is the poet suggesting that there are some people who derive comfort from just remaining the same, who do not welcome change ('He will not go behind his father's saying')?

The tone of the poem changes as the easy, neighbourly sociability of a shared task is replaced by a **feeling of tension**, first in the effort to keep the tumbling wall upright, and then in the opposite attitudes of the two neighbours – the mischievous, questioning poet and the taciturn, unquestioning neighbour 'like an old-stone savage'. The desire for human co-operation is often stopped, not by outside circumstances, but by a lack of desire on the part of the people involved. This is the poet commenting on human dilemmas. The easy-going, almost ruminative tone of someone musing to himself is written in blank verse, unrhymed iambic pentameter. The colloquial conversational phrases are all tightly controlled throughout this thought-provoking poem.

ANALYSIS

Frost examines the distances between people in his work. In your opinion, how successfully is this done in the poem 'Mending Wall'?

SAMPLE PARAGRAPH

I think Frost has very successfully given us a picture of two opposite personalities in this poem. The moody neighbour who doggedly walks on his side of the wall, 'We keep the wall between us both as we go', is vividly described. Here is a person who accepts what was told to him without question 'Good fences make good neighbors'. It is as if he is reciting the two-times tables. This is fact. There is no need to question. He is comfortable and secure in his traditional mindset. 'He will not go behind his father's saying'. He almost mindlessly repeats it. The poet describes him in unflattering terms, referring to him as 'an old stone-armed savage'. He also states that he was one who moved 'in darkness'. Frost does not agree with this unquestioning attitude of his neighbour's. It is not only a wall which divides these two, there is a completely different mindset. The poet has a lively personality, making jokes as they work, 'Stay where you are until our backs are turned', regarding the work as a game. However, he is not lightweight, as he asks the fundamental question about any boundary, 'I'd ask to know/What I was walling in or out'. He also asks the rather sensitive question about who he was likely to give offence to, with his wall. The neighbour has no such finer feeling, and is portrayed as someone who keeps on going in the same route as always. This apparently simple poem, written in blank verse, sticks in the reader's mind long after the reading. Frost has written a poem which is hard to get rid of. We are left wondering, are walls natural or necessary? Must we break down barriers to live as good neighbours? What if we are over-run?

EXAMINER'S COMMENT

A solid response. The poem is examined in some detail. The questions at the conclusion are lively and show engagement with the poem. Some quotations are inaccurate and this reduces the overall standard. Grade B.

CLASS/HOMEWORK EXERCISES

1. Comment on Frost's use of imagery. Do you find it effective? Refer closely to the text in your answer.
2. Copy the table below into your own notes and fill in critical comments about the last two quotations.

Key Quotes

Something there is that doesn't love a wall	The unnatural barriers erected by people are often pushed aside by nature.
We keep the wall between us as we go	The two neighbours walk on their own side of the wall as they carry out repair work. It also acts as a metaphor for the barriers erected by people between themselves.
And to whom I was like to give offence	If a wall is erected, is the person who has been excluded entitled to feel offended?
He moves in darkness as it seems to me	
'Good fences make good neighbors'	

• Poetry Focus •

After Apple-Picking

Robert Frost

My long two-pointed ladder's sticking through a tree
Toward heaven still,
And there's a barrel that I didn't fill
Beside it, and there may be two or three
Apples I didn't pick upon some bough.   5
But I am done with apple-picking now.
Essence of winter sleep is on the night,
The scent of apples: I am drowsing off.
I cannot rub the strangeness from my sight
I got from looking through a pane of glass   10
I skimmed this morning from the drinking trough
And held against the world of hoary grass.
It melted, and I let it fall and break.
But I was well
Upon my way to sleep before it fell,   15
And I could tell
What form my dreaming was about to take.
Magnified apples appear and disappear,
Stem end and blossom end,
And every fleck of russet showing clear.   20
My instep arch not only keeps the ache,
It keeps the pressure of a ladder-round.
I feel the ladder sway as the boughs bend.
And I keep hearing from the cellar bin
The rumbling sound   25
Of load on load of apples coming in.
For I have had too much
Of apple-picking: I am overtired
Of the great harvest I myself desired.
There were ten thousand thousand fruit to touch,   30
Cherish in hand, lift down, and not let fall.
For all
That struck the earth,
No matter if not bruised or spiked with stubble,
Went surely to the cider-apple heap   35
As of no worth.
One can see what will trouble
This sleep of mine, whatever sleep it is.

Were he not gone,
The woodchuck could say whether it's like his   40
Long sleep, as I describe its coming on,
Or just some human sleep.

'Toward heaven still'

GLOSSARY

- 7 *Essence*: scent.
- 10 *glass*: ice.
- 12 *hoary*: covered in frost.
- 20 *russet*: reddish-brown.
- 22 *ladder-round*: rung or support on ladder.
- 34 *stubble*: remnant stalks left after harvesting.
- 40 *woodchuck*: groundhog, a native American burrowing animal.

EXPLORATIONS

1 Select one image that evokes the hard, physical work of apple-picking. Comment on its effectiveness.
2 What do you understand lines 27–29 to mean?
3 Write a short personal response to this poem.

Robert Frost

STUDY NOTES

> The poem is a lyrical evocation of apple harvesting in New England. Frost takes an ordinary experience and transforms it into a meditative moment. Harvesting fruit soon becomes a consideration of how life has been experienced fully but with some regrets and mistakes. Frost chose not to experiment but to use traditional patterns, or as he said, he preferred 'the old-fashioned way to be new'. 'After Apple-Picking' is not free verse, but it is among Frost's least formal works, containing forty-two lines varying in length, a rhyme scheme that is also highly irregular and no stanza breaks.

The speaker in the poem (either Frost himself or the farmer persona he often adopted) feels himself drifting off to sleep with the scent of apples in the air. He thinks of the ladder he has left in the orchard still pointing to 'heaven'. Is the poet suggesting that his work has brought him closer to God? The slow-moving rhythm and broad vowel sounds ('two-pointed', 'bough', 'drowsing') in the **opening lines** reflect his **lethargic mood**. Although he seems close to exhaustion, he is pleased that the harvest is complete: 'But I am done with apple-picking now'. Ironically, his mind is filled with random thoughts about the day's work. The drowsy atmosphere is effectively communicated by the poet's mesmerising description: 'Essence of winter sleep is on the night'.

This dream-like state releases Frost's imagination and he remembers the odd sensation he felt while looking through a sheet of ice he had removed earlier from a drinking trough. While the memory is rooted in reality, it appears that he has experienced the world differently: 'I cannot rub the strangeness from my sight'. As he is falling asleep, he is conscious that his dreaming will be associated with **exaggerated images of harvesting**: 'Magnified apples appear and disappear'. The poet emphasises the sensuousness of what is happening. The vivid apples display 'every fleck of russet' and he can feel the pressure of the 'ladder-round' against his foot. He hears the 'rumbling sound' of the fruit being unloaded. The images suggest abundance: 'load on load of apples', 'ten thousand thousand'. Frost's use of repetition, both of evocative sounds and key words, is a prominent feature of the poem that enhances our appreciation of his intense dream.

Physically and mentally tired, the poet also relives the anxiety he had felt about the need to save the crop from being 'bruised or spiked with stubble', and not to lose them to 'the cider-apple heap'. In the poem's **closing lines**, which seem deliberately vague and distorted, Frost wonders again about the nature of consciousness: 'This sleep of mine, whatever sleep it is'. Like so many of his statements, the line is rich in possible interpretations. For some critics, the poem appears to be exploring the art and craft of writing. Others take a broader view, seeing it as a metaphor for how human beings live their lives. The poet's own final thoughts are of the woodchuck's winter retreat, before he eventually surrenders to his own mysterious 'sleep'.

'After Apple-Picking' is typical of Frost's work. Despite the apparent cheerfulness of much of the writing, it has **undertones of a more sober vision of life**. As always, there is a thoughtful quality to the poem. The reference to the approach of winter hints at the constant presence of mortality. Frost's question about what kind of sleep to anticipate suggests untroubled oblivion or possibly some kind of renewal, just as the woodchuck reawakens in the springtime after its long hibernation.

ANALYSIS

How would you describe the dominant mood in 'After Apple-Picking'? Refer closely to the poem in your answer.

SAMPLE PARAGRAPH

In his famous dramatic monologue, 'After Apple-Picking', Robert Frost creates a mood of otherworldliness. At the start, his accurate description of the orchard is realistic. But some of the poem seems symbolic – such as the mention of the ladder pointing to heaven which might suggest Frost's religious feelings. The setting is calm and the poet feels tired but satisfied after his demanding physical work – 'there's a barrel that I didn't fill'. But his tiredness soon makes his mood more dreamy – 'Essence of winter sleep is on the night'. The sibilance and slender vowels add to this languid atmosphere. I could trace a growing surreal quality to the poem as Frost drifts in and out of consciousness, remembering flashes of his work picking the apples – 'The scent of apples: I am drowsing off'. He mentions 'sleep' repeatedly, reflecting his deep weariness. The rhythm is slow and irregular, just like his confused thoughts about the apples he harvested or damaged. At times he is troubled, recalling his worries that some of the fruit would be 'bruised'. By the end of the poem, he is in a dream-like state, equally obsessed with apple-picking and his own need for sleep. He even wonders about 'whatever sleep is'. As he drifts off, he thinks of the animals that sleep through the winter and compares himself to the woodchuck. I think this kind of whimsical mood reflects his great interest in nature and is a characteristic of this great American poet.

EXAMINER'S COMMENT

This is an accomplished answer that ranges widely and shows some good personal engagement with the poem. There is an assured sense of the central mood and this is supported well with apt quotations. The references to Frost's style are also worthwhile. Grade A.

CLASS/HOMEWORK EXERCISES

1. Comment on the effectiveness of the poem's imagery in appealing to the senses. Refer closely to the text in your answer.
2. Copy the table below into your own notes and fill in critical comments about the last two quotations.

Key Quotes

But I am done with apple-picking now	It is ironic that although the harvesting itself has ended, its significance for Frost is just beginning.
I cannot rub the strangeness from my sight	Exhaustion has caused the poet's confusion. The strong sibilant effect adds emphasis to the mood.
Cherish in hand, lift down, and not let fall	The line reminds us of the speaker's care and devotion while harvesting. The punctuation slows down the rhythm, adding to the sense of pride in work.
Magnified apples appear and disappear	
I feel the ladder sway as the boughs bend	

The Road Not Taken

Robert Frost

Two roads diverged in a yellow wood,
And sorry I could not travel both
And be one traveler, long I stood
And looked down one as far as I could
To where it bent in the undergrowth;   5

Then took the other one, as just as fair,
And having perhaps the better claim,
Because it was grassy and wanted wear;
Though as for that, the passing there
Had worn them really about the same,   10

And both that morning equally lay
In leaves no step had trodden black.
Oh, I kept the first for another day!
Yet knowing how way leads on to way,
I doubted if I should ever come back.   15

I shall be telling this with a sigh
Somewhere ages and ages hence:
Two roads diverged in a wood, and I—
I took the one less traveled by,
And that has made all the difference.   20

'where it bent in the undergrowth'

GLOSSARY

1 *diverged*: separate and go in different directions.
5 *undergrowth*: small trees and bushes growing beneath larger trees in a wood.
7 *claim*: assertion that something is true.

EXPLORATIONS

1. In your opinion, is this a simple poem or does it have a more profound meaning? Outline your views, supporting them with relevant quotation.
2. Select one image from the poem that you consider particularly effective or interesting. Briefly justify your choice.
3. Frost has been described as someone who 'broods and comments on familiar country things … catching a truth in it'. In your view, what is the tone of this poem? Does it change or remain the same?

STUDY NOTES

> One of Frost's most popular poems, this was the opening poem from the collection *Mountain Interval* (1916). It was inspired by his friend, the poet Edward Thomas. Frost told Thomas, 'No matter which road you take, you'll always sigh, and wish you'd taken another'. Frost also said he was influenced by an event which happened to him at a crossroads after a winter snowstorm in 1912. He met a figure, 'my own image', who passed silently by him. Frost wondered at 'this other self'. The poem dramatises the choices we make in life and their consequences.

Huge themes are summarised in a simple narrative in this poem. In the **first stanza**, the speaker stands in a wood in autumn where two roads run off in different directions. He has to make a decision – which one will he take? The roads are 'about the same', so the emphasis is not on the decision, but on the **process of decision-making and its consequences**. The speaker decides that he cannot see where the first road is leading ('it bent in the undergrowth'), so he chooses the other one, though it is unclear why. The reference to the 'yellow wood' suggests that the poet is mature enough to realise the consequences of his decision. He won't have this opportunity again: 'I doubted if I should ever come back'. The beautiful image of the 'yellow wood' conjures up a picture of the autumn in New England, but it also has a deeper meaning and is tinged with regret. A person can't do everything in life; choice is part of the human condition.

Frost has said, 'I'm not a nature poet. There's always something else in my poetry'. Here, in this simple act, he is **exploring what it means to be human** and dramatises the decision-making process. There is the human desire to avoid making a decision ('sorry I could not travel both') and the consideration of the possible choices ('long I stood/And looked down one as far as I could'). The **regular rhyme scheme** mirrors the poet looking this way and that as he tries to decide which to choose (*abaab, cdccd, efeef, ghggh*). The unusual rhyme also underlines the unusual choice made. Frost felt that 'the most important thing about a poem ... is how wilfully, gracefully, naturally entertainingly and beautifully its rhymes are'.

Then, in **stanza two**, **he makes the decision**: he 'took the other one'. Why? Was it because it 'was grassy and wanted wear'? Is this someone who is individualistic and likes to do something different to the crowd? Does this suggest a desire for adventure? Then the poet becomes increasingly mischievous. When he sent the poem to his friend, Edward Thomas, Frost wrote: 'I don't know if you can get anyone to see the fun of the thing without showing them'. After pointing out the difference between the two roads, he now declares that they were not so different: 'the passing there/Had worn them really about the same'.

In the **third stanza**, he continues to **point out the similarity of the two roads**, which 'equally lay'. So is the idea that if you choose the less conventional route in life, you may not end up having adventures? The reader is now as confused as the poet was when trying to decide what to do. The second great truth is then revealed: no matter what we get, we always want what we don't have. The regret is palpable in the emphatic 'Oh, I kept the first for another day!' But there won't be another day, because time marches on and we cannot return to the past; we can only go on, as 'way leads on to way'.

In **stanza four**, the poet realises in **hindsight** that he will tell of this day in the future, 'ages and ages hence', though why 'with a sigh'? Has his choice resulted in suffering? Frost's own personal life was littered with suffering and tragedy. Does the repetition of 'I' and the inclusion of the dash suggest that the poet is asserting his maverick individuality as he resolutely declares: 'I took the one less traveled by,/And that has made all the difference'? Do you think he feels he made the right choice for himself? This common experience of choice and decision-making is caught succinctly in this simple narrative. It sounds like a person thinking aloud; the language seems ordinary. Yet upon closer examination, we become aware of the **musical sound effects**. The repeated 'e' sound, coupled with the sibilant 's' sounds ('it was grassy') and alliteration ('wanted wear') convey a calm, deliberating voice. Here is Frost's 'sound of sense'. This poem is inclusive rather than exclusive, as it invites the reader to share in the poet's decision-making.

ANALYSIS

'Frost uses traditional form not in an experimental way, but adapted to his purpose.' Discuss this statement with reference to 'The Road Not Taken'. Quote in support of your answer.

SAMPLE PARAGRAPH

Frost takes traditional subject matter similar to the Romantics, nature and man's relationship with nature, and tells us, 'There's plenty to be dark about, you know. It's full of darkness'. He forms his poems not in an experimental way, but in a deliberate way which suits his purpose. He uses iambic pentameter, a traditional metre used by Shakespeare, as it most closely resembles the English speaking voice, and it is an ironic, sceptical voice, 'yet knowing how way leads on to way', which resonates in 'The Road Not Taken'. The structure of the poem follows the deliberating process, as first the speaker tries to avoid making a choice, then considers the alternatives, 'long I stood'. The decision is made and almost immediately there is a sense of regret: 'Oh, I kept the first for another day'. The use of an unusual rhyme scheme adds to the excluded feel of the speaker. This is someone to whom individuality and self-sufficiency matters. 'I took the one less traveled by,/And that has made all the difference'. There is a sureness in the tone of the last lines which is like those of the early American pioneers: 'I did it and did it my way'. The rhyme scheme of the first stanza is *abaab*. The unusual rhyme scheme mirrors the unusual choice the poet made. Frost believed in the 'sound of sense', as he tells us that we can know what is going on even through a closed door by the sound, not necessarily the meaning of words. He also says that 'sound is the gold in the ore' of a poem. Consider the line, 'Because it was grassy and wanted wear'. The alliteration and the sibilance suggest an almost idyllic wilderness. So Frost structures the form of his poems for a purpose. In this poem the rhyme scheme mimics the glancing this way and that as the speaker tries to decide what route to take. These are some of the ways Frost uses form for purpose, rather than experimenting just for its own sake.

EXAMINER'S COMMENT

This thoroughly developed answer shows a deep sense of engagement with both the poem and poet. The well-sustained focus and integrated quoting ensure that the paragraph reached an impressive A grade standard.

CLASS/HOMEWORK EXERCISES

1. Frost's ambition was to 'write a few poems it will be hard to get rid of'. Do you think he succeeded? Refer to the poem 'The Road Not Taken' in your response.
2. Copy the table below into your own notes and fill in critical comments about the last two quotations.

Key Quotes

And sorry I could not travel both/And be one traveler	The poet expresses a universal sorrow that it is not possible to be everyone and do everything.
the passing there/Had worn them really about the same	The poet is admitting that really there was little difference between the roads.
Yet knowing how way leads on to way	Once a course of action is decided upon, there is no going back. The repetition emphasises the decision.
I shall be telling this with a sigh	
I took the one less traveled by/And that has made all the difference	

• Poetry Focus •

Birches

Robert Frost

When I see birches bend to left and right
Across the lines of straighter darker trees,
I like to think some boy's been swinging them.
But swinging doesn't bend them down to stay
As ice storms do. Often you must have seen them					5
Loaded with ice a sunny winter morning
After a rain. They click upon themselves
As the breeze rises, and turn many-colored
As the stir cracks and crazes their enamel.
Soon the sun's warmth makes them shed crystal shells			10
Shattering and avalanching on the snow crust—
Such heaps of broken glass to sweep away
You'd think the inner dome of heaven had fallen.
They are dragged to the withered bracken by the load,
And they seem not to break; though once they are bowed		15
So low for long, they never right themselves:
You may see their trunks arching in the woods
Years afterwards, trailing their leaves on the ground
Like girls on hands and knees that throw their hair
Before them over their heads to dry in the sun.					20
But I was going to say when Truth broke in
With all her matter-of-fact about the ice storm,
I should prefer to have some boy bend them
As he went out and in to fetch the cows—
Some boy too far from town to learn baseball,					25
Whose only play was what he found himself,
Summer or winter, and could play alone.
One by one he subdued his father's trees
By riding them down over and over again
Until he took the stiffness out of them,						30
And not one but hung limp, not one was left
For him to conquer. He learned all there was
To learn about not launching out too soon
And so not carrying the tree away
Clear to the ground. He always kept his poise					35
To the top branches, climbing carefully
With the same pains you use to fill a cup
Up to the brim, and even above the brim.

Then he flung outward, feet first, with a swish,
Kicking his way down through the air to the ground.   40
So was I once myself a swinger of birches.
And so I dream of going back to be.
It's when I'm weary of considerations,
And life is too much like a pathless wood
Where your face burns and tickles with the cobwebs   45
Broken across it, and one eye is weeping
From a twig's having lashed across it open.
I'd like to get away from earth awhile
And then come back to it and begin over.
May no fate willfully misunderstand me   50
And half grant what I wish and snatch me away
Not to return. Earth's the right place for love:
I don't know where it's likely to go better.
I'd like to go by climbing a birch tree,
And climb black branches up a snow-white trunk   55
Toward heaven, till the tree could bear no more,
But dipped its top and set me down again.
That would be good both going and coming back.
One could do worse than be a swinger of birches.

'birches bend to left and right'

GLOSSARY

1 *birches*: deciduous trees with smooth, white bark.
7 *click*: tapping sound made by the branches when they touch.
9 *crazes their enamel*: cracks the ice on the trees.
10 *crystal shells*: drops of melting ice on branches.
11 *avalanching*: collapsing.
14 *bracken*: fern leaves.
31 *limp*: loose; wilted.
39 *swish*: whoosh.
50 *willfully*: deliberately.

EXPLORATIONS

1. Choose one image from the poem that you found particularly interesting or effective. Briefly explain your choice.
2. Comment on Frost's use of contrast in the poem.
3. Do you find the poet's overall outlook optimistic or pessimistic? Refer to the text in your answer.

STUDY NOTES

'Birches' was first published in 1915, and like so much of Robert Frost's popular work, there is far more happening within the poem than first appears. The poem has been viewed as an important expression of his philosophical outlook on life. With its formal perfection, its opposition of the internal and external worlds and its occasional dry wit, it is one of the best examples of everything that was interesting and engaging about Frost's poetry.

The opening description of the leaning birches is interesting, as Frost compares them to the 'straighter darker trees'. The scene immediately brings him back to his childhood and he likes to think that 'some boy's been swinging them'. This tension between what has actually happened and what the poet would like to have happened – between the real world and the world of the imagination – runs through much of the poem. Throughout **lines 1–20**, he wonders why the birches are bent 'to left and right'. He accepts that the true reason is because of the ice weighing them down. The poet's **precise, onomatopoeic language** – particularly the sharp 'c' effect in 'cracks and crazes their enamel' – echoes the tapping sound of the frozen branches. Vivid, sensual imagery brings the wintry scene to life: 'crystal shells', 'snow crust', 'withered bracken'. Frost's conversational tone is engaging: 'You'd think the inner dome of heaven had fallen'. Characteristically, he adds a beautiful simile, comparing the bent branches 'trailing their leaves on the ground' to girls who are drying their cascading hair in the sunshine.

In the poem's second section (**lines 21–40**), Frost resists the accurate explanation ('Truth') for the bent trees, preferring to interpret the scene imaginatively. He visualises a lonely boy ('too far from town to learn baseball') who has learned to amuse himself among the forest birches. In simple, factual terms, the poet describes the boy as he 'subdued his father's trees'. We are given a sense of his youthful determination to 'conquer' them all until 'not one was left'. His persistence teaches him valuable lessons for later life. Swinging skilfully on the trees, the boy learns 'about not launching out too soon'. Readers are left in no doubt about the rich **metaphorical significance of the birches**. In highlighting the importance of 'poise' and 'climbing carefully', Frost reveals his belief in discipline and artistry as the important elements of a successful life ('to fill a cup/Up to the brim'). Such symbolism is a common feature of his writing.

Lines 41–59 are more nostalgic in tone. Frost recalls that he himself was once 'a swinger of birches' and extends the metaphor of retreating into the world of imagination and poetry. The similarities between climbing birches and writing poetry becomes more explicit: 'I'd like to get away from earth'. However, he stresses that he does not wish for a permanent escape because 'Earth's the right place for love'. Is this what poets do when they withdraw into their imaginations and reflect on reality in an attempt to explore the beauty and mystery of life? They are dreamers, idealists. The birch trees are similarly grounded, but they also reach '*Toward* heaven'. The emphatic image (the italics are Frost's) suggests his continuing aspiration for **spiritual fulfillment through the poetic imagination**: 'That would be good both going and coming back'. Frost ends his poem by stating his satisfaction with overcoming challenges and benefiting from the desire to achieve by writing: 'One could do worse than be a swinger of birches'.

ANALYSIS

Based on your study of 'Birches', comment on the poet's use of detailed description. Refer closely to the text in your answer.

SAMPLE PARAGRAPH

Frost's detailed use of language makes 'Birches' one of the poet's most accessible poems. The simple images and colloquial expression create a natural connection between the poet and his readers. I very much liked the closely observed descriptions of the ice-covered branches: 'the sun's warmth makes them shed crystal shells'. The sibilance here adds to the beauty of the language. There are so many impressive images in the poem. Using onomatopoeia, Frost captures the subtle sounds of the forest in the bitter weather. The trees 'click upon themselves'. The poet obviously loved nature and had a keen eye for its beauty. I also liked his comparison of the trail of leaves to the 'girls on hands and knees that throw their hair'. It was dramatic, fresh and unusual. The boy's movement playing on the trees is dynamic: 'Then he flung outward, feet first, with a swish'. Near the end of the poem, Frost describes a harsher side of the forest when 'your face burns and tickles with the cobwebs'. As someone who spent my childhood in the country, I could relate to this tactile image. For me, Frost is a wonderful writer whose poems give a clear sense of the New England landscape. 'Birches' is a very successful piece of description, mainly due to the poet's precise choice of words and the vivid imagery.

EXAMINER'S COMMENT

This paragraph showed a good knowledge of the text and a clear appreciation of Frost's writing skills. There was a strong sense of personal engagement with the poem and the comments on imagery were very convincing. Grade A.

CLASS/HOMEWORK EXERCISES

1. In your opinion, what is the central theme or message in 'Birches'? Support your answer with reference to the text.
2. Copy the table below into your own notes and fill in critical comments about the last two quotations.

Key Quotes

the stir cracks and crazes their enamel	Onomatopoeia and alliteration combine to echo the wintry atmosphere and bitter, sharp frost.
You'd think the inner dome of heaven had fallen	Colloquial and metaphorical language are used to suggest that the picturesque scene has been destroyed.
Then he flung forward, feet first, with a swish	The punctuation and interrupted rhythm imitate the boy's abrupt movement.
Shattering and avalanching on the snow crust	
Where your face burns and tickles with the cobwebs	

'Out, Out—'

Robert Frost

The buzz saw snarled and rattled in the yard
And made dust and dropped stove-length sticks of wood,
Sweet-scented stuff when the breeze drew across it.
And from there those that lifted eyes could count
Five mountain ranges one behind the other   5
Under the sunset far into Vermont.
And the saw snarled and rattled, snarled and rattled,
As it ran light, or had to bear a load.
And nothing happened: day was all but done.
Call it a day, I wish they might have said   10
To please the boy by giving him the half hour
That a boy counts so much when saved from work.
His sister stood beside them in her apron
To tell them 'Supper.' At the word, the saw,
As if to prove that saws knew what supper meant,   15
Leaped out at the boy's hand, or seemed to leap—
He must have given the hand. However it was,
Neither refused the meeting. But the hand!
The boy's first outcry was a rueful laugh,
As he swung toward them holding up the hand,   20
Half in appeal, but half as if to keep
The life from spilling. Then the boy saw all—
Since he was old enough to know, big boy
Doing a man's work, though a child at heart—
He saw all spoiled. 'Don't let him cut my hand off— 25
The doctor, when he comes. Don't let him, sister!'
So. But the hand was gone already.
The doctor put him in the dark of ether.
He lay and puffed his lips out with his breath.
And then—the watcher at his pulse took fright.   30
No one believed. They listened at his heart.
Little—less—nothing!—and that ended it.
No more to build on there. And they, since they
Were not the one dead, turned to their affairs.

'Sweet-scented stuff when the breeze drew across it'

GLOSSARY

'*Out, Out—*': phrase from a speech which Macbeth, King of Scotland, made on hearing of the death of his wife and when he was surrounded by enemies. He was commenting on the brevity and fragility of life: 'Out, out brief candle. Life's but a walking shadow'. (Shakespeare)

4 *lifted eyes*: reference to Psalm 21 – 'I will lift up mine eyes unto the hills' – but the people here don't. The sunset is ignored.

6 *Vermont*: a state in New England, America.

28 *ether*: form of anaesthetic.

EXPLORATIONS

1 What kind of world is shown in the poem? Consider the roles of adults and children. Use reference from the poem in your response.
2 In your opinion, why does the poet tell the story in chronological order? How does it affect your understanding of the story?
3 Comment on the use of colloquial language in the poem. Refer closely to the text in your answer.

STUDY NOTES

> Based on an actual event that occurred in 1910, the poem refers to a tragic accident when the son of a neighbour of Frost's was killed on his father's farm. By chance, he had hit the loose pulley of the sawing machine and his hand was badly cut. He died from heart failure due to shock. The event was reported in a local paper.

This **horrifying subject matter**, the early violent death of a young boy, was, in Frost's opinion, 'too cruel' to include in his poetry readings. The title, which is a reference to a speech from Shakespeare's *Macbeth*, is a telling comment on how tenuous our hold on life is. The scene is set on a busy timber yard: 'a world of actual hard, rattling, buzz saw, snarling action' (Seamus Heaney). In **line 1**, Frost's rasping onomatopoeic sounds give a vivid sound picture of the noisy, dangerous yard. The **long, flowing, descriptive lines** paint a picture of a place full of menace and physical reality where work has to be done. But there is beauty in the midst of this raw power: 'Sweet-scented stuff when the breeze drew across it'. The soft sibilant 's', the assonance of the long 'e' and the compound word 'Sweet-scented stuff' all go to show the surprising beauty to be found in the midst of the practical 'stove-length sticks of wood'.

The **surroundings are also beautiful**, if only the people would look up. But they, unlike the poet, are unaware of 'Five mountain ranges one behind the other/Under the sunset far into Vermont', as their focus is on the work. The repetition of the verbs 'snarled and rattled, snarled and rattled' mimics the action of the repeated sawing. The detail 'As it ran light, or had to bear a load' shows how the saw pushed through the wood to get it cut, then lightly ran back through the cut. **Line 9** tells us that the day was 'all but done'. A **foreshadowing of the impending tragedy** is given in 'I wish they might have said'. This is the only time in the whole poem when the personal pronoun 'I' is used. The poet's compassionate understanding for the young boy is evident as he explains how much it matters to a boy to be given precious time off from such hard work: 'That a boy counts so much'. The colloquial language in **line 10**, 'Call it a day', brings the reader right into this rural scene, rooting the poem in ordinary day-to-day life. The irony shimmers from the line, for soon there will be no more days for the boy.

A domestic detail adds to the reality of this scene as the boy's sister appears 'in her apron/To tell them "Supper."' In this central episode in **line 14**, the saw suddenly becomes personified, as if it too 'knew what supper meant'. The **jagged language**, 'Leaped out at the boy's hand, or seemed to leap—', reminds us of the jagged teeth of the saw as it seeks its prey. The mystifying accident is referenced in 'seemed to'. How could it have happened? 'He must have given the hand.' The helplessness of the victim, the boy, is shown: 'Neither refused the meeting'. We are reminded of someone almost paralysed into inaction at the split second of a horrific accident. Was this destiny? Is the poet adversely commenting on the mechanisation of farming, or on the practice of getting a boy to do a man's job? **All the attention is now focused on the hand**: 'But the hand!' The pity of the event is palpable in this climactic phrase.

The boy's reaction is chilling and poignant. He holds up the hand, 'spilling' its life blood. He pathetically asks for help, begging his sister not to let the doctor amputate his hand: 'Don't let him'. Now the poet interjects: 'So'. What more is to be said? It is like a drawn-out breath after the tension of the awful accident. The harsh reality is there for all to see: 'the hand was gone already'. The boy realised this when he 'saw all'. Without the use of his hands, there would be no man's work for him any more: 'He saw all spoiled'.

The closing section in **lines 33–39** shows the details of the medical help: the 'dark of ether', the boy's breath 'puffed'. Now **the lines break up into fragments** as the terrible final act of the tragedy unfolds: 'No one believed'. The heartbeats ebbed away: 'Little—less—nothing!' There are echoes of the *Macbeth* speech when Macbeth says, 'It is a tale told by an idiot ... signifying nothing'. The **sober reality hits home**: 'and that ended it'. The realisation that there is now no future for the boy is grasped: 'No more to build on there'. Frost has said that the reality of life is that 'it goes on'. And so the people there, because they were not the one dead, 'turned to their affairs'. No matter what horror happens in life, a new day comes. Neither the people nor the poet are being callous and unfeeling. Seamus Heaney calls it the 'grim accuracy' of the poem's end. The long line length also signals the return to normality.

The tone in this narrative poem shades from the anger and menace of the saw, to the calm of the beautiful rural countryside, to the wistful wishes of the poet and on to the fear and horror of the accident. In the end, Frost's ironic tone gives way to the cold fear of the finality of death, when all is changed forever.

ANALYSIS

Seamus Heaney commented, 'Here was a poet who touched things as they are, somehow'. Discuss this statement with reference to the poem 'Out, Out—'.

SAMPLE PARAGRAPH

This poem touched me deeply, as it reminded me of the Elton John song 'A Candle in the Wind', which he wrote for another young person whose life was as cruelly snuffed out in a terrible accident, just like this young boy. Many people are horrified at the poet and the people at the end of the poem, as they 'turned to their affairs'. Yet this is what life is like; after an accident, people put the kettle on. This does not mean they don't care, it means that the reality of life is, as Frost once said, 'It goes on'. I think it was very brave of the poet to just say things as they are, rather than pretending that life is not dark sometimes. I also felt as if I were actually in the timber yard as the saw 'snarled and rattled' in Vermont. The detail of sound and smell, 'Sweet-scented stuff', brought me there. It reminded me of Kavanagh, our Irish poet, who could see beauty in the most ordinary places. Frost, it seems to me, is also commenting negatively on the practice of having a young boy perform a man's job. The wistful 'I wish they might have said' condemns those who insisted on getting the job finished at the expense of the boy. It was too much to ask of a 'big boy', a 'child at heart'. The reality of the boy's life fading away was vividly captured by the poet in the line 'Little—less—nothing!' The punctuation adds to the effect of the heartbeat becoming weaker and finally stopping. This poet dared to say what life is like. He 'touched things as they are'. He achieved this by his craftsmanship as a poet, and his compassionate eye as a human being.

EXAMINER'S COMMENT

A thoughtful, personal exploration of the poem, using quotations that are well integrated into the answer, which results in an A grade. Contemporary references illustrate the continuing relevance of Frost as a realistic voice.

CLASS/HOMEWORK EXERCISES

1. It has been said that Frost's poems are 'little voyages of discovery'. Write a personal response to this poem, using quotations from the poem to support your answer.
2. Copy the table below into your own notes and fill in critical comments about the last two quotations.

Key Quotes

The buzz saw snarled and rattled in the yard	The harsh reality of farm life is graphically portrayed in this onomatopoeic line.
the saw,/As if to prove saws knew what supper meant	Personification adds to the horror of the accident. It is as though the saw is like a predatory animal.
Since he was old enough to know	The boy was old enough to know the meaning of the tragedy that had happened to him; he would no longer be able to do a man's work, now or in the future.
No one believed	
And they, since they/Were not the one dead, turned to their affairs	

• Poetry Focus •

Spring Pools

Robert Frost

These pools that, though in forests, still reflect
The total sky almost without defect,
And like the flowers beside them, chill and shiver,
Will like the flowers beside them soon be gone,
And yet not out by any brook or river,   5
But up by roots to bring dark foliage on.

The trees that have it in their pent-up buds
To darken nature and be summer woods—
Let them think twice before they use their powers
To blot out and drink up and sweep away   10
These flowery waters and these watery flowers
From snow that melted only yesterday.

GLOSSARY
2 *defect*: blemish; flaw.
5 *brook*: small stream.
6 *foliage*: plants; undergrowth.

'darken nature'

EXPLORATIONS

1. What aspects of the spring pools are conveyed in the first stanza? Refer to the text in your answer.
2. Choose one image from the poem that you found particularly striking. Briefly explain your choice.
3. Write your own personal response to the poem.

STUDY NOTES

'Spring Pools' captures a moment at the end of winter during which the poet reflects on the natural cycle of growth, decay and renewal. Rain falls from the sky, settles in pools and is then drawn up into the trees. In recalling the origins of this beautiful lyric poem, Frost commented, 'One night I sat alone by my open fireplace and wrote "Spring Pools". It was a very pleasant experience, and I remember it clearly, although I don't remember the writing of many of my other poems'.

The poem's title seems to celebrate new growth and regeneration. Ironically, **stanza one** focuses mainly on the fragility of nature. As always, Frost's **close observation of the natural world is evident** from the start. The clear pool water mirrors the overhead sky 'almost without defect'. While the simple images of the forest and flowers are peaceful, there is no escaping the underlying severity of 'chill and shiver'. The entire stanza of six lines is one long sentence. Its slow-moving pace, repetition and assonant vowels ('pools', 'brook', 'roots') enhance the sombre mood. Pool water will be absorbed by the tree roots to enrich the leaves and create 'dark foliage' and water and flowers will all 'soon be gone'. Frost pays most attention to the interdependence within the natural world and the transience of the beauty around him.

In **stanza two**, the poet addresses the trees directly, warning them to 'think twice before they use their powers'. He personifies them as an intimidating presence, associating them with dark destructiveness and 'pent-up' energy to 'blot out and drink up and sweep away'. Such forceful language combines with a resurgent rhythm to emphasise the power of the trees. The **tone becomes increasingly regretful in the final lines**. We are left with another evocative image of how nature's beauty is subject to constant change: 'snow that melted only yesterday'.

Frost's **poem is typically thought provoking**, touching on familiar themes regarding the mysteries of nature and the passing of time. Some critics interpret 'Spring Pools' as a metaphor for the creative process – water has long been a symbol of inspiration. Frost's own writing is wonderfully controlled, in keeping with the sense of order within the natural world that he describes. Both stanzas mirror each other perfectly and the *aabcbc* rhyme scheme completes the fluency of the lines.

ANALYSIS

How would you describe the dominant mood or atmosphere in 'Spring Pools'?

SAMPLE PARAGRAPH

There is a deep sense of loss going through much of Frost's poem 'Spring Pools'. It struck me first in the negative language of the opening stanza. Frost refers to the perfect sky 'without defect', implying that something might soon destroy the perfection. The peaceful setting of the winter flowers beside the pools is also spoiled when the poet points out that they 'chill and shiver'. The mood is downbeat – everything in nature will end inevitably and 'soon be gone'. The image of the trees ('dark foliage') adds to my sense of this depressing feeling. In the second part of the poem, Frost points out the irony of springtime as a season of decay just as much as of growth. To some degree, I think this is a realistic view, but it does take away from the joy of spring. The mood deteriorates as the poem continues. The trees are seen as agents of destruction, drying up the water from the pools and removing the flowers. They 'darken nature' – a dramatic way of summing up the overall mood of this poem.

EXAMINER'S COMMENT

This focused paragraph uses quotations very effectively to communicate the central mood of the poem. Some further discussion of style, particularly tone and rhythm, would have helped the answer. Overall, a basic B grade.

CLASS/HOMEWORK EXERCISES

1. In your view, what is the central theme or message of 'Spring Pools'? Refer closely to the poem in your answer.
2. Copy the table below into your own notes and fill in critical comments about the last two quotations.

Key Quotes

The total sky almost without defect	At the start of the poem, the setting is still and tranquil.
And like the flowers beside them, chill and shiver	Frost introduces a more disturbing element – the vulnerability of nature, as personified by the verbs.
darken nature and be summer woods	The trees in summer will blot out the light on the forest floor – one of the many ironies of the natural cycle.
dark foliage	
These flowery waters and these watery flowers	

Acquainted with the Night

I have been one acquainted with the night.
I have walked out in rain—and back in rain.
I have outwalked the furthest city light.

I have looked down the saddest city lane.
I have passed by the watchman on his beat   5
And dropped my eyes, unwilling to explain.

I have stood still and stopped the sound of feet
When far away an interrupted cry
Came over houses from another street,

But not to call me back or say good-by;   10
And further still at an unearthly height
One luminary clock against the sky

Proclaimed the time was neither wrong nor right.
I have been one acquainted with the night.

Robert Frost

'I have looked down the saddest city lane'

GLOSSARY

12 *luminary clock*: moon; a real clock shining with reflected light; simply passing time.
13 *Proclaimed ... wrong nor right*: this ambiguous message that the clock brings leaves us with more questions than answers. Why is the time neither wrong nor right? For whom is it so? For what is the time neither right nor wrong?

EXPLORATIONS

1. Does the shape of the poem add to or subtract from the poem's message? Comment on how the stanzas are arranged. Refer to the text in your answer.
2. Is there a sense of climax or anticlimax in this poem? Look at the rhyme scheme, the prevalence of end-stopped lines and the repetition. Refer to the text in your answer.
3. Write your own personal response to the poem.

STUDY NOTES

'Acquainted with the Night' is a sonnet from Frost's collection of poetry called *West-Ring Brook* (1928). Unusually for Frost, it is set in a bleak city rather than the countryside. This is one of Frost's darkest poems and portrays a solitary, isolated figure filled with despair. It is reminiscent of the Modernist poets, such as T.S. Eliot, or the American artist Edward Hopper, whose paintings frequently showed a solitary individual.

The twentieth century was a time of huge social upheaval and warfare, and was primarily focused on material progress rather than spiritual awareness. It was the century of the individual, rather than the community. Many people became alienated, lonely and confused. The certainty that institutions bring was lost, moral codes were abandoned and the traditional comforts of extended family and community began to disappear. The poem begins with a declaration: 'I have been one acquainted with the night'. It is a frank statement, rather like the declarations made at an AA meeting. It is also reminiscent of the Old Testament reference to **one who was despised and rejected by men**, a man of sorrows 'acquainted with grief'. The second line in this first stanza shows the direction that the poem will take. There are two journeys: the body travels outwards towards the edge of the city ('I have walked out in rain') while the mind travels inwards to the edge of the psyche ('and back in rain').

This **alienation is echoed in the form of the poem**, which is not a conventional fourteen-line sonnet (either three quatrains and a rhyming couplet, or an octet and sestet); here there is a terza rima format. The poet uses a three-line rhyming stanza, concluding with a rhyming couplet (*aba, bcb, cdc, ded, ff*). The terza rima was used by the great Italian poet Dante in his famous poem *The Divine Comedy* to describe the descent into hell. Is Frost using this structure in his poem because he is describing his own descent into his own private hell? (His own life had included many personal tragedies.) Is he using this format because nothing is conventional any more? This is a highly personal poem, as it uses 'I' at the beginning of seven of its fourteen lines. The rhythm imitates a slow walking movement: 'I have outwalked the furthest city light'. The poet has now gone beyond the last visible sign of civilisation. The use of iambic pentameter is the metre closest to the speaking voice in English, and the measured flow underlines the poet's melancholy mood.

The **solemn, sombre mood** of overwhelming anxiety is shown in the long vowel sounds of the **second stanza**: 'I have looked down the saddest city lane'. The broad vowels 'a' and 'o' lengthen the line and show the world-weariness of one who has seen and experienced too much. Although it is set at night, the traditional time for romance and lovers, we are presented with never-ending rain and gloom. A listless mood is created by the repetition of 'I have'. The run-on line suggests the ongoing trudging of this weary man who is too caught up in his own dark thoughts to even bother communicating with the 'watchman'. He is 'unwilling to explain' and is jealously guarding his privacy. Is this walk symptomatic of his inner state? Can nothing penetrate this extreme loneliness?

The use of the run-on line continues in the **third stanza**. Frost comes to an abrupt stop on his journey as an 'interrupted cry' rings out across the **desolate urban landscape**. Who cried? Why? And why was the cry 'interrupted'? Is something awful happening to someone? We, and the poet, don't know. Can anything be done about it? No. The poet just remarks in the next stanza that it has nothing to do with him, 'not to call me back or say good-by'. This is the chilling aspect of living in a big city: the sense of just being another person nobody cares about. These others have no substance, being reduced to the 'sound of feet' or a 'cry'.

In the **fourth stanza**, the poet speaks of a 'luminary clock'. This could be the moon or a real clock that is reflecting light. Is it symbolic of time passing relentlessly? Why is it at an 'unearthly height'? Is it because time rules the human world and nothing can change this? The **final couplet** proclaims that the 'time was neither wrong nor right'. We are left wondering what the time was neither right nor wrong for – what was supposed to happen? There is a real **sense of confusion** here, and echoes of Hamlet's declaration that 'the time is out of joint'. The poem ends as it begins: 'I have been one acquainted with the night'. We have come full circle, though **nothing has been achieved**. We have experienced the darkness with the poet. There is no sense of comfort or guidance, only the realisation of a hostile world.

ANALYSIS

This poem has been described as a 'dramatic lyric of homelessness'. Do you agree or disagree with this statement? Support your view with references from the text.

SAMPLE PARAGRAPH

The sense of homelessness is palpable in this unconventional sonnet of Robert Frost's. The individual in the poem seems to be always on his own, not connected either with family, friend or acquaintance, a real loner in a big anonymous city. The form of the poem mirrors this individualism. It is a maverick sonnet, just like in the great American tradition of cowboy films or gangster movies: the hero is the loner who never quite fits in. There is no network to comfort this man, no community to offer help and encouragement. This emphasis on self comes at a price. The hero does not want to engage, 'And dropped my eyes'. He wanders through town like the tumbleweed of old, with no roots to hold it still. The poem is like a mini drama as the main character plays out his exterior action: 'I have walked out in rain', and his interior journey, 'unwilling to explain'. The verbs carry the action of this sad man: 'outwalked', 'looked', 'passed by', 'stood', 'stopped'. This man is going nowhere. The setting is vividly realised as the bleak urban landscape is drawn with its endless rain and strange noises. So there is character, action, setting and mood. A lyric is a short musical poem which deals with feelings. The music of this lyrical poem is the rhythm of a slow walk as the steady iambic pentameter tempo steps out a hypnotic beat: 'I have outwalked the furthest city light.' The broad vowels add to this sombre music as the poem grinds on relentlessly: 'I have looked down the saddest city lane.' The regular rhyme scheme adds to the dull, hopeless feeling the character seems to be experiencing. This is indeed dark mood music, as the drawn-out vowel sounds 'lane', 'explain', 'beat' and 'feet' tap out the despair of this lonely man. So, in conclusion, I do agree with the statement that 'Acquainted with the Night' is indeed a dramatic lyric of homelessness.

EXAMINER'S COMMENT

This paragraph addresses the three elements of the question (homelessness, dramatic and lyric). It shows a real appreciation of poetic technique, as the terms are not only explained, but are well-examined in relation to the poem. Grade A.

CLASS/HOMEWORK EXERCISES

1. Seamus Heaney describes this poem as 'dark'. What type of darkness is there? Is it literal or metaphorical or both? Refer to the text in your answer.
2. Copy the table below into your own notes and fill in critical comments about the last two quotations.

Key Quotes

I have been one acquainted with the night	Frost tells us that he has known bad times – in an almost biblical fashion. But we are left with a mystery: what were those bad times?
I have outwalked the furthest city light	There are now no signs of civilisation. The poet has reached a place where there is no guiding light.
I have passed by the watchman on his beat/ And dropped my eyes	It was not just the city's fault that this man was alone. He made no effort to communicate with anyone.
But not to call me back or say good-by	
Proclaimed the time was neither wrong nor right	

• Poetry Focus •

Design

Robert Frost

I found a dimpled spider, fat and white,
On a white heal-all, holding up a moth
Like a white piece of rigid satin cloth—
Assorted characters of death and blight
Mixed ready to begin the morning right,   5
Like the ingredients of a witches' broth—
A snow-drop spider, a flower like a froth,
And dead wings carried like a paper kite.

What had that flower to do with being white,
The wayside blue and innocent heal-all?   10
What brought the kindred spider to that height,
Then steered the white moth thither in the night?
What but design of darkness to appall?—
If design govern in a thing so small.

'a dimpled spider, fat and white'

GLOSSARY

The poem's title refers to the argument that the natural design of the universe is proof of God's existence.
1. *dimpled*: indented.
2. *heal-all*: plant (once used as a medicine).
4. *blight*: disease in plants; evil influence.
6. *witches' broth*: revolting recipes used to cast spells.
12. *thither*: to there, to that place.
13. *appall*: horrify (to make pale, literally).

EXPLORATIONS

1. How important a part does the colour white play in this poem? Refer to the text in your answer.
2. Select one comparison from the poem that you consider particularly effective. Briefly explain your choice.
3. Describe the poet's tone in the octave. How does it compare with the tone in the sestet?

STUDY NOTES

> 'Design' explores our attempts to see order in the universe – and our failure to recognise the order that is present in nature. Frost's sonnet raises several profound questions. Is there a design to life? Is there an explanation for the evil in the world? The poet was fascinated by nature from a philosophical point of view. His choice of the traditional sonnet form allows him to address such an important theme in a controlled way.

In the **opening line**, Frost describes how he finds a 'dimpled spider, fat and white' on a flower, 'holding up a moth' it has captured. The adjective 'dimpled' usually has harmless connotations far removed from the world of arachnids, but in this context, and combined with the word 'fat', it suggests an unattractive image of venomous engorgement. The colour white (used four more times in this short poem) also tends to have positive overtones of innocence and goodness. But most spiders are brown or black, and purity here quickly gives way to pale ghastliness. Indeed, the **tone becomes increasingly menacing** as the octave proceeds. The unwary moth has been lured to its grizzly death on the 'white heal-all' flower, which makes the situation even more deceitful.

Frost's chilling similes reflect the deathly atmosphere. The hapless moth is held 'Like a white piece of rigid satin cloth'. The 'characters of death' in this grim drama are compared to the 'ingredients of a witches' broth'. **Lines 7–8** are particularly ironic. Frost then revises his view of the grotesque scene, seeing the **tragic coincidence** involving the 'snow-drop spider' and 'a flower like a froth'. While the images appear attractive, there is a lingering suggestion of gloom and ferocity.

The focus changes in the **sestet** as the tone grows passionately angry. Frost uses a series of **rhetorical questions demanding an explanation** for what he has witnessed: 'What had that flower to do with being white'? Is this implying that nature isn't so innocent after all? He reruns the sequence of events and wonders what 'steered the white moth thither in the night'. The possibility that such a catastrophic event might be part of a great 'design of darkness' appals the poet. However, the poem's **final line** ('If design govern in a thing so small') is the most intriguing of all. The word 'if' leaves the possibility that there is no grand plan for the universe, that it is all accidental. Whether predestination or chance is the more terrifying reality is left for readers to consider.

ANALYSIS

In your view, what image of nature does Frost present in his poem 'Design'? Refer closely to the text in your response.

SAMPLE PARAGRAPH

In his poem 'Design', Robert Frost takes an ironic approach to nature. Unlike other poems (e.g. 'The Tuft of Flowers'), where he ends up being reassured by the beauty and mystery of his natural environment, 'Design' is decidedly disquieting. The first few lines describe a repulsive side of nature's basic law – kill or be killed. I found the image of the bloated spider quite revolting: 'fat and white'. The poet cleverly conveys a strong sense of the violence and death that takes place when nature begins 'the morning right'. Dead moths are routine – often in beautiful settings. Nature is full of such contradictions. The image of the moth like a 'white piece of rigid satin cloth' suggested the lining of a coffin and reminded me that we see signs of our own mortality all around us. At the same time, Frost seems to be realistic about nature. Even in violent situations, there are beautiful creatures. The 'dead wings' are compared to a graceful 'paper kite'. Under different circumstances, I could imagine a more attractive 'snow-drop' or the 'wayside blue' of a wild flower. Overall, I think the poet probably shows a less attractive side to nature in the poem, but it is not altogether bleak or depressing. I found his ideas interesting and liked the way he managed simple language to raise deep and disturbing questions about our natural world.

EXAMINER'S COMMENT

The paragraph addressed the question very well. The response was balanced but clear, demonstrating a good understanding of the poem. References and quotations were carefully chosen and used effectively. Varied, confident expression throughout. Grade A.

CLASS/HOMEWORK EXERCISES

1. Sonnets often move from description to reflection ('sight to insight'). To what extent is this true of 'Design'? Refer closely to the poem in your answer.
2. Copy the table below into your own notes and fill in critical comments about the last two quotations.

Key Quotes

I found a dimpled spider, fat and white	Frost takes a matter-of-fact, narrative approach, using his characteristic colloquial diction.
And dead wings carried like a paper kite	The juxtaposition of a disturbing image alongside a childlike simile is a common feature of this poem's ambivalence.
innocent heal-all	Irony plays a central part in this poem. The moth was attracted to its death by the white flowers of a plant that is usually associated with healing.
Assorted characters of death and blight	
design of darkness	

Provide, Provide

Robert Frost

The witch that came (the withered hag)
To wash the steps with pail and rag
Was once the beauty Abishag,

The picture pride of Hollywood.
Too many fall from great and good   5
For you to doubt the likelihood.

Die early and avoid the fate.
Or if predestined to die late,
Make up your mind to die in state.

Make the whole stock exchange your own!   10
If need be occupy a throne,
Where nobody can call *you* crone.

Some have relied on what they knew,
Others on being simply true.
What worked for them might work for you.   15

No memory of having starred
Atones for later disregard
Or keeps the end from being hard.

Better to go down dignified
With boughten friendship at your side   20
Than none at all. Provide, provide!

'Was once the beauty Abishag'

GLOSSARY

3 *Abishag*: beautiful young woman who comforted King David in his old age.

12 *crone*: witchlike; old, withered woman.

17 *Atones*: make amends (for sin or wrongdoing).

20 *boughten*: bought.

EXPLORATIONS

1 Is the advice given in the poem to be taken seriously or humorously, or a mixture of both? Discuss, using reference from the poem to support your answer.

2 What elements in the poem resemble a fairytale or fable? Pick your favourite element and explain why you like it.

3 What conclusion, if any, does the poem come to? Do you agree or disagree with the view expressed? Refer to the poem to support your view.

STUDY NOTES

> This poem was written at the height of Frost's fame, in a collection called *A Further Rage* (1936). It was based on a real woman he had seen cleaning steps. The poem contrasts with most of Frost's work, as the tone is bitter and the emphasis is on material success. The Great Depression, a time of mass unemployment in America, was taking place. Is Frost suggesting that self-sufficiency is the answer?

The **first stanza** advises us to **plan for the future**. Why? A cold, bleak scene of a withered old woman doing a menial job of washing steps is given as a salutary picture of what happens if you don't provide. This is what happened to Abishag. The reference to the Biblical character adds a timeless element – this is a truth for all generations. We don't know what is to be. In this poem, old age equals diminishing beauty and success.

In **stanza two**, the destructive element of time is stressed as the poem comes to the present, 'Hollywood'. Even in the 'dream factory', beauty does not last. The tone of the poem is one of **addressing a public audience**, as if at an evangelical rally: 'For you to doubt the likelihood'. Fortune is fickle, as we all know.

The poem now offers **mock advice: the only solution is to die young** ('Die early'). Images of icons hover in our minds of tragic, famous deaths of the young and beautiful, such as James Dean and Marilyn Monroe. In the **third stanza**, **the only other solution is to become wealthy** and 'die in state'. An imperative verb, 'Make', in the **fourth stanza** shouts at us to grab material success: 'Make the whole stock exchange your own!' The exclamation mark captures the mood of exhortation that pervades this unusual poem of Frost's. The quaint image of the throne adds to the timeless element of this poem, as it is a universal symbol of power and wealth. Only political power, privilege and riches provide protection against the harsh reality of ageing. If 'you' don't want the same fate as Abishag, 'you' must be alert.

Independence was very important to Frost. Now, in **stanza six**, the poem cautions us that even if our early lives were wonderful, 'having starred', that memory is not a safeguard against the misfortune that might happen later in life. Black humour in the **final stanza** suggests, with wry, unsentimental honesty, that it is better to **buy friendship** ('boughten') than suffer loneliness at the end of life. Is this cynical view that bought friends are better than none realistic? The poem concludes with great urgency: 'Provide, provide!' Frost did not believe in a benevolent God ruling the universe, but rather takes the view that there is an indifferent God and we are subject to random darkness. This is not an affirmative poem.

Frost favoured **traditional poetic structures**, declaring that he was 'one of the notable craftsmen of this time'. Here the full rhyme of *aaa, bbb, ccc, ddd*, etc. does not seem strained. We hardly notice it in this carefully crafted poem of seven triplets. The rhythmic pattern of blank verse, i.e. four short–long beats, set against the irregular variations of colloquial speech gives this poem its energy. The use of the imperative for the verbs, especially 'Provide, provide', demands that the reader take this message on board. Frost presents **painful ideas** – in this instance a cynical view of fame and success – **in a controlled form**. He has said, 'The poems I make are little bits of order'.

ANALYSIS

'Poetry is a momentary stay against confusion.' Discuss this statement in relation to the poem, 'Provide, Provide'. Use references from the poem to support your views.

SAMPLE PARAGRAPH

The bleak, cold situation painted in this poem by Frost is very different from his other poems where a quiet, sensible speaking voice alerts us to the beauties of nature. Here the focus is on 'look out for your old age, as no one is going to want you'. I wonder if Frost was uncomfortable about his decision to commit himself to being famous? Did he, like so many contemporary stars today, find the whole fame business tacky and shallow? He enjoyed giving performances of his poems: 'Words exist in the mouth, not books,' he declared. When he read this poem in public, he usually added a line, 'Or somebody else'll provide for you!/And how'll you like that?' He is condemning those who take 'handouts', social benefits. Frost suffered many emotional tragedies in his long life, and I also wonder if the fact that his father died at thirty-four, and his mother had only eight dollars to bury him contributed to this bleak view of providing for hard times and old age? The poem is stating that change is the only certainty and vehemently exhorts us to get ourselves in order if we don't want to have a miserable time when looks and youth are gone. I like the mock serious tone in which this message is delivered: 'If need be occupy a throne,/Where nobody can call *you* crone'. I think this wry, dry, cynical tone appeals especially to today's reader who is saturated with this 'fame' issue. I also think that humour is very effective in delivering a message, particularly one as unpalatable as this. The airbrushed perfection of the groomed Hollywood stars is captured perfectly in the alliterative phrase: 'The picture pride of Hollywood'. Frost has arranged this line as carefully as the lighting technician has arranged the lighting of a star, so that all seems picture perfect. But the poet knew that this is not how it is – 'the end' is 'hard'. Frost said, 'If you suffer any sense of confusion in life, the best thing you can do is make little poems'. Here is the human's need for order in a terrifying universe. In this poem, Frost has succeeded in 'making a momentary stay against confusion'.

EXAMINER'S COMMENT

This response (to a very challenging question) has taken a ruminative view of Frost's poetry, connecting his views on poetry and life as well as his own personal circumstances into the discussion. However, it over-relies on biographical references and is not sufficiently rooted in the text. B grade.

CLASS/HOMEWORK EXERCISES

1. 'A poem begins in delight and ends in wisdom.' Is this a valid statement in relation to the poem 'Provide, Provide'? Use quotation from the poem in your explorations.
2. Copy the table below into your own notes and fill in critical comments about the last two quotations.

Robert Frost

Key Quotes

The witch that came	This is a reference to an old washing woman Frost saw at Harvard University
Die early and avoid the fate	Mock serious advice given in the poem. Note the imperative tone.
What worked for them might work for you	You can usually learn from the experiences of others. More wry advice.
No memory of having starred / Atones for later disregard	
Better to go down dignified/ With boughten friendship at your side/ Than none at all	

LEAVING CERT SAMPLE ESSAY

> **Q** 'We enjoy poetry for its ideas and language.'
>
> Using the above statement as your title, write an essay on the poetry of Robert Frost. Support the points by reference to the poetry of Robert Frost on your course.

MARKING SCHEME GUIDELINES

Expect candidates to deal with both elements of the question – ideas and language – but not necessarily separately. Take 'ideas' to mean themes, subjects, attitudes, issues and so on. Take 'language' to mean style, manner, phraseology, appropriate vocabulary, imagery, etc.

The level of engagement with the poetry will serve as an implicit treatment of what 'we enjoy' in the poetry of Robert Frost.

Some of the following areas might provide material for candidates:
- Poet's views on life/experience.
- Habitual concerns in the poems.
- Elegant plainness of his expression.
- Typical patterns of imagery/language.
- Variety of registers in the texts, etc.

SAMPLE ESSAY
(We Enjoy Frost's Poetry for Its Ideas and Language)

1 *How could you not enjoy the work of a man whose favourite book was* Robinson Crusoe? Here is a quiet, sensible speaking voice dealing with human suffering, isolation, loneliness and our relations with the world around us. No wonder his poems were sent to inspire soldiers in the Second World War, or that he was chosen to speak at the inauguration of JFK. 'Mending Wall' deals with an annual event where two neighbours check and mend their boundary wall ritualistically each spring. The communal activity joins people, but this poem is also about gaps in understanding between people. The speaker delights in mischief, in contrast to his neighbour, who 'walks in darkness' because he is traditional and is content to repeat received wisdom from previous generations without question: 'Good walls make good neighbors'.

2. *Civilisation needs boundaries and order. Respecting rules is necessary in society, otherwise there is chaos. We must respect equality, but also difference. Each remains on his own land, 'One on a side'. So Frost's single event contains a complex issue: boundaries connect and divide. The two neighbours can also be seen as reflecting the two contrasting facets of Frost – the wall toppler who delights in wildness, breaking rules, being disruptive; and the builder who abides by strict rules, form, grammar and the traditional structure of poems. Such insights are what attracts me to Frost's work.*

3. *I also enjoyed the idea that there is a force in nature that does not like the way men construct boundaries. When I think of the Native Americans who did not believe in land ownership but rather guardianship and care of Mother Earth, I agree that 'Something there is that doesn't love a wall'. I think it was a particularly good poem to read to President Khrushchev, particularly at a time of the Cold War and the Iron Curtain: 'I'd ask to know what I was walling in or walling out'.*

4. *The Romantic influence can be seen in the subject matter of 'The Road Not Taken'. Nature is the stimulus for an insight. This poem deals with decisions taken when young. We are all facing tough decisions now regarding study, points and careers and will we be like Frost's friend who inspired this poem, and regret decisions we have made? Will we be thinking of things that might have been: 'I shall be telling this with a sigh'? When we look at our classmates and know that we will all take different roads and may not meet again for quite some time, don't the lines 'Yet knowing how way leads on to way, I doubted if I ever should come back' ring very true?*

5. *Nature provides a beautiful but passive background to the horrific event in 'Out, Out–'. Frost never read this poem at his readings as he regarded it as too cruel. It was inspired by a newspaper account about a young boy whose hand was amputated by a saw as he was doing a man's job and who subsequently died. This reminded me of how Bob Geldof created Live Aid from an item of TV news. Like the Victorians, Frost believed that there was no benevolent God compassionately caring for the world. Terrible things happen. For me, the most shocking thing in this poem was not the chainsaw as it became an animal and devoured the boy's hand; rather it was how the onlookers who 'since they were not the one dead, turned to their affairs'. This is chilling. But Frost believed one thing about life: 'It goes on'. When I consider the tragic life Frost lived, I can see how he understood the importance of endurance, however cold it may seem.*

6 Frost's simple subject matter covers complex issues: 'There's always something else in my poetry.' His language allows us access to them. He did not follow the fashion of the time. Instead, he adopted the persona of the New England farmer inspired by natural events. But underpinning the colloquial language is a strict adherence to traditional forms and patterning. To him, free verse was like 'playing tennis without a net'. He used blank verse and iambic pentameter, which has rhythm but not rhyme: 'Something there is that doesn't love a wall'. There is a tension between the ordinary subject matter and the colloquial voice, as it is constrained by poetic patterning.

7 Frost believed in the sound of a poem, he said poems rather than read them, believing the sound carried the meaning. I see this clearly in 'The buzz saw snarled and rattled in the yard'. The sound of this line suggests a menacing element in the midst of beauty. The dust is beautifully described as 'sweet-scented stuff when the breeze blew across it'. The gentle 's' sound conveys the harmony in the timber yard, in contrast to the strident sound of the saw. I also enjoyed Frost's use of drama in his poetry, the moment of decision in 'The Road Not Taken' when he wrote: 'Two roads converged in a yellow wood' and the strange 'interrupted cry' in 'Acquainted with the Night' which left me wondering who had cried and why. No wonder I am just one of millions who enjoy Frost's poetic ideas and language.

(approx. 870 words)

```
GRADE: A1
P     =  15/15
C     =  15/15
L     =  15/15
M     =  5/5
Total =  50/50
```

EXAMINER'S COMMENT

A detailed exploration of the question and well-developed points on both subject matter and style supported by succinct quotations. The essay ranged widely and showed very good personal engagement with the poetry. Expression was varied and confidently managed throughout. A very assured response.

Robert Frost

SAMPLE LEAVING CERT QUESTIONS ON FROST'S POETRY
(45–50 MINUTES)

1. 'The appeal of Robert Frost's poetry for a young audience.'
   Write an essay on this statement, focusing particular attention on his themes and how he expresses them. Support the points you make by reference to the poetry of Robert Frost on your course.

2. What impact did the poetry of Robert Frost make on you as a reader? In shaping your answer, you might like to consider the following:
   - Your overall sense or outlook of the poet.
   - The poet's use of language and imagery.
   - Your favourite poem or poems.

3. 'Life by the throat' is a phrase often associated with the poetry of Robert Frost. How does the poetry catch life by the throat? Discuss, referring both to the content and style of the poems by Frost on your course.

SAMPLE ESSAY PLAN (Q2)

What impact did the poetry of Robert Frost make on you as a reader? In shaping your answer, you might like to consider the following:

- Your overall sense or outlook of the poet.
- The poet's use of language and imagery.
- Your favourite poem or poems.

•	*Intro:*	Interesting themes, individualistic style. His fascination with nature and human nature. Favourite poem – 'The Road Not Taken'.
•	*Point 1:*	Family – background tragic, yet it is the still, calm voice which sounds from the poem. He extends the invitation, 'you come too', as he explores man's relationship with nature.
•	*Point 2:*	'Sound of sense' – 'Writing with your ear to the voice'. Use of first person in 'Out, Out—'. Use of first person pronoun in 'The Road Not Taken'.
•	*Point 3:*	Formal patterning and rhyme – traditionalist, good craftsman, art deceptive, rhyme scheme in 'The Road Not Taken'. Terza rima in 'Acquainted with the Night'.

•	*Point 4:*	Metaphors – 'poetry is simply made up of metaphors'. Doesn't force, allows the metaphors to speak for themselves, e.g. road is a metaphor for a journey in 'The Road Not Taken'.
•	*Point 5:*	Other themes – natural world, endurance, ordinary life, etc.
•	*Conclusion:*	Wrote about ordinary people living ordinary lives. View of nature bleak. Aware of time and effect on human beings.

EXERCISE

Develop one of the above points into a paragraph.

POINT 5 – SAMPLE PARAGRAPH

The subject matter of Frost's poetry is rooted in the natural world. He believed that 'man has need of nature, but nature has no need of man'. But it was nature which was thought-provoking, a stimulus for the poet, leading to insight and revelation: 'A poem begins in delight and ends in wisdom'. This was in keeping with the Romantic poets, such as Wordsworth, and was in contrast to the Modernist movement that was in vogue at this time. They were urban poets who used classical references and were often obscure. Frost was and is accessible. He was influenced by current events – just like Geldof was inspired by a news item to create Live Aid, so Frost was inspired by a newspaper article to write the chilling poem of injured innocence, 'Out, Out–'. Frost believed in endurance: 'In three words I can sum up everything I've learned about life – it goes on'. He was influenced also by the Victorian poets like Hardy who did not believe in a world ruled by a benevolent God. Darkness erupts in a random manner with tragic consequences, as in 'Out, Out–'. He wrote about ordinary people living ordinary lives. But his view of the human condition was bleak and cold. He was aware of time and its effect on human beings.

EXAMINER'S COMMENT

As part of a full essay answer, the student has written a general exploration that shows a real understanding of Frost's aims. The paragraph focuses on the insight to be gained from a mature perception of nature. Grade A.

Last Words

'Like a piece of ice on a hot stove, the poem must ride on its own melting.'
Robert Frost

'Robert Frost: the icon of the Yankee values, the smell of wood smoke, the sparkle of dew, the reality of farm-house dung, the jocular honesty of an uncle.'
Derek Walcott

'I'll say that again, in case you missed it first time round.'
Robert Frost

'Every poet must be original.'

Gerard Manley Hopkins
(1844–89)

Gerard Manley Hopkins, a priest and poet, was born in Stratford, outside London, in 1844. Throughout his youth, Hopkins demonstrated excellent academic and artistic talent. In 1863 he began studying classics at Balliol College, Oxford, where he wrote a great deal of poetry. Hopkins converted to Catholicism and was later ordained a Jesuit priest in 1877. It was while studying for the priesthood that he wrote some of his best-known religious and nature poems, including 'The Windhover' and 'Pied Beauty'. His compressed style of writing, especially his experimental use of language, sound effects and inventive rhythms, combined to produce distinctive and startling poetry. In 1884 Hopkins was appointed Professor of Greek at University College, Dublin. He disliked living in Ireland, where he experienced failing health and severe depression. A devout and ascetic Jesuit, he was caught between his religious obligations and his poetic talent. In 1885 he wrote a number of the so-called 'terrible sonnets', including 'No worst, there is none', which have desolation at their core. Hopkins died of typhoid fever in June 1889 without ever publishing any of his major poems. He is buried in Glasnevin Cemetery.

• Poetry Focus •

PRESCRIBED POEMS (HIGHER LEVEL)

1 'God's Grandeur' (p. 168)

Hopkins's sonnet welcomes the power of the Holy Ghost to rescue people from sin and hopelessness.

2 'Spring' (p. 172)

This poem celebrates the natural beauty of springtime. However, Hopkins also regrets man's loss of innocence because of sin.

3 'As kingfishers catch fire, dragonflies draw flame' (p. 177)

In recognising the uniqueness of everything that exists in the world, Hopkins praises God as the unchanging source of all creation.

4 'The Windhover' (p. 181)

This was one of Hopkins's favourite poems and describes a bird in flight. Its powerful Christian theme focuses on the relationship between God and mankind.

5 'Pied Beauty' (p. 186)

This short poem again celebrates the diverse delights of nature and human nature, all of which owe their existence to a changeless Creator.

6 'Felix Randal' (p. 190)

An engaging narrative poem about the life and death of one of Hopkins's parishioners. At a deeper level, it celebrates the significance of living a good Christian life.

7 'Inversnaid' (p. 195)

Another nature poem rejoicing in the unspoiled beauty of the remote Scottish landscape. It concludes with the poet's heartfelt appeal to preserve the wilderness.

8 'I wake and feel the fell of dark, not day' (p. 199)

One of the 'terrible sonnets' in which Hopkins reveals his personal torment, self-disgust and despair. Some critics argue that the poet is attempting to renew his religious faith.

9 **'No worst, there is none' (p. 203)**

Hopkins explores the experience of unbearable depression, guilt and the awful sense of feeling abandoned by God. Only sleep or death offer any relief.

10 **'Thou art indeed just, Lord, if I contend' (p. 207)**

In this intensely personal poem, Hopkins wonders why good people suffer while the wicked seem to prosper. He ends by pleading with God to strengthen his own faith.

• Poetry Focus •

God's Grandeur

The world is charged with the grandeur of God.
　It will flame out, like shining from shook foil;
　It gathers to a greatness, like the ooze of oil
Crushed. Why do men then now not reck his rod?
Generations have trod, have trod, have trod;　　　　　　　　　　5
　And all is seared with trade; bleared, smeared with toil;
　And wears man's smudge and shares man's smell: the soil
Is bare now, nor can foot feel, being shod.

And for all this, nature is never spent;
　There lives the dearest freshness deep down things;　　　　10
And though the last lights off the black West went
　Oh, morning, at the brown brink eastward, springs –
Because the Holy Ghost over the bent
　World broods with warm breast and with ah! bright wings.

'nature is never spent'

GLOSSARY

Hopkins's philosophy emphasised the uniqueness of every natural thing, which he called *inscape*. He believed that there was a special connection between the world of nature and an individual's consciousness. Hopkins viewed the world as an integrated network created by God. The sensation of inscape (which the poet called *instress*) is the appreciation that everything has its own unique identity. The concept is similar to that of epiphanies in James Joyce's writing.

1　*charged*: powered; made responsible.
2　*foil*: shimmering gold or silver.
4　*Crushed*: compressed from olives or linseed.
4　*reck his rod*: pay heed to God's power.
6　*seared*: scorched; ruined.
6　*bleared*: blurred.
6　*toil*: industrialisation.
8　*shod*: covered; protected.
9　*spent*: exhausted.
11　*last lights*: the setting sun.

EXPLORATIONS

1. Describe Hopkins's tone in the first four lines of this poem. Refer closely to the text in your answer.
2. How are human beings portrayed in the poem? Support your points with reference.
3. Select two unusual images the poet uses. Comment on the effectiveness of each.

STUDY NOTES

> Hopkins wrote many Italian (or Petrarchan) sonnets (consisting of an octave and a sestet). The form suited the stages in the argumentative direction of his themes. Like many other Christian poets, Hopkins 'found' God in nature. His poetry is also notable for its use of sprung rhythm (an irregular movement or pace which echoed ordinary conversation). 'God's Grandeur' is typical of Hopkins in both its subject matter and style. The condensed language, elaborate wordplay and unusual syntax – sometimes like a tongue twister – can be challenging.

The poem's **opening quatrain** (four-line section) is characteristically dynamic. The **metaphor ('charged') compares God's greatness to electric power**, brilliant but hazardous. The visual effect of 'flame out' and 'shook foil' develops this representation of God's constant presence in the world. This image of oozing oil signifies a natural richness. The reference to electricity makes a subtle reappearance in **line 4**, where the 'rod' of an angry Creator is likened to a lightning bolt. The tone is one of energised celebration, but there is also a growing frustration: 'Why do men then now not reck his rod?' Hopkins seems mystified at human indifference to God's greatness.

The **second quatrain** is much more critical. We can sense the poet's own weariness with the numberless generations who have abandoned their spiritual salvation for the flawed material benefits of 'trade' and 'toil'. The laboured repetition of 'have trod' is purposely heavy-handed. The internal rhymes of the negative verbs ('seared', 'bleared' and 'smeared') in **line 6** convey his deep sense of disgust at a world blighted by industry and urbanisation. **Man's neglect of the natural environment is closely linked to the drift away from God.** Hopkins symbolises this spiritual alienation through the image of the 'shod' foot out of touch with nature and its Creator.

However, in response to his depression, the mood changes in **the sestet** (the final six lines of the sonnet). Hopkins's tone softens considerably and is aided by the gentle, sibilant effect in **line 10**: 'There lives the dearest freshness deep down things'. As in many of his religious poems, he takes comfort in conventional Christian belief. For him, 'nature is never spent'. The world is filled with 'freshness' that confirms God's presence. This **power of renewal** is exemplified in the way morning never fails to follow the 'last lights' of dark night.

The reassuring image in the **last line** is one of God guarding the world and promising rebirth and salvation. The source of this constant regeneration is 'the Holy Ghost' (God's grace) who 'broods' over a dependent world with the patient devotion of a bird protecting its young. In expressing his faith and surrendering himself to divine will, the poet can truly appreciate the grandeur of God. The final exclamations ('Oh, morning' and 'ah! bright wings') echo Hopkins's **sense of euphoria**.

ANALYSIS

What impression of God is presented in the poem? Refer to the text in your answer.

SAMPLE PARAGRAPH

Hopkins presents an image of a loving God caring for us all. Nature images are used as comparisons. God is seen at the end of the poem where he compares God to a female bird protecting its new-born fledglings in the nest. The image we get is of the hatchlings nestling under the 'warm breast'. Secure in the knowledge that they are being looked after. This is a simple but direct metaphor. Hopkins develops this image by referring to the 'bright wings' which might be a symbol of the glory of God's heavenly light. Something often referred to in the Bible. The poet obviously recognises the power of God. At the start of the sonnet, he compares God to a lightning rod, another nature comparison. Lightning is powerful but very dangerous, God is the Creator but has the power of Heaven and Hell. Overall, we get a balanced picture of God in the poem, but the main image is one of a caring protector who nurtures the world.

EXAMINER'S COMMENT

The paragraph includes some good discussion on the final positive image of God. However, a more thorough development of the lightning comparison would have helped raise the standard above a good C grade. The expression is note-like at times.

CLASS/HOMEWORK EXERCISES

1. Comment on Hopkins's use of sound in this poem. Refer closely to the text in your answer.
2. Copy the table below into your own notes and fill in critical comments about the last two quotations.

Key Quotes

The world is charged with the grandeur of God	Hopkins's metaphorical view of God's greatness as an electric force suggests both power and retribution.
And all is seared with trade; bleared, smeared with toil	The verbs emphasise a highly critical view of man's misuse of the earth.
nature is never spent	God possesses an infinite power of renewal. This is evident in the powerful cycle of nature.
nor can foot feel, being shod	
The Holy Ghost over the bent/World broods	

• Poetry Focus •

Spring

Gerard Manley Hopkins

Nothing is so beautiful as spring –
   When weeds, in wheels, shoot long and lovely and lush;
   Thrush's eggs look little low heavens, and thrush
Through the echoing timber does so rinse and wring
The ear, it strikes like lightnings to hear him sing;   5
   The glassy peartree leaves and blooms, they brush
   The descending blue; that blue is all in a rush
With richness; the racing lambs too have fair their fling.

What is all this juice and all this joy?
   A strain of the earth's sweet being in the beginning   10
In Eden garden. – Have, get, before it cloy,
   Before it cloud, Christ, lord, and sour with sinning,
Innocent mind and Mayday in girl and boy,
   Most, O maid's child, thy choice and worthy the winning.

'That blue is all in a rush/With richness'

GLOSSARY

2 *in wheels*: radiating out like spokes; rampant; pivoting movement.
2 *lush*: growing thickly, luxuriantly.
3 *Thrush's eggs*: songbird's eggs, which are light blue.
4 *rinse*: wash out with fresh water.
4 *wring*: to twist or squeeze; drain off excess water.
8 *have fair their fling*: the lambs are enjoying their freedom.
10 *strain*: a trace; streak; a segment of melody.
12 *cloud*: darken; depress.
13 *Mayday*: innocence of the young.
14 *Most*: the best choice.
14 *maid's child*: Jesus, son of Mary.

EXPLORATIONS

1. This poem opens with a confident statement. In your opinion, does the first section of the poem do justice to this declaration? Refer both to the style and content of the octet in your answer.
2. What is the mood in the second section of the poem? What reasons would you give for this change in the sestet? Use reference or quotation to support your point of view.
3. Hopkins preferred movement to stopping. What evidence for this statement is contained in the poem? Illustrate your response by referring to the expression and subject matter of the poem.

STUDY NOTES

> 'Spring' was written in May 1877. Hopkins had a special devotion to Mary, Queen of Heaven, and May is the month that is devoted to her. The poem was written after a holiday spent walking and writing poetry in Wales. He captures the exuberance of Nature bursting into life.

The simple opening sentence in the first section, 'Nothing is so beautiful as spring', is a deliberately exaggerated statement (hyperbole) used to emphasise a feeling. This Petrarchan sonnet's **octet** starts with an **ecstatic description of the blooming of nature in spring**. As we examine the poet's use of language, we can understand why it should be heard rather than read. Here in the second line – 'When weeds, in wheels, shoot long and lovely and lush' – the alliteration of 'w' and 'l', the assonance of 'ee' and the slow, broad vowels 'o' and 'u' add to this description of abundant growth. We can easily imagine the wild flowers growing before our eyes, as if caught by a slow-motion camera, uncurling and straightening as if to reach the heavens.

The **energy of the new plants** is contained in the verb 'shoot'. Just as the plants are shooting from the fertile earth, so one word seems to sprout out of another in the poem, e.g. 'thrush' springing from 'lush'. Now we are looking down, carefully examining a delicately beautiful sight among the long grasses: 'Thrush's eggs look little low heavens'. Note the speckled appearance of the eggs, similar to the dappling of blue and white in the sky. The oval shape is like the dome of the heavens.

The poet's **breathless excitement** at the sight of heaven on earth is caught by the omission of the word 'like'. Now we hear the song of the bird as the assonance of 'rinse' and 'wring' sings purely, like the bird cleansing our human ears with heavenly sounds. It has a powerful effect, like a bolt of lightning. The focus shifts to the gleam on the leaves of the pear tree, as its 'glassy' appearance is observed. Hopkins looked closely at objects to try to capture their essence (inscape). He once said, 'What you look hard at seems to look hard at you'.

Hopkins **pushes language** to its boundaries as nouns become verbs ('leaves' and 'blooms'). His unique style empowered modern poets to experiment to explore their own individuality. The sky seems to bend down to reach the growing trees: 'they brush/The descending blue'. The blueness of the sky is captured in the alliteration of 'all in a rush/With richness'. The little lambs are bounding happily, 'fair their fling'. This **octet** is a joyous exploration of a kaleidoscope of the colours, sounds and movement of spring. The poet's imagination soars as he strains language to encapsulate the immediacy of the moment.

In the sestet, **the mood becomes reflective** as the poet considers the significance of nature: 'What is all this juice and all this joy?' As he meditates, he decides it is 'A strain of the earth's sweet being', a fleeting snatch of melody from a perfect world 'In Eden garden', before it was sullied with sin. **Hopkins had a deep love of God**, especially as the Creator. His tone becomes insistent as he urges God to grasp the world in order to preserve it in its perfect state. The hard 'c' sound of 'cloy' and 'cloud' shows how the beauty will become stained and imperfect if God does not act swiftly. Hopkins desires virtue and purity: 'innocence', 'Mayday in girl and boy'. He refers to God as Mary's child ('O maid's child') as he attempts to persuade God that this world is worth the effort ('worthy the winning').

The regular rhyme scheme, *cdcdcd*, adds to the music of the poem as well as emphasising key words: 'joy', 'cloy', 'boy', 'beginning', singing', 'winning'. The poet was influenced by reading the theologian Duns Scotus, who said that the material world was an incarnation of God. Thus Hopkins felt justified in his preoccupation with the material world, as it had a sacramental value.

ANALYSIS

'Hopkins uses poetry to speak of the glory of God.' Write a paragraph in response to this statement, using reference or quotation to support your views.

SAMPLE PARAGRAPH

Hopkins had felt uneasy loving the natural world or a friend in case it distracted him from loving God, which was the main focus of his life. But after reading the theologian Duns Scotus, who maintained that the material world was a representation of God, Hopkins felt if he loved nature, he was loving its creator. This had swayed his 'spirits to peace'. So in giving us the glorious octet of this poem 'Spring', with the weeds spiralling 'long and lovely and lush', the blue of the sky in 'a rush/With richness', the thrush's eggs like 'little low heavens', Hopkins is worshipping God. In the sestet he becomes more reflective as he more closely links the poem to the glory of God as he meditates on the meaning of all this 'juice' and 'joy'. He thinks we have seen a glimpse, 'A strain', of the earth before the Fall of Adam and Eve. He asks God to preserve the world in its sinless state. We also see his devotion to the Mother of God, Our Lady in this poem. The references to 'O maid's child' and 'Mayday' confirm this. May is the month associated with the worship of Mary, Queen of Heaven. Never since the seventeenth century has a poet given a deeper poetic expression to religious belief than Hopkins as he celebrates the abundant world of nature. I agree that 'nothing is so beautiful as spring'.

EXAMINER'S COMMENT

The response has noted some of the influences on Hopkins in his decision to glorify God in his poetry. Close reading of the poem is evident. Quotations are used clearly to back up the opinions expressed. Grade A standard.

CLASS/HOMEWORK EXERCISES

1. Hopkins employs language in an energetic, intense and religious way. Do you agree? Use reference to the poem in your answer.
2. Copy the table below into your own notes and fill in critical comments about the last two quotations.

Gerard Manley Hopkins

Key Quotes

Nothing is so beautiful as spring	Hopkins emphatically declares his wonder about spring.
When weeds, in wheels, shoot long and lovely and lush	Sound effects (particularly alliteration) capture the luxuriant growth of wild flowers in springtime.
What is all this juice and all this joy?	The meaning of all this abundant growth is explored throughout the poem.
Have, get, before it cloy	
Most, O maid's child, thy choice and worthy the winning	

As kingfishers catch fire, dragonflies draw flame

As kingfishers catch fire, dragonflies draw flame;
  As tumbled over rim in roundy wells
  Stones ring; like each tucked string tells, each hung bell's
Bow swung finds tongue to fling out broad its name;
Each mortal thing does one thing and the same: 5
  Deals out that being indoors each one dwells;
  Selves – goes itself; myself it speaks and spells,
Crying What I do is me: for that I came.

I say more: the just man justices;
  Keeps grace: that keeps all his goings graces;   10
Acts in God's eye what in God's eye he is –
  Christ. For Christ plays in ten thousand places,
Lovely in limbs, and lovely in eyes not his
  To the Father through the features of men's faces.

Gerard Manley Hopkins

'dragonflies draw flame'

GLOSSARY

1 *kingfishers*: brilliantly coloured birds that hunt small fish.
1 *dragonflies*: brightly coloured insects with transparent wings.
3 *tucked*: plucked.
4 *Bow*: rim of bell that makes a sound when struck.
7 *Selves*: (used as a verb) defining or expressing its distinctiveness.
9 *justices*: (as a verb) acting justly.
10 *Keeps grace*: obeys God's will.

EXPLORATIONS

1. Comment on the nature images in the poem's opening line.
2. Select two interesting sound effects from the poem and briefly explain the effectiveness of each.
3. 'Celebration is the central theme in this poem.' Write your response to this statement, supporting your answer with reference to the text.

STUDY NOTES

> This poem is often cited as an example of Hopkins's theory of inscape, the uniqueness of every created thing as a reflection of God's glory. The poet believed that human beings had the uniqueness to recognise the divine presence in everything around us. This sonnet is written in an irregular ('sprung') rhythm that gives the poem a more concentrated quality.

The poem begins with two strikingly vivid images as Hopkins describes some of nature's most dazzling creatures. In **line 1**, he observes their vivid colour and dynamic movement (note the sharp alliteration and fast-paced rhythm) in the brilliant sunlight. The poet associates both the kingfisher and the dragonflies with fire. Aural images dominate **lines 2–4**. He takes great **delight in the uniqueness of existence** by listing a variety of everyday sounds: the tinkling noise of pebbles ('Stones ring') tossed down wells, the plucking of a stringed instrument and the loud ringing of a bell are all defined through their own distinctive sounds.

Hopkins is certain that the same quality applies to humans – 'Each mortal thing'. **We all express our unique inner selves.** Every individual does the same by presenting their inner essence (that dwells 'indoors'). The poet invents his own verb to convey how each of us 'Selves' (or expresses) our individual identity. The didactic tone of **lines 7–8** clearly reflects his depth of feeling, summed up by his emphatic illustration about our god-given purpose on earth: 'What I do is me: for that I came'.

Hopkins's enthusiasm ('I say more') intensifies at the start of the **sestet**. His central argument is that **people should fulfil their destiny by being themselves**. Again, he invents a new verb to illustrate his point: 'the just man justices' (good people behave in a godly way). Acting 'in God's eye' and availing of God's grace is our purpose on earth. The poet focuses on his belief that human beings are made in God's image and have the capacity to become like the omnipresent Christ.

Hopkins's **final lines** are filled with the devout Christian faith that **God will redeem everyone who 'Keeps grace'**. The poet repeatedly reminds us of the 'Lovely' personal relationship between God and mankind. It is Christ's presence within every human being that makes 'the features of men's faces' lovely in God's sight. Typically, Hopkins is convinced of the reality of Christ and the existence of the spirit world. He sees his own role as a 'kingfisher' catching fire – reeling in souls with his mystical poems of hope and spirituality.

Some critics have commented that the poem is too instructive and that Hopkins was overly concerned with getting across his message at the expense of method. The poet himself did not consider it a success. Yet there is no denying the poetic language of feeling and excitement in every line of the poem.

ANALYSIS

What aspects of this poem are typical of Hopkins's distinctive poetic style? Refer closely to the text in your answer.

SAMPLE PARAGRAPH

It seems to me that Hopkins the priest is the key speaker in 'As kingfishers catch fire'. To me, the poem is not as typical as 'Pied Beauty' or 'The Windhover'. However, his writing is unique. It is full of energy and unusual language patterns. It starts with lively images drawn from nature – 'As kingfishers catch fire, dragonflies draw flame'. In my opinion, no other poet on our course could write as precisely as this. There is an immediacy about his images that simply demands attention. The alliteration of 'f' and 'd' sounds suggest blinding flashes of colour, darting flames and dramatic movements – exactly what fish and insects do in their natural habitats. Hopkins uses very effective personification to show the vitality of the natural world – 'Stones ring'. He makes up new words of his own, such as 'justices'. Again, this is typical of his vibrant style. Hopkins does not bother with strict grammar either. He reduces sentences to childlike phrases to show his joy in being aware of the mystery of creation – 'For Christ plays in ten thousand places'. Even here, the alliteration adds energy to the rush of language. This is typical of so much of his poetry.

EXAMINER'S COMMENT

This is a well-illustrated answer, but is somewhat narrowly focused. Some of the features mentioned could have been developed further (e.g. Hopkins's use of 'new' words). However, there is worthwhile discussion of sound effects and the expression – although repetitive – is assured. A good B grade standard.

CLASS/HOMEWORK EXERCISES

1. Hopkins admitted that his poetry had an 'oddness' about it. Comment on his management of language in this poem. Refer closely to the text in your answer.
2. Copy the table below into your own notes and fill in critical comments about the last two quotations.

Key Quotes

dragonflies draw flame	Beautiful insects, such as the dragonfly, reflect their own – and God's – vivid presence in the world.
Stones ring	All that exists – even the pebble tossed into a well – is uniquely alive and makes us aware of its existence. Onomatopoeia enhances the effect.
Each mortal thing does one thing and the same	Hopkins believes that everything shares the common quality of uniqueness.
What I do is me: for that I came	
Christ plays in ten thousand places	

The Windhover

To Christ our Lord

I caught this morning morning's minion, king-
 dom of daylight's dauphin, dapple-dawn-drawn Falcon, in his riding
 Of the rolling level underneath him steady air, and striding
High there, how he rung upon the rein of a wimpling wing
In his ecstasy! then off, off forth on swing, 5
 As a skate's heel sweeps smooth on a bow-bend: the hurl and gliding
 Rebuffed the big wind. My heart in hiding
Stirred for a bird, – the achieve of, the mastery of the thing!

Brute beauty and valour and act, oh air, pride, plume here
 Buckle! AND the fire that breaks from thee then, a billion 10
Times told lovelier, more dangerous, O my chevalier!

 No wonder of it: sheer plod makes plough down sillion
Shine, and blue-bleak embers, ah my dear,
Fall, gall themselves, and gash gold-vermilion.

'how he rung upon the rein of a wimpling wing/ In his ecstasy!'

GLOSSARY

Windhover: a kestrel or small falcon; resembles a cross in flight.
1 *minion*: favourite; darling.
2 *dauphin*: prince, heir to French throne.
2 *dapple-dawn-drawn*: the bird is outlined in patches of colour by the dawn light, an example of Hopkins's use of compression.
4 *rung upon the rein*: circling movement of a horse at the end of a long rein held by a trainer; the sound of the bird pealing like a bell as it wheels in the sky.
4 *wimpling*: pleated.
6 *bow-bend*: a wide arc.
7 *Rebuffed*: pushed back; mastered.
7 *My heart in hiding*: the poet is afraid, unlike the bird.
10 *Buckle*: pull together; clasp; fall apart.
11 *chevalier*: medieval knight; Hopkins regards God as a knight who will defend him against evil.

GLOSSARY

12 *sheer plod*: back-breaking drudgery of hard work, similar to Hopkins's work as a priest.
13 *ah my dear*: intimate address to God.
14 *Fall, gall ... gash*: a reference to the Crucifixion of Christ as He fell on the way to Cavalry, was offered vinegar and gashed by a spear on the cross.
14 *gold-vermilion*: gold and red, the colours of Christ the Saviour and also of the Eucharist, the Body and Blood of Christ which offers redemption.

EXPLORATIONS

1 In your opinion, has the poet been as daring in his use of language as the bird has been in its flight? Support your view by referring closely to the poem.
2 The sonnet moves from description to reflection. What does the poet meditate on in the sestet? Support your response by reference to the text.
3 Would you consider the falcon's flight to symbolise the struggle against evil? Discuss this question, illustrating your answer by reference to the poem.

STUDY NOTES

'The Windhover' was Hopkins's favourite poem, 'the best thing I ever wrote'. It is dedicated to Christ, who died when he was thirty-three, and Hopkins was the same age when he wrote the poem in 1877. This is also the age when Jesuits are ordained. The poet celebrates the uniqueness of the bird and his own deep relationship with God the Creator.

The name of the bird comes from its custom of hovering in the air, facing the wind, as it views the ground for its prey. The opening lines of the **octet** are **joyful and celebratory** as Hopkins rejoices in the sight of the bird, 'daylight's dauphin'. The verb 'caught' suggests not just that the poet caught sight of the bird, but also that he 'caught' the essence of the bird on the page with words. This is an example of Hopkins's compression of language as he edges two meanings into one word or phrase. Hopkins shaped language by omitting articles, conjunctions and verbs to express the energy of the bird, 'off forth on swing'. **Movement fascinated the poet.** The bird is sketched by the phrase 'dapple-dawn-drawn'. A vivid image of the flecks of colour on his wings (as the dawn light catches him) is graphically drawn here.

The **momentary freshness** is conveyed by 'this morning', with the bird in flight beautifully captured by the simile 'As a skate's heel sweeps smooth on a bow-bend'. The 's' sound mimics the swish of the skater as a large arc is traced on the ice. This curve is similar to the strong but graceful bend of a bow stretched to loose its arrow, with all its connotations of beauty of line and deadly strength.

In the octet, there is typical **energetic language**: 'how he rung upon the rein of a wimpling wing/In his ecstasy!' This carries us along in its breathless description. It is not necessary for the reader to comprehend every word in order to appreciate the phrase's meaning. The word 'wimpling' refers to the beautiful, seemingly pleated pattern of the arrangement of the outstretched wings of the bird. The capital 'F' used for 'Falcon' hints at its symbolism for Christ. This very personal poem uses 'I' in the octet and 'my' in the sestet. Hopkins lavishes praise on the bird: 'dauphin' (young prince, heir) and 'minion' (darling). Run-on lines add to the poet's breathless excitement. He acknowledges that the bird has what he does not possess: power, self-belief and grace ('My heart in hiding'). The lively rhyme, such as 'riding'/'striding', never becomes repetitive because of the varying line breaks. The octet concludes with Hopkins's admiration of 'the thing', which broadens the focus from the particular to the general. All of creation is magnificent.

This leads to the sestet, where **God the Creator becomes central to the poem**. The essence (inscape) of the bird is exposed: 'air, pride, plume here'. The bird is strong, brave, predatory, graceful and beautiful. The word 'Buckle' is paradoxical, as it contains two contradictory meanings: clasp together and fall apart. The bird is holding the line as it rides the rolling wind and falls apart as it swoops down on its prey. Capital letters for the conjunction 'AND' signal a moment of insight: 'the fire that breaks from thee'. 'Thee' refers to God, whose magnificence is shown by 'fire'. The Holy Spirit is often depicted as a bird descending with tongues of flame. A soft tone of intimacy is revealed: 'O my chevalier!' It is as if Hopkins wants God to act as the honourable knight of old, to take up his cause and fight on his behalf against his enemy. God will be Hopkins's defender against evil.

The sestet concludes with **two exceptional images**, both entailing breaking apart to release their hidden brilliance. The ploughed furrow and the 'blue-bleak embers' of coal both reveal their beauty in destruction: 'sillion/Shine', 'gash gold-vermilion'. Christ endured Cavalry and Crucifixion, 'Fall, gall ... gash', and through his sacrifice, the 'fall', achieved redemption for us. So too the priest embracing the drudgery of his service embraces his destiny by submitting to the will of God. In doing so, he reflects the greatness of God.

Earthly glory is crushed to release heavenly glory. The phrase 'ah my dear' makes known the dominant force of Hopkins's life: to love God. The colours of gold and red are the colours of Christ the Saviour as well as the colours associated with the Eucharist, the Body and Blood of Christ. When Christians receive the sacrament of Holy Communion, they are redeemed. So, as the poem begins, 'dapple-dawn-drawn Falcon', it ends with 'gold-vermilion' in a triumph of glorious colour.

ANALYSIS

What do you think of Hopkins's reflections on Christ in 'The Windhover'? Consider his message and its expression in your response. Use quotation from the poem.

SAMPLE PARAGRAPH

In 'The Windhover', Hopkins uses the image of the falcon, which hovers in a cross-shape on the wind, as an emblem of Christ. He describes the bird's magnificent beauty, 'dapple-dawn-drawn', and its strength, 'rebuffed the big wind'. In the sestet, Hopkins calls God 'O my chevalier'. This gives me a vivid picture of a moral man who was both strong and who fought against evil. Hopkins also speaks of 'Buckle' which reminds me of the knight putting on his armour and falling in battle. Christ also fell on the way to Cavalry and because he was crucified. But from that a great glory resulted for us all, 'the fire that breaks from thee'. This won our salvation. Also, Hopkins felt it was right to focus on nature as it is evidence of the power and beauty of God. Hopkins believed that his vocation in life was to love God. In glorifying God through the emblem of the windhover, he is glorifying God's creation, and therefore God Himself. The flash of red and gold, with which the poem ends, reminds me that the lowly priest carrying out his humdrum duties is also revealing the beauty of God's creation. I also think Hopkins's reflections on Christ add a real spiritual dimension to his poetry.

EXAMINER'S COMMENT

Close reading of the poem is evident in this personal response. Quotations are very well used here to highlight Hopkins's commitment to his Christian faith. Overall, despite the lapses in expression, this is a good grade B standard.

CLASS/HOMEWORK EXERCISES

1. How does Hopkins adapt the Petrarchan sonnet for his own purposes here? Use reference to the poem in your answer.
2. Copy the table below into your own notes and fill in critical comments about the last two quotations.

Key Quotes

I caught this morning morning's minion	Hopkins was overwhelmed by the beauty and mystery of the falcon, the darling or favourite of morning.
the hurl/ and gliding/ Rebuffed the big wind	The strength and grace of the bird as it masters its element is conveyed as it is carried on the moving currents of air.
air, pride, plume, here/ Buckle!	The essence of the bird, which flies proudly through the air, is a powerfully dramatic emblem for Christ.
AND the fire that breaks from thee then	
sheer plod makes plough down sillion/ Shine	

• Poetry Focus •

Pied Beauty

Glory be to God for dappled things –
  For skies of couple-colour as a brinded cow;
    For rose-moles all in stipple upon trout that swim;
Fresh-firecoal chestnut-falls; finches' wings;
  Landscape plotted and pieced – fold, fallow, and plough;   5
    And all trades, their gear and tackle and trim.

All things counter, original, spare, strange;
  Whatever is fickle, freckled (who knows how?)
    With swift, slow; sweet, sour; adazzle, dim;
He fathers-forth whose beauty is past change: 10
    Praise him.

'skies of couple-colour'

GLOSSARY

    Pied: varied.
1 *dappled*: speckled, spotted.
2 *brinded*: streaked.
3 *rose-moles*: red-pink spots.
3 *stipple*: dotted.
4 *Fresh-firecoal chestnut-falls*: open chestnuts bright as burning coals.
5 *pieced*: enclosed.
5 *fold*: sheep enclosure.
5 *fallow*: unused.
6 *trades*: farmwork.
6 *gear*: equipment.
6 *tackle*: implements.
6 *trim*: fittings.
7 *counter*: contrasting.
7 *spare*: special.
8 *fickle*: changeable.
10 *He*: God.
10 *fathers-forth*: creates.

EXPLORATIONS

1. In your view, what is the central theme in this poem? Refer to the text in your answer.
2. Discuss the poet's use of sound effects in the poem. Support your answer with quotations.
3. Choose two striking images from the poem and comment on the effectiveness of each.

STUDY NOTES

> 'Pied Beauty' is one of Hopkins's 'curtal' (or curtailed) sonnets, in which he condenses the traditional sonnet form. It was written in the so-called sprung rhythm that he evolved, based on the irregular rhythms of traditional Welsh verse. The poem's energetic language – particularly its sound effects – reflects Hopkins's view of the rich, abundant diversity evident within God's coherent creation.

The simplicity of the prayer-like **opening line** ('Glory be to God') is reminiscent of biblical language and sets the poem's devotional tone. From the start, Hopkins displays a **childlike wonder** for all the 'dappled things' around him, illustrating his central belief with a series of vivid examples from the natural world.

Included in his panoramic sweep of nature's vibrant delights are the dominant blues and whites of the sky, which he compares to the streaked ('brinded') patterns of cowhide. The world is teeming with contrasting colours and textures, captured in **detailed images**, such as 'rose-moles all in stipple upon trout' and 'Fresh-firecoal chestnut-falls'.

For the exhilarated poet, everything in nature is linked. It is ironic, of course, that what all things share is their god-given individuality. In **line 4**, he associates broken chestnuts with burning coals in a fire, black on the outside and glowing underneath. In turn, the wings of finches have similar colours. Condensed imagery and compound words add even greater energy to the description.

Hopkins turns his attention to human nature in **lines 5–6**. The farmland features he describes reflect hard work and efficiency: 'Landscape plotted and pieced – fold, fallow, and plough'. The range of man's impact on the natural world is also worth celebrating, and this is reinforced by the **orderly syntax and insistent rhythm**. Human activity in tune with nature also glorifies God.

Hopkins's **final four lines** focus on the **unexpected beauty of creation** and further reveal the poet's passionate Christianity. As though overcome by the scale and variety of God's works – 'who knows how?' – the poet meditates on a range of contrasting adjectives ('swift, slow; sweet, sour; adazzle, dim'), all of which indicate the wonderful diversity of creation. As always, the alliteration gives an increased dynamism to this image of abundance and variety in nature.

The poem ends as it began – with a shortened version of the two mottoes of St Ignatius of Loyola, founder of the Jesuits: *Ad majorem Dei gloriam* (to the greater glory of God) and *Laus Deo semper* (praise be to God always). For Hopkins, **God is beyond change**. The Creator ('He fathers-forth') and all the 'dappled' opposites that enrich our ever-changing world inspire us all to 'Praise him'.

ANALYSIS

It has been said that the poem typifies Hopkins's appreciation of the energy present in the world. What evidence can you find to support this view?

SAMPLE PARAGRAPH

It seems to me that 'Pied Beauty' is more like a heartfelt prayer than an ordinary poem. It begins with the phrase 'Glory be to God' and continues to the final words 'Praise him'. In between, Hopkins lists a litany of examples of the variety of the 'dappled' natural environment. The pace of the poem is rapid, as though he is in a rush to explain his astonishment: 'Fresh-firecoal chestnut-falls'. There is a sheer sense of God's mystery and greatness. This is partly due to the compound phrases, such as 'couple-colour' and 'rose-moles', which make us more aware of the varied appearances of natural things. The energetic pace builds to a climax in the last line. This is short, direct and almost breathless – just one simple phrase that sums up Hopkins's awareness of God's creation: 'Praise him'. From start to finish, I can easily appreciate Hopkins's personal sense of the overpoweringly beautiful world around him.

EXAMINER'S COMMENT

This response is well focused and aptly supported. The paragraph ranges over a number of interesting features of Hopkins's style which convey the energy of nature. Points are clear and the expression is confident. Grade A standard.

CLASS/HOMEWORK EXERCISES

1. Compare and contrast the views expressed in 'Pied Beauty' with any other 'religious' poem by Hopkins from your course. Support your answer with reference to both poems.
2. Copy the table below into your own notes and fill in critical comments about the last two quotations.

Key Quotes

Glory be to God for dappled things	The poem has often been described as a hymn of praise to creation.
Whatever is fickle, freckled	Alliteration makes the language forceful and reflects the poet's tone of delight.
He fathers-forth whose beauty is past change	Hopkins reinforces his theme that God is the one constant creative force in the world.
Landscape plotted and pieced – fold, fallow, and plough	
Praise him	

• Poetry Focus •

Felix Randal

Gerard Manley Hopkins

Felix Randal the farrier, O he is dead then? my duty all ended,
Who have watched his mould of man, big-boned and hardy-handsome
Pining, pining, till time when reason rambled in it and some
Fatal four disorders, fleshed there, all contended?

Sickness broke him. Impatient he cursed at first, but mended   5
Being anointed and all; though a heavenlier heart began some
Months earlier, since I had our sweet reprieve and ransom
Tendered to him. Ah well, God rest him all road ever he offended!

This seeing the sick endears them to us, us too it endears.
My tongue had taught thee comfort, touch had quenched thy tears   10
Thy tears that touched my heart, child, Felix, poor Felix Randal;

How far from then forethought of, all thy more boisterous years,
When thou at the random grim forge, powerful amidst peers,
Didst fettle for the great grey drayhorse his bright and battering sandal!

'at the random grim forge, powerful amidst peers'

GLOSSARY

	Felix Randal: the parishioner's name was Felix Spenser. 'Felix' in Latin means 'happy'. Randal can also mean a lowly, humble thing or trodden on.
1	*farrier*: blacksmith.
1	*O he is dead then*: reaction of priest at Felix's death.
2	*hardy-handsome*: compound word describing the fine physical appearance of the blacksmith.
4	*disorders*: diseases.
4	*contended*: competitively fought over Felix.
6	*anointed*: sacraments administered to the sick by a priest.
7	*reprieve and ransom*: confession; penance; communion; redemption from sin.
8	*Tendered*: offered.
8	*all road ever*: in whatever way (local dialect).
13	*random*: casual; irregular.
14	*fettle*: prepare.
14	*drayhorse*: big horse used to pull heavy carts.
14	*sandal*: type of horseshoe.

EXPLORATIONS

1 'Hopkins is a poet who celebrates unique identities and experiences, their meaning and their value.' Discuss this statement with reference to the poem, illustrating your answer with quotations.
2 How does the octet differ from the sestet in this Petrarchan sonnet? Refer to theme, style and tone in your response. Use quotations in support of your views.
3 Choose two aural images that you found interesting and give reasons for their effectiveness.

STUDY NOTES

'Felix Randal' was written in Liverpool in 1880. This poem contrasts with others such as 'Spring'. Hopkins had been placed as a curate to the city slums of Liverpool, 'a most unhappy and miserable spot' in his opinion. He didn't communicate successfully with his parishioners and he didn't write much poetry, except this one poem about the blacksmith who died of tuberculosis, aged thirty-one.

The opening of the octet identifies the man with his name and occupation, 'Felix Randal the farrier'. Then the poet shocks us with the priest's reaction: 'O he is dead then? my duty all ended'. On first reading, this sounds both dismissive and cold. However, when we consider that the death was expected and that the priest had seen all this many times, we realise that the line rings with authenticity and professional detachment. Also, in the face of the big events of life, we articulate our feelings with thoughtless, numbed remarks. For Hopkins, 'duty' was a sacred office. **The farrier is recalled in his physical**

prime, using the alliteration of 'm', 'b' and 'h' in the phrase 'mould of man, big-boned and hardy-handsome'. The repetition of 'Pining, pining' marks his decline in health. His illness is graphically conveyed as his mental health deteriorated ('reason rambled') and the diseases attacked his body ('Fatal four disorders, fleshed there, all contended'). The **illnesses took possession of the body** and waged a horrific battle to win supremacy to kill Felix.

The use of the word 'broke' is suitable in this context, as in the world of horses it refers to being trained. Is Felix trained ('broke') through suffering? His realistic reaction to the news – 'he cursed' – changes when he receives the sacraments ('being anointed'). Felix was broken but is now healed by 'our sweet reprieve and ransom', the healing sacraments. **The tone changes** with the personal pronoun. The priest–patient relationship is acknowledged: we, both priest and layperson, are saved by God. A note of resigned acceptance, almost an anti-climax, is evident in the line 'Ah well, God rest him all road ever he offended!' The use of the Lancashire dialect ('all road') by the priest shows a developing relationship between the two men.

The detached priest's voice resurfaces in the sestet: 'This seeing the sick'. This section of the sonnet focuses on the reality of **sickness** and its effects. Both the sick man and the priest received something from the experience. We respond to the sick with sympathy ('the sick endears them to us'), but we also appreciate ourselves and our own health more ('us too it endears') as we face another's mortality. The priest comforted the sick man with words ('My tongue') and the Last Sacraments, anointing by 'touch'. The priest becomes a father figure to 'child' Felix. Is there a suggestion that one must become like a child to enter the kingdom of Heaven? The tercet (three-line segment) is intimate: 'thee', 'thy', 'Thy tears', 'my heart'. The last tercet explodes in a **dramatic flashback** to the energy of the young blacksmith in his prime, when there was little thought of death: 'How far from then forethought of'. Onomatopoeia and alliteration capture the lifeforce (inscapes) of the young Felix, 'boisterous' and 'powerful amidst peers'.

Sprung rhythm adds to the force of the poem as the six main stresses are interspersed with an irregular number of unstressed syllables. Felix did a man's job at the 'grim forge' as he made the 'bright and battering sandal' for the powerful carthorse, magnificently captured in the assonance of 'great grey drayhorse'. The poem ends not with Felix in heavenly glory, but in his former earthly glory: 'thou … Didst fettle'. God has fashioned Felix through his suffering as Felix had fashioned the horseshoe. Both required force and effort to bend them to the shape in which they can function properly. The poem is a celebration of God's creation of the man.

ANALYSIS

'Hopkins is a poet who celebrates unique identities and individual experiences, exploring their meaning and worth.' Discuss this statement in relation to one or more of the poems on your course, quoting in support of your points.

SAMPLE PARAGRAPH

Hopkins had been sent as curator of Liverpool, where he attended the sick as part of his duties. He was miserable there and wrote little poetry, except this one about one of his parishioners, Felix, who died of TB at the age of thirty-one. In 'Felix Randal', Hopkins captures the unique essence of the man and his inscape, a great big strong man struck down by illness. He was 'big-boned and hardy-handsome', and the alliteration emphasises the magnificence of his physique. His understandable reaction to his own misfortune is caught in 'he cursed at first', the assonance echoing the deep guttural oaths. The repeated 'f' of 'Fatal four disorders, fleshed there' conveys the impossible odds stacked against the man. Here Hopkins has given us the unique identity of the man and his individual experience. He also gives us the rather dismissive voice of the weary priest: 'O he is dead then? my duty all ended'. Here is a man who has seen too much suffering. His use of the Lancashire dialect 'all road' shows how he has tried to enter the world of his parishioners, but he quickly reverts back to his professional capacity: 'This seeing the sick'. He has a strong belief that the sacraments he is offering will help: 'sweet reprieve and ransom'. So Hopkins also gives us the individual essence of the weary priest trying his best for the sick in his care. The poem leaves us feeling that the priest has received as much from the sick man as the sick man has received from the priest: 'Thy tears that touched my heart'. The experience broke through the cold exterior of the priest to reveal his human capacity for compassion. Felix's acceptance of his lot and the priest's acceptance of his lot both show the value of the experience. We and they recognise God's design.

EXAMINER'S COMMENT

As part of a full essay answer, this paragraph has dealt comprehensively with the task set, i.e. to discuss both identity and experience and their worth. The close attention to the poet's use of language enhances the answer. Grade A standard.

CLASS/HOMEWORK EXERCISES

1. Hopkins deals with suffering in his poetry. Has this any relevance to the modern reader? Use reference to this poem in your answer.
2. Copy the table below into your own notes and fill in critical comments about the last two quotations.

Key Quotes

Sickness broke him	The fine man was reduced by physical suffering.
Ah well, God rest him all road ever he offended!	God grant him pardon for any offence he may have committed.
powerful amidst peers	Alliteration stresses the strength of the man in his prime, when he was admired by his own people.
our sweet reprieve and ransom	
Thy tears that touched my heart	

Inversnaid

This darksome burn, horseback brown,
His rollrock highroad roaring down,
In coop and in comb the fleece of his foam
Flutes and low to the lake falls home.

A windpuff-bonnet of fawn-froth   5
Turns and twindles over the broth
Of a pool so pitchblack, fell-frowning,
It rounds and rounds Despair to drowning.

Degged with dew, dappled with dew,
Are the groins of the braes that the brook treads through,   10
Wiry heathpacks, flitches of fern,
And the beadbonny ash that sits over the burn.

What would the world be, once bereft
Of wet and of wildness? Let them be left,
O let them be left, wildness and wet;   15
Long live the weeds and the wilderness yet.

'the fleece of his foam'

GLOSSARY

Inversnaid is a remote area located near Loch Lomond in the Scottish Highlands.
1 *burn*: stream.
3 *coop*: hollow.
3 *comb*: moving freely.
4 *Flutes*: grooves; whistles.
6 *twindles*: spins.
7 *fell*: fiercely.
9 *Degged*: sprinkled about.
10 *groins of the braes*: sides of hills.
11 *heathpacks*: heather outcrops.
11 *flitches*: ragged tufts.
12 *beadbonny*: mountain ash tree with bright berries.
13 *bereft*: deprived.

EXPLORATIONS

1. From your reading of the first stanza, explain how the poet conveys the stream's energy.
2. Sound effects play a key part in the second and third stanzas. Choose two aural images that convey Hopkins's excited reaction to the mountain stream. Comment on the effectiveness of each.
3. Write your own personal response to the poem, referring closely to the text in your answer.

STUDY NOTES

'Inversnaid' was written in 1881 after Hopkins visited the remote hillsides around Loch Lomond. He disliked being in cities and much preferred the sights and sounds of the wilderness. The poem is unusual for Hopkins in that there is no direct mention of God as the source of all this natural beauty.

The opening lines of stanza one are dramatic. Hopkins compares the brown, rippling stream ('This darksome burn') to a wild horse's back. The forceful alliteration – 'rollrock highroad roaring' – emphasises the power of this small and dismal stream as it rushes downhill, its course directed by confining rocks. A sense of immediacy and energy is echoed in the **vigorous onomatopoeic effects**, including end rhyme ('brown', 'down'), repetition and internal rhyme ('comb', 'foam'). This is characteristic of Hopkins, as is his use of descriptive details, likening the foamy 'fleece' of the water to the fluted surface ('Flutes') of a Greek or Roman column.

Stanza two begins with another effective metaphor. The poet compares the yellow-brown froth to a windblown bonnet (hat) as the water swirls into a dark pool on the riverbed. The **atmosphere is light and airy**. Run-on lines reflect the lively pace of the noisy stream. However, the tone suddenly darkens with the disturbing image of the 'pitchblack' whirlpool which Hopkins sees as capable of drowning all in 'Despair'. The sluggish rhythm in lines 7–8 reinforces this menacing mood.

Nature seems much more benign in stanza three. The language is softer sounding – 'Degged with dew, dappled with dew' – as Hopkins describes the **steady movement of the water** through 'the groins of the braes'. Enclosed by the sharp banks, the stream sprinkles nearby branches of mountain ash, aflame with their vivid scarlet berries. As always, Hopkins delights in the unspoiled landscape: 'Wiry heathpacks, flitches of fern,/And the beadbonny ash'. Throughout the poem, he has also used traditional Scottish expressions ('burn', 'braes') to reflect the lively sounds of the Highlands.

The language in **stanza four** is rhetorical. Hopkins wonders what the world would be like without its wild qualities. The tone is personal and plaintive: 'O let them be left, wildness and wet'. While repetition and the use of the exclamation add a sense of urgency, his plea is simple: let nature remain as it is. The final appeal – 'Long live the weeds and the wilderness yet' – is reminiscent of his poem 'Spring'. Once again, there is no doubting Hopkins's **enthusiasm for the natural beauty of remote places** and the sentiments he expresses are clearly heartfelt. Although written in 1881, the poem has obvious relevance for today's generation.

ANALYSIS

Write a paragraph summing up your impression of Hopkins himself as revealed in the poem 'Inversnaid'. Support your points with close reference or quotation.

SAMPLE PARAGRAPH

The most immediate thing that emerges about Hopkins is his extraordinary closeness to nature. This is evident in all his poems. He seems to have a heightened awareness of the sights and sounds of the remote mountain 'burn' in 'Inversnaid'. He details the colours of the water. It is 'darksome', 'horseback brown' and 'fawn-froth'. Hopkins is always excited by his natural environment. To him, the river is alive. It is 'roaring down'. He describes the Scottish rowan trees as 'the beadbonny ash', referring to their attractive red berries. Everything he says suggests his love for the natural world. In the last section of the poem, Hopkins openly states his fears for nature. He begs us to preserve the 'wildness and wet'. For him, all of nature deserves respect. He ends the poem with his own slogan, 'Long live the weeds and the wilderness'. Hopkins strikes me as being a lonely man who preferred the secluded Scottish hills where he could appreciate the natural world rather than being in a crowded city. Nature obviously inspired him and he seems to be deeply moved by the beauty of places such as Inversnaid. He repeats the words 'wet' and 'wildness' a number of times in the final lines, leaving us in no doubt about how much the natural landscape meant to him.

• Poetry Focus •

Gerard Manley Hopkins

EXAMINER'S COMMENT

This is a well-sustained response focusing clearly on the image of Hopkins that emerges from the poem. The evidence is firmly rooted in accurate textual references and the expression is fluent throughout. A grade standard.

CLASS/HOMEWORK EXERCISES

1. In your opinion, does the poem 'Inversnaid' have relevance to our modern world? Support the points you make with reference to the text.
2. Copy the table below into your own notes and fill in critical comments about the last two quotations.

Key Quotes

This darksome burn	The poet manages to associate the stream with a sense of danger and menace.
His rollrock highroad roaring down	Onomatopoeic effects and repetition convey the power and movement of the mountain stream.
O let them be left, wildness and wet	The heartfelt tone suggests a sense of foreboding. Hopkins's plea seems urgent and pessimistic.
A windpuff-bonnet of fawn-froth	
Degged with dew, dappled with dew	

I wake and feel the fell of dark, not day

Gerard Manley Hopkins

I wake and feel the fell of dark, not day.
What hours, O what black hours we have spent
This night! what sights you, heart, saw; ways you went!
And more must, in yet longer light's delay.
   With witness I speak this. But where I say   5
Hours I mean years, mean life. And my lament
Is cries countless, cries like dead letters sent
To dearest him that lives alas! away.

   I am gall. I am heartburn. God's most deep decree
Bitter would have me taste: my taste was me;   10
Bones built in me, flesh filled, blood brimmed the curse.
   Selfyeast of spirit a dull dough sours. I see
The lost are like this, and their scourge to be
As I am mine, their sweating selves; but worse.

'I wake and feel the fell of dark, not day'

GLOSSARY

1 *fell*: threat; blow; knocked down; past tense of fall (fall of Adam and Eve cast into darkness); also refers to the mountain.

7–8 *dead letters sent / To dearest him*: communication which is of no use, didn't elicit a response.

9 *gall*: bitterness; anger; acidity; vinegar.

9 *deep decree*: command that cannot easily be understood.

11 *Bones built in me, flesh filled, blood brimmed the curse*: the passive tense of the verb might suggest how God created Man, yet Man has sinned.

12 *Selfyeast of spirit a dull dough sours*: yeast makes bread rise; Hopkins feels he cannot become good or wholesome.

13 *The lost*: those condemned to serve eternity in Hell with no hope of redemption, unlike the poet.

EXPLORATIONS

1. How is the oppressive atmosphere conveyed in this sonnet? Quote in support of your response.
2. How does the poem conclude, on a note of hope or despair? Illustrate your answer by referring closely to the text.
3. Comment on the use of alliteration to convey Hopkins's sense of dejection. Mention at least three examples.

STUDY NOTES

> 'I wake and feel the fell of dark, not day' was written in Dublin, where Hopkins was teaching at UCD and was burdened by a massive workload of examination papers. He was there for six years and had over 1,300 scripts a year to correct. After a long silence, he wrote the 'terrible sonnets'. Hopkins said of these, 'If ever anything was written in blood, these were.' This sonnet was discovered among his papers after his death.

The last three sonnets on the course are called the 'terrible sonnets'. They are similar to Frost's 'Acquainted with the Night'. Here Hopkins reaches the **darkest depths of bleak despair**. The sonnet opens in darkness and the only mention of light in the whole poem is 'light's delay' in line 4, as it is postponed. He wakes to the oppressive blow of the dark ('the fell of dark'), not to the brightness of daylight. The heaviness of depression is being described, the oppressive darkness which Adam woke to after his expulsion from the Garden of Eden. Hopkins and his soul have shared these 'black hours' and they will experience 'more'. It is not just hours they have spent in darkness, but 'years', 'life'.

The formal, almost biblical phrase 'With witness I speak this' emphasises that what he has said is true. The hard 'c' sounds in 'cries countless' and the repetition of 'cries' keenly describe the **fruitless attempts at communication** ('dead letters'). There is no response: he 'lives alas! away' and cannot be reached by the poet. We can imagine the poet in the deep dark of the night attempting to gain solace from his prayers to God ('dearest him'), but they go unanswered.

Hopkins feels this deep depression intensely. **Note the repetition of 'I'**: 'I wake', 'I speak', 'I say', 'I mean', 'I am gall', 'I am heartburn', 'I see', 'I am'. He is in physical pain, bitter and burning. The language might well refer to Christ's Crucifixion, when he was offered a sponge soaked in vinegar to drink, and pierced through his side. However, the poet recognises that it is God's unfathomable decision that this is the way it should be: 'God's most deep decree'. **The poet is reviled by himself** in line 10: 'my taste was me'. He describes how he was fashioned: 'Bones built in me, flesh filled, blood brimmed'. The alliteration shows the careful construction of the body by the Creator, but Hopkins is full of 'the curse'.

Could this be read as full of original sin emanating from the fall of Adam and Eve? The deadening 'd' sound of 'dull dough' shows that there is no hope of rising. The body is tainted, soured. It does not have the capacity to 'Selfyeast', to resurrect or renew. Is it being suggested that he needs divine intervention? Is there an overtone of the bread of Communion, the wholesome Body of Christ? The scope of the poem broadens out at the end as the poet gains an **insight into the plight of others**. All those condemned to Hell are like this and in fact are worse off: 'but worse'. The horrific atmosphere of Hell is fixed in the phrase 'sweating selves'. For those 'lost', it is permanent. For Hopkins, perhaps it is just 'longer light's delay'. Some day **he will be redeemed**.

ANALYSIS

'Hopkins's poetry displays a deeply personal and passionate response to the human condition.' Discuss with reference to the poems on your course, illustrating your answer with relevant quotations.

SAMPLE PARAGRAPH

I was fascinated when reading about Hopkins's life to learn that he had to examine hundreds of scripts five or six times a year, and that his college lectures were conducted in uproar. He writes of a 'daily anxiety about work to be done', 'All impulse fails me'. Everyone can identify with this man suffering from depression. This is evident in 'I wake and feel the fell of dark, not day'. To me he is describing waking over and over again at night. The long vowel sounds in 'O what black hoürs' give an idea of the man tossing and turning, trying to sleep, his head in a whirl. Hopkins's personal and passionate relationship with God was the focus of his life. His passionate pleas to God, 'To dearest him', are useless, 'dead letters'. Usually God is written with a capital letter. I wonder if Hopkins is telling us that he doesn't even know how to address his Lord? So he is devastated and he uses the language of the Crucifixion to express that 'I am gall'. He, like all depressives, despises himself: 'the curse', 'dull dough'. The poem seethes with self-disgust. The only slight glimmer for the poet is that those condemned to Hell are in a worse situation 'and their scourge to be … their sweating selves; but worse'. Hopkins writes passionately about the human condition and a feeling of unworthiness. Sometimes people would say Hopkins is out of fashion, with his emphasis on sin and religion, but when I read of all the suicides today, I realise that Hopkins is describing a universal human condition, 'the deep night of the soul'.

EXAMINER'S COMMENT

The student gives a personal response to the assertion that Hopkins responds deeply and passionately to the human condition. Deep engagement with the poem is evident in the response. A very well written A grade standard.

CLASS/HOMEWORK EXERCISES

1. 'Hopkins charts an extraordinary mental journey in the "terrible sonnets".' Give a personal response to this statement, quoting in support of your opinions.
2. Copy the table below into your own notes and fill in critical comments about the last two quotations.

Key Quotes

I wake and feel the fell of dark, not day	The poet senses the oppression of the dark, rather than the optimistic brightness of day.
cries like dead letters sent/ To dearest him	Hopkins's pleas and prayers to God go unanswered.
Selfyeast of spirit a dull dough sours	He despises himself in this graphic metaphor of bread that does not have the capacity to rise.
But where I say/ Hours I mean years, mean life	
The lost are like this	

No worst, there is none

Gerard Manley Hopkins

No worst, there is none. Pitched past pitch of grief,
More pangs will, schooled at forepangs, wilder wring.
Comforter, where, where is your comforting?
Mary, mother of us, where is your relief?
My cries heave, herds-long; huddle in a main, a chief   5
Woe, world-sorrow; on an age-old anvil wince and sing –
Then lull, then leave off. Fury had shrieked 'No ling-
ering! Let me be fell: force I must be brief.'

O the mind, mind has mountains; cliffs of fall
Frightful, sheer, no-man-fathomed. Hold them cheap   10
May who ne'er hung there. Nor does long our small
Durance deal with that steep or deep. Here! creep,
Wretch, under a comfort serves in a whirlwind: all
Life death does end and each day dies with sleep.

'Frightful, sheer, no-man-fathomed'

GLOSSARY

1 *Pitched past pitch*: pushed beyond.
2 *pangs*: sudden pains.
2 *schooled at forepangs*: prepared by earlier sorrows.
3 *Comforter*: the Holy Spirit.
5 *main*: crowd.
8 *fell*: harsh; cruel.
8 *force*: perforce; therefore.
12 *Durance*: endurance; determination.
13 *whirlwind*: turmoil.

EXPLORATIONS

1 Comment on how Hopkins creates a sense of suffering and pessimism in the first four lines of the poem.
2 Discuss the effectiveness of the mountain images in lines 9–12.
3 In your opinion, is this a completely negative poem? Support your response by referring closely to the text.

• Poetry Focus •

Gerard Manley Hopkins

STUDY NOTES

> This Petrarchan sonnet was written in Hopkins's final years, at a time when he suffered increasingly from ill health and depression. It was one of a short series of sonnets of desolation, now known as the 'terrible sonnets' or 'dark sonnets'. In 'No worst, there is none', we see a man experiencing deep psychological suffering and struggling with his religious faith. The poem reveals a raw honesty from someone close to despair.

The **opening** is curt and dramatic, revealing the intensity of Hopkins's suffering: 'No worst, there is none'. He is unable to imagine any greater agony. The emphatic use of monosyllables in **line 1** reflects his **angry frustration**. Having reached what seems the threshold of torment, 'Pitched past pitch of grief', the poet dreads what lies ahead and the horrifying possibility that his pain ('schooled at forepangs') is likely to increase. The force of the verb 'Pitched', combined with the harsh onomatopoeic and alliterative effects, heighten the sense of uncontrollable anguish. Both 'pitch' and 'pangs' are repeated, suggesting darkness and violent movement.

The rhythm changes in **line 3**. The three syllables of 'Comforter' slow the pace considerably. This is also a much softer word (in contrast to the harshness of the earlier sounds) and is echoed at the end of the line by 'comforting'. Hopkins's desolate plea to the Holy Spirit and the Virgin Mary emphasises **his hopelessness**: 'where, where is your comforting?' The tone, reminiscent of Christ's words on the Cross ('My God, why hast thou forsaken me?'), is both desperate and accusatory.

The poet likens his hollow cries for help to a herd of cattle in **line 5**. The metaphor highlights his lack of self-worth – his hopeless prayers 'heave' and 'huddle in a main'. He feels that his own suffering is part of a **wider universal 'world-sorrow'**. There is an indication here that Hopkins recognises that experiencing a crisis of faith can affect any Christian from time to time. This possibility is supported by the memorable image of the anvil being struck in **line 6**. He realises that the Christian experience involves suffering the guilt of sin and doubt to achieve spiritual happiness: 'on an age-old anvil wince and sing'.

But for the poet, any relief ('lull') from suffering is short lived. His unavoidable feelings of shame and the pain of remorse are hauntingly personified: 'Fury had shrieked'. Once again, the severe sounds and the stretching of the phrase

'No lingering!' over two lines reinforce the relentlessness of **Hopkins's troubled conscience**.

This tormented tone is replaced by a more reflective one in the opening lines of the sestet, where Hopkins moves from the physical world of his 'cries' into the metaphorical landscape of towering mountains, with their dark, unknown depths. This **dramatic wasteland**, with its 'no-man-fathomed' cliffs, is terrifyingly portrayed. The poet reminds us that the terror of depression and separation from God cannot be appreciated by those 'who ne'er hung there'. The terror of being stranded on the 'steep or deep' rock face cannot be endured for long.

In the final lines, Hopkins resigns himself to the **grim consolation** that all the depression and pain of this world will end with death, just as everyday troubles are eased by sleep. The final, chilling image of the wretched individual taking refuge from the exhausting whirlwind is less than optimistic. There is no relief from the terrible desolation and Hopkins's distracted prayers have yet to be answered.

ANALYSIS

Write a paragraph tracing the development of Hopkins's tone throughout the course of the poem. Support the points you make with reference to the text.

SAMPLE PARAGRAPH

At the start of 'No worst, there is none', the tone is totally despondent. The first sentence is short and snappy, emphasising that Hopkins has reached rock bottom. Hopkins was a manic depressive and obsessed with religion. He also had issues with sexuality. In many ways he was caught between his role as a Jesuit priest and his human desires. Rhetorical questions highlight his dependence on his religious faith – 'Comforter, where, where is your comforting?' This gives a heartfelt tone. Hopkins uses effective images which always make us feel sympathy for him, for example 'My cries heave, herds-long'. His tone is sorrowful and this is emphasised by the way he uses comparisons. The prayers he offers to Heaven are just useless words which he says 'huddle' together like frightened cattle. He goes on to compare his sense of desperate danger from sin with being trapped on a steep mountain – 'O the mind, mind has mountains'. The use of the 'O' punctuation mark emphasises the tone of desperation. The end of the poem is even more negative. Hopkins obviously had issues with his own faith in God. He uses a strong tone of despair as he compares himself to a stranded wanderer finding shelter from a 'whirlwind'. His only comfort is sleep and eventually death, which will silence his inner pain. The last line emphasises his feelings of being tired with life – 'each day dies with sleep'. The tone is of complete hopelessness.

EXAMINER'S COMMENT

This response includes a number of relevant examples of tone throughout the poem. Quotations are well used in support. The answer drifted away from dealing with tone at times and the expression was awkward in places and there is overuse of the verb 'emphasises'. Otherwise, a solid B grade standard.

CLASS/HOMEWORK EXERCISES

1. Write your own personal response to 'No worst, there is none'. Refer closely to the text in your answer.
2. Copy the table below into your own notes and fill in critical comments about the last two quotations.

Key Quotes

Pitched past pitch of grief	Hopkins uses repetition and a forceful verb to convey his feelings of desolation.
Mary, mother of us, where is your relief?	The poet occasionally mentions other sufferers ('us') as well as himself. The plaintive tone here underpins the helplessness of those in pain.
Nor does long our small/Durance deal with that steep or deep	Hopkins contrasts man's 'small' or limited ability with the 'steep' challenges of life.
O the mind, mind has mountains	
Here! creep,/Wretch, under a comfort serves in a whirlwind	

• Leaving Certificate English •

Thou art indeed just, Lord, if I contend

Gerard Manley Hopkins

*Justus quidem tu es, Domine, si disputem tecum: verumtamen
justa loquar ad te: Quare via imporium prosperatur? &c.*

Thou art indeed just, Lord, if I contend
With thee; but, sir, so what I plead is just.
Why do sinners' ways prosper? And why must
Disappointment all I endeavour end?
Wert thou my enemy, O thou my friend, 5
How wouldst thou worse, I wonder, than thou dost
Defeat, thwart me? Oh, the sots and thralls of lust
Do in spare hours more thrive than I that spend,
Sir, life upon thy cause. See, banks and brakes
Now leaved how thick! laced they are again 10
With fretty chervil, look, and fresh wind shakes
Them; birds build – but not I build; no, but strain,
Time's eunuch, and not breed one work that wakes.
Mine, O thou lord of life, send my roots rain.

*'laced they are again/
With fretty chervil, look'*

GLOSSARY

Latin quotation: Indeed you are just, O Lord, if I dispute with you; yet I would plead my case before you. Why do the wicked prosper?
1 The first lines of the poem are a version of a Latin quotation that is taken from the Bible.
1 *contend*: dispute; argue; challenge.
7 *sots*: drunkards.
7 *thralls*: slaves.
9 *brakes*: thickets; groves of trees.
11 *fretty*: fretted; interlaced; the herb chervil has lacy leaves.
11 *chervil*: garden herb; the 'rejoicing leaf'.
13 *Time's eunuch*: a castrated male, incapable of reproducing.

EXPLORATIONS

1 List the questions put to God. What tone is evident in each – anger, rebelliousness, reverence, resentment, trust, despair, etc.?

2 Is there a real sense of pain in the poem? At what point is it most deeply felt? How does the abrupt, jerky movement of the poem contribute to this sense of pain? Quote in support of your points.
3 Is the image of God in the poem stern or not? Do you think that Hopkins had a good or bad relationship with God? Illustrate your answer with reference to this poem.

STUDY NOTES

> 'Thou art indeed just, Lord, if I contend' was written in 1889 at a time of great unhappiness for Hopkins in Dublin. He had written in a letter that 'all my undertakings miscarry'. This poem is a pessimistic yet powerful plea for help from God. It was written three months before he died.

This sonnet opens with the **formal language of the courtroom** as the poet, in clipped tones, poses three questions in the octet. With growing frustration, he asks God to explain why sinners seem to prosper. Why is he, the poet, continually disappointed? If God was his enemy instead of his friend, how could he be any worse off? God, he allows, is just, but he contends that his own cause is also just. The language is that of a coherent, measured argument: 'sir', 'I contend', I plead'. This is a contrast to the twisted, tortured grammar of the 'terrible sonnets', which echoes the deep, dark despair of the poet.

However, in lines 3–4, 'and why must/Disappointment all I endeavour end?', the inversion of the natural order makes the reader concentrate on the salient point that 'Disappointment' is the 'end' result of all the work the poet has done. But **the tone remains rational**, as he points out to 'Sir' that the worst doing their worse 'more thrive' than he does. But his frustration at his plight makes the line of the octet spill over into the sestet, as he complains that he has spent his life doing God's will ('life upon thy cause').

The sestet has the ring of the real voice breaking through as he urgently requests God to 'See', 'look'. Here is **nature busily thriving**, producing, building, breeding, growing. The movement and pace of continuing growth and regrowth is caught in the line 'Now leavèd how thick! lacèd they are again'. The **alliteration** of 'banks and braes', 'birds build' vividly portrays the abundance of nature, as does the **assonance** of 'fretty' and 'fresh'. **Flowing run-on lines** describe the surge of growing nature. Hopkins is the exception in this fertile scene. The negatives 'not', 'no', the punctuation of semi-colon and comma and the inversion of the phrase 'but not I build; no, but strain' depict the **fruitless efforts of the poet to create**. The terrible, dramatic, sterile image of 'Time's eunuch', the castrated male, contrasts the poet's unhappy state of unsuccessful effort with the ease of fruitful nature. Time is kind to nature, enabling it to renew, but the poet cannot beget one work: 'not breed one work that wakes'.

The last line of the poem, the shortest, pleads for help and rescue. An image of a drought-stricken plant looking for life-giving water is used to describe the poet's plight of unsuccessful poetic creativity. **He looks to the 'lord of life' for release.** Hopkins had written in one of his final letters, 'If I could produce work ... but it kills me to be time's eunuch and never to beget'. It is intriguing that someone of such great faith can argue ('contend') so vehemently with God. Hopkins stretches the disciplined structure of the sonnet form to echo his frustration as he strains to create. He died unknown as a poet, his body of work not even mentioned in his obituary. But the irony is that he did 'breed' 'work that wakes'.

His friend, Robert Bridges, submitted some of his poems for an anthology of nineteenth-century poetry and it attracted a favourable review which commented on how it possessed a 'poignant, even a passionate sincerity'. Thus, Hopkins finally found his place in the early twentieth century, a time of innovation and technical experimentation. His 'roots' had been sent 'rain'.

ANALYSIS

'Hopkins's poetry deals with the theme that God's will is a mystery to us.' Discuss this statement, illustrating your response with relevant quotation from the poetry on your course.

SAMPLE PARAGRAPH

How interesting to hear a man of great faith, a Jesuit priest, argue so openly and directly with God! As we see all the man-made and natural tragedies in the world, which of us has not thought, why has God allowed this to happen? Using the highly disciplined form of the sonnet, Hopkins charges God with accusations in the form of questions. How is it that sinners 'prosper'? Why 'must/Disappointment all I endeavour end?' The poet is frustrated, as we sometimes are; he does not know what is going on. God's will is a mystery to us. The tension at the centre of this sonnet is conveyed by Hopkins spilling the concerns of justice and morality into the sestet. He cannot contain himself. The mood of puzzlement continues in the sestet as he urgently points out ('See', 'look') how nature is thriving ('fretty chervil', 'birds build'). But he, in contrast, is not. He concludes the poem with the striking image of himself as the sterile 'Time's eunuch', a castrated slave unable to produce. He makes one final plea to God to nourish his parched 'roots' with 'rain'. The alliteration of 'roots rain' aligns him with the fertile world of nature, 'banks and brakes'. God is the 'lord of life', his divine plan a mystery to us, but we have the capacity to pray to Him.

EXAMINER'S COMMENT

Some personal engagement with the poem comes through in this response. Close reading of the poem is evident. Quotations are reasonably well used to illustrate how the poet deals with the theme. Grade B standard.

CLASS/HOMEWORK EXERCISES

1. Hopkins's innovative stylistic techniques make his work accessible to the modern reader. How true is this of 'Thou art indeed just, Lord, if I contend'? Use reference to the poem in your answer.
2. Copy the table below into your own notes and fill in critical comments about the last two quotations.

Key Quotes

But, sir, so what I plead is just	The poet is complaining that he is being treated badly by God.
Oh, the sots and thralls of lust/ Do in spare hours more thrive than I	The central argument of the poem is that sinners wasting their time sinning are doing better than he is. Sibilance suggests self-indulgence.
birds build – but not I	The world of nature is able to be creative and productive, unlike Hopkins.
Time's eunuch, and not breed one work that wakes	
Mine, O thou lord of life, send my roots rain	

LEAVING CERT SAMPLE ESSAY

Q 'There are many reasons why the poetry of Gerard Manley Hopkins appeals to his readers.' In response to the above statement, write an essay on the poetry of Hopkins. Your essay should focus clearly on the reasons why the poetry is appealing and you should refer to the poetry on your course.

MARKING SCHEME GUIDELINES

Answers to the question must contain clear evidence of engagement with the poetry on the course. Allow that candidates might focus, in part at least, on reasons why the poetry does not appeal to readers. Allow that an intensive treatment of a single dominant reason could be sufficient for full marks.

Expect a wide variety of approaches in the candidates' answering. Some of the following areas might provide material:
- Stylistic features such as sound, imagery, language.
- Poet's expression of feelings, doubts, beliefs.
- Descriptive power of the poetry.
- Innovative approaches and originality.
- Extension and development of traditional forms.
- Ideas – views on God, religion, life, etc.

SAMPLE ESSAY
(Appeal of Hopkins)

1 *Gerard Manley Hopkins was a fresh poet of innovative thinking. He honestly and openly expressed himself through his poetry and that is an admirable quality. As a poet, Hopkins focused on nature and the beauty of God's creation. He openly confessed his own faults and is easily identifiable with when he feels unworthy and hurt by God when he has dedicated his life to Him. His nature poems are beautifully descriptive and give a great sense of the wonder of the natural world.*

2. One such poem is 'Spring'. Here Hopkins states his awe and admiration at the world in springtime. He begins with a confident sentence which grabs your attention: 'Nothing is more beautiful than spring'. This sense of immediacy lets us know that this is what Hopkins believes and no one can dispute him. No one could argue against him, especially after reading his beautiful discription of the season. The line 'when weeds in wheels shoot long and lovely and lush' is a wonderful line. It is original and has a freshness to it. The 'l' and 'w' sounds remind me of rivers and luscious juices and the idea of dew on grass on an early spring morning. 'Weeds in wheels' suggest wild and wonderful plants growing untamed and natural.

3. 'Thrush's eggs look like little low heavens' is also a line you would not find in any poem. The way Hopkins can bring heaven to earth in the form of a bird's eggs is so unique and original. Our sense of hearing is appealed to in the lines 'and thrush does so rinse and wring the ear, it strikes like lightning to hear him sing'. We can imagine this bird in spring, with a song so good we just have to stop to listen.

4. Hopkins ends this poem with a question, 'What is all this juice and joy?' and he confidently gives a prompt answer, 'a strain of Eden's garden in the very beginning'. He feels we are privaleged to witness the beauty of Eden garden in spring and hope that man will preserve this beauty in the youth.

5. Another of his poems shows the poet's great apreciation for life. When you first read the poem it seems as if Hopkins is not troubled by Randal's death, 'oh he is dead then'. I feel that he was just reacting to his parishioner's death as most people react to a death; they feel strange don't know what to say and say empty statements that may seem selfish but are a disguise of how they really feel. In this way, Hopkins to me, is easily identifiable with and we can feel the same insecuraties as him.

6. Hopkins proceeds to describe Randal as 'big-boned and hardy-handsome' and it is clear that Felix Randal meant a lot to Hopkins in his heart rending cry 'touch had quenched thy tears; thy ears that touched my heart, child Felix, poor Felix Randal'. He speaks of Randal as a child showing deep affection for the farrier and his admiration is apparent in his discription of Randal's work at the forge, putting the 'sandal' on the 'big dray grey horse'.

7 One of the darker sonnets, 'Thou art indeed just Lord, if I contend' still does not deter me from my tremendous admiration for GM Hopkins. He feels he has been wronged by God, whom he loves and obeys. Again I can identify with him when he expresses his despair at doing right and getting nowhere, and others sinning and thriving. He wonders if God were his enemy would he treat the poet worse; 'Wert thou my enemy, how wouldst thou defeat, thwart me?' Although he is frustrated and extremely disappointed Hopkins remains faithful and says 'sir' as he knows his place in their relationship. He despairs at the 'sots and thralls' of lust in 'spare hours' thriving more than him spending his life on God's cause is pitiful as all Hopkins wants to do is serve his Creator.

8 There are various reasons why Hopkins's poetry is appealing and just by reading a short selection of it one can see the originality and outstanding talent that this poet had.

(approx. 700 words)

SPELLCHECKER
- description
- privileged
- appreciation
- insecurities
- disappointed

GRADE: C2
P   = 9/15
C   = 9/15
L   = 8/15
M   = 4/5
Total = 30/50

EXAMINER'S COMMENT

This is an example of an answer where over-reliance on notes has taken precedence over personal engagement with the text. There is a lack of control and organisation evident in the rambling opening, random paragraphing and inaccurate quoting. The expression is awkward and there are some spelling and grammar errors. However, the candidate had a reasonable knowledge of the poems and attempted to fulfil the task.

LEAVING CERT QUESTIONS ON HOPKINS'S POETRY (45–50 MINUTES)

1. 'Hopkins uses language in a startling and unique way.' Would you agree? Quote in support of your views from the poems on your course.

2. 'Hopkins's poetry can range from delight to despair.' Discuss this statement with reference to the poems on your course.

3. 'Loneliness, frustration and despair are themes in Hopkins's later poems.' How relevant is this to a reader from the twenty-first century? Discuss, using reference to the poetry of his on your course.

SAMPLE ESSAY PLAN (Q1)

'Hopkins uses language in a startling and unique way.' Would you agree? Quote in support of your views from the poems on your course.

- *Intro:* A personal examination is required of the imaginative, innovative techniques used by the poet, and also a reference to their purpose. These include sound effects, vivid imagery, bending words and coining new ones.

- *Point 1:* 'Spring' – sound effects, alliteration, assonance, onomatopoeia, run-on lines all reflect the exuberance of spring.

- *Point 2:* 'Pied Beauty' – compound words suggest dappling effect and ecstatic elation.

- *Point 3:* 'No worst, there is none' – repetition recreates the fear of the poet as he descends into desolation when he feels abandoned by God.

- *Point 4:* 'The Windhover' – sprung rhythm, pushing many unstressed syllables into the line, creates a childlike enthusiasm. His patent sincerity moves us.

- *Conclusion:* Like the Impressionists with paint, Hopkins bent his raw material into new shapes and textures with words so that readers can experience the world from a unique and starling perspective.

EXERCISE

Develop one of the above points into a paragraph.

POINT 2 – SAMPLE PARAGRAPH

Hopkins loved movement rather than rest. This is evident from the poem 'Pied Beauty'. Alliteration ('Fresh-firecoal', 'plotted and pieced', 'Fold, fallow'), assonance ('finches' wings') and compound words ('chestnut-falls') all celebrate the diversity of God's creation. This poem in particular reminds me of the Impressionist painters as they dabbed and speckled paint to recreate the varying light effects in nature. Hopkins uses his compound words in a similar way: 'couple-colour', 'rose-moles'. We sweep across the great patterns in nature which are 'adazzle', 'dim'. We see man working in harmony with nature: 'And all trades, their gear and tackle and trim'. There is a glorious orderly disorder – 'counter, original, spare, strange' – in this 'dappled' place of God's creation ('he fathers-forth'). Hopkins was a Jesuit and it was the custom for the Jesuit schools to start and finish their written work with praise to God. 'For the greater glory of God' is shortened to 'Glory be to God', while the ending 'Praise God always' is shortened to a more emphatic 'Praise him'. Hopkins succeeds, in my opinion, in capturing the mystery ('who knows what?') and the wonder ('whose beauty is past change') of God's creation through his innovative techniques.

EXAMINER'S COMMENT

As part of a full essay answer, the student has written a personal response to Hopkins's techniques focusing on one of his trademarks, his use of compound words. An in-depth exploration very well supported with quotation. Grade A.

Last Words

'What you look hard at seems to look hard at you.'
G.M. Hopkins

'Hopkins is more concerned with putting across his perceptions than with fulfilling customary expectations of grammar.'
Robert Bernard Martin

'Design, pattern, or what I am in the habit of calling inscape is what I above all aim at in poetry.'
G.M. Hopkins

'Poetry has to do with the reality of spirit.'

Patrick Kavanagh (1904–67)

Born in 1904 near Inniskeen, Co. Monaghan, in the shadow of Ulster's 'hungry hills', **Patrick Kavanagh** left school at the age of thirteen, apparently destined to plough the 'stony-grey soil' rather than write about it. But his interest in literature won out – 'I dabbled in verse,' he said, 'and it became my life'. Many of his poems celebrate the simple beauty and mystery of nature. In 1936, his first book of verse, *Ploughman and Other Poems*, was published, and in 1938 he followed this up with the autobiographical *The Green Fool*. For over twenty years, Kavanagh worked on the small family farm before moving to Dublin in 1939 to try and establish himself as a writer. However, Dublin's literary community saw him as a country farmer and cynics referred to him as 'That Monaghan Boy'. His epic poem, 'The Great Hunger', was published in 1942. Sombre, intense and emotive, it presented a disturbing view of rural poverty and repression. Kavanagh's reputation as a poet is based largely on the lyrical quality of his work, his mastery of language and form and his ability to transform the ordinary into something of significance. He is regarded by many as one of the most influential Irish poets, whose main achievement was to give an authentic voice to the peasant culture of rural Ireland during the insular de Valera era.

• Poetry Focus •

PRESCRIBED POEMS (HIGHER LEVEL)

Patrick Kavanagh

1 'Inniskeen Road: July Evening' (p. 220)

This well-known sonnet focuses on Kavanagh's role as a poet and his relationship with the local rural community in Co. Monaghan.

2 'Shancoduff' (p. 224)

One of Kavanagh's favourite poems, it illustrates his poetic appreciation of the ordinary life of the Monaghan countryside.

3 *from* 'The Great Hunger' (p. 229)

This long, powerful piece traces the life and times of Patrick Maguire, an elderly bachelor farmer. Kavanagh's critical view of Irish rural society is grim and disturbing.

4 'Advent' (p. 237)

Originally titled 'Renewal', the poem uses a two-sonnet structure to explore Kavanagh's religious experience of the Advent season.

5 'A Christmas Childhood' (p. 242)

Kavanagh describes a memorable Christmas when he was six years old and recalls how his 'child poet' associated the occasion with the birth of Christ in Bethlehem.

6 'Epic' (p. 248)

Based on an actual dispute over a small area of land in Co. Monaghan, the poem addresses wider aspects of conflict and the theme of poetic inspiration.

7 'Canal Bank Walk' (p. 252)

Written after a lengthy stay in hospital, the poet is keen to enjoy the wonderful gifts of nature, poetry and the overwhelming experience of being alive.

8 'Lines Written on a Seat on the Grand Canal, Dublin' (p. 256)

Another sonnet expressing Kavanagh's wish to be commemorated in one of his favourite places. Characteristically, he celebrates the wonder and greatness of ordinary things.

9 'The Hospital' (p. 260)

After recovering from a serious illness, the poet considers his newfound appreciation of natural beauty and the mystery of life itself while time allows.

10 'On Raglan Road' (p. 264)

Set on the streets of Dublin, this bittersweet ballad of unrequited love reveals much that is of interest about Kavanagh's own personality.

• Poetry Focus •

Patrick Kavanagh

Inniskeen Road: July Evening

The bicycles go by in twos and threes –
There's a dance in Billy Brennan's barn tonight,
And there's the half-talk code of mysteries
And the wink-and-elbow language of delight.
Half-past eight and there is not a spot   5
Upon a mile of road, no shadow thrown
That might turn out a man or woman, not
A footfall tapping secrecies of stone.

I have what every poet hates in spite
Of all the solemn talk of contemplation.   10
Oh, Alexander Selkirk knew the plight
Of being king and government and nation.
A road, a mile of kingdom, I am king
Of banks and stones and every blooming thing.

'a mile of kingdom'

GLOSSARY

The townland of Mucker near Inniskeen, Co. Monaghan was Kavanagh's birthplace. He lived there on the small family farm until the late 1930s.

2 *Billy Brennan's barn*: a local farmhouse where country dances took place.

10 *solemn talk of contemplation*: poets regard themselves as deep thinkers.

11 *Alexander Selkirk*: famous Scottish sailor (1676–1721) marooned on an uninhabited Pacific island for five years. His experience was the model for Daniel Defoe's novel, *Robinson Crusoe*.

14 *blooming*: flowering; also a colloquial expletive for impatience.

EXPLORATIONS

1. There is a lively mood of excitement in the poem's opening lines. How does Kavanagh's use of language achieve this effect?
2. Comment on the effectiveness of the comparison with Alexander Selkirk.
3. In your opinion, what are the feelings expressed by Kavanagh in the last two lines of the poem?

STUDY NOTES

> Taken from Kavanagh's first collection, *Ploughman and Other Poems*, this sonnet provides an interesting presentation of the poet's relationship with nature and the local community as well as providing a glimpse of Irish rural life in the 1930s. Kavanagh's dual role – as both a member of and a commentator on society – is succinctly dramatised. The octave (first eight lines) focuses on the local environment, while the sestet (final six lines) sums up Kavanagh's own reflections on his life as a poet.

Lines 1–2 set the scene as young people from Kavanagh's parish make their way to the local dance. **Colloquial language and energetic rhythms echo everyday speech**: 'There's a dance in Billy Brennan's barn tonight'. The alliterative 'b' sound and use of the present tense add to the mood of lively anticipation. Kavanagh's diction becomes more poetic in **lines 3–4** as he makes a sceptical observation about 'the half-talk code of mysteries/And the wink-and-elbow language of delight'. In distancing himself from the groups cycling to the dance, the poet emphasises his own sense of exclusion. Examine the tone Kavanagh uses – is it ironic, cynical, superior, self-pitying? It's difficult to know if he is enjoying the excited gestures of the carefree passers-by or if he is envious of them – or both.

The social atmosphere and relaxed camaraderie of the opening quatrain is followed by a more **reflective commentary** in **lines 5–8**. Left alone on the roadside, Kavanagh is drawn by the intense solitude ('no shadow thrown') of his surroundings. There is a certain poignancy to his loneliness, especially since he seems all too aware of the nature of his isolation. But although the poet is detached from human company ('man or woman'), he has the comfort of being close to nature – the 'secrecies of stone'. Of course, the secrets are never disclosed. Is Kavanagh thinking about the wonders of the natural world or the secret lives of the young dance-goers? Or even of his own poetic imagination? We can only guess. At any rate, the slower pace of this second quatrain, combined with the broad vowel assonance, contribute much to the pensive tone and mood of bittersweet alienation.

The **sestet** offers the poet's own explanation for most of the questions raised in the opening eight lines. Addressing the reader directly, Kavanagh outlines the reality of what it means to be a poet – and for him it is a **double-edged sword**. He 'hates' the popular perception that poets are introspective philosophers constantly immersed in serious 'contemplation'. In **line 11**, he compares himself to the marooned sailor, Alexander Selkirk. While the reference seems to be only half-serious, it serves to highlight the artist's role and relationship with society. Writing is a solitary occupation (a 'plight'), but it also guarantees the freedom and independence 'Of being king and government and nation'.

The ironic tone of **lines 13–14** reminds readers of the **contradictions of the poet's life**. As the self-styled 'king' of 'every blooming thing', Kavanagh illustrates the contradictory aspects of a literary life. The pun on 'blooming' underlines both the positive and negative sides of being a writer. Kavanagh may be somewhat removed from his own community, but he is gifted with a creative imagination which allows him to appreciate the wonders of nature.

ANALYSIS

From your reading of 'Inniskeen Road: July Evening', what do you learn about Kavanagh himself? Refer to the text in your answer

SAMPLE PARAGRAPH

Kavanagh strikes me as a highly intelligent person and a shrewd judge. He understands his own life as a working writer and that he is different to his peer group, the other young men in his area. At the beginning, he sees himself as a loner, an outsider. His friends pass him by 'in twos and threes'. I think Kavanagh knows well that he is different and he admits that he is outside the circle, cut off from what he calls 'the wink-and-elbow language of delight'. But he acknowledges that this is the price a poet must pay. He is an observer and he seems to almost enjoy being unlike the others. He has special status. At the same time, he is honest enough to admit that it is a lonely life. He is like the great explorer Alexander Selkirk who was abandoned on a desert island. The ending of the poem tells me most about Kavanagh. He seems resigned to his 'plight' because he is at one with nature. In fact he jokes that he is 'king/Of banks and stones and every blooming thing'. I find the tone of this to be good-humoured and proof that he was happy enough with the simple joys of Inniskeen. He has come to terms with his loneliness and is really making the most of his life even though it isn't perfect.

EXAMINER'S COMMENT

This is a clear, well-sustained response that ranges over the text in search of appropriate evidence about the poet's personality. There is some good personal engagement and a lively style throughout. A little more thorough analysis would have raised the standard above a basic B grade.

CLASS/HOMEWORK EXERCISES

1. One literary critic described 'Inniskeen Road: July Evening' as 'a love poem to a place, written towards the end of the affair'. Write your response to this comment, using close reference to the text of the poem.
2. Copy the table below into your own notes and fill in critical comments about the last two quotations.

Key Quotes

The bicycles go by in twos and threes	Kavanagh conveys a sense of excitement through the use of colloquial language and alliteration.
A footfall tapping secrecies of stone	While the phrase suggests Kavanagh's isolation, it also highlights his poetic imagination.
Of all the solemn talk of contemplation	Kavanagh's self-deprecating tone reflects his mock-serious attitude to the myth that poets are moody intellectuals who enjoy their own company.
the half-talk code of mysteries	
A road, a mile of kingdom	

• Poetry Focus •

Shancoduff

Patrick Kavanagh

My black hills have never seen the sun rising,
Eternally they look north towards Armagh.
Lot's wife would not be salt if she had been
Incurious as my black hills that are happy
When dawn whitens Glassdrummond chapel.　　　5

My hills hoard the bright shillings of March
While the sun searches in every pocket.
They are my Alps and I have climbed the Matterhorn
With a sheaf of hay for three perishing calves
In the field under the Big Forth of Rocksavage.　　　10

The sleety winds fondle the rushy beards of Shancoduff
While the cattle-drovers sheltering in the Featherna Bush
Look up and say: 'Who owns them hungry hills
That the water-hen and snipe must have forsaken?
A poet? Then by heavens he must be poor'.　　　15
I hear and is my heart not badly shaken?

'My black hills have never seen the sun rising'

GLOSSARY

Shancoduff: Old Black Hollow, from the Irish words '*sean*' (old) and '*dubh*' (black).

3 *Lot's wife*: reference to the Bible story where the wife of Lot was turned into a pillar of salt for disobeying God.

6 *shillings*: small silver coins from old Irish currency.

8 *Matterhorn*: the highest peak of the Alps, a mountain range in Switzerland.

11 *sleety*: icy rain.

14 *snipe*: marshland bird.

EXPLORATIONS

1 There are two distinct views of Shancoduff. Who holds these opposing views and why do you think they are different? Refer to the poem in your answer.
2 What effect does the naming of local places have on the poem? What does it tell you about Kavanagh and his relationship with Shancoduff?
3 What evidence is there of Kavanagh's self-deprecating humour in this poem? Why do you think he uses this?

STUDY NOTES

Kavanagh had a love–hate relationship with the place he grew up in, Inniskeen. Shancoduff, a north-facing hill, is shown in winter. Kavanagh's family had bought a small farm there, not far from his home. His brother, Peter, said Kavanagh regarded it as 'wonderland'. The view stretched fifteen miles to the Mourne Mountains.

Like an indulgent lover, Kavanagh turns the negatives of this hostile place into positives, just as a lover refuses to see bad in his loved one. The hills may be drab and 'Incurious' and mean (they 'hoard'), but they are his. The ownership is stressed in the protective, possessive adjective 'My': 'My black hills', 'My hills', 'my Alps'. He recognises that the land will remain 'Eternally' while the people come and go.

He personifies this land with verbs and adjectives: 'look', 'Incurious', 'happy', 'hoard'. Kavanagh loves the local. He sees magic here as he describes dawn breaking over the little country church in **line 5**: 'dawn whitens Glassdrummond chapel'. The place becomes luminous and radiant. These hills can't be bothered to look at the sun; 'they look north'. The poet turns their lack of curiosity into a positive, saying look at what happened to Lot's wife for her curiosity – she looked at a forbidden sight, the destruction of the sinning cities Sodom and Gomorrah, and was turned into a pillar of salt. Kavanagh, like his hills, also turned his face, refusing to accept the literary scene in Dublin.

• Poetry Focus •

Patrick Kavanagh

The **litany of place names**, rather like the proud parent naming the names of her children or the naming of saints in a religious ceremony, is a feature of Kavanagh's poetry, and points to the pride he had in Shancoduff. To him, these hills were as important and as impressive as the Alps, the famous mountain range in Switzerland. The polysyllabic sounds of these place names are masculine, tough, threatening, full of the fierce pride of a border place as they stand like heroes in an old film, surveying all before them. An ordinary act of feeding the calves becomes a heroic feat in this place in **line 8**: 'I have climbed the Matterhorn'. This is an example of Kavanagh's use of **hyperbole**. These hills are rebellious; they won't follow the rhythm of nature, they don't change in tune with the seasons. Like misers, they 'hoard' the bright pockets of ice and snow while the sun desperately tries to thaw the land, as it is springtime. The exasperation of the sun's effort is vividly caught in the description of the sun searching the pockets of the hills. These miserly hills won't give up their 'shillings', yet Kavanagh praises their thriftiness.

The tenderness of the lover is caught in the verb 'fondle', as Kavanagh again personifies this bleak place in **line 11**: the 'rushy beards of Shancoduff'. But **a negative note is struck as the drovers and farmers sneer** at 'them hungry hills'. They look dispassionately at this place, as the hills won't produce. The use of direct speech brings the conflict flickering into life, as they criticise not only the land but the profession of the owner, 'a poet'. To these men, he must be mad. **The rhetorical question at the end shows the poet's devastation at this criticism**, rather like a lover being made to face the reality that his loved one is ugly. Reality, like the biting winds, is piercing the poet's illusions: 'I hear and is my heart not badly shaken?' Is it the lack of potential for farming or the fear that these hills will not provide sufficient creative stimulus that leaves the poet 'badly shaken'? Whatever the answer, these places pushed Irish poetry into a new direction, showing that an emphasis on the ordinary (and even banal) is a worthwhile subject for poetry.

ANALYSIS

'The relationship between place and person is central to the poetry of Patrick Kavanagh.' Discuss this statement in relation to the poem 'Shancoduff'.

SAMPLE PARAGRAPH

Although Kavanagh has a love-hate relationship with his birthplace, Inniskeen, it is this very conflict that inspired Kavanagh to write. At this time, in the 1930s and 1940s in rural Ireland, the poet was looked at as someone strange and odd. He didn't quite fit into the rural scene. We hear this in the direct speech, in this poem, of the cattle-drovers, as they looked disparagingly at the bleak hill of Shancoduff and its owner. 'Who owns them hungry hills ... A poet?' They speak as if he wouldn't know what to do with the land. This criticism stung Kavanagh: 'I hear and is my heart not badly shaken?' To him, Shancoduff was a magical place, a 'wonderland', his brother tells us. This protective attitude of a caring lover, the poet, is evident in the repetition of the possessive adjective 'my'. He excuses all faults of the loved one; he thinks it is good that the hills are 'Incurious'. He feels they are happy once they see the chapel of Glassdrummond shining incandescently in the dawn light. They don't have to see the sun. He even delights in the miserliness of the hills that won't give up the last patches of ice that the sun is frantically trying to thaw: 'the sun searches in every pocket'. The love he has for the place is evident as we see the importance he places on the poor little hill, 'my Alps'. A common event is transformed into something heroic because it takes place there. Feeding the 'shivering' calves is now 'I have climbed the Matterhorn', the most dangerous peak in the Alps. Shancoduff is not beautiful, with its 'rushy beards', but to the poet, it is. So he imagines the sleety winds 'fondle' the small hill. This poem is firmly rooted in the harsh countryside of Monaghan, and this place is firmly rooted in Kavanagh's heart. Under the poet's loving gaze, this ordinary hill has become extraordinary.

EXAMINER'S COMMENT

A sensitive reading of the poem. A grade standard, strongly supported throughout with relevant quotations. The candidate has discussed the importance of this place to the poet, and has therefore fulfilled the required task.

CLASS/HOMEWORK EXERCISES

1. Would you consider the poetry of Kavanagh to be the poetry of 'rediscovery and celebration'? Discuss this statement in relation to the poem 'Shancoduff'.
2. Copy the table below into your own notes and fill in critical comments about the last two quotations.

• Poetry Focus •

Patrick Kavanagh

Key Quotes

My black hills have never seen the sun rising	Shancoduff faces north and the sun rises in the east, so the hills only see the reflection of the dawn.
My hills hoard the bright shillings of March	Ironically, Kavanagh uses the metaphor of miserliness to show his delight in the beauty of the season.
They are my Alps	These hills are as important to Kavanagh as the great mountain ranges of Europe.
The sleety winds fondle the rushy beards of Shancoduff	
I hear and is my heart not badly shaken?	

from **The Great Hunger**

Patrick Kavanagh

Clay is the word and clay is the flesh
Where the potato-gatherers like mechanized scare-crows move
Along the side-fall of the hill – Maguire and his men.
If we watch them an hour is there anything we can prove
Of life as it is broken-backed over the Book   5
Of Death? Here crows gabble over worms and frogs
And the gulls like old newspapers are blown clear of the hedges, luckily.
Is there some light of imagination in these wet clods?
Or why do we stand here shivering?
                          Which of these men   10
Loved the light and the queen
Too long Virgin? Yesterday was summer. Who was it promised marriage to himself
Before apples were hung from the ceilings for Hallowe'en?
We will wait and watch the tragedy to the last curtain,
Till the last soul passively like a bag of wet clay   15
Rolls down the side of the hill, diverted by the angles
Where the plough missed or a spade stands, straitening the way.

A dog lying on a torn jacket under a heeled-up cart,
A horse nosing along the posied headland, trailing
A rusty plough. Three heads hanging between wide-apart   20
Legs. October playing a symphony on a slack wire paling.
Maguire watches the drills flattened out
And the flints that lit a candle for him on a June altar
Flameless. The drills slipped by and the days slipped by
And he trembled his head away and ran free from the world's halter,   25
And thought himself wiser than any man in the townland
When he laughed over pints of porter
Of how he came free from every net spread
In the gaps of experience. He shook a knowing head
And pretended to his soul   30
That children are tedious in hurrying fields of April
Where men are spanging across wide furrows,
Lost in the passion that never needs a wife –
The pricks that pricked were the pointed pins of harrows.

Children scream so loud that the crows could bring 35
The seed of an acre away with crow-rude jeers.
Patrick Maguire, he called his dog and he flung a stone in the air
And hallooed the birds away that were the birds of the years.
Turn over the weedy clods and tease out the tangled skeins.
What is he looking for there? 40
He thinks it is a potato, but we know better
Than his mud-gloved fingers probe in this insensitive hair.

'Move forward the basket and balance it steady
In this hollow. Pull down the shafts of that cart, Joe,
And straddle the horse,' Maguire calls. 45
'The wind's over Brannagan's, now that means rain.
Graip up some withered stalks and see that no potato falls
Over the tail-board going down the ruckety pass –
And *that's* a job we'll have to do in December,
Gravel it and build a kerb on the bog-side. Is that Cassidy's ass 50
Out in my clover? Curse o' God –
Where is that dog?
Never where he's wanted.' Maguire grunts and spits
Through a clay-wattled moustache and stares about him from the height.
His dream changes like the cloud-swung wind 55
And he is not so sure now if his mother was right
When she praised the man who made a field his bride.

Watch him, watch him, that man on a hill whose spirit
Is a wet sack flapping about the knees of time.
He lives that his little fields may stay fertile when his own body 60
Is spread in the bottom of a ditch under two coulters crossed in Christ's Name.

He was suspicious in his youth as a rat near strange bread
When girls laughed; when they screamed he knew that meant
The cry of fillies in season. He could not walk
The easy road to his destiny. He dreamt 65
The innocence of young brambles to hooked treachery.
O the grip. O the grip of irregular fields! No man escapes.
It could not be that back of the hills love was free
And ditches straight.

No monster hand lifted up children and put down apes 70
As here.
                         'O God if I had been wiser!'
That was his sigh like the brown breeze in the thistles.
He looks towards his house and haggard. 'O God if I had been
    wiser!'
But now a crumpled leaf from the whitethorn bushes 75
Darts like a frightened robin, and the fence
Shows the green of after-grass through a little window,
And he knows that his own heart is calling his mother a liar.
God's truth is life – even the grotesque shapes of its foulest fire.

The horse lifts its head and cranes 80
Through the whins and stones
To lip late passion in the crawling clover.
In the gap there's a bush weighted with boulders like morality,
The fools of life bleed if they climb over.

The wind leans from Brady's, and the coltsfoot leaves are holed
    with rust, 85
Rain fills the cart-tracks and the sole-plate grooves;
A yellow sun reflects in Donaghmoyne
The poignant light in puddles shaped by hooves.

Come with me, Imagination, into this iron house
And we will watch from the doorway the years run back, 90
And we will know what a peasant's left hand wrote on the page.
Be easy, October. No cackle hen, horse neigh, tree sough, duck
    quack.

'The drills slipped by and the days slipped by'

GLOSSARY

The 'Great Hunger' was a common name for the 1840s famine. Kavanagh used the term symbolically to refer to the hunger for fulfilment and satisfactory relationships.

1 *Clay is the word*: the phrase echoes the Biblical account of creation: 'In the beginning was the Word'.
6 *gabble*: cry, squabble noisily.
11–12 *the queen ... Virgin*: the poet personifies the barren farmland.
18 *heeled-up*: upended.
22 *drills*: ploughed potato rows.
25 *halter*: restraint for controlling a horse.
32 *spanging*: jumping; striding.
34 *harrows*: ploughing implements.
39 *skeins*: root strands.
47 *Graip*: dig with a small fork.
48 *ruckety*: uneven.
54 *clay-wattled*: soiled; unclean.
59 *a wet sack*: used by farmers to keep their clothes dry.
61 *coulters*: plough blades.
73 *haggard*: storage area for fodder.
85 *coltsfoot*: creeping yellow weed.
86 *sole-plate*: horseshoe; underside of farm implement.
87 *Donaghmoyne*: parish near Inniskeen.
91 *what a peasant's left hand wrote*: probably refers to Kavanagh himself as the authentic voice of rural Ireland.
92 *sough*: sigh.

EXPLORATIONS

1 What impression of Maguire and his men do you get from lines 1–9 of the poem? Refer to the text in your answer.
2 Describe the mood in the last eight lines of the poem. How does Kavanagh create this mood?
3 In your view, how effective is Kavanagh's description of rural Ireland? Refer closely to the poem in your answer.

STUDY NOTES

'The Great Hunger' was written in 1942 when Kavanagh was living in Dublin. This epic narrative reveals the harsh realities of rural Irish life and focuses primarily on one character's relationship with the land. The poem also explores the effects of grinding poverty and sexual inhibition. Kavanagh challenges the romantic notion of the happy-go-lucky peasant that had been promoted elsewhere in Ireland's literary tradition. Throughout the poem, Kavanagh uses a narrator to present Patrick Maguire and to link key scenes in the character's unfulfilled life.

The extract's opening section (**lines 1–17**) portrays Patrick Maguire and his farm labourers in their natural element – 'Along the side-fall of the hill'. The sluggish rhythm and mock-serious biblical tone ('Clay is the word and clay is the flesh') reflect the helplessness of these men who are, in every sense, stuck in the mud. They are depicted as less than human, 'like mechanized scare-crows', in a **relentlessly desolate setting**. This hostile environment of 'wet clods' has left them 'broken-backed'. Kavanagh's imagery suggests a primitive world where 'crows gabble over worms and frogs'. The narrative voice informs us of the emptiness of life here and invites us to observe Maguire's 'tragedy to the last curtain'. Particular emphasis is placed on loneliness and sexual longing ('Who was it promised marriage to himself'). Forlorn rhetorical questions echo the men's deep feelings of regret. Their despair is succinctly expressed in the evocative sentence 'Yesterday was summer', a devastatingly bleak acceptance of lost opportunity.

Immediately following this prologue to Maguire's story, **lines 18–38** include several **images of failure**: 'a torn jacket', a 'rusty plough', a 'Flameless' candle. Although the sexual allusions are somewhat overstated, Maguire's frustration is still as pitiful as it is easy to mock. Kavanagh's extended lines, delivered largely at a plodding pace, suggest a monotonous existence: 'The drills slipped by and the days slipped by'. Yet despite being tied down like a tethered horse, Maguire deludes himself that he is happy and considers himself 'wiser than any man in the townland'. He even sneers at family life ('children are tedious'), but it is all pretence, as much of an empty act of bravado as his vain gesture when he 'flung a stone in the air' to scare away 'the birds of the years'.

The narrator's attitude to Maguire is somewhat ambivalent: it is seemingly sympathetic and yet highly critical at times. Consider, for instance, the tone of **line 41**: 'He thinks it is a potato, but we know better'. Is the voice superior and patronising, or sincere and understanding? Maguire speaks for himself in **lines 43–57** and confirms our initial impressions of a boorish man whose entire life revolves around farming. His curt utterances reflect the realistic rhythms of country life: 'Pull down the shafts of that cart'. This picture of a rough, hard-working farmer who 'grunts and spits' is convincingly constructed. But **Kavanagh also explores Maguire's secret life**. Deep down, the ageing bachelor is plagued by doubts about the sacrifices he has made for the sake of the land and 'is not so sure now if his mother was right/When she praised the man who made a field his bride'. While the brooding introspection is not completely unexpected, it is nonetheless a compelling expression of the human tragedy that affected an entire generation of men like Patrick Maguire.

The softer tone of narrative comment in **lines 58–61** is in keeping with Kavanagh's essential sympathy for **people whose emotional, sexual and spiritual needs were being stifled**. Maguire's depressed spirit is compared to 'a wet sack flapping about the knees of time'. The metaphor conveys a disconcerting sense of the ageing farmer's futile struggle. Ironically, he will give up his own happiness so that 'his little fields may stay fertile'. Such a sacrifice is hardly glorious. The image of Maguire's corpse buried 'under two coulters crossed in Christ's Name' provides a final symbol of depression. Throughout much of this section, Kavanagh controls the rhythm carefully, maintaining a funeral pace in line with the poem's sombre atmosphere.

Lines 62–79 take us back to Maguire's youthful years, a time of embarrassment and confusion which he has come to regret: 'O God if I had been wiser!' The poet's negative language ('suspicious', 'treachery', 'irregular', 'frightened') underlines a scathing **tone of bitter recrimination**. Repetition and the use of exclamations add to the feeling of resentment towards an earlier culture of ignorance and insensitivity: 'O the grip. O the grip of irregular fields!' Images of 'a crumpled leaf' and 'a frightened robin' symbolise the powerlessness of young people growing up in a narrow-minded era of deprivation.

Maguire again singles out one person for particular attention: 'And he knows that his own heart is calling his mother a liar'. **Kavanagh is probably using the figure of the Irish mother to represent powerful institutions of official Ireland that he was critical of**, such as the Catholic Church, the family and the country's education system. The poet's message could not be more lucid. For Kavanagh, Irish society's traditional repression of human sexuality was a denial that 'God's truth is life – even the grotesque shapes of its foulest fire'.

Lines 80–87 include a number of natural images from the familiar Irish landscape. **The poet's cinematic technique is atmospheric**, creating a mood of yearning and endurance, evoked by glimpses of the 'poignant light' of a 'yellow sun'. Despite the pervading sense of despondency, there is a recognition of the timeless beauty that typifies Kavanagh's sense of place. In **lines 89–92**, readers are asked to use their imaginations to watch 'the years run back' on Patrick Maguire's sullen life. The final hushed tone is reassuringly lyrical, echoing the voice of an elderly man at work on his farm: 'Be easy, October. No cackle hen, horse neigh'. The scene is set for the rest of Maguire's tragic story.

ANALYSIS

How effective is Kavanagh's portrayal of Irish rural society in Part I of 'The Great Hunger'? Refer to the text of the poem in your answer.

SAMPLE PARAGRAPH

Of the Kavanagh poems I have studied, the extract from 'The Great Hunger' gave me the best insight into what Irish rural life was like during the early decades of the twentieth century. The first word in the poem is 'Clay'. It sets the downbeat tone simply and directly. 'Clay is the word and clay is the flesh' told me that Kavanagh saw farm work almost as a type of religion. His central character is Patrick Maguire, a mature farmer who has never married. Maguire was typical of tens of thousands of lonely bachelors who gave their lives to the land in the 'hungry' 1930s and 1940s. The poet really brought Maguire to life for me and I imagined him as a grumpy workaholic who lived and breathed farming. He 'grunts and spits' and puts on an act in public that he is content with his lonely life. I disliked him as a character, but also felt sorry for him. The very fact that I took Maguire seriously at all is proof of how convincing a portrait Kavanagh created. The poet's detailed description is dramatic and very effective. Maguire and his men work like 'mechanized scare-crows'. Maguire laughs 'over pints of porter'. But it's all false. Kavanagh lets us hear Maguire's own sad voice, saying, 'O God if I had been wiser'. By the end of the poem, it's clear that he really is desperately lonely, filled with regret and anger because of his wasted life. He calls his mother 'a liar' and resents the waste of his youth. Kavanagh fills the poem with powerful images of decay: 'weedy clods', 'whins and stone', a 'rusty plough'. To me these create an atmosphere of a rural Ireland that was failing and depressed. It is a negative picture, but a very compelling one.

EXAMINER'S COMMENT

This is a successful individual response that shows clear engagement with the poem. The answer remains focused on the question throughout. Discussion points are well supported with references and short quotations. Grade A.

CLASS/HOMEWORK EXERCISES

1. In your view, does the poet feel sympathy for Maguire? Refer closely to the text of the poem in your answer.
2. Copy the table below into your own notes and fill in critical comments about the last two quotations.

Patrick Kavanagh

Key Quotes

life as it is broken-backed	Kavanagh's vivid physical image describes the bent-over potato-gatherers at work while also symbolising their oppressed lives.
'O God if I had been wiser!'	Maguire's mantra is poignant and pathetic, a searing indictment of a heartbreaking waste of human life.
we will know what a peasant's left hand wrote	The poet's individual account of Maguire's brutalised life will expose the truth about the effects of frustration and lack of fulfilment.
He was suspicious in his youth as a rat near strange bread/When girls laughed	
And he knows that his own heart is calling his mother a liar	

Advent

Patrick Kavanagh

We have tested and tasted too much, lover—
Through a chink too wide there comes in no wonder.
But here in this Advent-darkened room
Where the dry black bread and the sugarless tea
Of penance will charm back the luxury   5
Of a child's soul, we'll return to Doom
The knowledge we stole but could not use.

And the newness that was in every stale thing
When we looked at it as children: the spirit-shocking
Wonder in a black slanting Ulster hill   10
Or the prophetic astonishment in the tedious talking
Of an old fool will awake for us and bring
You and me to the yard gate to watch the whins
And the bog-holes, cart-tracks, old stables where Time begins.

O after Christmas we'll have no need to go searching   15
For the difference that sets an old phrase burning—
We'll hear it in the whispered argument of a churning
Or in the streets where the village boys are lurching.
And we'll hear it among simple decent men too
Who barrow dung in gardens under trees,   20
Wherever life pours ordinary plenty.
Won't we be rich, my love and I, and please
God we shall not ask for reason's payment,
The why of heart-breaking strangeness in dreeping hedges
Nor analyse God's breath in common statement.   25
We have thrown into the dust-bin the clay-minted wages
Of pleasure, knowledge and the conscious hour—
And Christ comes with a January flower.

'The why of heart-breaking strangeness in dreeping hedges'

• Poetry Focus •

GLOSSARY

Advent: the four weeks before Christmas, which in Kavanagh's time was a period of penance and fasting in preparation for the coming of Christ.
1 *lover*: soul; spiritual self.
4 *dry black bread*: eaten during Advent penance.
6 *we'll return to Doom*: we will discard as useless.
13 *whins*: furze/gorse bushes.
14 *Time begins*: after the birth of Christ, the calendar was changed and BC became AD.
16 *difference ... burning*: allows us to see wisdom in an old saying.
17 *churning*: cream is stirred and turned until butter is made.
23 *reason's payment*: rational explanation.
24 *dreeping*: dripping.
26 *clay-minted wages*: useless payment.
28 *January flower*: symbol of the return of innocence.

EXPLORATIONS

1 In the first stanza, the poet wishes to leave the world of adult experience and return to a world of childhood innocence. How do you interpret the phrase 'the luxury/Of a child's soul'?
2 Why does Kavanagh consider 'wonder' and 'astonishment' to be so important? What is the opposite of these? Why does he dislike the opposite?
3 Which vivid detail strikes you most in the second sonnet, lines 15–28? Why does this detail appeal to you?

STUDY NOTES

This poem was first published on Christmas Eve 1942 in *The Irish Times* and was originally called 'Renewal'. It concerns Kavanagh's early years in Dublin. He was a man of little formal education, as he had left school at thirteen to work the land, and here he is remaking his soul and announcing, in these two sonnets, that he is a poet of wonder. He finds that in order to go on, he must go back.

The sound of **world-weary, jaded senses** are vividly caught in the first sonnet's **opening**: 'We have tested and tasted too much'. The hard repetitive 't' sound and the use of the past tense capture the empty round of excess partying and too much drink. The reference to 'lover' suggests an intimate presence in the poet's life, whether a friend or his spiritual self. He has done too much, seen too much. He longs for the simple life. The poem is set in Advent, the four weeks prior to Christmas. This was a time of self-denial when people fasted and did penance to purify themselves in readiness for the coming of Christ at Christmas. They denied themselves sugar and butter as a penance ('dry black bread and the sugarless tea'). The short, gloomy evenings of winter are shown in the phrase 'Advent-darkened room'.

Kavanagh has written that 'revelations come as an aside'. Here, the 'chink' offers a tantalising glimpse into another mysterious world. He is saying that when everything is laid out in front of you, there is no desire for it. **This is what he doesn't want**. What he does want is the 'luxury/Of a child's soul'. The ability to look at things with breathless curiosity and awestruck wonder is what he desires now. He has experienced much, but like Adam and Eve in the Garden of Eden, he has knowledge that he cannot use. He wants to return it 'to Doom'. Innocence has gone and knowing is worthless.

In the next seven lines, **the poet tells us what he wants**, using a striking paradox: 'the newness that was in every stale thing'. **He wants to look again at the world through the eyes of a child** so that his soul can be shocked by an experience: 'the spirit-shocking/Wonder in a black slanting Ulster hill'. As a child, he could see the menacing threat in the dark hill silhouetted against the dying light of the sky. Paradoxes graphically show this poetic rebirth so that listening to a repetitive old man becomes a source of childish surprise, rather than the cynical reaction of an adult that this talking is boring. The sonnet concludes with a wonderful image of 'You and me' leaning over a gate, waiting, observing and realising that in the most ordinary things, lies the extraordinary. An old stable was where Christ was born and time was refigured.

In the second sonnet, the tense now moves to the future as he imagines with the expressive, heartfelt 'O' what will happen if he opens himself up to experiencing the **'ordinary plenty'**. He will understand the wisdom in an old saying, 'the difference that sets an old phrase burning'. The onomatopoeia allows us to hear it, along with the poet, in the line 'We'll hear it in the whispered argument of a churning'. The simple sights of corner boys and men tending their gardens are all shown to be where life is pouring out its riches. The intimate tone of the poet continues in the phrase 'Won't we be rich, my love and I' as he asks us **not to over-analyse, but rather experience**.

The beauty of a damp December evening on a remote Irish road is shown vividly in the 'heart-breaking strangeness of dreeping hedges'. Kavanagh coins a new word, 'dreeping', to convey the saturated weight of water on the hedgerow. But we are not to ask 'The why'. Our language ('common statement') is not adequate enough to comprehend 'God's breath'. Instead, we will discard what is useless, 'the clay-minted wages' of the senses, 'pleasure, knowledge'. We will leave aside knowingness, 'the conscious hour'. The second sonnet concludes in the present tense with the birth of Christ: 'And Christ comes with a January flower'. The innocence of childhood and purity has been regained and the creative impulse is in full bloom.

ANALYSIS

The original title of this poem was 'Renewal'. What type of renewal was Kavanagh seeking and why? Support your response with quotation from the poem.

SAMPLE PARAGRAPH

Kavanagh moved to Dublin, after thirty years spent in Monaghan, and he described it as the 'worst mistake of my life'. He was uneducated and was called, disparagingly, 'The Monaghan Boy' by the literati of the day in Dublin. He overindulged and felt empty and as if he had betrayed what was good and special about himself. This is why the poem begins with its tired, jaded phrase, recognising, almost as if at an AA meeting, the real truth, 'We have tested too much, lover'. He needed to go back to go forward. He needed to recapture the innocent eye of childhood, 'the luxury/Of a child's soul', so the he could experience the world without asking for 'reason's payment'. He wants to be moved, 'spirit-shocking', 'astonished'. He doesn't want to know things and be aware, 'knowledge and the knowing hour'. He looks forward to a rebirth, just as the people of his time purified themselves so that they were worthy to receive the sacraments on Christmas Day. The enjambment adds to the air of excitement in this process of renewal. The shining simplicity of the last line, 'And Christ comes with a January flower', with its use of the present tense, suggests that Kavanagh has realised this rebirth, from the cynical excesses of the pleasures of the flesh and the intellect, to the more mysterious gifts of the imagination and creative impulse. The use of the first person plural 'We' and the phrase 'You and I' include the reader in this journey towards rebirth, and the genius of Kavanagh allows us to see what he saw, the 'dreeping' hedges, and hear what he heard, 'whispered arguments of churning'. This enables us to share in this rebirth and renewal.

• Leaving Certificate English •

Patrick Kavanagh

EXAMINER'S COMMENT

This answer has responded in a clear way to the task of exploring what renewal meant for the poet. The answer focused less on why this was important to Kavanagh. There were also some misquotes. Overall, a solid B grade performance.

CLASS/HOMEWORK EXERCISES

1. What connection exists in Kavanagh's mind between penance, innocence, wonder and happiness? Refer to the text in your answer.
2. Copy the table below into your own notes and fill in critical comments about the last two quotations.

Key Quotes

Through a chink too wide there comes in no wonder	Kavanagh's metaphor suggests that when everything is displayed, there is no mystery and thus no interest.
And the newness that was in every stale thing/When we looked at it as children	The poet wishes to capture the experience of looking at the world with the innocent eyes of a child who appreciates the world's wonders.
Wherever life pours ordinary plenty	This is Kavanagh's poetic manifesto.
And please/God we shall not ask for reason's payment	
And Christ comes with a January flower	

• Poetry Focus •

A Christmas Childhood

Patrick Kavanagh

I

One side of the potato-pits was white with frost—
How wonderful that was, how wonderful!
And when we put our ears to the paling-post
The music that came out was magical.

The light between the ricks of hay and straw   5
Was a hole in Heaven's gable. An apple tree
With its December-glinting fruit we saw—
O you, Eve, were the world that tempted me

To eat the knowledge that grew in clay
And death the germ within it! Now and then   10
I can remember something of the gay
Garden that was childhood's. Again

The tracks of cattle to a drinking-place,
A green stone lying sideways in a ditch
Or any common sight the transfigured face   15
Of a beauty that the world did not touch.

II

My father played the melodeon
Outside at our gate;
There were stars in the morning east
And they danced to his music.   20

Across the wild bogs his melodeon called
To Lennons and Callans.
As I pulled on my trousers in a hurry
I knew some strange thing had happened.

Outside in the cow-house my mother   25
Made the music of milking;
The light of her stable-lamp was a star
And the frost of Bethlehem made it twinkle.

A water-hen screeched in the bog,
Mass-going feet 30
Crunched the wafer-ice on the pot-holes,
Somebody wistfully twisted the bellows wheel.

My child poet picked out the letters
On the grey stone,
In silver the wonder of a Christmas townland, 35
The winking glitter of a frosty dawn.

Cassiopeia was over
Cassidy's hanging hill,
I looked and three whin bushes rode across
The horizon—the Three Wise Kings. 40

An old man passing said:
'Can't he make it talk'—
The melodeon. I hid in the doorway
And tightened the belt of my box-pleated coat.

I nicked six nicks on the door-post 45
With my penknife's big blade—
There was a little one for cutting tobacco.
And I was six Christmases of age.

My father played the melodeon,
My mother milked the cows, 50
And I had a prayer like a white rose pinned
On the Virgin Mary's blouse.

'the wonder of a Christmas townland'

> **GLOSSARY**
>
> 3 *paling-post*: wooden support for wire fence.
> 5 *ricks*: large stacks of hay or straw.
> 6 *Heaven's gable*: a gable is the side wall of a house. As a child, Kavanagh imagined a bright part of the sky as a lit window in heaven's gable.
> 8–9 *O you ... knowledge*: in the Bible account of the Garden of Eden, Eve tasted the forbidden fruit and then gave it to Adam. For disobeying God, they lost their innocence and were banished from paradise.
> 15 *transfigured*: glorified; spellbound.
> 17 *melodeon*: small accordion.
> 30 *Mass-going feet*: the sound of the poet's Catholic neighbours on their way to mass.
> 32 *wistfully*: quietly and sadly.
> 32 *bellows wheel*: used to keep traditional turf and coal fires alight.
> 37 *Cassiopeia*: 'W'-shaped group of stars.

EXPLORATIONS

1 To what extent is 'A Christmas Childhood' a religious poem? Refer to the text in your answer.

2 Select any two images from the poem that you find particularly interesting. Briefly explain your choice in each case.

3 From your reading of the poem, what evidence can you find in Kavanagh's childhood that suggests he would become a poet in later life?

STUDY NOTES

> **Originally published as two separate poems, 'A Christmas Childhood' recreates Kavanagh's memories of a magical occasion when he was six years old. While he celebrates the intense feelings he had as a child for his parents, nature and his Christian faith, the poet is also aware of the passing of time and the loss of innocence.**

Part 1 opens with a vivid image from Kavanagh's childhood: 'One side of the potato-pits was white with frost'. This enduring memory is followed immediately by the adult poet's **nostalgic reflection**: 'How wonderful that was, how wonderful!' This pattern of commenting on early experiences continues throughout the poem. The mysterious beauty of nature is central to Kavanagh's time as a child on the family farm and his most enduring memories are of colours, light and music.

For the innocent six-year-old boy, reverberating sounds from the wires between paling-posts created 'magical' music. A gap of sky between the high hay ricks became 'a hole in Heaven's gable'. He imagined an ordinary apple tree as the Tree of Knowledge which led to Adam and Eve's original sin and their expulsion from the Garden of Eden. The adult voice that dominates lines 9–16 is filled with **regret at the loss of innocence**. He seems to resent adulthood, contrasting it with the 'Garden that was childhood's'. Part I ends with two 'common' recollections – the 'tracks of cattle' and a 'green stone lying sideways in a ditch' – both fixed in his memory as timeless images of 'a beauty that the world did not touch'.

Kavanagh's adult voice is almost entirely absent from Part II of the poem. Instead, we experience the excitement of Christmas through the child's eyes: 'I knew some strange thing had happened'. In particular, **he recalls people and music**, often together: 'My father played the melodeon', 'my mother/Made the music of milking'. Simple language and vivid images convey a clear sense of eager anticipation. Kavanagh remembers that even the stars in the sky 'danced'. The special atmosphere of the festive occasion affected every family ('Lennons and Callans') in the close-knit parish.

Religious imagery becomes increasingly prominent as the young narrator makes connections between his own Christmas in Co. Monaghan and Christ's nativity. The lamp in the farm outhouse becomes 'a star/And the frost of Bethlehem made it twinkle'. The **rich onomatopoeia** in lines 29–32 is characteristic of Kavanagh's musical effects. Carefully chosen verbs, such as 'screeched' and 'Crunched', are especially evocative. The gentle sibilance of 'Somebody wistfully twisted the bellows wheel' gives us a quiet sense of Irish country life a century ago.

The final stanzas continue to dramatise 'the wonder of a Christmas townland'. In retrospect, the poet recognises the first indications of his poetic imagination, his 'child poet', picking out the shapes of letters on frosted stones. **The mystery of creation always absorbed Kavanagh** and he can never forget the fascination of the night sky in winter: 'Cassiopeia was over/Cassidy's hanging hill'.

The poem concludes with a remarkable self-portrait of a wide-eyed child, 'six Christmases of age', a young boy who is intensely aware of the sensation of each moment of being alive. We see him gazing out at the great big world ('I hid in the doorway') as he tests his new penknife: 'I nicked six nicks on the door-post'. The colloquial language and flowing rhythm of lines 45–48 echo the child's newfound sense of his place in life. The last stanza provides an impressive overview of **the poet's closeness to his family**, especially his mother: 'And I had a prayer like a white rose pinned/On the Virgin Mary's blouse'. The clarity and simplicity of the image (white roses are rare and very beautiful), together with the poet's reverential tone, leave us with a memorable sense of Kavanagh's tender feelings.

ANALYSIS

It has been said that Kavanagh's poetry has been primarily concerned with a sense of loss. To what extent is this true of 'A Christmas Childhood'?

SAMPLE PARAGRAPH

I would agree that feelings of loss and regret are central to many of the Kavanagh poems I have studied. The title of 'A Christmas Childhood' is itself nostalgic. The life of the grown-up poet has been shaped by his vivid youthful experiences in Inniskeen. He always seems to be yearning for a return to those happy times, the innocent experiences of what he calls 'the gay garden of childhood'. Growing up in the remote countryside in 1910, Kavanagh's life was very simple, dominated by his Catholic religion. It is clear from the poem that he was an inquisitive child, lively and full of wonder. This is what he misses most – the innocence he experienced. The poem is filled with ordinary memories which were once great mysteries to him – the strange look of frosty potato-pits, the unexplained 'music' from the paling-posts and images of the first Christmas story which he imagined around the farm, such as the three whin bushes (the 'Wise Kings'). The whole poem is written in a nostalgic and wistful tone, suggesting deep loss. His parents play a key role in the flashbacks. He has fond memories of his father and mother, and he associates them both with music – 'My father was playing the melodeon', 'my mother made the music of milking'. He compares his mother to Christ's mother at the end of the poem in a moving metaphor which shows his love and loss – 'I had a prayer like a white rose on the Virgin Mary's blouse'. This poignant conclusion suggests yearning for an earlier innocent time.

EXAMINER'S COMMENT

Reveals a reasonably good understanding of the poem. Quotations are slightly inaccurate, but help to support key points well. A little more analysis of the poet's tone would have improved the answer. Grade B.

CLASS/HOMEWORK EXERCISES

1. What similarities and/or differences can you find between the two sections of the poem? Refer to both theme and style of writing in your answer.
2. Copy the table below into your own notes and fill in critical comments about the last two quotations.

Key Quotes

And death the germ within it	The poet compares his adulthood to Adam and Eve's fall from grace. For him, it is the death of innocence.
I looked and three whin bushes rode across / The horizon—the Three Wise Kings	Kavanagh associates sights and sounds from childhood with the story of Christ's birth, as seen in the vivid personification.
An old man passing said:/ 'Can't he make it talk'	The poem celebrates traditional rural culture and colloquial language.
My child poet picked out the letters/ On the grey stone	
And I had a prayer like a white rose pinned/ On the Virgin Mary's blouse	

• Poetry Focus •

Patrick Kavanagh

Epic

I have lived in important places, times
When great events were decided who owned
That half a rood of rock, a no-man's land
Surrounded by our pitchfork-armed claims.
I heard the Duffys shouting 'Damn your soul'　　　5
And old McCabe stripped to the waist, seen
Step the plot defying blue cast-steel—
'Here is the march along these iron stones'
That was the year of the Munich bother. Which
Was more important? I inclined　　　10
To lose my faith in Ballyrush and Gortin
Till Homer's ghost came whispering to my mind
He said: I made the *Iliad* from such
A local row. Gods make their own importance.

'I made the Iliad from such / A local row.'

GLOSSARY

Epic: (noun) long poem about heroic events; (adj) ambitious; impressive.

3 *half a rood*: small portion of land – a rood is a quarter of an acre.

7 *Step the plot*: traditional method of measuring the land by walking it.

8 *march*: boundary.

9 *Munich bother*: the poet's wry description of a crisis just before the outbreak of World War Two.

10 *most important*: Kavanagh is hesitating between the importance of the local or international row.

11 *Ballyrush and Gortin*: townlands near Inniskeen, Co. Monaghan.

12 *Homer*: Greek epic poet who wrote the *Iliad* about a dispute between the Greeks and the Trojans which led to the long, bloody Trojan Wars.

• Leaving Certificate English •

EXPLORATIONS

1 At first the reader is not sure whether the poet is making a sarcastic joke about the local row. What phrases indicate that he is serious?
2 Do you think the title of the poem is misleading or mischievous? What leads you to that opinion?
3 How effective do you think the reference to Homer at the end of the poem is? What importance did Homer have for the poet? Refer to the text in your answer.

STUDY NOTES

This poem was written about a local row. Kavanagh's brother, Peter, recalls 'the row over half-a-rood of rock in 1938'. This poem was set before the poet made the decision to move to Dublin, and just before the outbreak of the Second World War. Kavanagh believed in the importance of the local.

Epic poetry is usually very long, telling of great heroic exploits over a vast area and involving thousands of people. This small sonnet opens on a grand, authoritative scale, declaring that the poet had 'lived in important places' (**line 1**) and had been witness to great decisions. **Wryly humorous**, the poet then describes a local row between two Irish farmers over an eighth of an acre of stony ground. Yet all the fire and passion of a real conflict is there, as McCabe defiantly steps out the land, shouting, 'Here is the march'.

The use of real names for the people and the places adds **a sense of immediacy and authenticity** to this event. They almost take on a magical significance. The quoted outbursts, such as 'Damn your soul' (**line 5**), add drama and excitement as we feel that we are really hearing the bitterness and passion overflow in this parochial quarrel. However, the use of the phrases 'no-man's land' and 'armed claims' broaden the scope of the poem, showing it to be a microcosm of what is being played out on an international scale ('the Munich bother'). This careless, casual remark referring to the row over international boundaries which led to the Second World War also leads to the central question of the sonnet: 'Which/Was more important?' The poet begins to hesitate, and the assured tone of the opening starts to waver ('I inclined/To lose my faith') in the importance of the local row at a time of international crisis.

Suddenly, the ghost of Homer appears to reassure the poet that great works such as the *Iliad* were made from 'such/A local row'. The onomatopoeia of the word 'whispering' suggest a hidden secret being passed between two poets. The poet regains his former confidence and realises that **it is the poet who decides on the significance of the event**: 'Gods make their own importance' **(line 14)**. The use of the run-on lines in this poem shows the literal spilling over of boundaries and also cleverly hides the normal rhyme of the sonnet form. In times of war, all boundaries fluctuate.

ANALYSIS

The poet Michael Longley has declared that Patrick Kavanagh is a 'mythologist of the ordinary'. How does Kavanagh bind together the ordinary and myth in this poem? How effective is it? Support your discussion with reference to and quotation from the poem.

SAMPLE PARAGRAPH

Kavanagh takes an ordinary local row and explores it in such a way that the parochial becomes universal. The use of the title 'Epic', which normally refers to a very long poem, often a thousand lines, to a short fourteen-line sonnet is evidence of this. The poem begins in a self-important way as the speaker announces that he has 'lived in important places' and also at times when 'great events were decided'. So the reader assumes that the speaker is someone who has travelled widely and knows about world affairs at close hand. The immediacy of the scene is captured by the use of real names of people, 'Duffys' and 'McCabe', and places, 'Ballyrush and Gortin'. The dialogue also adds to this real feeling. However, we are then brought into an international context with the carelessly tossed phrase 'the Munich bother', referring to events which led to the outbreak of war. He wonders is the local or the international row more important? Both were about boundaries. He hesitates about the local issue: 'I inclined/To lose my faith' until he receives assurances from Homer, the Greek poet, who whispers that he had composed his great epic work, the *Iliad*, from 'such/A local row'. Kavanagh's confidence is restored in the right of the poet to determine the great value of an event. 'Gods make their own importance.' In this way, the ordinary and the mythic are interwoven to state the justification Kavanagh had in his own ability to mythologise the parochial, to see the extraordinary in the ordinary.

EXAMINER'S COMMENT

The weaving together of the ordinary and the mythic are ably examined in this response. A little more attention might have been given to the 'effective' element of the question. Overall, a very good, solid performance underpinned by succinct quotations and impressive expression. Grade A.

CLASS/HOMEWORK EXERCISES

1. In your opinion, is the mood of this poem confident and assertive, or hesitant and diffident? Refer closely to the text in your response.
2. Copy the table below into your own notes and fill in critical comments about the last two quotations.

Key Quotes

a no-man's land/Surrounded by our pitchfork-armed claims	A reference to a contested area of land between two opposing forces.
That was the year of the Munich bother	Kavanagh casually refers to one of the leading events of the outbreak of the Second World War in a throw-away line, rather like the use of the term 'the Troubles' to refer to the conflict in Northern Ireland.
Which/Was more important?	The poet hesitates about deciding which event was of greatest significance. The rhetorical question involves the reader.
Homer's ghost came whispering to my mind	
Gods make their own importance	

• Poetry Focus •

Canal Bank Walk

Patrick Kavanagh

Leafy-with-love banks and the green waters of the canal
Pouring redemption for me, that I do
The will of God, wallow in the habitual, the banal,
Grow with nature again as before I grew.
The bright stick trapped, the breeze adding a third   5
Party to the couple kissing on an old seat,
And a bird gathering materials for the nest for the Word,
Eloquently new and abandoned to its delirious beat.
O unworn world enrapture me, encapture me in a web
Of fabulous grass and eternal voices by a beech,   10
Feed the gaping need of my senses, give me ad lib
To pray unselfconsciously with overflowing speech
For this soul needs to be honoured with a new dress woven
From green and blue things and arguments that cannot be proven.

'Leafy-with-love banks and the green waters'

GLOSSSARY

1 *the canal*: the Grand Canal, Dublin.
2 *Pouring redemption*: the poet feels cleansed and renewed, like a baptised child.
3 *wallow*: relish; surrender to.
3 *the banal*: everyday or mundane things.
4 *Grow with nature again*: after recovering from ill health, the poet feels reborn.
7 *the Word*: biblical reference to the will of God, the Creator.
11 *ad lib*: innocence; spontaneity.
13 *a new dress*: freshness; simplicity.
14 *green and blue things*: nature; earth, sky and water.
14 *arguments*: beliefs; religious faith.

EXPLORATIONS

1. In your own words, explain what you understand by the 'redemption' Kavanagh mentions in line 2.
2. Select one image from the poem that you found particularly interesting and effective. Justify your choice.
3. Comment on the effectiveness of the poet's use of verbs in the sestet.

STUDY NOTES

> This sonnet was written in the mid-1950s after Kavanagh had been seriously ill. He spent much of his time convalescing by the banks of Dublin's Grand Canal. It was a time of spiritual and poetic renewal for the poet and he began to celebrate all the wonders of creation. As he wrote in his *Self-Portrait* (1964), 'as a poet, I was born in or about 1955, the place of my birth being the banks of the Grand Canal'. He added that this period of time marked a return to the simplicity of his earliest poems.

The poem begins on an enthusiastic note: 'Leafy-with-love'. This innovative phrase has a vivid, childlike quality that sets the upbeat mood of the sonnet. Throughout the first **quatrain, Kavanagh finds a sense of redemption** in 'the green waters of the canal' and feels inspired to do the 'will of God'. Water is used in both a literal and metaphorical way. It is free and fast-flowing, but it also purifies the poet's soul and restores his spirit, like the sacramental water of baptism. Along with the present tense, the energetic pace and run-through lines (enjambment) work to produce an exuberant atmosphere. The poet is eager to share his desire to 'wallow' in the canal's miraculous surroundings so that he can 'Grow with nature again'. Sensing that he has been given a second chance at life, he is determined to appreciate every moment.

The **second quatrain** focuses even more closely on Kavanagh's immediate environment and illustrates **the poet's observational skill**. Everything around him takes on an astonishing freshness, almost as though he is conscious of the world for the first time: 'Eloquently new and abandoned to its delirious beat'. He seems spellbound by the most common sights in nature (the 'bright stick') and in human nature ('the couple kissing'). His avid mood is explained by the crucial reference to divine creation: 'the Word'. Like other 'nature poets', Kavanagh intuitively recognises God's presence in the natural world. This is adroitly expressed in the invigorating image of the small bird in its element, 'gathering materials for the nest'.

Patrick Kavanagh

The **sestet** is more obviously reverential in tone: 'O unworn world enrapture me, encapture me'. The emphasis comes from a combination of the exclamatory 'O', internal rhyme and repetition. Urgent verbs add further intensity to the **sincerity of feeling** in **lines 9–14**. The poet is anxious to retain his heightened awareness of nature, with its 'fabulous grass and eternal voices by a beech'. But he has another hope – that he can 'pray unselfconsciously', using language in the same simple way as the overflowing canal water.

The sonnet ends confidently. **Lines 13–14** are extended, the rhythm relaxed and leisurely. In imagining his own rebirth, Kavanagh returns to the earlier baptism image: 'this soul needs to be honoured with a new dress'. In his case, the baptismal clothes will be made 'From green and blue things and arguments that cannot be proven'. The language has a refreshing quality that echoes his rediscovered passion for life. He is finally conte**nt to accept the mysteries of nature and God's will** without question. From now on, Kavanagh's poetry will celebrate the beauty and wonder of creation through innocent eyes.

ANALYSIS

To what extent do you agree that 'Canal Bank Walk' celebrates ordinary life through the use of everyday language? Refer to the poem in your response.

SAMPLE PARAGRAPH

To some extent this is a very true statement. Patrick Kavanagh had just come out of hospital after a very serious operation. He then started to see life as extremely precious, something to live one day at a time. To him, it was really like a religious experience. The language he uses is very simple especially when he is talking about the colours and sounds of the canal water. Colour images are very important in his description e.g. 'green waters of the canal'. He also uses ordinary childish expressions e.g. 'leafy-with-love' and 'green and blue things'. The kind of simple language a young child would come out with. I think his language is like Wordsworth's. He also becomes very aware of God as the Creator of all the world. Kavanagh describes everyday objects and then finds the ordinary to be extraordinary e.g. the 'bright stick'. An old stick lying along the canal bank is not exactly a thing of beauty, but it is to Kavanagh. Everything in the universe is mystical, part of God's work. Not all of his language is colloquial e.g. 'enrapture me' but many of his descriptions e.g. the 'couple kissing' are very ordinary and add realism to the poem.

EXAMINER'S COMMENT

Some reasonable attempts at examining the poet's use of language are made. The expression was flawed in places – both 'very' and 'e.g.' are overused. Some analysis of rhythm or sound would have improved the answer. An average C grade.

CLASS/HOMEWORK EXERCISES

1. Comment on Kavanagh's use of imagery, rhythm and sound in 'Canal Bank Walk'. Refer closely to the text in your answer.
2. Copy the table below into your own notes and fill in critical comments about the last two quotations.

Key Quotes

Pouring redemption for me	The phrase suggests the movement of the canal water, but also refers to Kavanagh's own spiritual renewal, similar to baptism.
abandoned to its delirious beat	The poet felt liberated and at one with nature, and sensed that his own soul became part of the universal spirit.
enrapture me, encapture me	Kavanagh uses hyperbole (exaggerated statements) to express his feelings. Rhyme and repetition also add intensity.
wallow in the habitual, the banal	
arguments that cannot be proven	

• Poetry Focus •

Patrick Kavanagh

Lines Written on a Seat on the Grand Canal, Dublin

'Erected to the Memory of Mrs Dermot O'Brien'

O commemorate me where there is water,
Canal water preferably, so stilly
Greeny at the heart of summer. Brother
Commemorate me thus beautifully
Where by a lock niagarously roars   5
The falls for those who sit in the tremendous silence
Of mid-July. No one will speak in prose
Who finds his way to these Parnassian islands.
A swan goes by head low with many apologies,
Fantastic light looks through the eyes of bridges – 10
And look! a barge comes bringing from Athy
And other far-flung towns mythologies.
O commemorate me with no hero-courageous
Tomb – just a canal-bank seat for the passer-by.

'just a canal bank seat for the passer-by'

GLOSSSARY

The memorial seat to Mrs Dermot O'Brien still stands on the canal bank. After Kavanagh's death, his friends erected a canal bank seat in memory of him, as he had wished.

2–3 *stilly/Greeny*: new words made up by Kavanagh, a stylistic feature of his poetry.

5 *niagorously*: Kavanagh often invented words. This refers to the famous Niagara Falls waterfall.

8 *Parnassian*: Mount Parnassus, near Delphi in Greece, was sacred to the god Apollo and the Muses, and is seen as the source of poetry and music.

12 *mythologies*: stories of people and events that are out of the ordinary.

13 *O commemorate me*: Kavanagh wished to be remembered beside canal water.

EXPLORATIONS

1. Look at the new words in the poem that Kavanagh coined, such as 'stilly', 'Greeny', 'niagorously', 'hero-courageous'. How do they help to communicate the central message of the poem?
2. In your view, how effective is Kavanagh's image of the swan? How is it relevant to the central theme of the poem?
3. Would you consider the tone of this poem to be solemn or celebratory? Support your answer with relevant quotation.

STUDY NOTES

> This poem was written while Kavanagh was convalescing from lung cancer, contracted in 1955. The poet, in a new mood of serenity and calm, admired the idea of having a seat as a symbol of remembrance. This poem is the conclusion of his poetic journey.

Kavanagh wishes that his memory should be honoured beside the canal. The Grand Canal in Dublin was a place of contentment and acceptance of life for the poet. He believed water purified, just as it does in the sacrament of baptism, causing a rebirth so that the child may come to a state of grace. The colour green recalls the natural world. The phrase 'stilly/Greeny' seems childish and almost silly at first, but the poet wanted to **view things as he had as a child**, with wonder and amazement. He also wanted us to share this view with him. The poem is set in the 'heart of summer' (line 3). The canal bank occupies a special place in the heart of the poet. He addresses humanity as 'Brother'. The old bitterness of the early poems has gone; now he is filled with love towards his fellow man. He humorously imagines the roar of the lock on the canal in Dublin as having the force of Niagara Falls. This is typical of Kavanagh's wry use of hyperbole. The onomatopoeia of 'roars' coupled with the newly coined polysyllabic word 'niagorously' effectively communicates the powerful *whoosh* of the water through the lock gate. All this movement and noise is contrasted with the great stillness of mid-summer: 'the tremendous silence'.

This wish to be commemorated is not an act of pride, but one of generosity. He wants others to share this positive experience of rebirth, which he had the privilege of undergoing beside the canal. He feels that they, too, will be inspired: 'No one will speak in prose' (line 7). He likens the stretch of canal to Mt Parnassus, the famous Greek mountain, a source of inspiration to all those involved in the arts. This hyperbole is similar to that used in the poem 'Shancoduff', when he refers to 'my Alps'. There are wonderful simple pleasures to be experienced on the canal, such as the 'bridges', the 'swan' and the 'barge', but these simple sights are transformed by the power of the poet's creativity. 'Fantastic light' is seen spilling from the personified bridges: 'through the eyes of bridges'. We, too, can see the sharp, shooting light searing through the bridge arches. The graceful curve of the swan's neck is highlighted by the phrase 'head low with many apologies'. The simple barge incorporates the heroic deeds and strange tales of the past: 'far-flung towns mythologies' (line 12).

Yeats wrote an epitaph for himself: 'Horseman, pass by'. Kavanagh wished to distance himself from what he regarded as the self-importance of Yeats. He did not want the viewer to look at the memorial, the seat, but rather at the view from the seat. Then **the viewer could see the same stretch of water** which had 'Pour[ed] redemption' for Kavanagh. He hoped others would benefit from this, as he had done. The opening and ending of the sonnet forms what seems like the black edge of the memorial card for the dead, 'O commemorate me' (line 13). This sense of place is very important to Gaelic poets. Kavanagh is paying tribute not to a place in the past, but to one in the present on the Grand Canal of Dublin.

ANALYSIS

Kavanagh wrote of how he had come 'back to where I started'. His poetic journey ends on the canal bank. Discuss this view with reference to the poem 'Lines Written on a Seat', using references and quotations to back up your opinion.

SAMPLE PARAGRAPH

Kavanagh sat quietly in the 'tremendous silence' of 'mid-July' and let the sounds and sights of the canal bank make him feel born again. He learns to look with a wondering, child's eye at the great elements of nature. His childish phrase, 'stilly/Greeny' water, masks a deeper meaning. We must learn to look with the innocent eye of a child if we wish to be saved. He makes us hear the lock 'roar' as he uses his new word, 'niagorously'. All the power and flow of the great Niagara Falls is likened to the water gushing through the lock gate in Dublin. Here, he has regained his poetic inspiration: 'No one will speak in prose'. Why? He is able to appreciate the beauty and grace in ordinary things, such as the swan with its 'head low with many apologies'. The serenity of the swan is deftly captured with a few well-chosen words. He makes us look, as children, with wonder at the 'Fantastic light'. We are coming back to where we started off, seeing stories, 'far-flung towns mythologies', everywhere. The poetic journey for Kavanagh ends here as he invites us to study the scene before us from the vantage view of a seat commemorating his memory.

EXAMINER'S COMMENT
A very well-expressed response which focuses clearly on the assigned task to discuss the poetic journey of Kavanagh. Short quotations are used effectively. Clear and to the point throughout. Grade A.

CLASS/HOMEWORK EXERCISES
1. Kavanagh felt one should not take oneself too 'sickly seriously', so he uses 'outrageous rhyming' such as 'bridges' and 'courageous'. Comment on Kavanagh's use of unusual words elsewhere in this sonnet, considering whether they contribute to or detract from the poem.
2. Copy the table below into your own notes and fill in critical comments about the last two quotations.

Key Quotes

O commemorate me where there is water	Kavanagh's simple wish for remembrance.
Where by a lock niagorously roars/The falls	The poet uses hyperbole to suggest the importance of the locks to him.
No one will speak in prose	He is enthusiastic about nature. After these wonderful experiences, everyone will be inspired.
Fantastic light looks through the eyes of bridges	
just a canal bank seat for the passer-by	

• Poetry Focus •

The Hospital

Patrick Kavanagh

A year ago I fell in love with the functional ward
Of a chest hospital: square cubicles in a row,
Plain concrete, wash basins – an art lover's woe,
Not counting how the fellow in the next bed snored.
But nothing whatever is by love debarred,   5
The common and banal her heat can know.
The corridor led to a stairway and below
Was the inexhaustible adventure of a gravelled yard.

This is what love does to things: the Rialto Bridge,
The main gate that was bent by a heavy lorry,   10
The seat at the back of a shed that was a suntrap.
Naming these things is the love-act and its pledge;
For we must record love's mystery without claptrap,
Snatch out of time the passionate transitory.

'I fell in love with the functional ward'

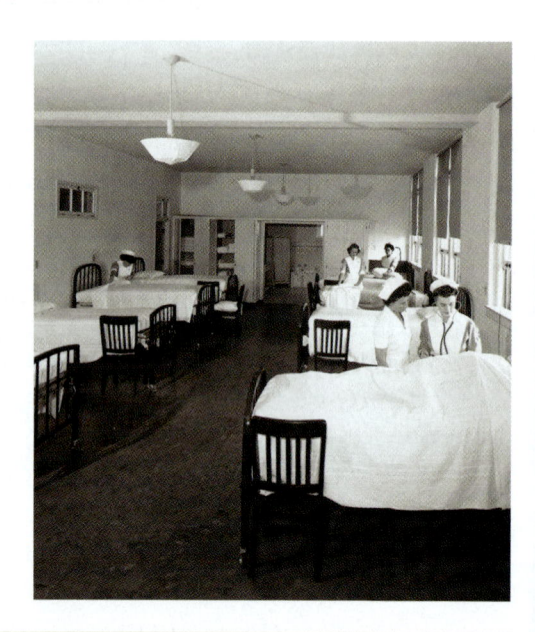

GLOSSARY

2 *a chest hospital*: the Rialto Hospital, Dublin, where Kavanagh was a patient for two months in 1955.
5 *debarred*: forbidden; excluded.
6 *banal*: common; mundane.
13 *claptrap*: foolishness; insincerity.
14 *the passionate transitory*: significant moments; deep feelings.

EXPLORATIONS

1. From your reading of the poem, what is your impression of the hospital ward that Kavanagh describes?
2. Comment on the main tone (or tones) that you can identify in the octave (lines 1–8).
3. In your opinion, what is the central message of the poem?

STUDY NOTES

'The Hospital' is an unusual love poem. Nondescript wards are unlikely objects of affection. Kavanagh wrote the sonnet in 1956 while recovering from a lengthy stay in Dublin's Rialto Hospital. His experience as a patient had a profound effect on him. He became much more positive about life and regained some of the innocent wonder of his childhood. To a large extent, the poem is about himself and his attitude to writing poetry.

Kavanagh's **opening lines** are clearly meant to surprise. He casually announces his latest romance: 'A year ago I fell in love with the functional ward/Of a chest hospital'. The picture he paints, however, could hardly be less passionate: 'Plain concrete, wash basins – an art lover's woe'. This **mock-serious posture** is also evident in his disclosure that 'the fellow in the next bed snored'.

In **lines 5–8**, the poet's true voice emerges and his earlier flippancy is replaced with a more focused tone: 'But nothing whatever is by love debarred'. Kavanagh wants us to know that love transcends all expectations and has no limits. He personifies the emotion – 'The common and banal her heat can know' – to highlight the intensity of love. What is important to Kavanagh is the experience of love as an expression of **appreciating the world in a fresh and positive way**. The seemingly unremarkable hospital itself is just one of countless wonders around him, such as 'the inexhaustible adventure of a gravelled yard'.

In the **sestet**, Kavanagh considers the far-reaching effects of love. As in the Canal Bank sonnets, he lists some of the ordinary things that would not be immediately seen as suitable subjects for love poetry – the Rialto Bridge, a damaged gate, a secluded garden seat. The poet's own beliefs are summed up in **line 12**: 'Naming these things is the love-act and its pledge'. By creating poems out of ordinary life, **Kavanagh can express his own appreciation of the world's simple wonders**. Poetry even gives them a certain immortality.

The tone of **lines 13–14**, in which Kavanagh speaks on behalf of other writers, is more forceful and didactic: 'we must record love's mystery without claptrap'. For the poet, **love is a sense of natural integration with all of creation**. In turn, love poems should be realistic and sincere, written in direct, unpretentious language ('without claptrap'). He illustrates this in the **final line**, where he recognises that because love is subject to time, love poetry (which registers such intense feelings) is all the more important. The poet's primary role, therefore, is to 'Snatch out of time the passionate transitory'.

ANALYSIS

In your view, is 'The Hospital' a love poem? Refer closely to the text of the poem in your answer.

SAMPLE PARAGRAPH

Patrick Kavanagh includes the word 'love' at least five times in 'The Hospital'. He starts off by shocking us slightly with his claim that he has fallen 'in love with the functional ward/Of a chest hospital'. We know he is just being funny in a sardonic sort of way, but it is enough to get our attention. He then makes fun of the place with its concrete walls and ugly washrooms. What soon becomes clear, though, is that it isn't the actual building he's in love with at all. He is actually in love with life itself. I know of a few people who have had life-threatening illnesses and they are transformed by it. That is why I see the poem as a love poem. Kavanagh really is aware that precious time is slipping away. So even the most ordinary and ugly things – what he calls 'common and banal' – are suddenly worthy of love. I find his tone to be sincere when he says that 'nothing whatever is by love debarred'. He now fully understands the magic of ordinary, everyday things – buildings, bridges, an old gravel yard. He talks about the 'inexhaustible adventure' of such things. As a poet, his duty is to write about commonplace subjects without any 'claptrap'. For him, this is a true 'love-act'. Kavanagh has written an interesting love poem, but his tone is passionate – especially at the end where he advises poets like himself to follow their hearts and celebrate 'love's mystery'.

EXAMINER'S COMMENT

This is a well-written, clear response that handles quotations effectively. There is some good personal engagement with the poem and the final sentence offers a succinct overview. A deserved A grade.

CLASS/HOMEWORK EXERCISES

1. Nature and human nature are central to much of Kavanagh's poetry. To what extent is this true of 'The Hospital'? Support the points you make by close reference to the poem.
2. Copy the table below into your own notes and fill in critical comments about the last two quotations.

Key Quotes

square cubicles in a row	The image of a functional ward reflects Kavanagh's ironic attitude that, depending on one's mood, it is possible to love anything.
the inexhaustible adventure of a gravelled yard	The poet develops his theme of how love can bring people into touch with the magical and the mystical.
we must record love's mystery without claptrap	By the end of the poem, Kavanagh is certain about the function of poetry. His use of the colloquial 'claptrap' emphasises his point that poetry should be unpretentious.
But nothing whatever is by love debarred	
Naming these things is the love-act and its pledge	

On Raglan Road

Patrick Kavanagh

(Air: 'The Dawning of the Day')

On Raglan Road on an autumn day I met her first and knew
That her dark hair would weave a snare that I might one day rue;
I saw the danger, yet I walked along the enchanted way,
And I said, let grief be a fallen leaf at the dawning of the day.

On Grafton Street in November we tripped lightly along the ledge   5
Of the deep ravine where can be seen the worth of passion's pledge,
The Queen of Hearts still making tarts and I not making hay —
O I loved too much and by such, by such, is happiness thrown away.

I gave her gifts of the mind, I gave her the secret sign that's known
To the artists who have known the true gods of sound and stone   10
And word and tint. I did not stint for I gave her poems to say
With her own name there and her own dark hair like clouds over fields of May.

On a quiet street where old ghosts meet I see her walking now
Away from me so hurriedly my reason must allow
That I had wooed not as I should a creature made of clay —   15
When the angel woos the clay he'd lose his wings at the dawn of day.

'On a quiet street where old ghosts meet'

GLOSSARY

	Raglan Road was a tree-lined street off Pembroke Road where Kavanagh lived for a time.
2	*snare*: trap with a noose.
2	*rue*: feel regret for.
6	*ravine*: narrow, steep-sided valley gouged out by a stream.
6	*pledge*: solemn promise.
7	*Queen of Hearts*: reference to a nursery rhyme character; also the name of a card.
10–11	*sound and stone/And word and tint*: art forms; music, sculpture, literature, painting.
11	*not stint*: was not miserly with.
14	*my reason must allow*: thinking logically.

EXPLORATIONS

1 What do you think Kavanagh's opinion of love is in the opening of 'On Raglan Road'? Support your answer with references from the poem.

2 Would you regard the poet as a proud man? Give evidence from the poem to support your view.

3 In your opinion, what is the poet's mood at the end of the poem: resigned, distraught, bitter, angry, nostalgic, etc.? Give reasons for your response, based on close reference to the text.

STUDY NOTES

This rare love poem of Kavanagh's, with its bittersweet lament for lost love, was first published on 3 October 1946 in *The Irish Press*. It was inspired by a beautiful young medical student, Hilda Moriarty. It has been recorded as a sung ballad by many artists to the tune of 'The Dawning of the Day'.

The poet's disappointment in love leads him to warn against placing trust in love and against loving too much. One of the strengths of this poem is its firm rooting of time and place, which adds to the authenticity of the experience. The action takes place on an autumn day in Dublin on Raglan Road. This is where he first saw and fell in love with a dark-haired beauty. Throughout the **first stanza**, he presents himself as naïve; he knew it was dangerous, but he continued and was willing to accept 'grief'. He seems helpless, lured by beauty and the possibility of love: 'the enchanted way'. He is resigned to the possibility of sorrow, representing it as a natural outcome, as real as a 'fallen leaf' in autumn at dawn: 'let grief be a fallen leaf at the dawning of the day'.

The **second stanza** moves to winter. The couple seem oblivious to the dangers ('tripped lightly') as they walk along Grafton Street. The assonance of the slender vowel sound 'i' and the repetition of the 'l' in 'lightly along the ledge' capture the carefree spirit of early love. However, this is a dangerous balancing act – someone could get hurt and go hurtling into 'the deep ravine' if 'passion's pledge' proves to be worthless. Is there a suggestion that this is an obsessive love, unrealistic, as it places the loved one on a pedestal? 'The Queen of Hearts' refers to the nursery rhyme and also to the card from a deck of cards. This is a successful woman who is in control of her destiny, whereas the poet, blinded by love, is not attending to his business: 'not making hay'. Kavanagh has gambled heavily on love ('O I loved too much') and lost ('and by such, by such, is happiness thrown away'). The ballad form of four-line stanzas with its regular rhyme, in this case *aabb*, is admirably suited to this simple yet universal tale of lost love. The rhythm is taken from the song 'The Dawning of the Day'. The long, winding lines captivate the reader/listener as effectively as Kavanagh was ensnared all those years before. The use of internal rhyme ('hair'/'snare', 'grief'/'leaf') comes from the old bardic tradition of Gaelic poetry.

This poem is written entirely from the poet's perspective, and in **stanza three**, Kavanagh proudly declares all the gifts he gave her: 'I gave her gifts of the mind'. He gave her something very precious, 'the secret sign', which is known only to artists, those who have been in communication with the gods of music, sculpture, literature and painting: 'the artists who have known the true gods of sound and stone'. She was allowed into this special community. The poet also says he was not mean, as he gave her poems with her name in them. The reader becomes a little uneasy as he suggests what more could she possibly want. Notice the frequent use of the first-person singular pronoun 'I'. What is this suggesting about Kavanagh's attitude? However, the sweet longing for love is beautifully captured in the image of her hair as billowing dark clouds sailing over the bright fields in early summer: 'and her own dark hair like clouds over fields in May'. The broad vowels of this line suggest the volume and cascading beauty of his beloved's hair. Suddenly, our sympathy returns to the awkward countryman hopelessly in love.

The **closing stanza** returns to the present. The relationship has ended and now Kavanagh sees her walking quickly away from him. Ruefully, he has to conclude that he did not love her as an ordinary human being, but as someone to be worshipped. He decides that she did not deserve this. He dismissively calls her 'a creature made of clay'. He adopts a much grander persona for himself, regarding himself as an angel, someone not entirely of this world. Kavanagh had a great sense of the importance of the place of the poet. He concludes the poem by saying that the poet loses his special gifts ('lose his wings') if he courts the woman in this way. Are we still sympathetic to the poet's plight at the end of the poem?

ANALYSIS

'Kavanagh takes the local and ordinary and makes it of universal significance.' Discuss this statement in relation to the poems on your course and quote in support of your opinions.

SAMPLE PARAGRAPH

Countless singers have performed this ballad, with its universal theme of lost love. The four four-line stanzas tell of a particular day and place, the 'local and the ordinary'. Here on an autumn day in 1940s Dublin on Raglan Road an awkward forty-year-old Monaghan man who had left school at thirteen saw the beautiful twenty-two-year-old medical student, Hilda Moriarty, and fell head over heels in love. The spell of female beauty is evocatively captured in the phrase 'her dark hair would weave a snare'. Yet the love-struck poet walks willingly to his destiny: 'I saw the danger, yet I walked along the enchanted way'. What person has not fallen for someone totally out of their reach, yet with the blindness of love, foolishly continued the pursuit? The carefree joy of early love is suggested by the assonance of the slender vowels 'tripped lightly' as the pair went along Grafton Street. But the danger is always there, the 'deep ravine'. It is possible to fall in love and end up being very hurt. The gamble of love is shown in the naming of the girl as 'The Queen of Hearts'. All lovers give their beloveds beautiful gifts, and Kavanagh is no exception: 'I gave her gifts of the mind'. The last line of this third stanza is, to my mind, one of the most beautiful as he recalls that he 'gave her poems to say/With her own name there and her own dark hair like clouds over fields of May'. The internal rhyme 'there'/'hair', reminiscent of old Gaelic poetry, makes the line soar, as his heart must have soared as he became entangled in Hilda's clouds of dark black hair. Sadly, they drifted apart, and who has not met a former love who is only too anxious to hurry away, 'walking now/Away from me'? The nostalgic tone of lost love echoes from 'On a quiet street where old ghosts meet'. I think this ballad is timeless. Its content with its warning against loving too much, 'O I loved too much', reminds me of Yeats's poem 'The Sally Gardens' as 'she bid me take love easy'. The imagery makes us nod ruefully as we recognise the universal experience of lost love, which is unfortunately as natural a process as 'a fallen leaf' on an autumn morning.

• Poetry Focus •

Patrick Kavanagh

EXAMINER'S COMMENT

This detailed response shows a real engagement with the poem as the answer traces how the local is made universal by the poet's skill. The style and control of the answer merits an A grade.

CLASS/HOMEWORK EXERCISES

1. 'Kavanagh's poetry is pervaded by a deep sense of loss.' Do you agree or disagree with this statement? Support the points you make with reference to the text.
2. Copy the table below into your own notes and fill in critical comments about the last two quotations.

Key Quotes

That her dark hair would weave a snare that I might one day rue	The poet is aware that this relationship could end in tears for him.
And I said, let grief be a fallen leaf at the dawning of the day	Kavanagh is resigned to the possibility that this relationship may not work out, but he is willing to risk it.
the deep ravine where can be seen the worth of passion's pledge	A promise made when in love becomes worthless when the relationship is ended. The alliterative 'p' emphasises the passion.
I gave her the secret sign	
When the angel woos the clay he'd lose his wings at the dawn of day	

LEAVING CERT SAMPLE ESSAY

Q Imagine you were asked to select one or more of Patrick Kavanagh's poems from your course for inclusion in a short anthology entitled *The Essential Kavanagh*. Give reasons for your choice, quoting from or referring to the poem or poems you have chosen.

MARKING SCHEME GUIDELINES

Expect the focus of the answer to be on the reason(s) given for including the poem(s) in the anthology. Evidence of genuine engagement with the poetry should be rewarded.

The range of reasons offered might include the following:
- Early poems provide an insight into rural Irish life.
- Poems celebrate the ordinary, familiar world.
- They reveal an ironic affection for the local surroundings.
- Engaging mood/atmosphere of the poems.
- Distinctive patterns of language and imagery, etc.

SAMPLE ESSAY (The Essential Kavanagh)

1 Kavanagh protrays Irish rural life in 'Inniskeen Road', and the feelings of both belonging and isolation resonate from this sonnet. We all know the tremendous pleasure of a shared joke among friends, so vividly captured by the poet in the phrase 'the wink-and-elbow language of delight', which describes the young people as they go to the local dance. For someone who is not a part of this scene, it is 'the half-talk code of mysteries' as he, like Kavanagh, is not part of the group. When a person is alone, the world seems made up of couples and groups, 'The bicycles go by in twos and threes'. The poet is the outsider, the observer, he is left alone at half-past eight 'Upon a mile of road, no shadow thrown'. A silent stone is transformed by the onomatopoeia in the line 'A footfall tapping out secrecies of stone'. He is in splendid isolation, because he has chosen to be a poet, regarded then by the locals as something strange. He rules over 'banks and stones', alone. In the sestet, he lets us know the price he has paid for his proffesion, 'hates, 'plight'.

2 In 'Advent', the modern reader is brought back to the weeks before Christmas, the season of Advent, when it was customary for Catholics to fast. Now people sometimes abstain from drink, before they overindulge at Christmas. This sense of excess is captured by Kavanagh as he uses the alliteration of 't' in 'We have tasted too much'. He wrote this poem about his experiances in Dublin. He suggests the atmosphere of a dull, November evening, 'Advent darkened room', as the shorter days pass. Two details suggest a time of penance, 'dry black bread and sugarless tea'. He wants to return to innocence, 'the luxury of a child's soul', so that he could experiance 'the newness that was in every stale thing'. Kavanagh then recreates for us what it is like to look at the world through the unspoiled eyes of a child, 'spirit-shocking, black slanting Ulster hill'. I can relate to Kavanagh contemplating 'bog-holes, cart-tracks,' suddenly realising that Time as we measure it (AD) began with the birth of Christ in an old stable. Again we are shown the extraordinary in the ordinary.

3 In the last section of the poem he shows, through the use of onomatopoeia, how to look at life, 'the whispered arguement of a churning'. The soft slapping sound the milk makes as it is being made into butter is there for us to hear. Just experiance it, Kavanagh is telling us, don't 'analyse God's breath'. Leave aside knowledge, he tells us, 'the conscious hour', and then you won't have to go 'searching', as 'Christ comes with a January flower'. Nowadays we read of people finding themselves, and they explore lots of different ways of living. Kavanagh is telling us to be still and look around us. It is all there. 'Won't we be rich'? We miss it because we are too busy with our 'clay-minted wage'. Kavanagh places it in front of us as he shows us the 'heart-breaking strangeness in dreeping hedges'.

4 In 1955 Kavanagh contracted cancer. He beat the illness and emerged with a new outlook on life. The poem 'Canal Bank Walk' reflects this new serenity. The word 'Leafy-with-love' captures the goodness of nature. He feels saved as he sits on the canal bank, recuperating. He feels the joy of nature, and the green water of the canal 'pouring redemption'. He has got what he wished for in the previous poem, he is enjoying the simple things, 'a bright stick trapped'. He prays eloquently, 'enrapture me'. We are given stunning visions of ordinary things, 'fabulous grass'. I can imagine lying in the long grass as it stretches, green against the blue sky. He longs for spontaineity 'give me ad lib', not to be reasoning. Instead he will honour his soul with 'green and blue things'. His spiritual side will be fed from the abundance of nature.

5 *Kavanagh makes up words, if he feels there is not one to fit what he wishes to describe. 'niagorously' in 'Lines Written' refers to the water which spills from the lock of the Grand Canal, as if it were the great waterfall, Niagora Falls. The word gives us a hint of the dry humour of the poet, that this little lock gate is thundering, 'roars', like the famous waterfall. This is similar to 'Epic', where he likens a dispute between two farmers to Homer's poem, the Iliad, 'I made the Iliad from such a local row', he has Homer's ghost telling him. I think he wants us to realise that we have the wonders of the whole world spread out in front of us if we just sit and observe. 'A barge comes bringing from Athy'. Kavanagh is not as he described himself, 'a proud one', but one who understood the importance of idleness, the things that really matter are insignificant little things. Today he has got his wish, 'O commemorate me where there is water', and a canal seat adorns the side of the Grand Canal in Dublin, with a seated figure of Kavanagh, inviting us to leave the busy, weary world a while, and sit and be still, so that we can 'Feed the gaping need' of our senses. This to me is the 'Essential Kavanagh'.*

(approx. 900 words)

SPELLCHECKER
- portrays
- profession
- experience
- argument
- spontaneity

GRADE: A2
P   = 15/15
C   = 13/15
L   = 11/15
M   = 4/5
Total = 43/50

EXAMINER'S COMMENT

This is a very personal and well-sustained response to the exploration of the essential Kavanagh. References are used succinctly, and a genuine awareness of the poet and his work is communicated throughout. Some spelling errors and inaccurate quotations were penalised.

• Poetry Focus •

Patrick Kavanagh

SAMPLE LEAVING CERT QUESTIONS ON KAVANAGH'S POETRY (45–50 MINUTES)

1 'Kavanagh's poetry celebrates the local and the ordinary.' To what extent do you agree with this view? Support the points you make by quotation from or reference to the poems by Kavanagh on your course.

2 'An autobiography in poetry form.'
Write a response to the view that the poetry of Patrick Kavanagh reflects the highs and lows of his life. Support the points you make with the aid of suitable reference to the poems you have studied.

3 'Kavanagh's poetry has continuing relevance for the modern reader.' Discuss this statement, supporting your points with reference to the poems by Kavanagh on your course.

SAMPLE ESSAY PLAN (Q2)

2 **'An autobiography in poetry form.'**

Write a response to the view that the poetry of Patrick Kavanagh reflects the highs and lows of his life. Support the points you make with the aid of suitable reference to the poems you have studied.

- *Intro:* Kavanagh's poetry is a journey from Monaghan to the banks of the Grand Canal, a journey of discovery and exploration, filled with highs and lows.
- *Point 1:* 'Inniskeen Road' and 'Shancoduff' – early years in Inniskeen, rural setting and farming, love–hate relationship with the land.
- *Point 2:* 'Advent' – early Dublin years, 'the worst mistake of my life', loss of childlike wonder, realisation of the need for a spiritual dimension to his life.
- *Point 3:* 'Canal Bank Walk' – love poem to a place, rebirth after illness.
- *Point 4:* 'On Raglan Road' – bittersweet love poem of unrequited love, poet's belief in himself.
- *Point 5:* 'Lines Written' – gratitude to God, lack of ego.
- *Point 6:* Style – lyrical, rhythmic use of language, word fusion, imagery, sonnet, ballad 'the lines that speak the passionate heart'.
- *Conclusion:* Reader accompanies Kavanagh, 'that Monaghan boy', on his journey from love–hate to ecstatic appreciation of the beauty of nature, and finally to calm serenity.

EXERCISE

Develop one of the above points into a paragraph.

POINT 4 – SAMPLE PARAGRAPH

Kavanagh wrote this rare love poem, which has been made famous by the singer Luke Kelly of The Dubliners. It is a love poem tinged with regret. He describes himself as an innocent who has been unable to resist 'a snare' of 'her dark hair'. He loved not wisely, but too well. The image of the Queen of Hearts suggests a gamble, in this case an unsuccessful one. Kavanagh comes across as quite arrogant as he declared he gave her 'gifts of the mind'. He even named her in some of his poems. He decides she did not deserve his love, 'a creature made of clay'. He, on the other hand, was an 'angel' who 'lost his wings'. But although we may take this view of the poem, nevertheless it is the music in the mid-line rhyme, from Gaelic poetry, which remains echoing in our hearts: 'hair'/'snare', 'grief'/'leaf', 'woos'/'lose'. This is what leaves the lament, sung to the tune 'The Dawning of the Day', hanging in the air, while the long lines flow dreamily and sweetly as 'On Grafton Street in November we tripped lightly along the ledge/Of the deep ravine where can be seen the worth of passion's pledge'. Here, indeed, is a low point in Kavanagh's life.

EXAMINER'S COMMENT

A successful examination of a low in Kavanagh's life, when love is lost. Good use is made of quotations. One or two of the ideas could have been developed more effectively. However, there is a sensitive awareness of the musical effects used in this poem, while acknowledging the questionable attitude of the poet himself. B grade.

Last Words

'Kavanagh gave you permission to dwell without cultural anxiety among the usual landmarks of your life. He brought us back to where we came from.'
Seamus Heaney

'At his memorial seat on the Grand Canal, visitors are asked to sit with their backs to the memorial description, reading instead the scene before them.'
Antoinette Quinn

'I've often wondered if I'd be different if I had been brought up to love better things.'
Patrick Kavanagh

Adrienne Rich   (1929–)

Adrienne Rich's most recent books of poetry are *Telephone Ringing in the Labyrinth: Poems 2004–2006* and *The School Among the Ruins: 2000–2004*. A selection of her essays, *Arts of the Possible: Essays and Conversations*, appeared in 2001. She edited Muriel Rukeyser's *Selected Poems* for the Library of America. In spring 2009, Norton will publish *A Human Eye: Essays on Art in Society*. She is a recipient of the National Book Foundation's 2006 Medal for Distinguished Contribution to American Letters, among other honours. She lives in California.

• Poetry Focus •

Adrienne Rich

PRESCRIBED POEMS (HIGHER LEVEL)

1. 'Aunt Jennifer's Tigers' (p. 277)
2. 'The Uncle Speaks in the Drawing Room' (p. 279)
3. 'Power' (p. 281)
4. 'Storm Warnings' (p. 283)
5. 'Living in Sin' (p. 285)
6. 'The Roofwalker' (p. 287)
7. 'Our Whole Life' (p. 289)
8. 'Trying to Talk with a Man' (p. 291)
9. 'Diving into the Wreck' (p. 293)
10. 'From a Survivor' (p. 297)

> For copyright reasons, it has not been possible to include detailed study notes on the poetry of Adrienne Rich.

Aunt Jennifer's Tigers

Aunt Jennifer's tigers prance across a screen,
Bright topaz denizens of a world of green.
They do not fear the men beneath the tree;
They pace in sleek chivalric certainty.

Aunt Jennifer's fingers fluttering through her wool   5
Find even the ivory needle hard to pull.
The massive weight of Uncle's wedding band
Sits heavily upon Aunt Jennifer's hand.

When Aunt is dead, her terrified hands will lie
Still ringed with ordeals she was mastered by.   10
The tigers in the panel that she made
Will go on prancing, proud and unafraid.

GLOSSARY

1 *prance*: walk with exaggerated, bouncing steps.
1 *screen*: surface on which an image is formed; a movable structure used to conceal.
2 *topaz*: semi-precious stone, yellow or light blue.
2 *denizens*: inhabitants.
4 *sleek*: glossy; smooth; shiny.
4 *chivalric*: behaving in a courteous way.
6 *ivory*: hard, white bony substance that forms the tusks of elephants.
10 *ordeals*: painful or difficult experiences.

EXPLORATIONS

1 What aspects of Aunt Jennifer's character are revealed by Adrienne Rich's use of verbs in the poem?
2 This poem illustrates the power of a symbol. Comment on Rich's choice of symbols.
3 Do you regard the ending of the poem as positive or negative? Explain your answer with reference to the text.
4 'Rich challenges us with her ideas on relationships.' To what extent is this true in 'Aunt Jennifer's Tigers'?
5 Write your own personal response to the poem.

• Poetry Focus •

Adrienne Rich

CLASS/HOMEWORK EXERCISE

1 Copy the table below into your own notes and fill in critical comments about the quotations.

Key Quotes	
Aunt Jennifer's tigers prance across a screen	
They pace in sleek chivalric certainty	
The massive weight of Uncle's wedding band	
her terrified hands will lie/Still ringed with ordeals	
prancing, proud and unafraid	

The Uncle Speaks in the Drawing Room

I have seen the mob of late
Standing sullen in the square,
Gazing with a sullen stare
At window, balcony, and gate.
Some have talked in bitter tones, 5
Some have held and fingered stones.

These are follies that subside.
Let us consider, none the less,
Certain frailties of glass
Which, it cannot be denied, 10
Lead in times like these to fear
For crystal vase and chandelier.

Not that missiles will be cast;
None as yet dare lift an arm.
But the scene recalls a storm 15
When our grandsire stood aghast
To see his antique ruby bowl
Shivered in a thunder-roll.

Let us only bear in mind
How these treasures handed down 20
From a calmer age passed on
Are in the keeping of our kind.
We stand between the dead glass-blowers
And murmurings of missile-throwers.

Adrienne Rich

GLOSSARY

Drawing Room: room where visitors are entertained.
1 *mob*: disorderly crowd.
2 *sullen*: unwilling to talk.
7 *follies*: foolish actions or ideas.
9 *frailties*: physical flaws or moral weaknesses.
12 *crystal*: clear and brilliant glass.
13 *missiles*: objects or weapons thrown or launched at a target.
16 *grandsire*: an old-fashioned word for grandfather.
16 *aghast*: overcome with amazement or horror.
17 *ruby bowl*: deep red glass bowl.
22 *in the keeping of our kind*: in the care and charge of people like us.
23 *glass-blowers*: people who make glass objects by shaping molten glass.

Adrienne Rich

EXPLORATIONS

1. The voice in the poem belongs to the uncle. What type of man do you think he is? Consider what he says and how he speaks.
2. Choose two symbols or metaphors that are used in this poem and explain what you think each represents.
3. Do you think the formal structure of the poem suits its subject matter? Look at the layout, rhyme and rhythm of the poem.
4. What do you learn from the contrasting moods inside and outside the house?
5. 'Poets draw on everyday events and experiences to make complex ideas accessible.' Discuss this statement with reference to 'The Uncle Speaks in the Drawing Room'.

CLASS/HOMEWORK EXERCISE

1. Copy the table below into your own notes and fill in critical comments about the quotations.

Key Quotes	
I have seen the mob of late	
These are follies that subside	
Certain frailties of glass	
To see his antique ruby bowl/ Shivered in a thunder-roll	
We stand between the dead glass-blowers/ And murmurings of missile-throwers	

Power

Adrienne Rich

Living   in the earth-deposits   of our history

Today a backhoe divulged   out of a crumbling flank of earth
one bottle   amber   perfect   a hundred-year-old
cure for fever   or melancholy   a tonic
for living on this earth   in the winters of this climate   5

Today I was reading about Marie Curie:
she must have known she suffered   from radiation sickness
her body bombarded for years   by the element
she had purified
It seems she denied to the end   10
the source of the cataracts on her eyes
the cracked and suppurating skin   of her finger-ends
till she could no longer hold   a test-tube or a pencil

She died   a famous woman   denying
her wounds   15
denying
her wounds   came   from the same source as her power

GLOSSARY

2	*backhoe*: mechanical digger.	7	*radiation sickness*: illness caused by damaging radioactive rays.
2	*flank*: side.		
3	*amber*: orange-yellow colour.	8	*bombarded*: attacked.
4	*melancholy*: deep sadness.	11	*cataracts*: medical condition causing blurred vision.
6	*Marie Curie*: pioneering scientist.		
		12	*suppurating*: festering.

EXPLORATIONS

1. Briefly explain what you understand by the first line of the poem.
2. From your reading of the poem, what image do you get of Marie Curie?
3. How would you describe the tone in the final stanza? Refer to the text in your answer.
4. Write a paragraph on how this poem addresses the issue of power. Support your points with close reference to the text.
5. What impact did the poem 'Power' have on you? Refer closely to the text in your response.

CLASS/HOMEWORK EXERCISE

1. Copy the table below into your own notes and fill in critical comments about the quotations.

Key Quotes	
Living in the earth-deposits of our history	
in the winters of this climate	
her body bombarded for years	
she could no longer hold a test-tube or a pencil	
a famous woman	

Storm Warnings

Adrienne Rich

The glass has been falling all the afternoon,
And knowing better than the instrument
What winds are walking overhead, what zone
Of gray unrest is moving across the land,
I leave the book upon a pillowed chair   5
And walk from window to closed window, watching
Boughs strain against the sky

And think again, as often when the air
Moves inward toward a silent core of waiting,
How with a single purpose time has traveled   10
By secret currents of the undiscerned
Into this polar realm. Weather abroad
And weather in the heart alike come on
Regardless of prediction.

Between foreseeing and averting change   15
Lies all the mastery of elements
Which clocks and weatherglasses cannot alter.
Time in the hand is not control of time,
Nor shattered fragments of an instrument
A proof against the wind; the wind will rise,   20
We can only close the shutters.

I draw the curtains as the sky goes black
And set a match to candles sheathed in glass
Against the keyhole draught, the insistent whine
Of weather through the unsealed aperture.   25
This is our sole defense against the season;
These are the things that we have learned to do
Who live in troubled regions.

GLOSSARY

1 *glass*: barometer.
7 *Boughs*: branches.
9 *core*: centre.
11 *undiscerned*: unseen.
15 *averting*: avoiding.
16 *elements*: weather.
25 *aperture*: opening.

EXPLORATIONS

1 Using reference to the opening stanza, comment on the way Adrienne Rich conveys the atmosphere as the storm approaches.
2 In your opinion, what does the poem suggest about people's attempts to control their environment? Support the points you make by quotation or reference.
3 Choose two images from the poem that you consider particularly interesting and briefly explain why you chose each one.
4 How would you describe the tone of stanza four? Support your opinion using reference to the poem.
5 Write your own personal response to 'Storm Warnings'. Refer closely to the text in your answer.

CLASS/HOMEWORK EXERCISE

1 Copy the table below into your own notes and fill in critical comments about the quotations.

Key Quotes	
The glass has been falling all the afternoon	
I leave the book upon a pillowed chair	
We can only close the shutters	
And set a match to candles sheathed in glass	
This is our sole defense against the season	

Living in Sin

Adrienne Rich

She had thought the studio would keep itself;
no dust upon the furniture of love.
Half heresy, to wish the taps less vocal,
the panes relieved of grime. A plate of pears,
a piano with a Persian shawl, a cat   5
stalking the picturesque amusing mouse
had risen at his urging.
Not that at five each separate stair would writhe
under the milkman's tramp; that morning light
so coldly would delineate the scraps   10
of last night's cheese and three sepulchral bottles;
that on the kitchen shelf among the saucers
a pair of beetle-eyes would fix her own—
envoy from some village in the moldings...
Meanwhile, he, with a yawn,   15
sounded a dozen notes upon the keyboard,
declared it out of tune, shrugged at the mirror,
rubbed at his beard, went out for cigarettes;
while she, jeered by the minor demons,
pulled back the sheets and made the bed and found 20
a towel to dust the table-top,
and let the coffee-pot boil over on the stove.
By evening she was back in love again,
though not so wholly but throughout the night
she woke sometimes to feel the daylight coming   25
like a relentless milkman up the stairs.

GLOSSARY

1 *studio*: one-room studio flat with small kitchen and bathroom.
3 *heresy*: judgement contrary to accepted opinion.
6 *picturesque*: pleasant to look at; forming a picture.
8 *writhe*: twisting movement of extreme pain.
10 *delineate*: to show by outlining either in a drawing or by words.
11 *sepulchral*: gloomy; melancholy.
14 *moldings*: decorative edging made of wood or plaster.
19 *demons*: evil spirits; people who do something with great energy or skill.
26 *relentless*: ongoing; merciless; without compassion.

EXPLORATIONS

1. 'Living in sin' is not an expression often used today. What did this phrase originally mean? Has society's views on this matter changed? How?
2. Why do you think the poet uses both ordinary, everyday language and metaphorical language? Pick an example of each type of language that you found effective and give reasons for your choice.
3. Based on your reading of the poem, comment on the poet's use of contrast. Refer to the text in your answer.
4. It has been said that Adrienne Rich's poetry flows in more than one direction. To what extent is this true of 'Living in Sin'?
5. Write a personal response to this poem, referring to both its theme and the stylistic techniques employed. Support your answer with reference.

CLASS/HOMEWORK EXERCISE

1. Copy the table below into your own notes and fill in critical comments about the quotations.

Key Quotes	
Half heresy, to wish the taps less vocal	
A plate of pears, / a piano with a Persian shawl	
envoy from some village in the moldings	
jeered by the minor demons	
By evening she was back in love again, / though not so wholly	

The Roofwalker

—for Denise Levertov

Over the half-finished houses
night comes. The builders
stand on the roof. It is
quiet after the hammers,
the pulleys hang slack.   5
Giants, the roofwalkers,
on a listing deck, the wave
of darkness about to break
on their heads. The sky
is a torn sail where figures   10
pass magnified, shadows
on a burning deck.

I feel like them up there:
exposed, larger than life,
and due to break my neck.   15

Was it worth while to lay—
with infinite exertion—
a roof I can't live under?
—All those blueprints,
closings of gaps,   20
measurings, calculations?
A life I didn't choose
chose me: even
my tools are the wrong ones
for what I have to do.   25
I'm naked, ignorant,
a naked man fleeing
across the roofs
who could with a shade of difference
be sitting in the lamplight   30
against the cream wallpaper
reading—not with indifference—
about a naked man
fleeing across the roofs.

Adrienne Rich

GLOSSARY

Dedication: Denise Levertov (1923–97) is a post-war Anglo-American poet.
5   *pulleys*: wheel and rope device for lifting weights.
7   *listing*: leaning.
7   *deck*: floor of ship.
17 *infinite exertion*: non-stop effort.
19 *blueprints*: plans; models.

EXPLORATIONS

1. Comment on the use of the poet's choice of adjectives in the first stanza. What do they suggest about the speaker's state of mind?
2. Look carefully at the poem's shape on the page. Can you suggest a reason for placing lines 13–15 on their own?
3. How do you respond to Adrienne Rich's use of metaphors in 'The Roofwalker'? Use quotation from the poem to support your views.
4. In your opinion, is there a definite conclusion reached at the end? Would you regard the poem as optimistic or pessimistic? Support your response with quotations from the poem.
5. What do you think the choice facing the speaker at the end of the poem is? Support your response with quotations from the poem.

CLASS/HOMEWORK EXERCISE

1. Copy the table below into your own notes and fill in critical comments about the quotations.

Key Quotes	
shadows/on a burning deck	
and due to break my neck	
A life I didn't choose/chose me	
a naked man fleeing/across the roofs	
sitting in the lamplight	

Our Whole Life

Adrienne Rich

Our whole life a translation
the permissible fibs

and now a knot of lies
eating at itself to get undone

Words bitten thru words   5

meanings burnt-off like paint
under the blowtorch

All those dead letters
rendered into the oppressor's language

Trying to tell the doctor where it hurts   10
like the Algerian
who walked from his village, burning

his whole body a cloud of pain
and there are no words for this

except himself   15

GLOSSARY

1 *translation*: interpretation.
2 *permissible fibs*: acceptable untruths.
7 *blowtorch*: lamp for removing paint.
8 *dead letters*: useless language; undelivered mail.
9 *rendered*: turned into.
9 *oppressor's language*: words used by tyrants.

EXPLORATIONS

1 Comment on the effectiveness of the poem's title.
2 The poet mentions 'fibs' and 'lies' in the opening lines of the poem. What do you think she really means by this?
3 How would you describe the poet's tone in lines 3–7?
4 Write a paragraph in which you comment on Adrienne Rich's use of imagery in this poem. Support the points you make with close reference to the text.
5 Write your own personal response to 'Our Whole Life'.

- Poetry Focus -

Adrienne Rich

CLASS/HOMEWORK EXERCISE

1. Copy the table below into your own notes and fill in critical comments about the quotations.

Key Quotes	
Our whole life a translation	
a knot of lies/eating at itself to get undone	
All those dead letters/rendered into the oppressor's language	
Trying to tell the doctor where it hurts	
his whole body a cloud of pain	

Trying to Talk with a Man

Adrienne Rich

Out in this desert we are testing bombs,

that's why we came here.

Sometimes I feel an underground river
forcing its way between deformed cliffs
an acute angle of understanding 5
moving itself like a locus of the sun
into this condemned scenery.

What we've had to give up to get here—
whole LP collections, films we starred in
playing in the neighborhoods, bakery windows 10
full of dry, chocolate-filled Jewish cookies,
the language of love-letters, of suicide notes,
afternoons on the riverbank
pretending to be children

Coming out to this desert 15
we meant to change the face of
driving among dull green succulents
walking at noon in the ghost town
surrounded by a silence

that sounds like the silence of the place 20
except that it came with us
and is familiar
and everything we were saying until now
was an effort to blot it out—
coming out here we are up against it 25

Out here I feel more helpless
with you than without you
You mention the danger
and list the equipment
we talk of people caring for each other 30
in emergencies—laceration, thirst—
but you look at me like an emergency

• Poetry Focus •

Adrienne Rich

Your dry heat feels like power
your eyes are stars of a different magnitude
they reflect lights that spell out: EXIT   35
when you get up and pace the floor

talking of the danger
as if it were not ourselves
as if we were testing anything else.

GLOSSARY

1 *desert*: the Nevada desert where nuclear weapons were tested during the 1940s and 1950s.	9 *LP collections*: long-playing music discs.
4 *deformed*: misshapen.	17 *succulents*: desert plants; cacti.
6 *locus*: position.	31 *laceration*: flesh wound; gash.
7 *condemned*: poisoned landscape.	34 *magnitude*: size; measure.

EXPLORATIONS

1 Comment on the effectiveness of the poem's title in relation to the themes addressed by the poet.
2 How would you describe the atmosphere in this poem? Refer closely to the text in your answer.
3 Choose two images from the poem that you found particularly effective. Comment on your choice in each case.
4 Based on your reading of lines 8–14, what was the couple's relationship like in the past?
5 How does the poem make you feel? Give reasons for your response, supporting the points you make with quotation or reference.

CLASS/HOMEWORK EXERCISE

1 Copy the table below into your own notes and fill in critical comments about the quotations.

Key Quotes	
Out in this desert we are testing bombs	
What we've had to give up to get here	
walking at noon in the ghost town	
Out here I feel more helpless/with you than without you	
Your dry heat feels like power	

Diving into the Wreck

Adrienne Rich

First having read the book of myths,
and loaded the camera,
and checked the edge of the knife-blade,
I put on
the body-armor of black rubber   5
the absurd flippers
the grave and awkward mask.
I am having to do this
not like Cousteau with his
assiduous team   10
aboard the sun-flooded schooner
but here alone.

There is a ladder.
The ladder is always there
hanging innocently   15
close to the side of the schooner.
We know what it is for,
we who have used it.
Otherwise
it's a piece of maritime floss   20
some sundry equipment.

I go down.
Rung after rung and still
the oxygen immerses me
the blue light   25
the clear atoms
of our human air.
I go down.
My flippers cripple me,
I crawl like an insect down the ladder   30
and there is no one
to tell me when the ocean
will begin.

First the air is blue and then
it is bluer and then green and then   35

black I am blacking out and yet
my mask is powerful
it pumps my blood with power
the sea is another story
the sea is not a question of power   40
I have to learn alone
to turn my body without force
in the deep element.

And now: it is easy to forget
what I came for   45
among so many who have always
lived here
swaying their crenellated fans
between the reefs
and besides   50
you breathe differently down here.

I came to explore the wreck.
The words are purposes.
The words are maps.
I came to see the damage that was done   55
and the treasures that prevail.
I stroke the beam of my lamp
slowly along the flank
of something more permanent
than fish or weed   60

the thing I came for:
the wreck and not the story of the wreck
the thing itself and not the myth
the drowned face always staring
toward the sun   65
the evidence of damage
worn by salt and sway into this threadbare beauty
the ribs of the disaster
curving their assertion
among the tentative haunters.   70

This is the place.
And I am here, the mermaid whose dark hair
streams black, the merman in his armored body
We circle silently
about the wreck   75
we dive into the hold.
I am she: I am he

whose drowned face sleeps with open eyes
whose breasts still bear the stress
whose silver, copper, vermeil cargo lies   80
obscurely inside barrels
half-wedged and left to rot
we are the half-destroyed instruments
that once held to a course
the water-eaten log   85
the fouled compass

We are, I am, you are
by cowardice or courage
the one who find our way
back to this scene   90
carrying a knife, a camera
a book of myths
in which
our names do not appear.

GLOSSARY

1 *myths*: ancient tales; folklore.
5 *body-armor*: wetsuit.
9 *Cousteau*: Jacques Cousteau (1910–97), the famous French underwater explorer and documentary film-maker.
10 *assiduous*: methodical; professional.
11 *schooner*: sailing ship.
20 *maritime*: naval; related to the sea.
20 *floss*: thread.
21 *sundry*: varied; miscellaneous.
48 *crenellated*: having ridges or notches.
49 *reefs*: outcrops of jagged rocks.
56 *prevail*: survive.
58 *flank*: side.
67 *threadbare*: worn; shabby.
70 *tentative*: unsure; timid.
70 *haunters*: divers who repeatedly explore wrecks.
72 *mermaid*: mythical sea creature (part woman and part fish).
73 *merman*: male version of a mermaid.
80 *vermeil*: precious metal; gilded silver or gold.
85 *log*: day-to-day ship's record.

Adrienne Rich

EXPLORATIONS

1. What does the title of the poem suggest to you?
2. How would you describe the atmosphere in the opening stanza?
3. At one level, this poem is about exploring a shipwreck. In your view, what else is the speaker exploring? Refer closely to the text in your answer.
4. From your reading of the poem, what do you understand by the phrase 'threadbare beauty' (line 67)?
5. Write a paragraph on the poet's description of the underwater world. Refer closely to the text, commenting on the effectiveness of the language used.

CLASS/HOMEWORK EXERCISE

1. Copy the table below into your own notes and fill in critical comments about the quotations.

Key Quotes

Quote	
The ladder is always there	
I crawl like an insect	
swaying their crenellated fans/between the reefs	
worn by salt and sway into this threadbare beauty	
a book of myths/in which/our names do not appear	

From a Survivor

The pact that we made was the ordinary pact
of men & women in those days

I don't know who we thought we were
that our personalities
could resist the failures of the race   5

Lucky or unlucky, we didn't know
the race had failures of that order
and that we were going to share them

Like everybody else, we thought of ourselves as special

Your body is as vivid to me   10
as it ever was: even more

since my feeling for it is clearer:
I know what it could do and could not do

it is no longer
the body of a god   15
or anything with power over my life

Next year it would have been 20 years
and you are wastefully dead
who might have made the leap
we talked, too late, of making   20

which I live now
not as a leap
but a succession of brief, amazing moments

each one making possible the next

GLOSSARY
1 *pact*: formal agreement.
18 *wastefully dead*: gone without achieving.

EXPLORATIONS

1. Consider the shape of the poem on the page. Is the fragmented order being used by the poet to say anything about life?
2. Why do you think the poet uses '&' between 'men' and 'women' in line 2? What does this suggest to you?
3. How would you describe the tone in 'From a Survivor'? Does it change at any point? Refer to the text in your answer.
4. Do you think the poem's ending is optimistic or pessimistic? Look at the absence of punctuation at the end. Why do you think Adrienne Rich chose to do this?
5. Write your own personal response to the poem.

CLASS/HOMEWORK EXERCISE

1. Copy the table below into your own notes and fill in critical comments about the quotations.

Key Quotes	
The pact that we made was the ordinary pact	
Like everybody else, we thought of ourselves as special	
since my feeling for it is clearer	
Next year it would have been 20 years	
each one making possible the next	

SAMPLE LEAVING CERT QUESTIONS ON RICH'S POETRY

1. 'Adrienne Rich's poetry is interesting both for its modern and universal themes and for its conventional and experimental use of language.' Discuss this statement with reference to the poems on your course.

2. 'I like (or do not like) to read the poetry of Adrienne Rich.' Respond to this statement, referring to the poetry by Adrienne Rich on your course.

3. Do you consider the poetry of Adrienne Rich to be a 'succession of brief, amazing moments'? Consider this question in relation to the poetry of Adrienne Rich that you have studied on your course.

4. Adrienne Rich has said, 'The desire to be heard – that is the impulse behind writing poems for me.' Does Rich's poetry speak to you? Write your personal response to the poems of Rich that do/do not speak to you.

Last Words

'What is possible in this life? What does love mean, this thing that is so important? What is this other thing called "freedom" or "liberty" – is it like love, a feeling?'
Adrienne Rich

'Adrienne Rich's poems speak quietly but do not mumble ... do not tell fibs.'
W.H. Auden

'Formalism was part of the strategy like asbestos gloves, it allowed me to handle materials I couldn't pick up barehanded.'
Adrienne Rich

'The world is too much with us.'

William Wordsworth
(1770–1850)

William Wordsworth was one of the most influential of England's Romantic poets. Like his friend, the poet Samuel Taylor Coleridge, he explored the inner self and looked for knowledge through the imagination. As a young man, Wordsworth developed a profound love of nature, a theme reflected in many of his poems. He believed that poetry was created from 'emotion recollected in tranquillity'. In 1799, he and his sister, Dorothy, settled in Grasmere in the Lake District, and it was there that he wrote his most famous poem, 'I Wandered Lonely as a Cloud', in 1804. His masterpiece is generally considered to be *The Prelude*, a semi-autobiographical poem of his early years which the poet revised many times. Wordsworth was England's Poet Laureate from 1843 until his death in 1850.

• Poetry Focus •

William Wordsworth

PRESCRIBED POEMS (HIGHER LEVEL)

1 'To My Sister' (p. 304)

Wordsworth's simple invitation to his sister, Dorothy, to join him on a day of 'idleness' illustrates his deep sense of discovering divine creation in nature.

2 'A slumber did my spirit seal' (p. 309)

This short, thought-provoking poem (one of the 'Lucy poems') explores the mystery of life, time, death and eternity.

3 'She dwelt among the untrodden ways' (p. 313)

Another of the 'Lucy poems'. Although we learn little about the life and death of this child of nature, she had a profound effect on Wordsworth.

4 'Composed Upon Westminister Bridge' (p. 317)

This well-known sonnet captures and celebrates the calm early morning view from Wordsworth's vantage point of Westminster Bridge in the centre of London.

5 'It is a beauteous evening, calm and free' (p. 321)

The poem was written after Wordsworth met with his estranged daughter in France. He associates the beauty of the evening with the child's innate closeness to God.

6 'The Solitary Reaper' (p. 325)

Because the words of the reaper's song are incomprehensible, the speaker in the poem is free to focus on its expressive beauty and the blissful mood it creates in him.

7 *from The Prelude:* 'The Stolen Boat' (p. 330)

A seemingly harmless childhood adventure returns to haunt Wordsworth and teaches him that human behaviour is subject to nature's moral laws.

8 *from The Prelude:* 'Skating' (p. 335)

This memory of skating with his friends on a frozen lake is much more positive. However, the poet is still drawn towards the greater beauty and mystery of his natural surroundings.

9 'Tintern Abbey' (p. 340)

After five years' absence, Wordsworth revisits the abbey ruins in the beautiful Welsh valley of the River Wye. This lengthy, reflective monologue celebrates the abbey's pastoral setting and highlights the poet's intimate relationship with nature.

• Poetry Focus •

To My Sister

William Wordsworth

It is the first mild day of March:
Each minute sweeter than before,
The redbreast sings from the tall larch
That stands beside our door.

There is a blessing in the air,   5
Which seems a sense of joy to yield
To the bare trees, and mountains bare,
And grass in the green field.

My sister! ('tis a wish of mine)
Now that our morning meal is done,   10
Make haste, your morning task resign;
Come forth and feel the sun.

Edward will come with you; and, pray,
Put on with speed your woodland dress;
And bring no book: for this one day   15
We'll give to idleness.

No joyless forms shall regulate
Our living calendar:
We from to-day, my Friend, will date
The opening of the year.   20

Love, now a universal birth,
From heart to heart is stealing,
From earth to man, from man to earth:
—It is the hour of feeling—

One moment now may give us more   25
Than years of toiling reason:
Our minds shall drink at every pore
The spirit of the season.

Some silent laws our hearts will make,
Which they shall long obey: 30
We for the year to come may take
Our temper from to-day.

And from the blessed power that rolls
About, below, above,
We'll frame the measure of our souls: 35
They shall be tuned to love.

Then come, my Sister! come, I pray,
With speed put on your woodland dress;
And bring no book: for this one day
We'll give to idleness.   40

'The redbreast sings'

GLOSSARY

3 *redbreast*: common name for the robin.
13 *Edward*: Wordsworth and his sister were taking care of a friend's son whose real name was Basil Montague.

33–34 *And from the blessed ... above*: a similar idea is found in lines 100–102 of 'Tintern Abbey'.

• Poetry Focus •

EXPLORATIONS

1. Comment on the poet's tone in lines 9–16.
2. What does the poem reveal to you about Wordsworth's own personality? Use reference to the text in your response.
3. In your opinion, do the views expressed by Wordsworth in 'To My Sister' have any relevance to our modern world? Give reasons to support your response.

STUDY NOTES

A bright spring morning will almost certainly lift our spirits and make us feel glad to be alive. 'To My Sister' was written in 1798, when Wordsworth was living near the beautiful Quantock Hills in Somerset. The scene is a March morning at the start of a mild English spring. All the poet does is ask his sister to wear her warm outdoor clothes, bring the young boy they were caring for and join him in taking the day off. The poem is made up of ten four-line stanzas, each with a regular *abab* rhyme scheme.

In the **first two stanzas**, Wordsworth uses simple and direct description to convey a vibrant sense of the new spring season – 'the first mild day of March'. Vivid images of the 'redbreast' and the 'green field' are evidence of his closeness to nature. The poet's **conversational language** is engaging and his **enthusiastic tone** ('Each minute sweeter than before') increases as he acknowledges 'a blessing in the air'. It seems as though nature itself, in all its god-given wonder and beauty, is inviting him to embrace this great 'sense of joy'.

Wordsworth is obviously **keen to share his feelings** with his sister, Dorothy, to whom he seems devoted. In **stanza three**, he urges her to forget about work and hurry outside to 'feel the sun'. The emphatic tone of the exclamation ('My sister!') echoes his sense of urgency. She should also dress for the outdoors ('your woodland dress') and 'bring no book'. The run-on line ('for this one day/We'll give to idleness') adds to the energetic rhythm and emphasises Wordsworth's eagerness that they should seize the moment while they can. It's clear that the poet feels there is a great deal more to be learned out of doors than from any book. For him, life's sensual pleasures (the sights and sounds of the great outdoors) are what are most important.

From **stanza five** onwards, the poet reflects on the intimate relationship between people and nature. He dismisses the restrictive routines of daily life as 'joyless forms' and looks forward to a new 'living calendar'. For Wordsworth, the mysteries and delights of nature will be both **an emotional and spiritual experience**. Springtime is a new birth, an astonishing stirring of 'universal' love. This 'hour of feeling' will bring him into harmony with a greater love, a cosmic force that enriches the whole of creation – nature and human nature – 'From earth to man, from man to earth'.

The poet develops this idealistic theme of **nature's positive influence** in **stanzas seven to nine** by contrasting the limitations of people's 'toiling reason' with the limitless delights on offer in our natural surroundings, which 'Our minds shall drink at every pore'. Wordsworth is equally convinced of nature's beneficial effects, not just in allowing us to get in touch with our feelings, but in humanising society's 'laws' and transforming all our lives so that 'They shall be tuned to love'.

In the **final stanza** (almost identical to stanza four), the poet again asks his sister to join him in enjoying the pleasures of nature. The relaxed tone, brisk rhythm and regular end-rhymes leave us in no doubt about Wordsworth's increasingly cheerful mood. Throughout the poem, he has used simple, conversational language to **celebrate the beauty of creation**. It is ironic that planning a whole day of 'idleness' could produce such worthwhile lessons for the poet – especially the belief in the way our senses can recognise the 'blessed power' of creation.

ANALYSIS

It has been said that there is a vitality to Wordsworth's language. Do you agree that this quality is evident in 'To My Sister'? Give reasons for your answer, illustrating your points with reference or quotation.

SAMPLE PARAGRAPH

'To My Sister' is typical of much of Wordsworth's poetry. The writing is conversational, especially the opening verse where he sets the scene on a fresh spring morning – 'It is the first mild day of March'. But immediately he fills in the scene with lively images of the robin singing and the 'tall larch' outside his door. The simplicity of his language is what gives it life. The tone becomes more enthusiastic and imperative in stanza three, where Wordsworth persuades Dorothy to accompany him on a day of idleness.

William Wordsworth

'My sister!' and 'Make haste' reflect his excitement at the thought of exploring the great outdoors. The dynamic rhythm also gives the poem energy and there is a vigorous balance in some of the lines – 'From earth to man, from man to earth'. There are also a number of upbeat images, such as when he describes nature as 'Our living calendar'. There is additional energetic repetition – for example, when he mentions the 'blessed power' that exists 'About, below, above'. To a large extent, the strength of Wordsworth's writing is its simplicity. His use of language keeps the poem moving along at a strident pace, making his enthusiasm for nature infectious.

EXAMINER'S COMMENT

A well-focused A grade response that addresses the question directly. Selected key quotations are handled with assurance to illustrate the energy and originality of Wordsworth's writing. The expression is varied and controlled throughout.

CLASS/HOMEWORK EXERCISES

1. Wordsworth set out to use 'language actually spoken' by ordinary people. In your view, did he succeed in doing this in 'To My Sister'? Support your answer with reference to the text of the poem.
2. Copy the table below into your own notes and fill in critical comments about the last two quotations.

Key Quotes

The redbreast sings from the tall larch	The simplicity of this lively image is typical of Wordsworth's writing.
There is a blessing in the air	Wordsworth found a sense of divine creation in nature.
It is the hour of feeling	The poem celebrates the sensual delights of nature.
Put on with speed your woodland dress	
And bring no book	

A slumber did my spirit seal

A slumber did my spirit seal;
  I had no human fears:
She seemed a thing that could not feel
  The touch of earthly years.

No motion has she now, no force;   5
  She neither hears nor sees;
Rolled round in earth's diurnal course,
  With rocks, and stones, and trees.

'With rocks, and stones, and trees'

GLOSSARY

1	*slumber*: sleep.	1	*seal*: close up.
1	*spirit*: non-physical aspect of a person; soul.	4	*motion*: movement.
		7	*diurnal*: daily.

EXPLORATIONS

1 Is the identity of 'She' important or relevant to an appreciation of the poem?
2 In your opinion, is the poem's focus on stillness or movement? Explain your response, using textual support.
3 Do you think the broad vowel sounds contribute to the mood of the poem? Do they add lightness or heaviness to the sound of the poem? Does this connect in any way with the movement of the earth? Your answer should make close reference to the text.

William Wordsworth

STUDY NOTES

This poem is part of the collection known as the 'Lucy poems' and was regarded by Coleridge, a fellow Romantic poet, as a 'most sublime epitaph'. An elegy is usually written for someone famous who has achieved great things in his/her life. This elegy is written for the unknown Lucy, whose importance was her effect on the poet. The poem suggests Lucy's qualities and how Wordsworth was affected by her death. There is a great sense of the never-ending turning of the world.

The 'Lucy poems' cannot be related to one specific person, although it is often thought that Wordsworth's sister Dorothy, with whom he had a very close relationship, may be the inspiration for these poems. But it is not clear if they actually refer to a real person or someone imagined. The opening image in the **first stanza** is one of the poet falling into a pleasant sleep. The alliteration of the soft 's' sound induces a relaxed feeling. The poet is now in another state, one of **suspended animation**, where there are no 'human fears'. He is beyond considerations of passing time, loss and death. The use of the past tense shows that this is a **recollected incident**. 'She' suggests a mystery. We are given no details except that she is beyond the reach of time: 'could not feel/The touch of earthly years'. It appeared ('seemed') as if she did not grow old. We are left wondering if this is a delusion.

In **stanza two**, the change of tense unsettles: 'No motion has she now'. **Time has touched her.** There has been a radical change in her condition. Lucy is incapable of action or strength. The use of the negative suggests a stopping of what once was. But now we are left with another enigmatic mystery: although she herself is incapable of movement, she is moving as she is 'Rolled round'. **Now she is part of the great force of nature** and its continuum. She is no longer an individual. The alliteration of 'r' and the word 'diurnal' (the only word in the poem that has more than two syllables) add to this feeling of continuous movement of the earth as it spins on its axis. Lucy has been able to connect with nature in a way that the poet cannot.

Wordsworth believed that if a poet's 'works be good, they contain within themselves all that is necessary, to their being comprehended and relished'. In that case, the identity of 'She' is irrelevant. The poet ends with an **acceptance that transience is inevitable and natural**, yet also mysterious and ambiguous. The punctuation of the final line causes the reader to pause and reflect on life and death. This little lyric is deceptive, as contained within its eight lines is a complex exploration of life, transience, mortality and eternity. As the earth revolves on its axis, so the poem revolves on two musical words, 'slumber' and 'diurnal', and shows us reality.

ANALYSIS

Wordsworth's poems move from personal relevance to universal relevance. In your reading of this poem, would you consider this statement to be true? Support your response with references from the text.

SAMPLE PARAGRAPH

Whether the poem refers to the death of Mary Hutchinson, the younger sister of Wordsworth's wife, or the imagined moment of his sister Dorothy's passing is not relevant to our appreciation of this delightful, short lyric, which deals with the poet's response to loss and his acceptance of change. This simple poem, with its regular eight lines and even rhythm, deals with huge and lofty themes, transience and death. In the first stanza, 'She' is above the march of time, 'could not feel/The touch of earthly years'. There is a false sense of security, 'I had no human fears'. She is not real, a 'thing' which does not age. The change occurs in the second stanza as she can no longer move. She has no energy, no 'force'. She is no longer aware, 'neither hears nor sees'. She is not a conscious individual, but part of the bigger picture of the world as she is 'Rolled round'. The alliteration emphasises the fact that as the earth goes through its daily course she is moved, as are the 'rocks, and stones, and trees'. The interconnectedness of all things is being stressed, as all move around according to the laws of nature. The use of the present tense encourages the reader to view her as part of nature's grand plan of continuity. She is nothing, yet she is part of everything. The highly personal feeling of loss felt by everyone at some point in their lives is translated into a universal acceptance of transience.

EXAMINER'S COMMENT

A thoughtful response to a challenging question. Very good engagement with both theme and style. The candidate shows that it is not the explanation of individual details which are important here, but the enigmatic ambiguity of life and death as is experienced by humanity. A grade.

CLASS/HOMEWORK EXERCISES

1. 'A slumber did my spirit seal' is an example of a poem that is both sad and uplifting at the same time. Discuss with reference to the text.
2. Copy the table below into your own notes and fill in critical comments about the last two quotations.

Key Quotes

A slumber did my spirit seal	Sleep closed tightly around the poet's consciousness. The sibilant 's' adds to the drowsy effect.
She seemed a thing that could not feel / The touch of earthly years	She appeared to be a separate entity beyond mortality, as she could not be touched by time, or so the poet assumed.
She neither hears nor sees	She is no longer an individual, but has merged with the earth.
Rolled round in earth's diurnal course	
With rocks, and stones, and trees	

She dwelt among the untrodden ways

She dwelt among the untrodden ways
   Beside the springs of Dove,
A Maid whom there were none to praise
   And very few to love:

A violet by a mossy stone   5
   Half hidden from the eye!
—Fair as a star, when only one
   Is shining in the sky.

She lived unknown, and few could know
   When Lucy ceased to be;   10
But she is in her grave, and, oh,
   The difference to me!

'But she is in her grave'

GLOSSARY

1   *untrodden*: remote; unspoiled.
2   *Dove*: an English river.
3   *Maid*: young girl.

EXPLORATIONS

1   Choose one image from the poem that you find particularly effective. Briefly explain your choice.
2   From your own reading of the poem, what is your impression of Lucy?
3   Comment on the tone of the last two lines. Is it optimistic or pessimistic? Give reasons for your answer.

• Poetry Focus •

STUDY NOTES

'She dwelt among the untrodden ways' is the best-known of Wordsworth's short series of 'Lucy poems'. These were probably written during the winter of 1799 when he was living in Germany. This short poem combines the beauty and simplicity that is the hallmark of Wordsworth's work. It is written with a sparseness that captures Lucy's plain character and natural way of life. While Lucy remains an enigmatic figure, it seems clear that the poet is deeply affected by her death.

In the **opening stanza**, Wordsworth chooses very **simple language** (mainly one-syllable words) to describe the isolated area where Lucy lived. Her anonymity is emphasised from the start – she is 'A Maid whom there were none to praise'. No details are given. Instead, her sincerity and gentleness are suggested. Although she is a solitary figure and somewhat unappreciated, she is one of nature's children. The poet also highlights her loneliness – she had 'very few to love'. He himself admires her rustic simplicity and seems to believe that more sophisticated people can learn a lot from her.

The **second stanza** explores Lucy's innocence and beauty through **contrasting images**. Wordsworth sees her as a 'violet by a mossy stone' in harmony with her rustic world. However, he balances this view of a simple country girl with a more forceful simile. She is also 'Fair as a star, when only one/Is shining in the sky'. These vivid comparisons are both drawn from nature to highlight Lucy's modest charm and striking individuality. They might also reflect Wordsworth's own deep sense of the mystery in all of creation.

This idea is developed further in the **third stanza** with a renewed **focus on Lucy's 'unknown' life**. While Wordsworth is clearly affected by Lucy's life and death, we are left to guess about his own thoughts and feelings. The final lines are emphatic, perhaps suggesting pain and loss at her death. However, the poet does not clarify the 'difference' Lucy's passing has made. Is the tone mournful or celebratory – or both? Is he simply reminding us that we can never fully know another person?

'She dwelt among the untrodden ways' contains several features associated with traditional folk ballads and fairytales, which often told unhappy stories of young maids in a dramatic style. Tragic tales of young lives were also a common feature of the Romantic poets. Wordsworth's account of Lucy is much more restrained (she simply 'ceased to be') and concentrates on his own reaction to her death. The use of regular rhyme along with a quietly dignified rhythm contributes much to the poem's **attractive musical qualities** – and to the mysterious appeal of Lucy herself.

ANALYSIS

'"She dwelt among the untrodden ways" closely identifies human beings with the natural world.' Discuss this statement, supporting your answer with reference to the poem.

SAMPLE PARAGRAPH

I would agree with this view of Wordsworth's poem. Lucy is the central figure and she is portrayed as a personification of nature. She is described as living in the unspoiled wilderness 'among the untrodden ways'. Wordsworth celebrates her closeness to the earth – she grows up alongside the riverbank – 'the springs of Dove'. Lucy is likened to a violet, one of nature's most unimportant but beautiful flowers. There is a childlike quality to Wordsworth's writing which links the simplicity of his language to the humble life Lucy led amid the remote English countryside. But Lucy is also compared to a single star 'shining in the sky'. The word 'shining' suggests the vivid beauty of her life and the great impact it has made on the poet. This comparison also shows her uniqueness. She is the 'only one' in the sky. This suggests that every human life is equally important as part of God's creation. Wordsworth believed in a shared spirit throughout all of nature. In her grave, Lucy has returned to this universal spirit. In both life and death, she is part of nature.

EXAMINER'S COMMENT

This is a reasonably well-focused B grade paragraph which makes clear points in response to the question. Quotations are used effectively throughout. The style is a little repetitive and awkward in places, but the final point is confidently expressed.

CLASS/HOMEWORK EXERCISES

1. What are the characteristic features of Wordsworth's style that are present in 'She dwelt among the untrodden ways'? Illustrate your answer with reference to the poem.

• Poetry Focus •

William Wordsworth

2 Copy the table below into your own notes and fill in critical comments about the last two quotations.

Key Quotes	
Beside the springs of Dove	All through the poem, Wordsworth emphasises Lucy's place within her natural surroundings.
And very few to love	There is an underlying sense of sadness that Lucy was unappreciated during her lonely life.
Half hidden from the eye	The poet also hints at her shyness and modesty.
A violet by a mossy stone	
The difference to me!	

• Leaving Certificate English •

Composed Upon Westminster Bridge

3 September 1802

William Wordsworth

Earth has not anything to show more fair:
Dull would he be of soul who could pass by
A sight so touching in its majesty:
This City now doth, like a garment, wear
The beauty of the morning; silent, bare,
Ships, towers, domes, theatres, and temples lie   5
Open unto the fields, and to the sky;
All bright and glittering in the smokeless air.
Never did sun more beautifully steep
In his first splendour, valley, rock, or hill;   10
Ne'er saw I, never felt, a calm so deep!
The river glideth at his own sweet will:
Dear God! The very houses seem asleep;
And all that mighty heart is lying still!

'This City now doth, like a garment, wear/ The beauty of the morning'

GLOSSARY

1 *fair*: beautiful; fine.
4 *doth*: does.
6 *towers, domes, theatres, temples*: the panoramic view of London, including the Houses of Parliament, Westminster Abbey and the dome of St Paul's Cathedral.
9 *steep*: soak; saturate.

EXPLORATIONS

1 What type of language is Wordsworth using in the opening line of the poem? Would you describe it as emphatic, monosyllabic, assertive, persuasive, etc.? In your opinion, what effect is he trying to achieve?
2 Wordsworth is known as a poet who loves nature. Are you surprised that in this poem he is celebrating a cityscape? What is it about this scene that he finds appealing? Support the points you make by quotation or reference.
3 Does the ending of the poem suggest uneasiness or calm? Does the poet feel that this moment will soon be gone or that it will always remain?

• Poetry Focus •

William Wordsworth

STUDY NOTES

> Written, according to Wordsworth, 'on the roof of a coach' as he set out for France to visit his daughter Caroline and her mother, the poet succeeds in capturing the freshness and beauty of a city before the day's rush begins. His sister Dorothy accompanied him and wrote of the scene in her journal: 'The City, St Paul's, with the River and a multitude of little boats, made a most beautiful sight as we crossed Westminster Bridge'. Wordsworth uses the strict form of the Petrarchan sonnet as he meditates on the scene, which Dorothy describes as having 'the purity of one of nature's own grand spectacles'.

The poem **opens** with the confident assertion that **the world has no sight more beautiful than this early-morning scene of London**: 'Earth has not anything to show more fair'. The strong **monosyllables underline the statement** and create a note of expectancy in the reader that entices him/her to read on. The poet then goes on to claim that only a person who was lacking in intelligence and spirit would not find this scene emotionally moving. Although the poem is set in a particular place and time – London on 3 September 1802 – the scope of the poem, like the city, moves beyond its boundaries to celebrate the beauty of nature. The word 'majesty' suggests that the scene has the grandeur of both king and God. In **line 4**, the focus of the poem moves from the general to the particular, signalled by the word 'This'. The city is given a capital letter, as if it were a person, and **personification** is used to show how the city assumes this beauty: 'This City now doth, like a garment, wear/The beauty of the morning'. People wear magnificent clothes to create an impression, but clothes are changed frequently and this suggests that the beauty of the city is only temporary, as it can be cast aside like an item of clothing.

Wordsworth did not like cities; he regarded them as dehumanising places full of noise. Notice how the adjectives used reinforce this idea: 'silent, bare'. The panoramic sweep of the city from Westminster Bridge is described: 'Ships, towers, domes, theatres, and temples'. These 'lie/Open' – the city has the capacity to expand, bringing in its surroundings, the 'fields' and the 'sky'. He shows us the interconnectedness of city and nature. Even the buildings appear 'bright and glittering'. The air is 'smokeless'. Why? The capital is quiet and tranquil before the morning rush of people, factories and transport turn it into the ugly, chaotic place Wordsworth hated. He regarded the 'hum of cities torture'. This is why the image of the 'garment' is so apt. **Unlike the beauty of nature, which is permanent, the beauty of the city is transient**. This concludes the **octet** of this fourteen-line Petrarchan sonnet.

In the **sestet**, the poet compares the perfection and attraction of the early-morning London scene to a country scene, where the sun saturates 'valley, rock, or hill' with its bright light, as if it were the first day of the world: 'In his first splendour'. He is **reacting positively** to this scene, and the use of the present tense throughout connects the reader to the immediacy of this scene and Wordsworth's response. As a Romantic, he delights in the world around him. The exclamation marks show his surprise at this experience. Here he uses the first-person personal pronoun 'I' as he states 'Ne'er saw I, never felt, a calm so deep!' The river echoes the peaceful state, as it is undisturbed by its busy traffic at this early hour in the morning.

The sound effect of the gentle rhythm of the **iambic pentameter** and the assonance of the slender vowel sound 'i' allow the reader to experience this serenity: 'The river glideth at his own sweet will'. The emotional intensity of the phrase 'Dear God!' is at odds with the calm. Is Wordsworth realising how temporary this beauty is? The personification continues as he describes the silence of the houses that 'seem asleep'. Again, appearance is stressed by the use of the word 'seem'. The final image encompasses the buildings and the inhabitants: 'all that mighty heart is lying still!' **This is how Wordsworth prefers the city, when it most closely resembles nature**. He does not passively observe – the sight raises questions within him which he shares with us.

ANALYSIS

Write a paragraph on why, in your opinion, Wordsworth chose the Petrarchan sonnet form for this poem. Consider how the form of the poem contributes to its message. Support the points you make by close reference to the text.

SAMPLE PARAGRAPH

The Petrarchan sonnet is a disciplined structure of fourteen lines consisting of an octet and sestet, and with a strict rhyming scheme of *abba abba cdcdcd*. This creates a calm and soothing effect on the reader, in my opinion. This poem celebrates the city of London in its quiet moments, before the hustle and bustle of human activity drives the city into its usual frenetic chaos. For Wordsworth, a city is an alien place, but here the regular rhythm of iambic pentameter and the assonance of the slender vowel 'i' contribute to the deep calm experienced by the poet as he observes the city. Rather than observing a strict demarcation of description of the sight in the octet and reflection in the sestet, Wordsworth intermingles the two. The 'fair' scene is evoked as he responds positively to it: 'Dull would he be of soul who could pass by/A sight so touching in its majesty'. This creates a fresh immediacy in the poem. It reminds me of Woody Allen's treatment of Manhattan, New York, in his films, where he allows you to both see the city and experience his response to the city with him. The rhyme scheme reinforces the subject matter as he states that the city is 'fair' because it is 'bare', without people. All objects 'lie' 'Open' to the 'sky'. So the city is able to operate at its 'own sweet will' because it is 'lying still'. I believe the structure, the rhyme scheme and the rhythm of the Petrarchan sonnet contribute and enrich the subject matter of this poem to such an extent that it is one of the most popular poems in the English language.

EXAMINER'S COMMENT

The paragraph shows a depth of analysis of the poem's structure that is combined with a real sense of personal engagement by the candidate. An interesting examination of the rhyme scheme lifts this response into an A grade.

CLASS/HOMEWORK EXERCISES

1. Wordsworth's subject matter comes from 'incidents and situations from common life'. Having studied this poem, would you agree or disagree with this statement? Refer closely to the text in your answer.
2. Copy the table below into your own notes and fill in critical comments about the last two quotations.

Key Quotes

A sight so touching in its majesty	A view so moving in its splendour.
All bright and glittering in the smokeless air	London was infamous for its fogs from the smoking chimneys. The slender vowels suggest the bright shards of morning light.
Never did sun more beautifully steep/ In his first splendour, valley, rock, or hill	The city is as fresh and beautiful as the first morning the sun soaked the countryside with light.
Dear God! The very houses seem asleep	
And all that mighty heart is lying still	

It is a beauteous evening, calm and free

William Wordsworth

It is a beauteous evening, calm and free,
The holy time is quiet as a Nun
Breathless with adoration; the broad sun
Is sinking down in its tranquillity;
The gentleness of heaven broods o'er the Sea: 5
Listen! the mighty Being is awake,
And doth with his eternal motion make
A sound like thunder—everlastingly.
Dear Child! dear Girl! that walkest with me here,
If thou appear untouched by solemn thought,   10
Thy nature is not therefore less divine:
Thou liest in Abraham's bosom all the year;
And worshipp'st at the Temple's inner shrine,
God being with thee when we know it not.

'The gentleness of heaven broods o'er the Sea'

GLOSSARY

9 *Dear Child*: Caroline, the daughter of Wordsworth and Annette Vallon.

12 *Abraham's bosom*: biblical reference for heaven.

13 *Temple's inner shrine*: the holiest place.

EXPLORATIONS

1. Select two images from the poem that effectively show the harmony and perfection of nature. Give reasons for your choice in each case.
2. In your view, what is the poet's attitude towards the 'mighty Being'? Support your answer with reference to the text.
3. From your reading of the poem, what is your impression of the young girl? Support your answer with reference to the text.

STUDY NOTES

'It is a beauteous evening' is thought to have originated from the reunion between Wordsworth and his estranged nine-year-old daughter. The poem was written after their visit to a beach near Calais in the autumn of 1802. It is a typical Petrarchan sonnet, consisting of an octave (eight lines) and a sestet (six lines). The form was popularly used by Petrarch, a fourteenth-century Italian writer. Other types of sonnets have less intricate rhyme patterns. The octave (or octet) usually describes a problem, while the sestet offers the resolution to it. The term 'sonnet' itself derives from the Italian *'sonetto'*, meaning 'little song'.

In the **opening lines** of 'It is a beauteous evening', Wordsworth is watching the sun set over the ocean. The evening is beautiful and calm, inspiring a mood of religious wonder, like 'a Nun/Breathless with adoration'. The explicit religious simile reflects the **poet's own intimate, spiritual relationship with nature**. There is an obvious emphasis on the reverential silence ('calm', 'quiet', 'gentleness') of the setting. This is further enhanced by the use of assonance, particularly the broad vowel sounds ('holy', 'adoration', 'broods') and by the measured rhythm of the early lines. In the midst of such tranquillity, Wordsworth's attention shifts and he suddenly notices the sound of the waves. The noise, 'like thunder', shows that the ocean is awake and its unceasing motion brings thoughts of eternity to the poet's mind.

In **lines 6–8**, we see the poet's **mystical view of nature**. The exclamation 'Listen!' signals his recognition of a mystical presence. The 'mighty Being' may refer to God or nature – or to God manifested through nature. At any rate, this indefinable force is in 'eternal motion' and 'everlastingly' omnipotent, making 'A sound like thunder'. Is it paradoxical that such a deafening spiritual insight should occur within the stillness of this sublime setting?

In the **final six lines**, Wordsworth addresses the young child ('Dear Child! dear Girl!') who walks with him by the sea. The repetition of 'dear' indicates his growing emotion and clearly suggests his great affection for her. Although she seems untouched by the 'solemn thought' that he is gripped by, this does not make her 'less divine'. He recognises the natural sanctity of childhood as a time when she 'worshipp'st at the Temple's inner shrine' – in other words, **she is always in the presence of God**. Is Wordsworth simply celebrating the child's instinctive spirituality? Or might he also be envious of her innate closeness to God?

The poem's conventionally Christian message is similar to the central theme of 'Composed Upon Westminster Bridge'. The religious references and biblical language ('beauteous', 'doth', 'thy', 'thee') are in keeping with the **dignified tone** throughout the sonnet. In the reverential **final lines**, Wordsworth seems to link the young girl's spiritual beauty with the evening itself, 'calm and free'. It is as though he senses that heaven is touching the earth and the child is as sacred as the beautiful sunset.

ANALYSIS

What is the poet's attitude to nature in 'It is a beauteous evening'?

SAMPLE PARAGRAPH

William Wordsworth is extremely positive about nature. The picture he paints is of a very hushed evening scene along the seashore. It is 'calm and free'. He associates nature with religion all through the poem. This is seen where he says the evening is a 'holy time'. Wordsworth finds great comfort in the stillness and tranquillity of nature. The beautiful image of the 'gentleness of heaven' over the sea creates a reassuring atmosphere. I can imagine the beauty of this peaceful moment when he gets a chance to think about life. Wordsworth seems to believe that nature and childhood are both divine. There is a common energy or power in the world of nature and in the young child who is accompanying him on his walk. He refers to this natural force as a 'mighty Being'. The same power is present in the child – 'God being with thee'. Although the poem is quite short, it is clear that Wordsworth finds intense spiritual significance in the natural world.

William Wordsworth

EXAMINER'S COMMENT

A clear response to a challenging question, well supported with suitable reference and quotation. There might have been some added comment on how the poet's style (especially tone and rhythm) reflects his appreciation of nature. However, the final sentence rounds off the paragraph succinctly. Overall, a B grade standard.

CLASS/HOMEWORK EXERCISES

1. How would you describe the dominant mood of this sonnet? Support your answer with reference to the text of the poem.
2. Copy the table below into your own notes and fill in critical comments about the last two quotations.

Key Quotes

It is a beauteous evening, calm and free	Wordsworth's opening description of the evening is simple and effective.
The holy time is quiet as a Nun	The simile immediately links the twin themes of nature and religion.
the mighty Being is awake	The poet found a sense of divine creation in nature.
The gentleness of heaven broods o'er the Sea	
Thy nature is not therefore less divine	

The Solitary Reaper

Behold her, single in the field,
Yon solitary Highland Lass!
Reaping and singing by herself;
Stop here, or gently pass!
Alone she cuts and binds the grain,   5
And sings a melancholy strain;
O listen! For the Vale profound
Is overflowing with the sound.

No Nightingale did ever chaunt
More welcome notes to weary bands   10
Of travellers in some shady haunt,
Among Arabian sands:
A voice so thrilling ne'er was heard
In spring-time from the Cuckoo-bird,
Breaking the silence of the seas   15
Among the farthest Hebrides.

Will no one tell me what she sings?—
Perhaps the plaintive numbers flow
For old, unhappy, far-off things,
And battles long ago: 20
Or is it some more humble lay,
Familiar matter of to-day?
Some natural sorrow, loss, or pain,
That has been, and may be again?

Whate'er the theme, the Maiden sang   25
As if her song could have no ending;
I saw her singing at her work,
And o'er the sickle bending;—
I listened, motionless and still;
And, as I mounted up the hill,   30
The music in my heart I bore,
Long after it was heard no more.

William Wordsworth

• Poetry Focus •

William Wordsworth

*'I saw her singing at her work/
And o'er the sickle bending'*

GLOSSARY

1	*Behold her*: look at her.	16	*Hebrides*: islands off the coast of Scotland.
2	*Yon*: over there.		
6	*strain*: melody.	18	*plaintive numbers*: sad verses.
7	*Vale profound*: deep valley.	21	*lay*: song.
9	*chaunt*: short, simple, repetitive melody.	28	*sickle*: curved blade used for cutting grass or grain.

EXPLORATIONS

1. Discuss Wordsworth's use of tone in the first stanza. In your response, consider his choice of verbs and use of punctuation.
2. How does the poet suggest that the girl is in harmony with nature?
3. In your opinion, why did the song have such a lasting impact on the poet? Refer to the text in your answer.

STUDY NOTES

On a tour of Scotland with his friend, the Romantic poet Coleridge, and his own sister Dorothy, Wordsworth came upon this lone girl in a field reaping and singing a sad song in Erse, a type of Gaelic dialect. Although he could not understand what she was singing about, the sound of the song made such an impact on the poet that he composed this poem about it two years later, as part of his collection ***Lyrical Ballads***. This poem

> praises the power of memory. The girl sings of events long ago, the poet remembers the girl's song and now we remember the song also. This is 'emotion recollected in tranquillity'.

The **poet addresses the reader directly**, 'Behold her ... O listen!' in the **opening**. This creates a sense of immediacy and intimacy between the poet and the reader, as the reader feels as if he/she is actually on the walk with Wordsworth, experiencing the same sights as he did. The use of the present tense adds to the freshness of the scene: 'she cuts and binds ... And sings'. This freshness challenged the poets of the time, the Augustans. The Romantic poets believed in using the **'language of conversation'** in their work, unlike the poetic diction that was the fashion. They were also obsessed with solitude – here, the girl is described as 'solitary', 'single', 'Alone'. The reaper is alone with nature. These poets focused on the individual. The liberal use of exclamation marks adds energy to the scene. When he offers the choice of stopping to listen or of 'gently' passing, the poet is suggesting that to move on would show a lack of spirit, as the music is so enticing.

The structure of the poem is that of a ballad – four stanzas with eight lines each. The regular rhyme scheme adds to the harmony of the scene. Stanzas one and four are *abcbddee*, and stanzas two and three are *abadccdd*. Stanzas one, three and four tell the story, and two gives his reaction to the scene. This use of two forms, the lyric and the ballad, was an experiment at the time. This flexible form is appropriate for the subject of personal emotion and experience, rather than the reasoned argument of the Augustan poets who were popular at this time.

The **second stanza**, which **deals with Wordsworth's reaction to the scene**, uses the imagery of birdsong. The nightingale singing in the heat of the desert ('Arabian sands') conjures up an exotic, magical place. The Romantics revelled in the allure of foreign places. The cuckoo is then described singing in a completely different scenario – the cold, hostile, windswept North Atlantic, 'the farthest Hebrides'. The singing causes a reaction in the listeners; the nightingale's song is full of 'welcome notes to weary bands'. The cuckoo breaks the 'silence of the seas' as he signals the return of spring. In hostile settings, the birds bring relief, comfort and hope. Does the 'Highland Lass' do the same? And for whom – the reader, Wordsworth or both?

Then, in the **third stanza**, we are brought back to the actual scene. A conversational tone invites us to **ponder what she is actually singing about**:

'Will no one tell me what she sings?' Again, the focus is on the listener rather than the song, which is sung in Erse. Perhaps she sings of 'old, unhappy, far-off things'. Others might hear a haunting song, telling of secrets hidden in the mists of time, a favourite topic of the Romantics. Although the song's subject matter is imperfectly understood, the mood is sensed: 'sorrow, loss, or pain'. The use of rhetorical questions invites the reader to muse with the poet over the interpretation of the song.

Finally, in the **fourth stanza**, the poet concludes that it doesn't matter what the theme is ('Whate'er the theme'), it is how she sang that stays with him. She sings in a free-flowing manner, 'As if her song could have no ending'. This might refer to the unfamiliar use of modes which are common in Gaelic tunes and which give a haunting and inconclusive sound. The lack of an ending also symbolises that this song will reverberate down the generations, both passed on through the oral traditions of the area and also because **it remains in Wordsworth's memory** and is then made into a poem that is passed onto the us, the readers: 'The music in my heart I bore,/Long after it was heard no more'. The poem concludes in the past tense. The scene surpasses time.

ANALYSIS

Wordsworth stated that poetry should 'treat of things not as they are, but as they appear, not as they exist in themselves, but as they seem to exist to the senses'. In your opinion, how relevant is this statement to the poem 'The Solitary Reaper?'

SAMPLE PARAGRAPH

In my opinion, it is not the actual event of hearing the girl alone in the fields singing which is the focus of this poem, but rather Wordsworth's reaction to the incident, and subsequently our reaction to his reaction. The impact this girl's song had on his senses is all important: 'I listened, motionless and still'. In stanza two, the poet uses the imagery of birdsong to explain this profound impact of the solitary Highland Lass's song. He uses, as he often does, two negatives to emphasise how deeply he was affected by the 'plaintive numbers'. He moves on from the song in the 'Vale profound' to a song in the heat of the desert, 'Arabian sands', and then to a song in the chill Atlantic, 'farthest Hebrides', as he stresses, through the imagery of birdsong, how comfort and hope is brought to listeners. But the tunes of these birds were not 'so thrilling' as the Maiden's song. The human voice is preferred. So, I believe, the emphasis in this poem is on 'The music in my heart I bore', the impact the music had on the poet's senses and its reverberations in the poet's memory. Although he describes her in stanza one, 'Alone she cuts and binds the grain,/And sings a melancholy strain', it is stanza two, reflecting and speculating on the song which remains with the reader. 'A voice so thrilling ne'er was heard'. This voice, with its enigmatic song, recollected in memory and in the poem, stays with the poet and the reader 'Long after it was heard no more'.

EXAMINER'S COMMENT

The candidate offers a personal opinion that is considered and articulate. Wordsworth's emphasis on speculation and remembrance is stressed with relevant quotation. This is a solid A grade standard.

CLASS/HOMEWORK EXERCISES

1. What elements of Romanticism are evident in 'The Solitary Reaper'? Support your answer with relevance to the text as you consider both the content and style of the poem.
2. Copy the table below into your own notes and fill in critical comments about the last two quotations.

Key Quotes

And sings a melancholy strain	The girl is singing a song that sounds sad.
Will no one tell me what she sings?	Wordsworth was intrigued by spoken Gaelic, a language he did not understand. The rhetorical question invites the reaader to wonder.
Some natural sorrow, loss, or pain,/ That has been, and may be again?	The poet speculates that her song may be about the continuing sorrows of life.
I listened, motionless and still	
The music in my heart I bore, Long after it was heard no more	

• Poetry Focus •

from *The Prelude*: The Stolen Boat

William Wordsworth

    One summer evening (led by her) I found
A little boat tied to a willow tree
Within a rocky cave, its usual home.
Straight I unloosed her chain, and stepping in
Pushed from the shore. It was an act of stealth   5
And troubled pleasure, nor without the voice
Of mountain-echoes did my boat move on;
Leaving behind her still, on either side,
Small circles glittering idly in the moon,
Until they melted all into one track   10
Of sparkling light. But now, like one who rows,
Proud of his skill to reach a chosen point
With an unswerving line, I fixed my view
Upon the summit of a craggy ridge,
The horizon's utmost boundary; for above   15
Was nothing but the stars and the grey sky.
She was an elfin pinnace; lustily
I dipped my oars into the silent lake,
And, as I rose upon the stroke, my boat
Went heaving through the water like a swan;   20
When, from behind that craggy steep till then
The horizon's bound, a huge peak, black and huge,
As if with voluntary power instinct
Upreared its head. I struck and struck again,
And growing still in stature the grim shape   25
Towered up between me and the stars, and still,
For so it seemed, with purpose of its own
And measured motion like a living thing,
Strode after me. With trembling oars I turned,
And through the silent water stole my way   30
Back to the covert of the willow tree;
There in her mooring-place I left my bark,—
And through the meadows homeward went, in grave
And serious mood; but after I had seen
That spectacle, for many days, my brain   35
Worked with a dim and undetermined sense
Of unknown modes of being; o'er my thoughts
There hung a darkness, call it solitude

Or blank desertion. No familiar shapes
Remained, no pleasant images of trees,   40
Of sea or sky, no colours of green fields;
But huge and mighty forms, that do not live
Like living men, moved slowly through the mind
By day, and were a trouble to my dreams.

'She was an elfin pinnace'

GLOSSARY

The *Prelude* is Wordsworth's longest poem. It is largely autobiographical and contains much of the poet's own ideas on poetry and on life.
1   *her*: nature.
13 *unswerving*: straight.
17 *elfin pinnace*: small boat.
22 *bound*: boundary.
23 *As if ... instinct*: as though it had special powers.
31 *covert*: shelter.
32 *bark*: boat.
36 *undetermined*: uncertain.
38 *solitude*: alienation.
42 *mighty forms*: terrifying dreams.

EXPLORATIONS

1 What impression of nature is given by the images in lines 1–11 of the poem?
2 A significant change of tone occurs after line 21. Explain the change. How does Wordsworth convey this change through his use of language?
3 Write your own personal response to the poem. Your answer should make close reference to the text.

• Poetry Focus •

William Wordsworth

STUDY NOTES

Taken from Wordsworth's long autobiographical poem, *The Prelude*, this extract narrates a childhood experience dominated by fear. Written in blank verse (unrhymed with a regular iambic pentameter rhythm), the poem recalls a memorable occurrence on a tranquil summer evening. In many of his poems, the poet seemed to be happiest when he had only nature for company. However, in 'The Stolen Boat', Wordsworth projects his own feelings onto a hostile landscape and discovers that nature is enforcing a moral lesson that was to affect the poet for the rest of his life.

The poem **opens** with a few well-chosen **narrative details** ('summer evening', 'little boat', 'rocky cave') that recreate this memorable scene from his early boyhood. Wordsworth remembers being captivated by the beauty of nature ('led by her') and it first seems that he is casually recalling a nostalgic moment from his past. However, the mood changes in **line 5**: 'It was an act of stealth'. The underlying sense of wrongdoing is emphasised by the phrase 'troubled pleasure', a further admission of disquiet.

Any guilty feelings are quickly replaced with a vivid description of the exquisite surroundings on that magical evening. The image of the child alone in the boat is powerfully evoked through vivid details, such as 'I dipped my oars into the silent lake' and 'Small circles glittering idly in the moon'. There is an increasing sense of the poet's close **affinity with his natural surroundings** as he grows aware of the 'sparkling light' all around him. By **line 12**, he imagines himself as a young romantic hero and thinks of the boat as 'an elfin pinnace' being spirited over the water. He is conscious also of his own strength confidently guiding the small craft. The simile ('heaving through the water like a swan') effectively captures all the delicacy and naturalness of the movement.

However, this sublime experience is dramatically interrupted in **lines 21–22** with the appearance of 'a huge peak, black and huge' towering before him. The child imagines it as a monstrous figure that 'Upreared its head'. **His terror grows out of his guilt**, which in turn causes him to invest the cliff with awesome, primitive powers. Ironically, the insistent repetition of 'I struck and struck again' underscores the boy's powerlessness. He is compelled to recognise nightmarish forces that he cannot control. Indeed, the more he tries to escape the 'grim shape', the more the mountains seem to shadow him.

The disturbing sequence is relieved with the child's shameful return to 'the covert of the willow tree'. But the menacing experience ('That spectacle') continues to haunt him and he tries to understand its significance 'for many days'. Through the rest of the poem, Wordsworth attempts to clarify his vague understanding ('a dim and undetermined sense') of the moral relationship between human beings and the natural world. He feels as if nature has punished him for his earlier wrongdoing in stealing the boat. An **uneasy mood of guilt and uncertainty** dominates **lines 39–44**. This is emphasised by a series of negatives ('no pleasant images of trees', 'no colours of green fields'). There is little doubt that the poet still finds difficulty coming to terms with such a traumatic event from his past. Only in composing the poem many years later does Wordsworth recognise the way such episodes have shaped his life. He can finally acknowledge that the experience was sublime.

ANALYSIS

How does Wordsworth present nature in 'The Stolen Boat'? Does it seem beautiful, benevolent, intimidating or mysterious?

SAMPLE PARAGRAPH

William Wordsworth is usually described as a great lover of nature. This is true of many of his poems. But it is not the case with 'The Stolen Boat'. At first, he presents what looks like a harmless childhood memory. He 'found' a little rowing boat one evening. The early description of the summer evening on the 'silent lake' seems relaxed. Nature is a watchful female figure and he is 'led by her'. But this doesn't last. The mountain overlooking the lake suddenly seems threatening – described as a 'craggy steep'. To his innocent mind, it becomes a 'living thing' looming over him. He is soon terrified. He retreats back to the shoreline where he tries to come to terms with stealing the small boat. His own guilt-ridden conscience is now like nature itself – 'a darkness'. The whole incident has taught him a lesson. Human nature is part of the natural world. Wordsworth believes that there is a definite link between our human moral laws and the harmony of nature. What he did as a young lad was wrong – the theft of a boat. In the end, he seems troubled by all that has happened and more respectful of nature.

William Wordsworth

EXAMINER'S COMMENT

This is an admirable attempt at quite a difficult question. There is a clear, cogent response, tracing the varying views of nature within the whole poem. Effective use is also made of textual illustrations. Despite the tendency towards short, note-like sentences, there is a solid B grade standard overall.

CLASS/HOMEWORK EXERCISES

1. 'The Stolen Boat' has been described as a highly dramatic poem. Do you agree with this view? Give reasons for your answer, supporting the points you make with reference to the text.
2. Copy the table below into your own notes and fill in critical comments about the last two quotations.

Key Quotes

One summer evening (led by her)	Wordsworth's dependent relationship with nature is central to the poem.
I dipped my oars into the silent lake	The image suggests both the forbidden thrill of his action and the disharmony he is causing.
Towered up between me and the stars	In his terror, the boy is overwhelmed by the vastness and power of nature.
With trembling oars I turned	
And through the silent water stole my way	

from The Prelude: **Skating**

William Wordsworth

   And in the frosty season, when the sun
Was set, and visible for many a mile
The cottage windows blazed through twilight gloom,
I heeded not their summons: happy time
It was indeed for all of us—for me   5
It was a time of rapture! Clear and loud
The village clock tolled six, —I wheeled about,
Proud and exulting like an untired horse
That cares not for his home. All shod with steel,
We hissed along the polished ice in games   10
Confederate, imitative of the chase
And woodland pleasures,—the resounding horn,
The pack loud chiming, and the hunted hare.
So through the darkness and the cold we flew,
And not a voice was idle; with the din   15
Smitten, the precipices rang aloud;
The leafless trees and every icy crag
Tinkled like iron; while far distant hills
Into the tumult sent an alien sound
Of melancholy not unnoticed, while the stars   20
Eastward were sparkling clear, and in the west
The orange sky of evening died away.
Not seldom from the uproar I retired
Into a silent bay, or sportively
Glanced sideway, leaving the tumultuous throng,   25
To cut across the reflex of a star
That fled, and, flying still before me, gleamed
Upon the glassy plain; and oftentimes
When we had given our bodies to the wind,
And all the shadowy banks on either side   30
Came sweeping through the darkness, spinning still
The rapid line of motion, then at once
Have I, reclining back upon my heels,
Stopped short; yet still the solitary cliffs
Wheeled by me—even as if the earth had rolled   35
With visible motion her diurnal round!
Behind me did they stretch in solemn train,
Feebler and feebler, and I stood and watched
Till all was tranquil as a dreamless sleep.

• Poetry Focus •

William Wordsworth

'It was a time of rapture!'

GLOSSARY

6   *rapture*: wonderful excitement; bliss.
8   *exulting*: rejoicing.
9   *shod with steel*: wearing skates.
10–11   *games/Confederate*: playing in groups.
15   *din*: loud noise.
16   *Smitten*: struck by.
25   *Glanced*: moved.
25   *tumultuous throng*: noisy crowd of skaters.
26   *reflex*: reflection.
28   *glassy plain*: smooth ice.
36   *diurnal*: daily.
37   *train*: line.

EXPLORATIONS

1   'It was a time of rapture!' How is the boy's feeling of 'rapture' conveyed throughout the poem?
2   What impression of Wordsworth himself as a young boy do you get from reading 'Skating'?
3   What picture of nature emerges from this poem? Support your answer with reference to the text.

STUDY NOTES

This extract from *The Prelude* is a fond memory of Wordsworth's schooldays. The poem describes an evening's ice-skating on the frozen surface of Esthwaite Water in the north-west of England. It was getting dark and the lights in the cottages plus the chiming of the clock reminded him that he should be indoors. However, his desire to continue skating with his friends was so strong that he decided to take no notice of time. For Wordsworth, the centre of this extraordinary experience is the way in which people and landscape are so closely interrelated.

In the **opening lines**, the poet invites us into the special world of his boyhood with a simple description of a memorable winter scene – 'the frosty season'. His personal narrative has a richly **nostalgic tone and the vivid imagery immediately sets the scene**: 'The cottage windows blazed through twilight gloom'. As the poet begins to relive the moment, his language reflects the intense sense of delight and freedom that he felt during that 'happy time'. The repetition and run-on lines emphasise the tremendous excitement he recalls: 'for all of us—for me/It was a time of rapture!'

Wordsworth goes on to describe the thrilling experience of skating in **lines 7–14**. What is most noticeable is the **vitality of the language**, particularly the dynamic verbs ('wheeled', 'hissed', 'flew'). Acutely observing the movement, he makes use of both the urgent rhythm and a powerful simile to capture his exhilaration: 'I wheeled about,/Proud and exulting like an untired horse'. The comparison is developed further when he describes the skaters as seemingly 'shod with steel'. Musical sibilance reinforces the importance of the memory: 'We hissed along the polished ice'. Caught up in the moment, the children imagine themselves as wild hounds pursuing a hare: 'The pack loud chiming'. Onomatopoeia ('We hissed along') conveys the fast movement. Speed is more obviously shown by the use of the verb 'flew'.

Indeed, **sound effects are used successfully throughout**, including **lines 15–22**, where the poet continues to bring the noisy scene to life: 'with the din/Smitten, the precipices rang aloud'. The activity ('uproar') is in contrast with the 'silent' landscape surrounding the skaters. Wordsworth remembers leaving 'the tumultuous throng' to seek out a quieter area where he skates round and round. When he stops, he feels the earth is still spinning on 'her diurnal round' and for a brief moment he feels connected to the wider universe surrounding him. Fascinated as always by the vast solitude, he takes time to reflect on the mysterious relationships between people and nature. The underlying sense of sadness is never explained. Perhaps the assonant phrase 'alien sound/Of melancholy' reflects the reality of time passing and that even echoes die.

After all the dramatic exuberance, the mood becomes subdued and reverential in the eloquent **final lines**. Overcome by the beauty and majesty of 'the shadowy banks on either side', Wordsworth tells us that he simply 'stood and watched'. Although the boy does not realise that he is learning about the transience of life, the adult poet does. 'All was tranquil as a dreamless sleep' might refer to the dying of day, just as other images (the sun setting and the child spinning in circles on his skates) signified the harmonious movement of the universe. To a large extent, the poem is about the passage of time, which is in itself a difficult concept. In the skating episode, the child Wordsworth is simply playing on a lake with his friends. However, such life-shaping memories (he later called them 'spots of time') made him see **nature as a formative shaper of conscience**.

ANALYSIS

From your reading of 'Skating', would you say that Wordsworth is a writer of great descriptive power? Support your answer with reference to the text of the poem.

SAMPLE PARAGRAPH

I think 'Skating' is remarkably descriptive. Wordsworth uses contrast to describe the cottage windows, which 'blazed through twilight gloom' and deftly weaves these with revelations about his own exited emotions – 'It was a time of rapture!' He really gives me a sense of the actual sensation of what it was like to be skating on ice. The feeling of moving gracefully at speed and yet being close to danger is suggested through lively phrases like 'I wheeled about', 'We hissed along' and 'sweeping through the darkness'. Wordsworth builds up a vivid picture of the landscape around the lake at dusk. There are 'leafless trees', an 'orange sky' and 'solitary cliffs'. He also uses comparisons to show the recklessness of the children playing. They are like a pack of wild dogs chasing 'the hunted hare'. Such descriptive details really bring out the excitement of the scene.

EXAMINER'S COMMENT

A good, focused B grade response very well supported by useful reference and quotations. The expression is varied but generally controlled. While some mention of sound effects would have been welcome, there is a convincing sense of engagement with how Wordsworth's descriptive power creates the mood of exhilaration in the poem.

CLASS/HOMEWORK EXERCISES

1 Comment on the roles of rhythm and movement in the poem, supporting your answer with reference to the text.
2 Copy the table below into your own notes and fill in critical comments about the last two quotations.

Key Quotes

I heeded not their summons	The young Wordsworth was so involved in the excitement of skating that he ignored everything else.
So through the darkness and the cold we flew	The rapid rhythm conveys the movement of the carefree skaters.
leaving the tumultuous throng	Nature always had a special attraction for the poet and he is drawn away from play.
The orange sky of evening died away	
I stood and watched/Till all was tranquil as a dreamless sleep	

William Wordsworth

Tintern Abbey

William Wordsworth

Five years have past; five summers, with the length
Of five long winters! and again I hear
These waters, rolling from their mountain-springs
With a soft inland murmur.—Once again
Do I behold these steep and lofty cliffs,   5
That on a wild secluded scene impress
Thoughts of more deep seclusion; and connect
The landscape with the quiet of the sky.
The day is come when I again repose
Here, under this dark sycamore, and view   10
These plots of cottage-ground, these orchard tufts,
Which at this season, with their unripe fruits,
Are clad in one green hue, and lose themselves
'Mid groves and copses. Once again I see
These hedge-rows, hardly hedge-rows, little lines   15
Of sportive wood run wild: these pastoral farms,
Green to the very door; and wreaths of smoke
Sent up, in silence, from among the trees!
With some uncertain notice, as might seem
Of vagrant dwellers in the houseless woods,   20
Or of some Hermit's cave, where by his fire
The Hermit sits alone.
                      These beauteous forms,
Through a long absence, have not been to me
As is a landscape to a blind man's eye:
But oft, in lonely rooms, and 'mid the din   25
Of towns and cities, I have owed to them,
In hours of weariness, sensations sweet,
Felt in the blood, and felt along the heart;
And passing even into my purer mind,
With tranquil restoration:—feelings too   30
Of unremembered pleasure: such, perhaps,
As have no slight or trivial influence
On that best portion of a good man's life,
His little, nameless, unremembered, acts
Of kindness and of love. Nor less, I trust,   35
To them I may have owed another gift,
Of aspect more sublime; that blessed mood

In which the burthen of the mystery,
In which the heavy and the weary weight
Of all this unintelligible world,   40
Is lightened:—that serene and blessed mood,
In which the affections gently lead us on,—
Until, the breath of this corporeal frame
And even the motion of our human blood
Almost suspended, we are laid asleep   45
In body, and become a living soul:
While with an eye made quiet by the power
Of harmony, and the deep power of joy,
We see into the life of things.
                         If this
Be but a vain belief, yet, oh! how oft—   50
In darkness and amid the many shapes
Of joyless daylight; when the fretful stir
Unprofitable, and the fever of the world,
Have hung upon the beatings of my heart—
How oft, in spirit, have I turned to thee,   55
O sylvan Wye! thou wanderer thro' the woods,
How often has my spirit turned to thee!

   And now, with gleams of half-extinguished thought,
With many recognitions dim and faint,
And something of a sad perplexity,   60
The picture of the mind revives again:
While here I stand, not only with the sense
Of present pleasure, but with pleasing thoughts
That in this moment there is life and food
For future years. And so I dare to hope,   65
Though changed, no doubt, from what I was when first
I came among these hills; when like a roe
I bounded o'er the mountains, by the sides
Of the deep rivers, and the lonely streams,
Wherever nature led: more like a man   70
Flying from something that he dreads than one
Who sought the thing he loved. For nature then
(The coarser pleasures of my boyish days,
And their glad animal movements all gone by)
To me was all in all.—I cannot paint   75

What then I was. The sounding cataract
Haunted me like a passion: the tall rock,
The mountain, and the deep and gloomy wood,
Their colours and their forms, were then to me
An appetite; a feeling and a love,   80
That had no need of a remoter charm,
By thought supplied, nor any interest
Unborrowed from the eye.—That time is past,
And all its aching joys are now no more,
And all its dizzy raptures. Not for this   85
Faint I, nor mourn nor murmur; other gifts
Have followed; for such loss, I would believe,
Abundant recompense. For I have learned
To look on nature, not as in the hour
Of thoughtless youth; but hearing oftentimes   90
The still, sad music of humanity,
Nor harsh nor grating, though of ample power
To chasten and subdue. And I have felt
A presence that disturbs me with the joy
Of elevated thoughts; a sense sublime   95
Of something far more deeply interfused,
Whose dwelling is the light of setting suns,
And the round ocean and the living air,
And the blue sky, and in the mind of man:
A motion and a spirit, that impels   100
All thinking things, all objects of all thought,
And rolls though all things. Therefore am I still
A lover of the meadows and the woods,
And mountains; and of all that we behold
From this green earth; of all the mighty world   105
Of eye, and ear, —both what they half create,
And what perceive; well pleased to recognise
In nature and the language of the sense
The anchor of my purest thoughts, the nurse,
The guide, the guardian of my heart, and soul   110
Of all my moral being.
                        Nor perchance,
If I were not thus taught, should I the more
Suffer my genial spirits to decay:
For thou art with me here upon the banks

Of this fair river; thou my dearest Friend, 115
My dear, dear Friend; and in thy voice I catch
The language of my former heart, and read
My former pleasures in the shooting lights
Of thy wild eyes. Oh! yet a little while
May I behold in thee what I was once, 120
My dear, dear Sister! and this prayer I make,
Knowing that Nature never did betray
The heart that loved her; 'tis her privilege,
Through all the years of this our life, to lead
From joy to joy: for she can so inform 125
The mind that is within us, so impress
With quietness and beauty, and so feed
With lofty thoughts, that neither evil tongues,
Rash judgements, nor the sneers of selfish men,
Nor greetings where no kindness is, nor all 130
The dreary intercourse of daily life,
Shall e'er prevail against us, or disturb
Our cheerful faith, that all which we behold
Is full of blessings. Therefore let the moon
Shine on thee in thy solitary walk; 135
And let the misty mountain-winds be free
To blow against thee: and, in after years,
When these wild ecstasies shall be matured
Into a sober pleasure; when thy mind
Shall be a mansion for all lovely forms, 140
Thy memory be as a dwelling-place
For all sweet sounds and harmonies; oh! then,
If solitude, or fear, or pain, or grief,
Should be thy portion, with what healing thoughts
Of tender joy wilt thou remember me, 145
And these my exhortations! Nor, perchance—
If I should be where I no more can hear
Thy voice, nor catch from thy wild eyes these gleams
Of past existence—wilt thou then forget
That on the banks of this delightful stream 150
We stood together; and that I, so long
A worshipper of Nature, hither came
Unwearied in that service: rather say
With warmer love—oh! with far deeper zeal

William Wordsworth • Poetry Focus •

Of holier love. Nor wilt thou then forget,   155
That after many wanderings, many years
Of absence, these steep woods and lofty cliffs,
And this green pastoral landscape, were to me
More dear, both for themselves and for thy sake!

'Lines Composed A Few Miles Above Tintern Abbey, On Revisiting the Banks of The Wye During A Tour. 13 July 1798' is the full title of the poem.

GLOSSARY

1 *Five years have past*: Wordsworth is now revisiting the ruins of Tintern Abbey and the River Wye, which he had first seen five years earlier on a walking tour.
11 *orchard tufts*: small groups of fruit trees.
20 *vagrant dwellers*: wandering gypsies.
38 *burthen of the mystery*: the weight of the mystery of life.
42 *affections*: feelings; sensations.
43 *corporeal frame*: body.
58 *half-extinguished thought*: memories that are half-forgotten.
86 *murmur*: complain in a quiet, continuous way.
94 *A presence*: an unseen being or influence.
96 *interfused*: filled with.
106–107 *both what ... perceive*: both what is taken in by the senses and transformed by the imagination.
115 *my dearest Friend*: Dorothy, the poet's sister. She accompanied him on this walk when the poem was composed.

EXPLORATIONS

1 What is the dominant mood of the opening section (lines 1–22)? What words and images are used to create this mood?
2 Which of these words would you use to describe the tone of the second section (lines 22–49): quiet, intense, contemplative, nostalgic, reverent? Choose two and explain your choice.

3   Wordsworth introduces his sister Dorothy into the landscape and meditation. What does the phrase 'what I was once' suggest about Dorothy's importance for the poet?

STUDY NOTES

> 'Tintern Abbey' comes at the end of the collection, *Lyrical Ballads*. It is an intensely personal poem and shows a new preoccupation with the poet's inner life, as it is explicitly autobiographical and contains Wordsworth's ideas about nature, perception and spiritual growth. It is a reflection on the importance of the natural world to the poet and the way in which his relationship with nature has changed since boyhood. The urge to explain his own life gave rise to his greatest poetry. Wordsworth wrote this poem at the age of twenty-eight in one day as he left Tintern Abbey: 'Not a line of it was altered ... and not any part of it written down till I reached Bristol'.

The **opening (lines 1–22)** describes the present moment when **the scene at the River Wye was revisited**. At first this seems to be a pictorial account of a landscape in the conventional eighteenth-century manner. However, on looking closer we realise that this description of **the rural scene is a projection of the poet's own mood of tranquillity**. The repetition of 'I' reminds us of his presence: 'I hear', 'I behold', 'I again repose'. The landscape is an emblem of the unity Wordsworth perceives in nature, as everything merges seamlessly: 'clad in one green hue, and lose themselves'. The tranquil mood is emphasised by the 'quiet of the sky', the 'soft inland murmur' of the river and the wreaths of smoke 'Sent up, in silence'. The **simple language** used records experience in a vivid, direct, clear manner rather than embroidering it, as was the fashion of the times. Wordsworth uses language in ebbs and flows as speech moves in natural conversation: 'These hedge-rows, hardly hedge-rows'. This was a dramatic move away from the formal poetic diction of contemporary poets.

The **second section (lines 22–49)** shows us **what the place meant to him** in the intervening years between his two visits. The memory of this landscape has been a 'tranquil restoration', as it has had a therapeutic effect on the poet in 'hours of weariness' in city life. It has had a moral influence on him as it encouraged acts of 'kindness and of love'. It also gave him the 'gift' of 'that serene and blessed mood' which enabled him to 'see into the life of things'. In this state of heightened perception, he becomes aware of an inner force which permeates the natural world and also himself. He becomes less aware of his bodily self, 'our human blood/Almost suspended'. The world then stops being oppressive and problematic: 'the weary weight .../Is lightened'. This 'blessed mood' is a state of suspension where insight occurs in a period of tranquillity. Wordsworth discovers a feeling of the unity of the universe and of being part of that unity: 'become a living soul'.

In **lines 49–57, the poet expresses doubts**: 'If this/Be but a vain belief, yet, oh!' The use of natural language speaks to us from the heart as moments of certainty give way to moments of hesitation, pauses to reflect or doubt. He is not sure whether he has really seen into the 'life of things'. There is a desperate need to believe so that he can grasp the meaning of a world that is otherwise 'unintelligible' to him. The repetitions and movement between past and present allow us to feel that we are following Wordsworth's thoughts as he tries to clarify and evaluate what nature has meant to him.

The phrase 'And now' returns the reader to the present, in **lines 58–111**, to stand alongside the poet as he remembers how this place sustained him in the past, how he is enjoying it now and how he realises that this view will sustain him in the future: 'there is life and food/For future years'. Thus past, present and future are fused together in this great harmony. He **recreates his 'boyish days' and traces his relationship with nature**, recalling his unthinking, physical enjoyment ('glad animal movements') and reliving the intense emotional and sensory delights ('aching joys' and 'dizzy raptures'). That is gone: 'That time is past'. Now he is aware of **an invisible force that unifies and drives nature**, a 'motion', a 'spirit' that 'rolls through all things'. The phrase 'I would believe' hints again at his uncertainty. Is he almost forcing himself to believe? Is his adult response to nature (the 'sense sublime') sufficient? Is it really an 'Abundant recompense' for losing 'thoughtless youth'?

In the final section, **lines 111–159, he examines his sister's relationship with nature** and dedicates his **prayer for her**. Dorothy is like a reincarnation of Wordsworth's former self – her 'wild eyes' and 'wild ecstasies' remind him of the 'aching joys' and 'dizzy raptures' of his youth: 'May I behold in thee what I was once'. He prays that nature will be a restorative force for her, helping her to deal with what life is: 'the dreary intercourse of daily life'. His sister's relationship with nature will change as his has done into a 'sober pleasure'. He now anticipates his own death as he looks into the future and hopes that he will live on in Dorothy's memory, 'on the banks of this delightful stream/We stood together'. The poem ends on a religious note. Wordsworth describes himself as 'A worshipper of Nature' and one capable of 'holier love', as he declares how 'this green pastoral landscape' meant so much to him for its own sake and also for Dorothy's sake. The reader is left with the landscape of the River Wye bound up with its impact on the poet and his responses to it. We view this place through Wordsworth's eyes forever.

ANALYSIS

Growth is a central preoccupation for Wordsworth. Discuss how Wordsworth explores the growth of his relationship with nature in the poem 'Tintern Abbey'.

SAMPLE PARAGRAPH

Wordsworth was very interested in the growth of his relationship with nature, how it influenced him at various points in his life and how his awareness of it changed. After describing the scenery of the Wye Valley and the influence this has had on him, the poet reaches back into the past and recollects his younger self, 'when like a roe/I bounded o'er the mountains'. Here Wordsworth distinguishes between two phases in his relationship with nature. He describes 'the coarser pleasures' of his boyhood. Satisfaction and enjoyment were derived from physical activity. The use of the word 'coarser' suggests that this experience is inferior to what is to come next. The use of the word 'animal' also suggests that something more refined was lacking. He traces the emotional intensity of his response to nature at this time, 'To me was all in all'. He responds to the 'colours' and 'forms' of the landscape, but his intellect was not engaged. In the second phase, he moves to include humanity in his adult response, 'the still sad music of humanity', and now he realises the essential unity in nature, the interconnectedness of 'all things'. He becomes aware of a dynamic, living force that 'impels' and 'rolls' through everything. This adult response to nature is reflective. But there is a note of regret for this 'remoter' response. He 'would believe' that it is adequate recompense for losing the 'aching joys' and 'dizzy raptures' of youth. But he is not certain. This former response of his is what he catches in Dorothy's 'shooting lights' in her 'wild eyes'. I think that, although he is saying that this more 'sober' response to nature is superior to his 'former pleasures', yet it is the 'sounding cataract' which has 'haunted' him 'like a passion', and Dorothy on her moonlit walks with the 'misty mountain-winds' which really impact on Wordsworth.

William Wordsworth

• Poetry Focus •

EXAMINER'S COMMENT

The candidate has discussed the various phases in Wordsworth's relationship with nature and has given a personal opinion on whether he was satisfied with the outcome. Quotations are skilfully used throughout the answer. This is a solid A grade standard.

CLASS/HOMEWORK EXERCISES

1. Seamus Heaney wrote that Wordsworth established how truly 'the child is father to the man'. Discuss how Wordsworth shows that our early life determines our adulthood. Support the points you make with reference to the text.
2. Copy the table below into your own notes and fill in critical comments about the last two quotations.

Key Quotes

These beauteous forms,/Through a long absence, have not been to me	Wordsworth has a use for this landscape, as a therapy, a moral guide and a vision.
with an eye made quiet by the power/ Of harmony	Nature's beauty invokes a tranquil mood in the poet so that he can make sense of the world.
Their colours and their forms, were then to me/An appetite	The young Wordsworth responded to nature in a primitive way, unlike the more intellectual response that came with maturity.
The guide, the guardian of my heart, and soul/Of all my moral being	
when thy mind/Shall be a mansion for all lovely forms	

• 348 •

• Leaving Certificate English •

William Wordsworth

LEAVING CERT SAMPLE ESSAY

Q **Wordsworth wanted to write poetry that would 'interest mankind permanently'. In studying the prescribed poems of Wordsworth, do you think he succeeded or failed in his aim 'to interest'? Write your personal response to the poems of Wordsworth which do/do not interest you.**

MARKING SCHEME GUIDELINES

Reward responses that show clear evidence of personal engagement/ involvement with the poetry of William Wordsworth.

Some of the following areas might be addressed:
- Subject matter comes from interesting 'situations from common life'.
- Compelling relationship with nature.
- Fresh, innovative imagery.
- Challenges poetic diction of the time, uses the language of the people effectively.
- Nature as a source of good, a comfort and teacher to man.
- Appealing autobiographical element, etc.

SAMPLE ESSAY
(Wordsworth's Poetry Interests You)

1 In the modern world, as we observe the climactic changes all around us – floods, hurricanes, melting ice caps – we are becoming more and more aware of the interconnectedness of the universe. We are realising that man and his environment have to be balanced so that each may survive in harmony. In my opinion, Wordsworth was way ahead of his time. While he celebrated the beauty of nature, he also presented nature as a teacher, a comforter, a means of developing insight into the meaning of life, a divine presence which encourages spiritual wisdom. As the Native Americans say, 'Mother Earth, Sister Moon and Brother Wind'.

2 In 'Tintern Abbey', although the opening appeals to our senses with a beautifully evoked pastoral landscape – a 'soft inland murmur' – it is the effect of the landscape on the poet that is the main focus. Memories of this beautiful place have comforted him in times of trouble: 'But oft, in lonely rooms, and 'mid the din/Of towns and cities'. All of us in the sanctuary of our own rooms have favourite pictures or photos of places where we were really happy. Even today in terms of stress management we are advised to close our eyes and remember the colours and sounds of a place where we were happy. Mr Wordsworth, we too are looking for that 'serene and blessed mood' which you evoke in this scene 'clad in one green hue'.

3. This same longing for peace in noisy cities is described in 'Composed Upon Westminster Bridge' as the poet praises the beauty of the city 'worn' briefly for a moment, like a precious garment before the hustle and bustle of people and transport disrupt this 'calm so deep'. We all know the frenetic rush of city traffic and how we long to escape its screeching uproar. Wordsworth captures the serenity of the early morning in the flowing line 'The river glideth at his own sweet will' as he describes the mighty Thames River gently rolling at nature's pace. I also think it is interesting that he wrote this 'on the roof of a coach, on my way to France' and that the long poem 'Tintern Abbey' was composed in a single day, and 'not a line of it altered'. This suggests someone inspired with the urge to get down on paper overwhelming emotions.

4. Wordsworth is indeed a challenging poet, and he causes controversy now, just as he did when he first published his poetry. What did he do to attract such criticism? He was an act similar to The Beatles, who changed popular music forever. He blew away an entire movement, the Augustan poets, by changing the subject matter to nature, which had never been seen as a suitable subject for poetry. He praised the rustic lifestyle as in 'The Solitary Reaper'. He prized imagination and feeling more than reason and intellect. He favoured the poetry of sensation, with all its 'aching joys' and 'dizzy raptures'. He focused on the individual rather than mythological themes. 'How oft, in spirit, have I turned to thee,/O sylvan Wye!' He favoured the language of everyday, with its repetitions and hesitancies, instead of the polished diction of the fashionable Augustan poets. 'Once again I see/These hedge-rows, hardly hedge-rows, little lines/Of sportive wood run wild'.

5. His legacy is such that the most popular literary destination for tourists is his beloved English Lake District, once regarded as wild and untamed and not

suitable for civilised people. Now tourists see this place through the eyes of Wordsworth and can appreciate 'its beauteous forms'. The modern visitor has been freed to hear 'The music', just like the poet, 'Long after it was heard no more'. Wordsworth is indeed the father of modern poetry, with its emphasis on feelings, poetry which 'thinks into the human heart'. So I disagree with those who dismiss him as self-indulgent, a poet for children. In the concluding passage of 'Tintern Abbey', Wordsworth has a prayer for his sister Dorothy, to whom he was very close: 'Therefore let the moon/Shine on thee in thy solitary walk'.

6 But Wordsworth is not just a poet who feels. He believed that a poet must think 'long and deep' about his subject as 'our feelings are modified by our thoughts'. In Dorothy he saw his former self, who responded emotionally to the sights and sounds of nature: 'May I behold in thee what I was once'. Contrast the writing of the brother and sister on the occasion of their visit to his daughter, Caroline, in France. Dorothy wrote of 'purple waves brighter than precious stones for ever melting away upon the sands'. Wordsworth wrote 'The gentleness of heaven broods o'er the Sea'. His is the more mature response who can see the 'sober pleasure' in these 'wild ecstasies', who can see 'A presence that disturbs me with the joy/Of elevated thoughts'. Wordsworth is a poet who interests and intrigues me. He has given me 'other gifts'.

(approx. 830 words)

```
GRADE: A1
P      =   15/15
C      =   1515
L      =   15/15
M      =   5/5
Total  =   50/50
```

EXAMINER'S COMMENT

An original and deeply felt response, showing a good engagement with and knowledge of the poetry of Wordsworth, both in terms of subject matter and style. The fluency of language and contemporary references added to the very high standard of the essay.

• Poetry Focus •

William Wordsworth

SAMPLE LEAVING CERT QUESTIONS ON WORDSWORTH'S POETRY (45–50 MINUTES)

1. Wordsworth 'saw new things, or he saw things in a new way'. Do you regard this poet as original? Support your response with quotations from the poetry of Wordsworth on your course.
2. The imagination was very important to William Wordsworth, as he regarded the mind as 'white paper void of all characters'. In your opinion, what function did the imagination have for this poet? In your discussion, refer to the poems by Wordsworth on your course.
3. 'Nature is the cornerstone of Wordsworth's poetry.' Discuss this view, supporting your answer by quotation from or reference to the poems you have studied by Wordsworth on your course.

SAMPLE ESSAY PLAN (Q3)

'Nature is the cornerstone of Wordsworth's poetry.' Discuss this view, supporting your answer by quotation from or reference to the poems you have studied by Wordsworth on your course.

- *Intro:* Readers coming to Wordsworth expecting detailed pictorial representation of nature will be disappointed. He is interested in the fundamental workings of nature and the relationship between man and nature.
- *Point 1:* 'Tintern Abbey' – meditation on the growth of his relationship with nature, detailing physical, emotional and contemplative response; sees nature as a process of continual growth, the past adds to the present.
- *Point 2:* 'The Stolen Boat' and 'Tintern Abbey' – nature as a moral guide.
- *Point 3:* 'A slumber' and 'Tintern Abbey' – awareness of ultimate unity of all living things. Nature as consoler.
- *Point 4:* Style – 'speaking from the heart', 'a man speaking to men'; blank verse, varied tones, etc.
- *Conclusion:* We enjoy Wordsworth's poetry for its original treatment of nature. He makes our 'eye quiet by the power of harmony' so that 'We see into the life of things'.

EXERCISE

Develop one of the above points into a paragraph.

POINT 3 – SAMPLE PARAGRAPH

In the second stanza of 'A slumber', Lucy is dead, unable to hear, move or see. Buried in the earth, she is as dead as the rocks or stones. Wordsworth is very aware of the impersonal forces of nature that govern the universe. They cannot be stopped in their course. Death is part of the natural cycle of things. Nothing escapes, not even Lucy, although he deludes himself in stanza one that she is a 'thing that could not feel/The touch of earthly years'. The word 'diurnal' conveys the reality. Lucy is now part of the process. She is free of human restraints, at one with the dynamic forces of the universe, 'Rolled round'. Similarly, in 'Tintern Abbey', Wordsworth is aware of an inner life that is part of the natural world. He 'sees into the life of things' because of the 'blessed mood' that nature's beauty bestows on him. He becomes aware of the ultimate unity of the universe and being part of that unity: 'the motion of our human blood/Almost suspended, we are laid asleep/In body'. Nature enables us to attain a state of suspended animation. Wordsworth believes that nature teaches us of the 'power of harmony', the interconnectedness of all: 'connect/The landscape with the quiet of the sky'. He is exploring the fundamental workings of nature and their relationship to man, rather than describing pretty pictures.

EXAMINER'S COMMENT

As part of a full essay answer, this is a lucid response that shows a real understanding of Wordsworth's aims. The paragraph focuses on the insight to be gained from a mature perception of nature. The answer also benefits from accurate and well-integrated quotations. Grade A.

Last Words

'Poetry ... takes its origin from emotion recollected in tranquillity.'
William Wordsworth

'Wordsworth's poetry is inevitable ... Nature not only gave him the matter for his poem, but wrote his poem for him.'
Matthew Arnold

'It is a thing unprecedented in literary history that a man should talk so much about himself.'
William Wordsworth

'I have spread my dreams under your feet.'

W.B. Yeats (1865–1939)

William Butler Yeats was born in Dublin in 1865. The son of a well-known Irish painter, John Butler Yeats, he spent much of his childhood in Co. Sligo. As a young writer, Yeats became involved with the Celtic Revival, a movement against the cultural influences of English rule in Ireland that sought to promote the spirit of our native heritage. His writing drew extensively from Irish mythology and folklore. Another great influence was the Irish revolutionary Maud Gonne, a woman as famous for her passionate nationalist politics as for her beauty. She rejected Yeats, who eventually married another woman, Georgie Hyde Lees. However, Maud Gonne remained a powerful figure in Yeats's writing. Over the years, Yeats became deeply involved in Irish politics and despite independence from England, his work reflected a pessimism about the political situation here. He also had a lifelong interest in mysticism and the occult. Appointed a senator of the Irish Free State in 1922, he is remembered as an important cultural leader, as a major playwright (he was one of the founders of Dublin's Abbey Theatre) and as one of the greatest twentieth century poets. Yeats was awarded the Nobel Prize in 1923 and died in 1939 at the age of seventy-three.

• Poetry Focus •

PRESCRIBED POEMS (HIGHER LEVEL)

'The Lake Isle of Innisfree' (p. 358)

Written when Yeats lived in London and was homesick for Ireland, the poem celebrates the simple joys of nature and the search for peace.

2 'September 1913' (p. 362)

In this nostalgic poem, Yeats contrasts the disillusionment he feels about the Ireland of his own day with the romanticised past.

3 'The Wild Swans at Coole' (p. 367)

Based on the symbolism of the swans, Yeats reviews his emotional state. He reflects on deep personal concerns: love, ageing and the loss of poetic inspiration.

4 'An Irish Airman Foresees his Death' (p. 372)

This war poem is written as a monologue in the 'voice' of Yeats's friend, Major Robert Gregory. Its themes include heroism, nationalism and the youthful desire for excitement.

5 'Easter, 1916' (p. 376)

Yeats explores a variety of questions and issues provoked by the 1916 Rising. In re-evaluating his own views, he struggles to balance heroic achievement with the tragic loss of life.

6 'The Second Coming' (p. 383)

The poem addresses the chaos brought about by violence and political change. Having witnessed war in Europe, he feared that civilisation would break down completely.

7 'Sailing to Byzantium' (p. 388)

Yeats's wide-ranging themes (including old age, transience, death, immortality and art) are all associated with the importance of finding spiritual fulfilment.

8. *from* **Meditations in Time of Civil War: 'The Stare's Nest by my Window'** (p. 394)

Written in response to the Irish Civil War, the poem tries to balance the destruction of conflict with the regenerative power of nature.

9. **'In Memory of Eva Gore-Booth and Con Markiewicz'** (p. 398)

Yeats's tribute to the Gore-Booth sisters is a lament for lost youth and beauty. He also reflects on the decline of the Anglo-Irish Ascendancy.

10. **'Swift's Epitaph'** (p. 403)

In this short translation from the original Latin inscription commemorating Jonathan Swift, Yeats honours a courageous writer who also came from the Anglo-Irish tradition.

11. **'An Acre of Grass'** (p. 406)

Yeats refuses to grow old quietly. Instead, he takes inspiration from William Blake and Michelangelo to continue using his creative talents in search of truth.

12. *from* **'Under Ben Bulben'** (p. 410)

Written shortly before his death, the poem is often seen as Yeats's last will and testament. It includes a summary of his beliefs and ends with the poet's own epitaph.

13. **'Politics'** (p. 414)

A short satirical poem in which Yeats rejects political activity, preferring romantic love.

• Poetry Focus •

The Lake Isle of Innisfree

W.B. Yeats

I will arise and go now, and go to Innisfree,
And a small cabin build there, of clay and wattles made:
Nine bean-rows will I have there, a hive for the honey-bee,
And live alone in the bee-loud glade.

And I shall have some peace there, for peace comes dropping
   slow,   5
Dropping from the veils of the morning to where the cricket sings;
There midnight's all a glimmer, and noon a purple glow,
And evening full of the linnet's wings.

I will arise and go now, for always night and day
I hear lake water lapping with low sounds by the shore;   10
While I stand on the roadway, or on the pavements grey,
I hear it in the deep heart's core.

'I hear lake water lapping with low sounds by the shore'

GLOSSARY

Innisfree: island of heather.
2 *clay and wattles*: rods and mud were used to build small houses.
7 *midnight's all a glimmer*: stars are shining very brightly in the countryside.
8 *linnet*: songbird.
10 *lapping*: gentle sounds made by water at the edge of a shore.
12 *heart's core*: essential part; the centre of the poet's being.

EXPLORATIONS

1. This poem was voted number one in a recent *Irish Times* poll of the top 100 poems. Why do you think it appeals to so many readers?
2. What does the poem reveal to you about Yeats's own state of mind? Use reference to the text in your response.
3. How does the second stanza describe the rhythm of the passing day? Use quotations to illustrate your response.

STUDY NOTES

'The Lake Isle of Innisfree' was written in 1890. Yeats was in London, looking in a shop window at a little toy fountain. He was feeling very homesick. He said the sound of the 'tinkle of water' reminded him of 'lake water'. He was longing to escape from the grind of everyday life and he wrote an 'old daydream of mine'.

This timeless poem has long been a favourite with exiles everywhere, as it **expresses a longing for a place of deep peace**. The tone in stanza one is deliberate, not casual, as the poet announces his decision to go. There are biblical overtones here: 'I will arise and go to my father,' the prodigal son announces. This lends the occasion solemnity. Then the poet describes the idyllic life of self-sufficiency: 'nine bean-rows' and 'a hive for the honey-bee'. These details give the poem a **timeless quality** as the poet lives 'alone in the bee-loud glade'.

Stanza two describes Innisfree so vividly that the future tense of 'I will arise' gives way to the present: 'There midnight's all a glimmer'. The **repetition** of 'peace' and 'dropping' suits the subject, as it lulls us into this tranquil place to which we all aspire to go at some point in our lives. **Beautiful imagery** brings us through the day, from the gentle white mists of the morning which lie like carelessly thrown veils over the lake to the blazing purple of the heather under the midday sun. The starry night, which can only be seen in the clear skies of the countryside, is vividly described as 'midnight's all a glimmer', with **slender vowel sounds** suggesting the sharp light of the stars. The soft 'l', 'm' and 'p' sounds in this stanza create a gentle and magical mood.

The third stanza repeats the opening, giving the air of a solemn ritual taking place. The **verbal music** in this stanza is striking, as the broad vowel sounds slow down the line, 'I hear lake water lapping with low sounds by the shore', emphasising peace and tranquillity. Notice the alliteration of 'l' and the assonance of 'o' all adding to the serene calm of the scene. The only **contemporary detail** in the poem is 'pavements grey', suggesting the relentless concrete of the city. The exile's awareness of what he loves is eloquently expressed as he declares he hears the sound 'in the deep heart's core'. Notice the monosyllabic ending, which drums home how much he longs for this place. Regular end rhyme (*abab*) and the regular four beats in each fourth line reinforce the harmony of this peaceful place.

ANALYSIS

What musical sounds did you find effective in this poem? Write a paragraph, illustrating your answer with references to the text.

SAMPLE PARAGRAPH

Yeats said that this poem was his 'first lyric with anything in its rhythm of my own music'. 'The Lake Isle of Innisfree' has a solemn, deliberate tone. It even has biblical overtones. The steady end rhyme ('Innisfree', 'honey-bee') adds to this stately music. The poet uses broad vowels to slow down the pace of the poem. This is an idyllic place where time almost stands still, 'alone in the bee-loud glade'. The repetition of 'peace' and 'dropping' creates a dreamy, soporific effect in this 'old daydream' of Yeats's. The brightly shining stars and the rapid movement of the bird's wings provide contrast as busy slender vowels in 'midnight's all a glimmer' and 'linnet's wings' tremble on the page. The soft 'l' sounds and alliteration in the line 'I hear lake water lapping with low sounds by the shore' bring us back to the calm, magical scene. I thought the consonance of 'la' and 'lo' also added to this effect. The final line beats out its message with five strong monosyllabic words: 'In the deep heart's core'. The phrase underlines the longing of the emigrant. This contrasts wonderfully with the slipping away of reality in 'pavements grey' as the exile relives his heart's desire.

EXAMINER'S COMMENT

A good understanding of the techniques used by a poet to create music and the effect this has on the poem is displayed in the answer. Quotations are very well used here to back up this personal response. Grade A standard.

CLASS/HOMEWORK EXERCISES

1. Pick out two images from the poem that appeal to you and discuss the reasons for their appeal.
2. Copy the table below into your own notes and fill in critical comments about the last two quotations.

Key Quotes

Nine bean-rows will I have there	Throughout the poem, Yeats is nostalgic for his homeland. He is yearning to return to the simple life he once enjoyed.
Dropping from the veils of the morning	The use of assonance emphasises the serene atmosphere of this magical place as the white mist lies over the lake.
noon a purple glow	The midday reflection of the heather in the water under the blazing midday sun is typical of the poet's effective visual imagery.
I will arise and go now	
I hear it in the deep heart's core	

• Poetry Focus •

September 1913

What need you, being come to sense,
But fumble in a greasy till
And add the halfpence to the pence
And prayer to shivering prayer, until
You have dried the marrow from the bone? 5
For men were born to pray and save:
Romantic Ireland's dead and gone,
It's with O'Leary in the grave.

Yet they were of a different kind,
The names that stilled your childish play, 10
They have gone about the world like wind,
But little time had they to pray
For whom the hangman's rope was spun,
And what, God help us, could they save?
Romantic Ireland's dead and gone, 15
It's with O'Leary in the grave.

Was it for this the wild geese spread
The grey wing upon every tide;
For this that all that blood was shed,
For this Edward Fitzgerald died, 20
And Robert Emmet and Wolfe Tone,
All that delirium of the brave?
Romantic Ireland's dead and gone,
It's with O'Leary in the grave.

Yet could we turn the years again, 25
And call those exiles as they were
In all their loneliness and pain,
You'd cry, 'Some woman's yellow hair
Has maddened every mother's son':
They weighed so lightly what they gave. 30
But let them be, they're dead and gone,
They're with O'Leary in the grave.

• W.B. Yeats

'Romantic Ireland's dead and gone'

GLOSSARY

1 *you*: merchants and business people.
8 *O'Leary*: Fenian leader, one of Yeats's heroes.
9 *they*: the selfless Irish patriots.
17 *the wild geese*: Irish independence soldiers forced into exile in Europe after 1690.
20 *Edward Fitzgerald*: eighteenth-century Irish aristocrat and revolutionary.
21 *Robert Emmet and Wolfe Tone*: Irish rebel leaders. Emmet was hanged in 1803. Tone committed suicide in prison after being sentenced to death in 1798.

EXPLORATIONS

1 Comment on the effectiveness of the images used in the first five lines of the poem.
2 How would you describe the tone of this poem? Is it bitter, sad, ironic, angry, etc.? Refer closely to the text in your answer.
3 Were the patriots named in the poem heroes or fools? Write a paragraph in response to Yeats's views.

STUDY NOTES

'September 1913' is typical of Yeats's hard-hitting political poems. Both the content and tone are harsh as the poet airs his views on public issues, contrasting the idealism of Ireland's heroic past with the uncultured present.

Yeats had been a great supporter of Sir Hugh Lane, who had offered his extensive art collection to the city of Dublin, provided the paintings would be on show in a suitable gallery. When the authorities failed to arrange this, Lane withdrew his offer. The controversy infuriated Yeats, who criticised Dublin Corporation for being miserly and anti-cultural. For him, it represented a **new low in the country's drift into vulgarity and crass commercialism**. The year 1913 was also a year of great hardship, partly because of a general strike and lock-out of workers. Poverty and deprivation were widespread at the time, particularly in Dublin's tenements.

The first stanza begins with a derisive **attack on a materialistic society** that Yeats sees as being both greedy and hypocritical. Ireland's middle classes are preoccupied with making money and slavish religious devotion. The rhetorical opening is sharply sarcastic, as the poet depicts the petty penny-pinching shopkeepers who 'fumble in a greasy till'. Yeats's tone is as angry as it is ironic: 'For men were born to pray and save'. Images of the dried bone and 'shivering prayer' are equally forceful – the poor are exploited by ruthless employers and a domineering Church. This disturbing picture leads the poet to regret the loss of 'Romantic Ireland' in the concluding refrain.

Stanza two develops the contrast between past and present as Yeats considers the **heroism and generosity of an earlier era**. Ireland's patriots – 'names that stilled' earlier generations of children – could hardly have been more unlike the present middle class. Yeats clearly relates to the self-sacrifice of idealistic Irish freedom fighters: 'And what, God help us, could they save?' These disdainful words echo the fearful prayers referred to at the start of the poem. The heroes of the past were so selfless that they did not even concern themselves with saving their own lives.

The wistful and nostalgic tone of stanza three is obvious in the rhetorical question about all those Irish soldiers who had been exiled in the late seventeenth century. Yeats's high regard for these men is evoked by comparing them to 'wild geese', a plaintive metaphor reflecting their nobility. Yet the poet's admiration for past idealism is diminished by the fact that **such heroic dedication was all for nothing**. The repetition of 'for this' hammers home Yeats's contempt for the pious materialists of his own imperfect age. In listing a roll of honour, he singles out the most impressive patriots of his own class, the Anglo-Irish Ascendancy. For the poet, Fitzgerald, Emmet and Tone are among the most admirable Irishmen. In using the phrase 'All that delirium of the brave', Yeats suggests that their passionate dedication to Irish freedom bordered on a frenzied or misplaced sense of daring.

This romanticised appreciation continues into the final stanza, where the poet imagines the 'loneliness and pain' of the heroic dead. His empathy towards them is underpinned by an **even more vicious portrayal of the new middle class**. He argues that the establishment figures of his own time would be unable to comprehend anything about the values and dreams of 'Romantic Ireland'. At best, they would be confused by the ludicrous self-sacrifice of the past. At worst, the present generation would accuse the patriots of being insane or of trying to impress friends or lovers. Perhaps Yeats is illustrating the cynical thinking of his time, when many politicians courted national popularity. 'Some woman's yellow hair' might well refer to the traditional symbol of Ireland as a beautiful woman.

The poet's disgust on behalf of the patriots is rounded off in the last two lines: 'But let them be, they're dead and gone'. The refrain has been changed slightly, adding further emphasis and a **sense of finality**. After reading this savage satire, we are left with a deep sense of Yeats's bitter disillusionment towards his contemporaries. The extreme feelings expressed in the poem offer a dispirited vision of an unworthy country. It isn't surprising that some critics have accused Yeats of over-romanticising the heroism of Ireland's past, of being narrow minded and even elitist. At any rate, the poem challenges us to examine the values of the state we are in, our understanding of Irish history and the meaning of heroism.

ANALYSIS

'September 1913' is based on contrasting images of meanness and generosity. Which set of images makes the greater impact? Write your response in a paragraph, referring closely to the text in your answer.

SAMPLE PARAGRAPH

Although W.B. Yeats ridicules the greedy shopkeepers and landlords of Dublin, he makes a much greater impression in describing the patriots of old Ireland – 'names that stilled your childish play'. The image stops us in our tracks. We can imagine how children used to hold men like Wolfe Tone and Robert Emmet in such great respect. Yeats uses the beautiful image of the wild geese spreading 'The grey wing upon every tide' to describe the dignified flight of Irish soldiers who refused to accept colonial rule. The poet's simple imagery is taken from the world of nature and has a vivid quality that makes us aware of the poet's high opinion of those heroes who were prepared to die for their beliefs.

EXAMINER'S COMMENT

Clearly written and very well supported, this B grade response addresses the question directly. There is evidence of close engagement with the poem. In addition, the expression is varied, fluent and controlled throughout. However, further development of key contrast points would be expected for a top grade.

CLASS/HOMEWORK EXERCISES

1. How relevant is 'September 1913' to present-day Ireland? Refer to the text of the poem when writing your response.
2. Copy the table below into your own notes and fill in critical comments about the last two quotations.

Key Quotes

What need you, being come to sense	Rhetorical questions satirise those smug people who knew how to exploit situations to their advantage.
Romantic Ireland's dead and gone	In his refrain, Yeats is caught between deep disillusionment towards his contemporaries and admiration for a more idealistic age.
All that delirium of the brave	The heroes of the past were extraordinarily courageous – but does the paradox suggest that they were also out of control?
You have dried the marrow from the bone	
For this that all that blood was shed	

The Wild Swans at Coole

The trees are in their autumn beauty,
The woodland paths are dry,
Under the October twilight the water
Mirrors a still sky;
Upon the brimming water among the stones   5
Are nine-and-fifty swans.

The nineteenth autumn has come upon me
Since I first made my count;
I saw, before I had well finished,
All suddenly mount   10
And scatter wheeling in great broken rings
Upon their clamorous wings.

I have looked upon those brilliant creatures,
And now my heart is sore.
All's changed since I, hearing at twilight,   15
The first time on this shore,
The bell-beat of their wings above my head,
Trod with a lighter tread.

Unwearied still, lover by lover,
They paddle in the cold   20
Companionable streams or climb the air;
Their hearts have not grown old;
Passion or conquest, wander where they will,
Attend upon them still.

But now they drift on the still water,   25
Mysterious, beautiful;
Among what rushes will they build,
By what lake's edge or pool
Delight men's eyes when I awake some day
To find they have flown away?   30

W.B. Yeats

• Poetry Focus •

W.B. Yeats

'The bell-beat of their wings above my head'

GLOSSARY

5 *brimming*: filled to the very top or edge.
12 *clamorous*: loud, confused noise.
18 *Trod ... tread*: walked lightly; carefree.
19 *lover by lover*: swans mate for life; this highlights Yeats's loneliness.
21 *Companionable*: friendly.
24 *Attend upon them still*: waits on them yet.

EXPLORATIONS

1 Why do you think the poet chose the season of autumn as his setting? What changes occur at this time of year? Where are these referred to in the poem?
2 In your opinion, what are the main contrasts between the swans and the poet? Describe two, using close reference to the text.
3 What do you think the final stanza means? Consider the phrase 'I awake'. From what does the poet awake?

STUDY NOTES

'The Wild Swans at Coole' was written in 1916. Yeats loved spending time in the West, especially at Coole, the home of Lady Gregory, his friend and patron. He was fifty-one when he wrote this poem, which contrasts the swans' beauty and apparent seeming immortality with Yeats's ageing, mortal self.

The poem opens with a tranquil, serene scene of **autumnal beauty** in the park of Lady Gregory's home in Galway. This romantic image is described in great detail: the 'woodland paths are dry'. It is evening, 'October twilight'. The water is 'brimming'. The swans are carefully counted, 'nine-and-fifty'. The use of the soft letters 'l', 'm' and 's' emphasise the calm of the scene in stanza one.

In stanza two, the poem moves to the personal as he recalls that it is nineteen years since he first counted the swans. The word 'count' links the two stanzas. The poet's counting is interrupted as these mysterious creatures all suddenly rise into the sky. Run-through lines suggest the flowing movement of the rising swans. Strong verbs ('mount', 'scatter') reinforce this elemental action. The great beating wings of the swans are captured in the onomatopoeic 'clamorous wings'. They are independent and refuse to be restrained. The ring is a symbol of eternity. The swans are making the same patterns as they have always made; they are unchanging. Stanza two is linked to stanza three by the phrases 'I saw' and 'I have looked'. Now the poet tells us his 'heart is sore'. He has taken stock and is **dissatisfied with his emotional situation**. He is fifty-one, alone and unmarried and concerned that his poetic powers are lessening: **'All's changed'**. All humans want things to remain as they are, but life is full of change. He has lost the great love of his life, the beautiful Irish activist, Maud Gonne. He also laments the loss of his youth, when he 'Trod with a lighter tread'. Nineteen years earlier, he was much more carefree. The noise of the beating wings of the swans is effectively captured in the compound word 'bell-beat'. The alliterative 'b' reinforces the steady, flapping sound. The poet is using his intense personal experiences to express universal truths.

The swans in stanza four are **symbols of eternity**, ageless, 'Unwearied still'. They are united, 'lover by lover'. They experience life together ('Companionable streams'), not on their own, like the poet. He envies them their defiance of time: 'Their hearts have not grown old'. They do what they want, when they want. They are full of 'Passion or conquest'. By contrast, he is indirectly telling us, he feels old and worn out. The **spiral imagery** of the 'great broken rings' is reminiscent of the spirals seen in ancient carvings representing eternity. Yeats believed there was a cyclical pattern behind all things. The swans can live in two elements, water and air, thus linking these elements together. They are living, vital, immortal, unlike their surroundings. The trees are yellowing ('autumn beauty') and the dry 'woodland paths' suggest the lack of creative force which the poet is experiencing. Yeats is heartbroken and weary. Only the swans transcend time.

Stanza five explores a **philosophy of life**, linked to the previous stanza by the repetition of 'still'. The swans have returned to the water, 'Mysterious, beautiful'. The poem ends on a speculative note as the poet asks where they will

'Delight men's eyes'. Is he referring to the fact that **they will continue to be a source of pleasure to someone else** long after he is dead? The swans appear immortal, a continuing source of happiness as they practise their patterns, whereas the poet is not able to continue improving his own writing, as he is mortal. The poet is slipping into the cruel season of winter while the swans infinitely 'drift on the still water'.

ANALYSIS

Poets use patterns to communicate their message. With reference to 'The Wild Swans at Coole', write a paragraph on Yeats's use of pattern, referring to imagery, sound effects, rhyme, etc.

SAMPLE PARAGRAPH

The rhyme scheme in 'The Wild Swans at Coole' is *abcbdd*. When I look at the words which these rhymes stress, I see another layer in this poem. The marked contrast between the dry woodland paths, which are so suggestive of the drying up of creativity, and the water which 'Mirrors a still sky' is very effective. The water is teeming with life. In the second stanza the poet is anchored to the land as he makes his 'count', while the swans are free to fly at a moment's notice, 'All suddenly mount'. When Yeats first went to Coole, he was suffering from a broken heart and this is echoed in the rhyming lines 'And now my heart is sore', 'The first time on this shore'. Although the swans are in the 'cold', they have not 'grown old'. Finally, he wonders where these 'Mysterious and beautiful' creatures will be: 'By what lake's edge or pool'. Similarly, another layer of meaning is created by the rhyme of the last two lines of each stanza. I particularly liked the rhyme in the last stanza: 'when I awake some day/To find they have flown away'. This sums up for me the sadness of the poet as he realises he is mortal, whereas they are immortal. It may even suggest his dread that his poetic inspiration, which is as mysterious and beautiful as the swans, may suddenly desert him too. I think examining the carefully worked patterns of the poem increases both our enjoyment of the poem as well as our understanding of the poet's message.

EXAMINER'S COMMENT

The student has engaged in a personal way to answer this question. Detailed attention has been given to the poet's use of rhyme. An effective, well-developed discussion that makes good use of quotations to sustain the argument. Confident expression adds to the A grade standard.

CLASS/HOMEWORK EXERCISES

1. Is the poem more concerned with the poet than the swans? Write a paragraph responding to this statement, referring to the text.
2. Copy the table below into your own notes and fill in critical comments about the last two quotations.

Key Quotes

The woodland paths are dry	Using symbolism, Yeats expresses his fears of ageing and the loss of his poetic imagination.
And now my heart is sore	Yeats admits to being dissatisfied with his life. The assonance adds to the poignancy.
All's changed	Political changes included World War I, the 1916 Rising and the Civil War. Personal changes included the loss of his great love (Maud Gonne) and his youth.
Unwearied still, lover by lover	
Mysterious, beautiful	

An Irish Airman Foresees his Death

I know that I shall meet my fate
Somewhere among the clouds above;
Those that I fight I do not hate,
Those that I guard I do not love;
My country is Kiltartan Cross,   5
My countrymen Kiltartan's poor,
No likely end could bring them loss
Or leave them happier than before.
Nor law, nor duty bade me fight,
Nor public men, nor cheering crowds,   10
A lonely impulse of delight
Drove to this tumult in the clouds;
I balanced all, brought all to mind,
The years to come seemed waste of breath,
A waste of breath the years behind   15
In balance with this life, this death.

'I balanced all'

GLOSSARY

The Irish airman in this poem is Major Robert Gregory (1881–1918), son of Yeats's close friend, Lady Gregory. He was shot down and killed while on service in Northern Italy.
3 *Those that I fight*: the Germans.
4 *Those that I guard*: Allied countries, such as England and France.
5 *Kiltartan*: townland near the Gregory estate in Co. Galway.
7 *likely end*: outcome.
12 *tumult*: turmoil; confusion.

EXPLORATIONS

1 'This poem is not just an elegy or lament in memory of the dead airman. It is also an insight into the excitement and exhilaration of warfare.' Write your response to this statement, using close reference to the text.
2 Write a paragraph on Yeats's use of repetition throughout the poem. Refer to the text in your answer.
3 Imagine you are Robert Gregory. Write a short diary entry reflecting your thoughts and feelings about becoming a fighter pilot. Base your comments on the text of the poem.

STUDY NOTES

> Thousands of Irishmen fought and died in the British armed forces during the First World War. Robert Gregory was killed in Italy at the age of thirty-seven. The airman's death had a lasting effect on Yeats, who wrote several poems about him.

Is it right to assume anything about young men who fight for their countries? Why do they enlist? Do they always know what they are fighting for? In this poem, Yeats expresses what he believes is the airman's viewpoint as he comes face to face with death. This **fatalistic attitude** is prevalent in the emphatic opening line. The poem's title also leads us to believe that the speaker has an intuitive sense that his death is about to happen. But despite this premonition, he seems strangely resigned to risking his life.

In lines 3–4, he makes it clear that he neither hates his German enemies nor loves the British and their allies. His thoughts are with the people he knows best back in Kiltartan, Co. Galway. Major Gregory recognises the irony of their detachment from the war. The ordinary people of his homeland are unlikely to be affected at all by whatever happens on the killing fields of mainland Europe. Does he feel that he is abandoning his fellow countrymen? What is the dominant tone of lines 7–8? Is there an underlying bitterness?

In line 9, the speaker takes time to reflect on why he joined the air force and immediately dismisses the obvious reasons of conscription ('law') or patriotism ('duty'). As a volunteer, Gregory is more openly cynical of the 'public men' and 'cheering crowds' he mentions in line 10. Like many in the military who have experienced the realities of warfare, **he is suspicious of hollow patriotism** and has no time for political leaders and popular adulation.

So why did Robert Gregory choose to endanger his life by going to war? The answer lies in the key comments 'A lonely impulse of delight' (**line 11**) and 'I balanced all' (**line 13**). The first phrase is paradoxical. The airman experiences not just the excitement, but also the isolation of flying. At the same time, his 'impulse' to enlist as a fighter pilot reflects both his **desire for adventure** as well as his regret.

The **last four lines** explain the real reason behind his decision. It was neither rash nor emotional, but simply a question of balance. Having examined his life closely, Gregory has chosen the heroism of a self-sacrificing death. It is as though he only feels truly alive during the 'tumult' of battle. Yeats's language is particularly evocative at this point. Awesome air battles are effectively echoed in such dynamic phrasing as 'impulse of delight' and 'tumult in the clouds'. This **sense of freedom and power** is repeatedly contrasted with the dreary and predictable security of life away from the war – dismissed out of hand as a 'waste of breath'. From the airman's perspective, as a man of action, dying in battle is in keeping with 'this life' that he has chosen. Such a death would be his final adventurous exploit.

Some commentators have criticised Yeats's poem for glorifying war and pointless risk-taking. Others have suggested that the poet successfully highlights Anglo-Irish attitudes, neither exclusively Irish nor English. The poet certainly raises interesting questions about national identity and ways of thinking about war. However, in elegising Robert Gregory, he emphasises **the airman's daring solitude**. Perhaps this same thrill lies at the heart of other important choices in life, including the creative activity of artists. Is there a sense that the poet and the pilot are alike, both of them taking calculated risks in what they do?

ANALYSIS

What do you think is the poem's dominant or central mood? Write your response in a paragraph, referring closely to the text in your answer.

SAMPLE PARAGRAPH

The title itself suggests fear. However, the airman accepts his impending death as if it is a natural result. 'Fate' suggests destiny, the unavoidable. The rest of the poem is dominated by a strong mood of resignation. The slow repetitive rhythm is like a chant or a prayer. This airman has a fatalistic temperament. He seems completely relaxed and reasonable when he says 'Those that I fight I do not hate'. In a way, he seems to have distanced himself from everything and everyone. He appears to have something of a death wish and his mood becomes very disillusioned towards the final section. For him, the past and future are a 'waste'. In general, his mood is quite resigned to death.

EXAMINER'S COMMENT

This candidate focuses well on the negative moods within the poem. Apt quotes are also effectively used in reference. The paragraph might have included some mention of the contrasting euphoria of war. The language towards the end is also slightly stilted. Overall, a B grade standard.

CLASS/HOMEWORK EXERCISES

1. Do you consider 'An Irish Airman Foresees his Death' to be an anti-war poem? Give reasons for your answer.
2. Copy the table below into your own notes and fill in critical comments about the last two quotations.

Key Quotes

I know that I shall meet my fate	The narrator, Robert Gregory, accepts that he will be killed in battle, yet his desire to take risks is more powerful.
My countrymen Kiltartan's poor	Examine the narrator's tone throughout the poem. Is it sincere, sympathetic, ironic, cynical?
A waste of breath	The speaker's disenchantment with ordinary life is emphasised. Is this disturbing?
Nor law, nor duty bade me fight	
In balance with this life, this death	

Easter, 1916

I have met them at close of day
Coming with vivid faces
From counter or desk among grey
Eighteenth-century houses.
I have passed with a nod of the head   5
Or polite meaningless words,
Or have lingered awhile and said
Polite meaningless words,
And thought before I had done
Of a mocking tale or a gibe   10
To please a companion
Around the fire at the club,
Being certain that they and I
But lived where motley is worn:
All changed, changed utterly: 15
A terrible beauty is born.

That woman's days were spent
In ignorant good-will,
Her nights in argument
Until her voice grew shrill.   20
What voice more sweet than hers
When, young and beautiful,
She rode to harriers?
This man had kept a school
And rode our wingèd horse;   25
This other his helper and friend
Was coming into his force;
He might have won fame in the end,
So sensitive his nature seemed,
So daring and sweet his thought.   30
This other man I had dreamed
A drunken, vainglorious lout.
He had done most bitter wrong
To some who are near my heart,
Yet I number him in the song;   35
He, too, has resigned his part
In the casual comedy;

He, too, has been changed in his turn,
Transformed utterly:
A terrible beauty is born.

Hearts with one purpose alone
Through summer and winter seem
Enchanted to a stone
To trouble the living stream.
The horse that comes from the road,
The rider, the birds that range
From cloud to tumbling cloud,
Minute by minute they change;
A shadow of cloud on the stream
Changes minute by minute;
A horse-hoof slides on the brim,
And a horse plashes within it;
The long-legged moor-hens dive,
And hens to moor-cocks call;
Minute by minute they live:
The stone's in the midst of all.

Too long a sacrifice
Can make a stone of the heart.
O when may it suffice?
That is Heaven's part, our part
To murmur name upon name,
As a mother names her child
When sleep at last has come
On limbs that had run wild.
What is it but nightfall?
No, no, not night but death;
Was it needless death after all?
For England may keep faith
For all that is done and said.
We know their dream; enough
To know they dreamed and are dead;
And what if excess of love
Bewildered them till they died?
I write it out in a verse –
MacDonagh and MacBride

W.B. Yeats • Poetry Focus •

And Connolly and Pearse
Now and in time to be,
Wherever green is worn,
Are changed, changed utterly:
A terrible beauty is born.   80

'All changed, changed utterly'

GLOSSARY

On 24 April 1916, Easter Monday, about 700 Irish Republicans took over several key buildings in Dublin. These included the Four Courts, Bolands Mills, the Royal College of Surgeons and the General Post Office. The rebellion lasted six days and was followed by the execution of its leaders. The Rising was a pivotal event in modern Irish history.

1 *them*: the rebels involved in the Rising.
14 *motley*: ridiculous clothing.
17 *That woman*: Countess Markiewicz, friend of Yeats and a committed nationalist.
24 *This man*: Padraig Pearse, poet and teacher, was shot as a leader of the Rising.
25 *wingèd horse*: Pegasus, the mythical white horse that flies across the sky, was a symbol of poetic inspiration.
26 *This other*: Thomas MacDonagh, writer and teacher, executed in 1916.
31 *This other man*: Major John MacBride was also executed for his part in the rebellion. He was the husband of Maud Gonne.
33 *most bitter wrong*: there were recurring rumours that MacBride had mistreated Maud Gonne.
67 *needless death*: Yeats asks if the Rising was a waste of life, since the British were already considering independence for Ireland.
76 *Connolly*: Trade union leader and revolutionary, executed in 1916.

EXPLORATIONS

1. Describe the atmosphere in the opening stanza of the poem. Refer closely to the text in your answer.
2. 'Easter, 1916' has many striking images. Choose two that you find particularly interesting and briefly explain their effectiveness.
3. On balance, does Yeats approve or disapprove of the Easter Rising? Refer to the text in your answer.

STUDY NOTES

> Yeats, who was in London at the time of the Rising, had mixed feelings about what had happened. He was clearly fascinated but also troubled by this heroic and yet in some ways pointless sacrifice. He did not publish the poem until 1920.

In the **opening stanza**, Yeats recalls how he used to meet some of the people who were later involved in the Easter Rising. He was unimpressed by their 'vivid faces' and he remembers routinely dismissing them with 'polite meaningless words'. His admission that he **misjudged these insignificant Republicans** as subjects for 'a mocking tale or a gibe' among his clever friends is a reminder of his derisive attitude in 'September 1913'. Before 1916, Yeats had considered Ireland a ridiculous place, a circus 'where motley is worn'. But the poet confesses that the Rising transformed everything – including his own condescending apathy. In the stanza's final lines, Yeats introduces what becomes an ambivalent refrain ending in 'A terrible beauty is born'.

This sense of shock and the need to completely re-evaluate his views is developed in **stanza two**. The poet singles out individual martyrs killed or imprisoned for their activities, among them his close friend Countess Markiewicz. He also mentions Major John MacBride, husband of Maud Gonne, who had refused Yeats's proposal of marriage. Although he had always considered MacBride as little more than a 'drunken, vainglorious lout', Yeats now acknowledges that he too has been distinguished by his bravery and heroism. The poet wonders about the usefulness of all the passion that sparked the rebels to make such a bold move, but his emphasis is on the fact that **the people as well as the whole atmosphere have changed**. Even MacBride, whom he held in utter contempt, has grown in stature.

In **stanza three**, Yeats takes powerful images from nature and uses them to explore the meaning of Irish heroism. The metaphor of the stubborn stone in the stream might represent the defiance of the revolutionaries towards all the forces around them. The poet evokes the constant energy and dynamism of the natural world, focusing on the changes that happen 'minute by minute'. Image after dazzling image conjures up a vivid picture of unpredictable movement and seasonal regeneration (as 'hens to moor-cocks call') and skies change 'From cloud to tumbling cloud'.

For the poet, the Rising presented many contradictions, as he weighs the success of the revolt against the shocking costs. In contrasting the inflexibility of the revolutionaries with the 'living stream', he indicates a reluctant admiration for the rebels' dedication. Does Yeats suggest that the rebels risked the loss of their own humanity, allowing their hearts to harden to stone? Or is he also thinking of Maud Gonne and blaming her cold-hearted rejection of him on her fanatical political views?

In the **final stanza**, the poet returns to the metaphor of the unmoving stone in a flowing stream to warn of the dangers of fanaticism. The rhetorical questions about the significance of the rebellion reveal **his continuing struggle to understand** what happened. Then he asks the single most important question about the Rising: 'Was it needless death after all', particularly as England 'may keep faith' and allow Ireland its independence, all of which would prompt a more disturbing conclusion, i.e. that the insurgents died in vain.

Yeats quickly abandons essentially unanswerable questions about the value of the Irish struggle for freedom. Instead, he simply pays tribute to the fallen patriots by naming them tenderly, 'As a mother names her child'. The final assertive lines commemorate the 1916 leaders in dramatic style. Setting aside his earlier ambivalence, Yeats acknowledges that these patriots died for their dreams. The hushed tone is reverential, almost sacred. The rebels have been transformed into martyrs who will be remembered for their selfless heroism 'Wherever green is worn'. The insistent final refrain has a stirring and increasingly disquieting quality. The poem's central paradox, 'A terrible beauty is born', concludes that **all the heroic achievements of the 1916 Rising were at the tragic expense of human life**.

ANALYSIS

Write a paragraph outlining Yeats's feelings about the Irish patriots as expressed in the final stanza of 'Easter, 1916'. Support the points you make with suitable reference or quotation.

SAMPLE PARAGRAPH

The final verse reveals many of Yeats's unanswered questions and confused thinking about the 1916 patriots. However, he sees that his own role is to record what he knows to be true and to 'write it out in a verse'. This allows him to pay his own tribute to the 1916 leaders whom he lists formally, almost like a graveside oration. The slow, deliberate rhythm is deeply respectful. The mood is serious, almost sombre, in keeping with the poet's newfound respect for the dead heroes. Yeats ends with the keynote comment, 'A terrible beauty is born'. This oxymoron derives its power from the obvious contrast between the terms. He believed that the Easter Rising was terrible because of all the unnecessary suffering that had occurred. Nevertheless, Yeats accepts that there was a transforming beauty that took the rebels, and perhaps many others, out of their lives of 'casual comedy' into the tragic drama of real life.

EXAMINER'S COMMENT

This short paragraph is well focused and supported. The candidate touches on several interesting aspects of the poet's mixed feelings about 1916. The references to features of style contribute much to this well-written A grade response.

CLASS/HOMEWORK EXERCISES

1 Yeats emphasises change of one kind or another throughout 'Easter, 1916'. List the main changes and comment briefly on them.
2 Copy the table below into your own notes and fill in critical comments about the last two quotations.

W.B. Yeats

Key Quotes

All changed, changed utterly:/ A terrible beauty is born	The 1916 Rising, in all its idealism and brutality, had transformed not just Ireland, but Yeats's own attitudes.
Enchanted to a stone	The poet uses the metaphor to show both the determination of the rebels and their unswerving fanaticism.
they dreamed and are dead	Yeats has been forced to accept that the 1916 rebels were idealists who made the ultimate sacrifice.
Polite meaningless words	
Being certain that they and I/ But lived where motley is worn	

The Second Coming

Turning and turning in the widening gyre
The falcon cannot hear the falconer;
Things fall apart; the centre cannot hold;
Mere anarchy is loosed upon the world,
The blood-dimmed tide is loosed, and everywhere   5
The ceremony of innocence is drowned;
The best lack all conviction, while the worst
Are full of passionate intensity.

Surely some revelation is at hand;
Surely the Second Coming is at hand.   10
The Second Coming! Hardly are those words out
When a vast image out of *Spiritus Mundi*
Troubles my sight: somewhere in sands of the desert
A shape with lion body and the head of a man,
A gaze blank and pitiless as the sun,   15
Is moving its slow thighs, while all about it
Reel shadows of the indignant desert birds.
The darkness drops again; but now I know
That twenty centuries of stony sleep
Were vexed to nightmare by a rocking cradle,   20
And what rough beast, its hour come round at last,
Slouches towards Bethlehem to be born?

'somewhere in sands of the desert/A shape with lion body and the head of a man'

W.B. Yeats

GLOSSARY

The Second Coming: This is a reference to the Bible. It is from Matthew and speaks of Christ's return to reward the good.

1 *in the widening gyre*: Yeats regarded a cycle of history as a gyre. He visualised these cycles as interconnecting cones that moved in a circular motion widening outwards until they could not widen any further, then a new gyre or cone formed from the centre of the circle created. This spun in the opposite direction to the original cone. The Christian era was coming to a close and a new disturbed time was coming into view. In summary, the gyre is a symbol of constant change.
2 *falcon*: a bird of prey, trained to hunt by the aristocracy.
2 *falconer*: the trainer of the falcon. If the bird flies too far away, it cannot be directed.
4 *Mere*: nothing more than; just; only.
4 *anarchy*: lack of government or order. Yeats believed that bloodshed and a worship of bloodshed were the end of an historical era.
5 *blood-dimmed*: made dark with blood.
12 *Spiritus Mundi*: Spirit of the World, the collective soul of the world.
14 *lion body and the head of a man*: famous statue in Egypt; an enigmatic person.
17 *desert birds*: birds of prey.
19 *twenty centuries*: Yeats believed that two thousand years was the length of a period in history.
20 *vexed*: annoyed; distressed.
20 *rocking cradle*: coming of the infant Jesus.
21 *rough beast*: the Anti-Christ.
22 *Bethlehem*: birthplace of Christ. It is usually associated with peace and innocence, and it is terrifying that the beast is going to be born there. The spiral has reversed its spinning. A savage god is coming.

EXPLORATIONS

1 This poem suggests that politics are not important. Does the poet convince you? Write a paragraph in response, with reference to the text.
2 Yeats uses symbols to express some of his most profound ideas. What symbols in this poem appeal to you? Use reference to the text in your response.
3 'Yeats is yearning for order, and fearing anarchy.' Discuss two ways in which the poem illustrates this statement. Support your answer with reference to the text.

STUDY NOTES

'The Second Coming' is a terrifying, apocalyptic poem written in January 1919 against a background of the disintegration of three great European empires at the end of the First World War, and against the catastrophic War of Independence in Ireland. These were bloody times. Yeats yearned for order and feared anarchy.

Sparked off by both disgust at what was happening in Europe as well as his interest in the occult, Yeats explores, in stanza one, what he perceives to be the failure at the heart of society: 'Things fall apart'. In his opinion, **the whole world was disintegrating** into a bloody, chaotic mess. This break-up of civilisation is described in metaphorical language. For Yeats, the 'gyre' is a symbol representing an era. He believed contrary expanding and contracting forces influence people and cultures and that the Christian era was nearing its end. Images of hunting show how the old world represented its failing – 'The falcon cannot hear the falconer'. We have lost touch with Christ, just as the falcon loses touch with the falconer as he swings into ever-increasing circles. This bird was trained to fly in circles to catch its prey. The circular imagery, with the repetitive '-ing', describes the continuous, swirling movement. Civilisation is also 'Turning and turning in the widening gyre' as it buckles and fragments.

The **tension** is reflected in a list of contrasts: 'centre' and 'fall apart', 'falcon' and 'falconer', 'lack all conviction' and 'intensity', 'innocence' and 'anarchy'. The strain is too much: 'the centre cannot hold'. The verbs also graphically describe this chaotic world: 'Turning and turning', 'loosed', 'drowned', 'fall apart'. Humans are changing amidst the chaos: 'innocence is drowned'. **Anarchy** is described in terms of a great tidal wave, 'the blood-dimmed tide', which sweeps everything before it. The compound word reinforces the overwhelming nature of the water. Yeats feels that the 'best', the leaders and thinkers, have no energy; they are indifferent and 'lack all conviction'. On the other hand, the 'worst', the cynics and fanatics, are consumed with hatred and violence, 'full of passionate intensity'.

Disillusioned, Yeats thinks **a new order has to be emerging**. He imagines a Second Coming. He repeats the word 'Surely' in a tone of both belief and fear in stanza two. 'The Second Coming' is usually thought of as a time when Christ will return to reward the good, but the image Yeats presents us with is terrifying. **A blank, pitiless creature emerges**. It is straight from the Book of Revelations: 'And I saw a beast rising out of the sea'. This was regarded as a sign that the end of the world was near. Such an unnatural hybrid of human and animal is the Anti-Christ, the opposite force of the gentle infant Jesus who signalled the end of the Greek and Roman Empires. The 'gaze blank' suggests its lack of intelligence. The phrase 'pitiless as the sun' tells us the creature has no empathy or compassion. It 'Slouches'. It is a brutish, graceless monstrosity.

The **hostile environment** is a nightmare scenario of blazing desert sun, shifting sands and circling predatory birds. The verbs suggest everything is out of focus:

'Reel', 'rocking', 'Slouches'. 'The darkness drops again' shows how disorder, disconnectedness and the 'widening gyre' have brought us to nihilism. This seems to be a prophetic statement, as fascism was to sweep the world in the mid-twentieth century. Then Yeats has a moment of epiphany: 'but now I know'. Other eras have been destroyed before. The baby in the 'rocking cradle' created an upheaval that resulted in the end of 'twenty centuries of stony sleep'.

Yeats believed that a **cycle of history** lasted two thousand years in a single evolution of birth, growth, decline and death. All change causes upheaval. The Christian era, with its qualities of innocence, order, maternal love and goodness, is at an end. The new era of the 'rough beast' is about to start. It is pitiless, destructive, violent and murderous. This new era has already begun: 'its hour come round at last'. It is a savage god who is coming, uninvited. The spiral has reversed its motion and is now spinning in the opposite direction. The lack of end rhyme mirrors a world of chaos. Yeats looks back over thousands of years. We are given a thrilling and terrifying prospect from a vast perspective of millennia.

ANALYSIS

Yeats declared that a poet should think like a wise man, but express himself as one of the common people. Write a paragraph in response to this view, using close reference to 'The Second Coming'.

SAMPLE PARAGRAPH

I feel that the themes of stability and anarchy are wisely considered by Yeats. When I look at the events of the mid to late twentieth century from the perspective of the twenty-first century, I see a very prophetic voice warning of the dangers of the cynic, 'lack all conviction', and the fundamentalist fanatic, 'while the worst/Are full of passionate intensity'. The rise of fascism, the Second World War, the Vietnam War, the atom bomb – none of these were known when Yeats wrote this poem in 1919. Things did 'fall apart' and 'darkness' did drop again. However, the human spirit, *Spiritus Mundi*, rose again, and I would suggest that he was wrong to be so gloomy. Out of the turmoil and chaos of the Second World War came a cry. 'Surely some revelation is at hand'. But it was not the 'rough beast' with a 'gaze blank and pitiless as the sun'. Instead we had the foundation of the European Union, which has led to a long peace and stability. So, unlike Yeats's doom-laden prophecy, I think the 'centre' did 'hold'. In my opinion, the references to the Bible, Matthew, 'The Second Coming', and the Book of Revelations, 'I saw a beast', the phrases 'widening gyre', *Spiritus Mundi* and the image of the Sphinx are not the language of the common man. It is very interesting to discover the meaning behind these phrases, but this is not the language of everyday speech. So although I do agree that Yeats did think like a wise man, I feel he was too pessimistic about the human race. I also think that although his expressions are powerful and thought provoking, they are not the language of the common man. This is in keeping with Yeats's view that the nobles and aristocrats should rule, not the masses.

EXAMINER'S COMMENT

This impressive response focused clearly on the task, which was to consider Yeats's wisdom and his ability to express himself as one of the common people. A real sense of individual engagement with the poem came across in this well-argued answer. A grade.

CLASS/HOMEWORK EXERCISES

1. This is a political poem. What kind of political vision does it convey? Illustrate your answer with reference to the text.
2. Copy the table below into your own notes and fill in critical comments about the last two quotations.

Key Quotes

Things fall apart	Yeats believes that civilisation is breaking up and a new, brutish order will be established.
The ceremony of innocence is drowned	This metaphor highlights that the rituals and celebration of goodness represented by the Christian era are swept away by anarchy.
When a vast image out of Spiritus Mundi/ Troubles my sight	The awesome sight that comes from the collective bank of memory of the human race.
Turning and turning in the widening gyre	
Surely the Second Coming is at hand	

Sailing to Byzantium

I

That is no country for old men. The young
In one another's arms, birds in the trees
– Those dying generations – at their song,
The salmon-falls, the mackerel-crowded seas,
Fish, flesh, or fowl, commend all summer long   5
Whatever is begotten, born, and dies.
Caught in that sensual music all neglect
Monuments of unageing intellect.

II

An aged man is but a paltry thing,
A tattered coat upon a stick, unless   10
Soul clap its hands and sing, and louder sing
For every tatter in its mortal dress,
Nor is there singing school but studying
Monuments of its own magnificence;
And therefore I have sailed the seas and come   15
To the holy city of Byzantium.

III

O sages standing in God's holy fire
As in the gold mosaic of a wall,
Come from the holy fire, perne in a gyre,
And be the singing-masters of my soul.   20
Consume my heart away; sick with desire
And fastened to a dying animal
It knows not what it is; and gather me
Into the artifice of eternity.

IV

Once out of nature I shall never take   25
My bodily form from any natural thing,
But such a form as Grecian goldsmiths make

Of hammered gold and gold enamelling
To keep a drowsy Emperor awake;
Or set upon a golden bough to sing   30
To lords and ladies of Byzantium
Of what is past, or passing, or to come.

'the holy city of Byzantium'

GLOSSARY

Sailing to Byzantium: for Yeats, this voyage would be one taken to find perfection. This country only exists in the mind. It is an ideal. The original old city of Byzantium was famous as a centre of religion, art and architecture.

1 *That*: Ireland – all who live there are subject to ageing, decay and death.
3 *dying generations*: opposites are linked to show that in the midst of life is death.
7 *sensual music*: the young are living life to the full through their senses and are neglecting the inner spiritual life of the soul.
9 *paltry thing*: worthless, of no importance. Old age is not valued in Ireland.
10 *tattered coat*: an old man is as worthless as a scarecrow.
10–11 *unless/Soul clap its hands and sing*: man can only break free if he allows his spirit the freedom to express itself.
13–14 *Nor is there ... own magnificence*: all schools of art should study the discipline they teach, while the soul should study the immortal art of previous generations.
17 *O sages*: wise men, cleansed by the holy fire of God.
19–24 *Come ... artifice of eternity*: Yeats asks the sages to teach him the wonders of Byzantium and gather his soul into the perfection of art.
19 *perne in a gyre*: spinning; turning very fast.
22 *fastened to a dying animal*: the soul trapped in a decaying body.
32 *past, or passing, or to come*: in eternity, the golden bird sings of transience (passing time).

• Poetry Focus •

EXPLORATIONS

1. This poem tries to offer a form of escape from old age. Does it succeed? Write a paragraph in response, with support from the text.
2. Why are the monuments of unageing intellect of such importance to Yeats? What does this imply about contemporary Ireland?
3. The poem is defiant in its exploration of eternity. Discuss, using reference or quotation.

STUDY NOTES

> 'Sailing to Byzantium' confronts the universal issue of old age. There is no easy solution to this problem. Yeats found the idea of advancing age repulsive and longed to escape. Here he imagines an ideal place, Byzantium, which allowed all to enjoy eternal works of art. He celebrates what man can create and he bitterly condemns the mortality to which man is subject.

Yeats wrote, 'When Irishmen were illuminating the Book of Kells … Byzantium was the centre of European civilization … so I symbolise the search for the spiritual life by a journey to that city.'

The poet declares the theme in the **first stanza** as he confidently declaims that the world of the senses is not for the old – they must seek another way which is timeless, **a life of the spirit and intellect**. The word 'That' tells us he is looking back, as he has already started his journey. But he is looking back wistfully at the world of the lovers ('the young/In one another's arms') and the world of teeming nature ('The salmon-falls, the mackerel-crowded seas'). The compound words emphasise the dynamism and fertility of the life of the senses, even though he admits the flaw in this wonderful life of plenty is mortality ('Those dying generations'). The life of the senses and nature is governed by the harsh cycle of procreation, life and death.

The poet asserts in the **second stanza** that **what gives meaning to a person is the soul**, 'unless/Soul clap its hands and sing'. Otherwise an elderly man is worthless, 'a paltry thing'. We are given a chilling image of the thin, wasting frame of an old man as a scarecrow in tattered clothes. In contrast, we are shown the wonders of the intellect as the poet tells us that all schools of art study what they compose, what they produce – 'Monuments of unageing intellect'. These works of art are timeless; unlike the body, they are not subject to decay. Thus, music schools study great music and art schools study great paintings. The life of the intellect and spirit must take precedence over the life of the senses. Yeats will no longer listen to the 'sensual music' that is appropriate only for the young, but will study the carefully composed 'music' of classic art.

In Byzantium, the buildings had beautiful mosaics, pictures made with little tiles and inlaid with gold. One of these had a picture of martyrs being burned. Yeats addresses these wise men ('sages') in **stanza three**. He wants them to whirl through time ('perne in a gyre') and come to **teach his soul how to 'sing'**, how to live the life of the spirit. His soul craves this ('sick with desire'), **but it is trapped in the decaying, mortal body** ('fastened to a dying animal'). This is a horrendous image of old age. The soul has lost its identity: 'It knows not what it is'.

He pleads to be saved from this using two interesting verbs, 'Consume' and 'gather'. Both suggest a desire to be taken away. A fire consumes what is put into it and changes the form of the substance. Yeats wants a new body. He pleads to be embraced like a child coming home: 'gather me'. But where will he go? He will journey into the cold world of art, 'the artifice of eternity'. 'Artifice' refers to the skill of those who have created the greatest works of art, but it also means artificial, not real. **Is the poet suggesting that eternity also has a flaw?**

The **fourth stanza** starts confidently as Yeats declares that 'Once out of nature', he will be transformed into the ageless perfect work of art, the **golden bird**. This is the new body for his soul. Now he will sing to the court. But is the court listening? The word 'drowsy' suggests not. Isn't he singing about transience, the passing of time: 'what is past, or passing, or to come'? Has this any relevance in eternity? So, is there a perfect solution to the dilemma of old age?

Yeats raises these questions for our consideration. He has explored this problem by contrasting the abundant life of the young with the 'tattered coat' of old age. He has shown us the golden bird of immortality in opposition to the 'dying animal' of the decaying body. The poet has lulled us with end-rhymes and half-rhymes. He has used groups of threes – 'Fish, flesh, or fowl', 'begotten, born, and dies', 'past, or passing, or to come' – to argue his case. At the end of the poem, do we feel that Yeats genuinely longs for the warm, teeming life of the senses with all its imperfections rather than the cold, disinterested world of the 'artifice of eternity'?

W.B. Yeats

ANALYSIS

'Yeats is often concerned with finding ways of escape from the sorrows and oppressions which are so much a part of life.' What evidence do you find for this statement in 'Sailing to Byzantium'?

SAMPLE PARAGRAPH

I believe that Yeats was preoccupied with the inescapable fact of ageing and death. This poem, 'Sailing to Byzantium', concerns a voyage to perfection. In ordinary life there is no perfection, a fact that Yeats recognises in the phrase 'dying generations'. All must die so that more can be born into the abundant, mortal world of nature. He rages against the weaknesses of old age: an old man is a 'tattered coat upon a stick', 'a paltry thing'. The body is a 'dying animal'. Terrible, grotesque imagery vividly describes the ravages of the ageing process. Yeats intends to turn his back on this and seek immortality, hence his journey to Byzantium. This city, in his opinion, is the perfect city, as it was the cradle of European civilisation and religious philosophy. He wants the figures that are in the golden mosaics to come and instruct him how to live this life of the intellect: 'gather me'. He wants to escape the sorrows and oppressions of ordinary life. Then he paints an idyllic picture of himself, now in the shape of a golden bird, singing his songs. But this world seems cold, 'artifice of eternity', lifeless and a poor contrast to the warm, heaving, teeming 'salmon-falls, mackerel-crowded seas' world of stanza one. I don't believe Yeats has found the perfect solution to the problem of ageing. Is there one?

EXAMINER'S COMMENT

A close reading of the poem is evident in this response to Yeats's search for escape. Engagement is evident in the response and was well supported by quotations. The student showed confidence in the concluding remarks. A grade standard.

CLASS/HOMEWORK EXERCISES

1. Yeats often places himself at the centre of his work. Do you find this to be true in 'Sailing to Byzantium'? Give reasons for your answer.
2. Copy the table below into your own notes and fill in critical comments about the last two quotations.

Key Quotes

That is no country for old men	Yeats feels that Ireland is not a suitable place to live when old.
all neglect/Monuments of unageing intellect	Young people, because they are in the vigour of their youth, are only concerned with living life through their senses, and have no time for matters of the mind or soul.
perne in a gyre	Twist in a spiralling motion. A spiral is an ancient symbol for immortality. The image suggests that Yeats will actively seek spiritual fulfillment.
Into the artifice of eternity	
I shall never take/My bodily form from any natural thing	

from Meditations in Time of Civil War: The Stare's Nest by my Window

W.B. Yeats

The bees build in the crevices
Of loosening masonry, and there
The mother birds bring grubs and flies.
My wall is loosening; honey-bees,
Come build in the empty house of the stare.   5

We are closed in, and the key is turned
On our uncertainty; somewhere
A man is killed, or a house burned,
Yet no clear fact to be discerned:
Come build in the empty house of the stare.   10

A barricade of stone or of wood;
Some fourteen days of civil war;
Last night they trundled down the road
That dead young soldier in his blood:
Come build in the empty house of the stare.   15

We had fed the heart on fantasies,
The heart's grown brutal from the fare;
More substance in our enmities
Than in our love; O honey-bees,
Come build in the empty house of the stare.   20

'days of civil war'

GLOSSARY

Stare is another name for the starling, a bird with distinctive dark brown or greenish-black feathers.
3 *grubs*: larvae of insects.
12 *civil war*: the Irish Civil War (1922–23) between Republicans who fought for full independence and supporters of the Anglo-Irish Treaty.
13 *trundled*: rolled.
17 *fare*: diet (of dreams).
18 *enmities*: disputes; hatred.

EXPLORATIONS

1 Comment on how Yeats creates an atmosphere of concern and insecurity in stanzas two and three.

2 In your opinion, how effective is the symbol of the bees as a civilising force amid all the destruction of war? Support your answer with close reference to the poem.

3 How would you describe the dominant mood of the poem? Is it positive or negative? Refer closely to the text in your answer.

STUDY NOTES

The Irish Civil War prompted Yeats to consider the brutality and insecurity caused by conflict. It also made him reflect on his own identity as part of the Anglo-Irish Ascendancy. The poet wrote elsewhere that he had been shocked and depressed by the fighting during the first months of hostilities, yet he was determined not to grow bitter or to lose sight of the beauty of nature. He wrote this poem after seeing a stare building its nest in a hole beside his window.

Much of the poem is dominated by the images of building and collapse. **Stanza one** introduces this tension between creativity ('bees build') and disintegration ('loosening'). In responding to the bitter civil war, Yeats finds suitable **symbols in the nurturing natural world to express his own hopes**. Addressing the bees, he asks that they 'build in the empty house of the stare'. He is desperately conscious of the political vacuum being presently filled by bloodshed. His desperate cry for help seems heartfelt in tone. There is also a possibility that the poet is addressing himself – he will have to revise his own attitudes to the changing political realities caused by the war.

In **stanza two**, Yeats expresses a sense of being **threatened by the conflict** around him: 'We are closed in'. The use of the plural pronoun suggests a community under siege. He is fearful of the future: 'our uncertainty'. Is the poet reflecting on the threat to his own immediate household or to the once-powerful Anglo-Irish ruling class? The constant rumours of everyday violence are highlighted in the stark descriptions: 'A man is killed, or a house burned'. Such occurrences almost seem routine in the grim reality of war.

Stanza three opens with a **haunting image**, the 'barricade of stone', an enduring symbol of division and hostility. The vehemence and inhumanity of the times is driven home by the stark report of soldiers who 'trundled down the road' and left one 'dead young soldier in his blood'. Such atrocities add greater depth to the plaintive refrain for regeneration: 'Come build in the empty house of the stare'.

In the **final stanza**, Yeats faces up to the root causes of war: 'We had fed the heart on fantasies'. Dreams of achieving independence have led to even greater hatred ('enmities') and intransigence than could have been imagined. It is a tragic irony that the Irish nation has become more divided than ever before. The poet seems despairing as he accepts the failure represented by civil conflict: 'The heart's grown brutal'. It is as though he is reprimanding himself for daring to imagine a brave new world. His **final plea for healing** and reconstruction is strengthened by an emphatic 'O' to show Yeats's depth of feeling: 'O honey-bees,/Come build in the empty house of the stare'.

ANALYSIS

'Images of ruin and renewal are in constant opposition in this poem.' Write a paragraph in response to this statement, supporting your points with reference from the text.

SAMPLE PARAGRAPH

'The Stare's Nest by my Window' is mainly about conflict, and particularly the Irish Civil War. It is not surprising that the poem contains many symbols and images of ruin and destruction. Yeats watches the bees are building a nest in 'loosening masonry' outside his window. It's ironic. Something new is happening among the ruins. The bees are constructing. Building for the future. It is symbolic that something positive is taking place. This is a key theme in the poem. Yeats is hopeful in spite of the war. The poet's use of symbolism contrasts the two forces of ruin and renewal when he says 'build in the empty house'. There are other images of ruin e.g. the 'house burned' and the ruined life of the 'young soldier in his blood'. These images remind us of what happens in wartime. But Yeats seems to argue that we can learn from nature. He hopes that just as the birds take care of their young, Ireland will recover from war. In the future there will be renewal after all the ruin.

EXAMINER'S COMMENT

There are a number of focused points made in this paragraph and there is a reasonable attempt to use supporting references. The expression is disjointed at times and the point about symbolism is repeated unnecessarily. A solid C grade standard.

CLASS/HOMEWORK EXERCISES

1. Repetition is an important feature in this poem. Comment on its effectiveness in enhancing our understanding of the poet's themes.
2. Copy the table below into your own notes and fill in critical comments about the last two quotations.

Key Quotes

The mother birds bring grubs and flies	Details of nurturing in nature are used as a contrast to the background violence and devastation of warfare.
Yet no clear fact to be discerned	Many Irish people were confused by the Civil War and families were sometimes bitterly divided.
Come build in the empty house of the stare	Yeats emphasises the need to rebuild the country after the conflict and establish a new civilised order.
My wall is loosening	
The heart's grown brutal	

• Poetry Focus •

In Memory of Eva Gore-Booth and Con Markiewicz

The light of evening, Lissadell,
Great windows open to the south,
Two girls in silk kimonos, both
Beautiful, one a gazelle.
But a raving autumn shears 5
Blossom from the summer's wreath;
The older is condemned to death,
Pardoned, drags out lonely years
Conspiring among the ignorant.
I know not what the younger dreams – 10
Some vague Utopia – and she seems,
When withered old and skeleton-gaunt,
An image of such politics.
Many a time I think to seek
One or the other out and speak 15
Of that old Georgian mansion, mix
Pictures of the mind, recall
That table and the talk of youth,
Two girls in silk kimonos, both
Beautiful, one a gazelle. 20

Dear shadows, now you know it all,
All the folly of a fight
With a common wrong or right.
The innocent and the beautiful
Have no enemy but time; 25
Arise and bid me strike a match
And strike another till time catch;
Should the conflagration climb,
Run till all the sages know.
We the great gazebo built, 30
They convicted us of guilt;
Bid me strike a match and blow.

'that old Georgian mansion'

GLOSSARY

1 *Lissadell*: the Gore-Booth family home in Co. Sligo.
3 *kimonos*: traditional Japanese robes.
4 *gazelle*: graceful antelope.
5 *shears*: cuts.
9 *Conspiring*: plotting; scheming.
11 *Utopia*: a perfect world.
22 *folly*: foolishness.
28 *conflagration*: blazing inferno.
29 *sages*: philosophers.
30 *gazebo*: ornamental summer house, sometimes seen as a sign of extravagance.

EXPLORATIONS

1 What mood does Yeats create in the first four lines of the poem? Explain how he achieves this mood.
2 Would you agree that this is a poem of contrasts? How does Yeats use contrasts to express his thoughts and feelings? Support your points with relevant reference.
3 What picture of Yeats himself emerges from this poem? Use close reference to the text to support the points you make.

STUDY NOTES

Yeats wrote this poem about the two Gore-Booth sisters shortly after their deaths. He was sixty-two at the time. Eva was a noted campaigner for women's rights and Constance was a revolutionary who took part in the 1916 Rising. She later became the first woman elected to the British House of Commons at Westminster. The poet had once been fascinated by their youthful grace and beauty, but he became increasingly opposed to their political activism. Although the poem is a memorial to the two women, it also reveals Yeats's own views about the changes that had occurred in Ireland over his lifetime.

• Poetry Focus •

W.B. Yeats

Stanza one begins on a nostalgic note, with Yeats recalling a magical summer's evening in the company of the Gore-Booth sisters. The details he remembers suggest **a world of elegance and privilege** in the girls' family home, Lissadell House, overlooking Sligo Bay. 'Great windows' are a reminder of the grandeur to be found in the Anglo-Irish 'Big House'. Eva and Constance are portrayed as being delicately beautiful, their elusive femininity indicated by the exotic 'silk kimonos' they wear. The poet compares one of the girls to 'a gazelle', stylishly poised and graceful.

The abrupt contrast of mood in **line 5** disrupts the tranquil scene. Yeats considers the harsh effects of time and how it changes everything. He describes autumn (personified as an overenthusiastic gardener) as 'raving' and uncontrollable. The metaphor illustrates the way **time destroys** ('shears') the simple perfection of youth ('Blossom'). Typically, Yeats chooses images from the natural world to express his own retrospective outlook.

In **lines 7–13**, the poet shows his **deep contempt** for the involvement of both the Gore-Booth sisters in revolutionary politics. As far as Yeats is concerned, their activism 'among the ignorant' was a great mistake. These beautiful young women wasted their lives for a 'vague Utopia'. The graphic image of one of the girls growing 'withered old and skeleton-gaunt' is also used to symbolise the unattractive political developments of the era. Repulsed by the idea, Yeats retreats into the more sophisticated world of Lissadell's 'old Georgian mansion'.

The **second stanza** is in marked contrast to the first. Yeats addresses the spirits ('shadows') of Eva and Constance. The tone of voice is unclear. It appears to be compassionate, but there is an undertone of weariness as well. He goes on to scold the two women for wasting their lives on 'folly'. Yeats seems angry that their innocence and beauty have been sacrificed for nothing. It is as though he feels **they have betrayed both their own femininity and their social class**. If they had only known it, their one and only enemy was time.

In the **final lines** of the poem, Yeats dramatises his feelings by turning all his **resentment against time** itself. He associates the failed lives of the women with the decay of the Anglo-Irish Ascendancy. The energetic rhythm and repetition reflect his fury as he imagines striking match after match ('And strike another till time catch') and is consumed in a great 'conflagration'. The poet imagines that the significance of this inferno will eventually be understood by those who are wise, the 'sages'. In the last sentence, Yeats considers how 'They' (the enemies of the Anglo-Irish Ascendancy) hastened the end of a grand cultural era in Ireland. The 'great gazebo' is a symbol of the fine houses and gracious living that were slowly disappearing. The poem ends on a defiant note ('Bid me strike a match and blow'), with Yeats inviting the ghosts of Eva and Constance to help him resist the devastating effects of time.

ANALYSIS

To what extent is the poem a lament for the loss of youth and beauty? Refer closely to the text in your answer.

SAMPLE PARAGRAPH

'In Memory of Eva Gore-Booth and Con Markiewicz' is largely focused on the effects of time as an agent of destruction. Yeats begins by describing the two sisters as 'two girls'. I think his nostalgic portrayal of the time he shared with them at Lissadell is filled with regret. He remembers the summer evenings relaxing together 'and the talk of youth'. Yeats contrasts the beautiful girls in their silk kimonos with the way they were in their later years – 'withered old and skeleton-gaunt'. The image is startling, evidence of how he views the ravages of time. It is all the more shocking when compared with the exquisite kimonos – symbols of lost beauty. I think Yeats is also regretful of his own lost youth. At the end of the poem, he shows his anger at ageing and argues that youth has 'no enemy but time'.

EXAMINER'S COMMENT

Although short, this is a well-focused paragraph which directly addresses the question. The references and quotes are carefully chosen and show a clear engagement with the poem. The use of the unnecessary 'I think' weakens the expression slightly. Otherwise, a good B grade response.

CLASS/HOMEWORK EXERCISES

1. From your reading of the poem, how would you describe Yeats's true feelings towards the two women? Support the points you make with reference and/or quotation.
2. Copy the table below into your own notes and fill in critical comments about the last two quotations.

W.B. Yeats

Key Quotes

The light of evening, Lissadell, / Great windows open to the south	These beautiful opening lines recreate the leisurely lifestyle associated with the Anglo-Irish gentry, the class to which Yeats belonged.
That table and the talk of youth	This is another reminder of the potential the sophisticated Gore-Booth sisters once had.
All the folly of a fight	In much of his poetry, Yeats was highly critical of the revolutionary activism of his time. This is underlined by the emphatic alliteration.
Two girls in silk kimonos	
Arise and bid me strike a match	

Swift's Epitaph

Swift has sailed into his rest;
Savage indignation there
Cannot lacerate his breast.
Imitate him if you dare,
World-besotted traveller; he   5
Served human liberty.

'Swift's Epitaph'

GLOSSARY

Swift: Jonathan Swift, satirist and clergyman, author of *Gulliver's Travels* and dean of St Patrick's Cathedral. The original inscription in Latin is on his memorial in the cathedral. Yeats liked to spend time there.
Epitaph: inscription for a tomb or memorial.
1 *his rest*: suggestion of afterlife; death is not an end.
2 *Savage indignation*: the driving force of Swift's satirical work. He believed in a society where wrong was punished and good rewarded.
3 *lacerate*: cut; tear.
5 *World-besotted*: obsessed with travelling, or with material concerns rather than spiritual matters.
5–6 *he | Served human liberty*: Yeats believed Swift served the liberty of the intellect, not liberty for the common people. Yeats associated democracy with organised mobs of ignorant people.

• Poetry Focus •

W.B. Yeats

EXPLORATIONS
1 How would you describe the tone of this poem?
2 Comment on the poet's use of the verb 'lacerate'. What do you think Yeats is trying to convey?

STUDY NOTES

> 'Swift's Epitaph' is a translation from the original Latin epitaph composed by Swift for himself. Yeats adds a new first line to the original. He regarded this epitaph as the 'greatest ... in history'.

W.B. Yeats admired Swift, who was proud and solitary and belonged to the Anglo-Irish tradition, as did Yeats himself. He regarded the Anglo-Irish as superior. He once said, 'We have created most of the modern literature of this country. We have created the best of its political intelligence'. **Yeats's additional first line** to the epitaph conveys a dignified sailing into the spiritual afterlife by the deceased Swift. The rest of the poem is a **translation** from the Latin original. Swift is now free from all the negative reactions he was subjected to when alive: 'Savage indignation there/Cannot lacerate his breast'. Swift's self-portrait conveys the impression of a man of fierce **independence and pride**. 'Imitate him if you dare' is the challenge thrown down like a gauntlet to the reader to try to be like him. 'World-besotted traveller' can be read as a man who has travelled extensively in his imagination, as well as in reality. His contribution to humanity is summed up in the final sentence: 'he/Served human liberty'. **He freed the artist** from the masses so that the artist could 'make liberty visible'. The tone of this short, compressed poem is proud and defiant, like Swift.

ANALYSIS

What impression of Swift do you get from this poem by Yeats? Write a paragraph in response, supporting your views with reference to the text.

SAMPLE PARAGRAPH

I thought that Swift was a confident, fearless man who dared to voice his own truth. The tone of the poem, from its opening, 'Swift has sailed into his rest', suggests a man who knew what he was doing and did it with style. It suggests a spiritual man, 'into his rest'. He is embarking on an afterlife of some sort. He was a man who braved the censure of the world, 'Savage indignation there/Cannot lacerate his breast'. He dared to say what he felt he had to say. A challenge is thrown down to the reader, 'Imitate him if you dare'. Obviously, both Swift and Yeats considered that Swift would be a hard act to follow. The phrase 'world-besotted traveller' could mean that the poet considered that modern man was too obsessed with material possessions, while Swift was concerned with loftier matters such as the moral good. The final sentence, 'he/Served human liberty', states that he improved the human condition by making us all free. This is where I, as a twenty-first-century reader, part company with the epitaph. Swift did not fight for freedom as we understand it. It could be argued that he only believed in liberty for a select few, the Anglo-Irish Protestants. Yeats's tone is one of admiration for this courageous man, but modern man would not agree with this elitist view of freedom for a select group. Also the confident challenge to the reader to match Swift 'if you dare' comes across to me as arrogance. While I admire Swift's fearlessness, I do not admire his elitism or arrogance.

EXAMINER'S COMMENT

An original A grade response to the question. The paragraph raises interesting discussion points about both writers. There is detailed support throughout and a fluent control of language in arguing the case vigorously.

CLASS/HOMEWORK EXERCISES

1. Is Yeats's use of the sailing metaphor effective? Briefly explain your answer.
2. Copy the table below into your own notes and fill in critical comments about the last two quotations.

Key Quotes

Swift has sailed into his rest	Swift has now entered the next life. The tone reflects Yeats's admiration and respect.
Savage indignation there/ Cannot lacerate his breast	He is free from criticism now. Ironically, Swift's own savage criticism is now also at rest.
Imitate him if you dare	A challenge is given to the reader. Is the tone confrontational or superior?
World-besotted traveller	
he/ Served human liberty	

An Acre of Grass

W.B. Yeats

Picture and book remain,
An acre of green grass
For air and exercise,
Now strength and body goes;
Midnight, an old house   5
Where nothing stirs but a mouse.

My temptation is quiet.
Here at life's end
Neither loose imagination,
Nor the mill of the mind   10
Consuming its rag and bone,
Can make the truth known.

Grant me an old man's frenzy.
Myself must I remake
Till I am Timon and Lear   15
Or that William Blake
Who beat upon the wall
Till Truth obeyed his call;

A mind Michael Angelo knew
That can pierce the clouds   20
Or inspired by frenzy
Shake the dead in their shrouds;
Forgotten else by mankind
An old man's eagle mind.

'An acre of green grass'

GLOSSARY

2 *acre*: the secluded garden of Yeats's home, where he spent his final years.
5 *an old house*: the house was in Rathfarnham, Co. Dublin.
9 *loose imagination*: vague, unfocused ideas.
13 *frenzy*: wildly excited state.
15 *Timon and Lear*: two of Shakespeare's elderly tragic heroes, both of whom raged against the world.
16 *William Blake*: English visionary poet and painter (1757–1827).
19 *Michael Angelo*: Michelangelo, Italian Renaissance artist (1475–1564).
22 *shrouds*: burial garments.

EXPLORATIONS

1 How does Yeats create a mood of calm and serenity in the opening stanza?
2 Briefly explain the change of tone in stanza three.

STUDY NOTES

Written in 1936 when Yeats was seventy-one, the poet expresses his resentment towards ageing gracefully. Instead, he will dedicate himself to seeking wisdom through frenzied creativity. People sometimes take a narrow view of the elderly and consider them completely redundant. In Yeats's case, he is determined not to let old age crush his spirit.

Stanza one paints a picture of retirement as a surrender to death. Yeats's life has been reduced to suit his basic needs. 'Picture and book' might refer to the poet's memories. Physically weak, he feels like a prisoner whose enclosed garden area is for 'air and exercise'. There is an underlying **feeling of alienation and inactivity**: 'nothing stirs'.

In stanza two, the poet says that it would be easy to give in to the stereotypical image of placid contentment: 'My temptation is quiet', especially since old age ('life's end') has weakened his creative powers. Yeats admits that his 'loose imagination' is not as sharp as it was when he was in his prime. He no longer finds immediate inspiration ('truth') in everyday experiences, which he compares to life's 'rag and bone'.

The third stanza opens on a much more dramatic and forceful note as the poet confronts his fears: 'Grant me an old man's frenzy'. Yeats's personal prayer is totally lacking in meekness. Instead, he urges himself to focus enthusiastically on his own creative purpose – 'frenzy'. **He pledges to 'remake' himself** in the image of such heroic figures as Timon, Lear and William Blake. The passionate tone and run-on lines add to his sense of commitment to his art.

In **stanza four**, Yeats develops **his spirited pursuit of meaningful old age** by reflecting on 'A mind Michael Angelo knew'. The poet is stimulated and encouraged to follow the great artist's example and 'pierce the clouds'. The image suggests the daring power of imagination to lift the spirit in the search for truth and beauty. The final lines build to a climax as Yeats imagines the joys of an 'old man's eagle mind'. Such intense creativity can 'Shake the dead' and allow the poet to continue experiencing life to its fullest.

ANALYSIS

Based on your reading of the poem, comment on Yeats's response to old age. Refer to the text in your answer.

SAMPLE PARAGRAPH

Yeats takes a highly unusual approach to ageing in 'An Acre of Grass'. He seems to be happy to sit reading in his quiet 'acre of grass'. Everything seems to be very organised, a little too organised for his liking. In the first few lines, we get a picture of someone close to second childhood, with his 'picture and book'. Late at night, he is awake and feels that 'nothing stirs but a mouse'. This is like the mind of a little child and it is what Yeats rebels against. He does not want to fade away. He really wants to keep being a poet and seek truth. To him, it is 'an old man's frenzy'. This suggests that he would prefer to be thought of as mad, but to keep producing his poems rather than fade away quietly. He wants to be like King Lear, the old king in Shakespeare's play who fought to the bitter end. Yeats wants to live life to the full, not fade away quietly. He wants to write his poetry and make use of his active mind until he takes his last breath. I admire his energy even though he seems a grumpy old man. His tone is fierce and defiant throughout most of the poem. He will not fade away on his acre of grass.

EXAMINER'S COMMENT

There is some very good discussion in this paragraph and a clear sense of individual engagement. The idea of Yeats rejecting second childhood is well supported. The style of writing lacks control at times and there are some awkward expressions and repetition ('fade away'). An average C grade.

CLASS/HOMEWORK EXERCISES

1. How would you describe the structure of this poem? Formal or informal? Regular or irregular? How does the poem's structure and form emphasise Yeats's message about old age?
2. Copy the table below into your own notes and fill in critical comments about the last two quotations.

Key Quotes

Midnight, an old house/Where nothing stirs but a mouse	Yeats creates an atmosphere of stillness and emptiness associated with lonely old age.
Here at life's end	Central to the poem is Yeats's awareness of death, which makes him determined to make the most of life.
the mill of the mind/Consuming its rag and bone	Yeats distils laanguage in this powerful observation which contains alliteration, personification and metaphor.
Grant me an old man's frenzy	
An old man's eagle mind	

• Poetry Focus •

from **Under Ben Bulben**

W.B. Yeats

V

Irish poets, learn your trade,
Sing whatever is well made,
Scorn the sort now growing up
All out of shape from toe to top,
Their unremembering hearts and heads   5
Base-born products of base beds.
Sing the peasantry, and then
Hard-riding country gentlemen,
The holiness of monks, and after
Porter-drinkers' randy laughter;   10
Sing the lords and ladies gay
That were beaten into the clay
Through seven heroic centuries;
Cast your mind on other days
That we in coming days may be   15
Still the indomitable Irishry.

VI

Under bare Ben Bulben's head
In Drumcliff churchyard Yeats is laid,
An ancestor was rector there
Long years ago, a church stands near,   20
By the road an ancient cross.
No marble, no conventional phrase;
On limestone quarried near the spot
By his command these words are cut:

      Cast a cold eye   25
      On life, on death.
      Horseman, pass by!

GLOSSARY
2 *whatever is well made*: great art.
6 *base*: low; unworthy.
16 *indomitable*: invincible; unbeatable.
17 *Under bare Ben Bulben's head*: defiant symbol of the famous mountain.
19 *ancestor*: the poet's great-grandfather.
27 *Horseman*: possibly a symbolic figure from local folklore.

'Under bare Ben Bulben's head'

EXPLORATIONS

1 Comment on the tone used by Yeats in giving advice to other writers. Refer to the text in your answer.
2 From your reading of the poem, explain the kind of 'Irishry' that Yeats wishes to see celebrated in poetry. Support the points you make with reference or quotation.
3 Describe the mood of Drumcliff churchyard as visualised by the poet. Use close reference to the text to show how Yeats uses language to create this mood.

STUDY NOTES

This was one of Yeats's last poems. Sections V and VI of the elegy sum up his personal views on the future of Irish poetry and also include the enigmatic epitaph he composed for his own gravestone. Using art as a gateway to spiritual fulfillment is characteristic of the poet.

Section V is a hard-hitting address by Yeats to his contemporaries and all the poets who will come after him. He encourages them to set the highest 'well made' standards for their work. His uncompromisingly negative view of contemporary writing ('out of shape from toe to top') is quickly clarified. The reason why modern literature is in such a state of confusion is that the poets' 'unremembering hearts and heads' have **lost touch with tradition**. The formality and discipline of great classic poetry have been replaced by unstructured writing and free verse. The authoritative tone becomes even more scathing as Yeats castigates the inferiority of his peers as 'Base-born products'.

It is not only intellectual artistic tradition that the poet admires; he finds another valuable tradition in the legends and myths of old Ireland. Yeats urges his fellow writers to 'Sing the peasantry'. But he also advises them to **absorb**

other cultural traditions. Here he includes the 'Hard-riding country gentlemen' of his own Anglo-Irish class and the 'holiness of monks' – those who seek truth through ascetic or spiritual means. Even the more sensuous 'randy laughter' of 'Porter-drinkers' can be inspirational. For Yeats, the peasant and aristocratic traditions are equally worth celebrating. Irish history is marked by a combination of joy, heroism, defeat and resilience. Yet despite (or perhaps because of) his harsh criticism of the present generation, there is little doubt about the poet's passionate desire to encourage new writing that would reflect the true greatness of 'indomitable Irishry'.

Section VI is a great deal less dogmatic. Writing in the third person, Yeats describes his final resting place in Drumcliff. The voice is **detached and dignified**. Using a series of unadorned images, he takes us to the simple churchyard at the foot of Ben Bulben. The mountain stands as a proud symbol of how our unchanging silent origins outlive human tragedy. It is to his Irish roots that the poet ultimately wants to return. His wishes are modest but curt – 'No marble'. Keen to avoid the well-worn headstone inscriptions, Yeats provides his own incisive epitaph. The three short lines are enigmatic and balance opposing views, typical of so much of his poetry. The poet's last warning ('*Cast a cold eye*') reminds us to live measured lives based on a realistic understanding of the cycle of life and death. The beautiful Christian setting, subdued tone and measured rhythm all contribute to the quiet dignity of Yeats's final farewell.

ANALYSIS

Some people have criticised this poem as 'a bitter old man's snobbish rant'. Write your response to this comment, supporting your views with reference to the text.

SAMPLE PARAGRAPH

It's easy to see why Yeats could be accused of being elitist and superior. As he nears death, he is clearly not concerned with political correctness. He knows his own worth as the leading Irish writer of his times. He gets straight to the point in advising younger poets – 'learn your trade'. If I was an unpublished writer, I would take him seriously, rather than feeling precious. Yeats does not suffer fools easily and he has no respect for shoddy work that is 'out of shape'. His tone can be harsh, even shrill on occasions, but he is stressing a basic lesson that good writing must be disciplined. Rather than seeing him as someone who is ranting, I appreciate the way Yeats shows his interest in standards. His attitude is actually inclusive. He wants young poets to learn from every source available to them – sacred texts, the Protestant and peasant Catholic traditions, and from the 'Porter-drinkers' of Ireland. I can see no bitterness here. His own funeral instructions are actually humble. He does not demand a hero courageous tomb, just a simple plot in a country graveyard. To me, Yeats comes across as a man who is neither arrogant nor snobbish, but as a legendary writer concerned about Irish literature.

EXAMINER'S COMMENT

This is a very spirited and well-sustained personal response that reflects a clear viewpoint. Points are supported robustly with apt quotations and the arguments range over the whole poem. In the main, expression is fluent and controlled. An impressive A grade standard.

CLASS/HOMEWORK EXERCISES

1 Is Yeats's epitaph in keeping with the views he expresses throughout the rest of the poem? Explain your answer using reference to the text.
2 Copy the table below into your own notes and fill in critical comments about the last two quotations.

Key Quotes

Irish poets, learn your trade	Yeats is enthusiastic about the need for poets to return to the formal, classical tradition that will again celebrate Ireland's heroic and spiritual values.
Base-born products of base beds	The poet is contemptuous of modern poetry, much of which he believed came from inferior writers. Repetition emphasises his disdain.
Sing the lords and ladies gay	Yeats associated aesthetic values and the place of art in society with the gracious lifestyle of the Anglo-Irish class.
By the road an ancient cross	
Cast a cold eye/ On life, on death	

• Poetry Focus •

W.B. Yeats

Politics

'In our time the destiny of man presents its meanings in political terms.' – Thomas Mann

How can I, that girl standing there,
My attention fix
On Roman or on Russian
Or on Spanish politics,
Yet here's a travelled man that knows　　　　　　　5
What he talks about,
And there's a politician
That has both read and thought,
And maybe what they say is true
Of war and war's alarms,　　　　　　　　　　　　10
But O that I were young again
And held her in my arms.

'But O that I were young again/And held her in my arms'

GLOSSARY

Politics: winning and using power to govern society.
Thomas Mann was a German novelist who argued that the future of man was determined by states and governments.
3–4 *On Roman or on Russian/Or on Spanish politics*: a reference to the political upheavals of Europe in the 1930s.

EXPLORATIONS

1 This poem suggests that politics are not important. Does the poet convince you? Write a paragraph in response, with reference to the text.
2 Where does the language used in the poem convey a sense of deep longing? How effective is this?

STUDY NOTES

'Politics' is a satire written in 1939 when Yeats was seventy-three in response to a magazine article. He said it was based on 'a moment of meditation'.

A **satire** uses ridicule to expose foolishness. A magazine article praised Yeats for his 'public' work. The poet was delighted with this word, as one of his aims had always been to 'move the common people'. However, the article went on to say that Yeats should have used this 'public' voice to address public issues such as politics. Yeats disagreed, as he had always regarded politics as dishonest and superficial. He thought professional politicians manipulated through 'false news'. This is evident from the ironic comment, 'And maybe what they say is true'. Here we see the poet's indifference to these matters.

This poem addresses **real truths**, the proper material for poems, the universal experience of **human relationships**, not the infinite abstractions that occupied politicians ('war and war's alarms'). Big public events, Yeats is suggesting, are not as important as love. The girl in the poem is more important than all the politics in the world: 'How can I ... My attention fix/On Roman or on Russian/Or on Spanish politics'? So Yeats is overthrowing the epigraph at the beginning of the poem where the novelist Thomas Mann is stating that people should be concerned with political matters. Politics is the winning and using of power to govern the state. Yeats is adopting the persona of the distracted lover who is unable to focus on the tangled web of European politics in the 1930s. This poem was to be placed in his last poetry collection, almost like a farewell, as he states again that what he desires is youth and love.

But this poem can also give another view. Is the 'she' in the poem Ireland? Yeats has addressed public issues in poems such as 'Easter, 1916' and 'September 1913' and he was already a senator in the Irish government. As usual, he leaves us with questions as he draws us through this deceptively simple poem with its **ever-changing tones** that range from the questioning opening to mockery, doubt and finally longing. The **steady rhyme** (the second line rhymes with the fourth and so on) drives the poem forward to its emphatic **closing wish**, the cry of an old man who wishes to recapture his youth and lost love.

ANALYSIS

Do you agree with Yeats that only youth and love matter? Discuss, using reference to the poem.

SAMPLE PARAGRAPH

I think Yeats is expressing a deep-seated desire in all of us. We all want to be concerned with our own lives ('My attention fix'), not on the mess that the political world seems to be in, 'Roman or on Russian/Or on Spanish politics'. It is the same today. How often have we turned off the news in disgust or because we just couldn't take any more 'Of war and war's alarms'? And yet I would like to suggest another view on this. We get the governments we deserve. Democracy is fragile when good people are inattentive. So although I agree with Yeats's sentiments and can fully understand his closing wish, 'But O that I were young again/And held her in my arms', I feel that we have to sometimes safeguard the destiny of man. We are the generation that is on watch now for the protection of the environment and the safety of humanity. I think Thomas Mann has a point as he says, 'In our time the destiny of man presents its meanings in political terms'.

EXAMINER'S COMMENT

The student has engaged personally with the question and has presented a considered argument using relevant quotations effectively. The answer reads well and adjectives (such as 'fragile' and 'inattentive') are well chosen. Grade A.

CLASS/HOMEWORK EXERCISES

1. Comment on the rhythm of the poem, paying particular attention to the use of run-on lines.
2. Copy the table below into your own notes and fill in critical comments about the last two quotations.

Key Quotes

How can I, that girl standing there,/My attention fix	The poet is declaring that his attention is on his personal concerns, rather than public concerns such as politics.
And maybe what they say is true/Of war and war's alarms	The poet is unsure of the truth of politicians' speeches.
On Roman or on Russian	The alliterative 'r' emphasises Yeats's tone of frustration.
And there's a politician/That has both read and thought	
But O that I were young again/And held her in my arms	

LEAVING CERT SAMPLE ESSAY

W.B. Yeats

> **Q** Write an article for a school magazine introducing the poetry of W.B. Yeats to Leaving Certificate students. Tell them what he wrote about and explain what you liked about his writing, suggesting some poems that you think they would enjoy reading. Support your points by reference to the poetry by Yeats that you studied.

MARKING SCHEME GUIDELINES

Candidates are free to adopt a register they consider appropriate to the task. The task contains three closely related elements, which may be addressed separately or together. It is not necessary that these elements be given equal treatment.
- What he wrote about (themes, concerns, subject matter).
- What you liked about his writing.
- Suggest enjoyable poems.

Reward responses that show clear evidence of engagement with the poems and/or poet.

Some of the following areas might be addressed:
- Political and personal perspective of the poems.
- Variety of the themes.
- Strength of Yeats's vision.
- Depth and range of his feelings.
- Features of style, such as language, imagery, symbolism, sound, etc.

SAMPLE ESSAY
(Introduction to Yeats)

1 *Allow me to introduce to you a man of passion with a love for art and a great admiration for Ireland's heroes. Seamus Heaney described this man as 'a dreamer, an idealist'. This man, just like many of you, longed for a retreat from all the pressures of civilisation, and I feel we can all identify with him. This man is W.B. Yeats.*

• Poetry Focus •

2 Many of you today may be feeling fed up with school, home, life in general. Yeats felt the same way and longed to escape oppressive city life. This retreat from the irksome routine of the everyday is evoked in Yeats's most well-known poem, 'The Lake Isle of Innisfree'. After you have read these lines, close your eyes and imagine the scene, the colours, 'midnight's all a glimmer, and noon a purple glow'. Imagine the sounds: 'I hear lake water lapping with low sounds by the shore'. The tranquil atmosphere is summoned by 'and peace comes dropping slow'. Suddenly we are in an idyllic paradise as the soothing effect of the lines quietens our frazzled brains. Yeats stored this hypnotic image in his mind and returned to it every time he needed escape, 'While I stand on the roadway, or on the pavements grey'. He heard it in 'the deep heart's core'. We all, like Yeats, have a place or long to have a place, either physical or mental, that we retreat to when the pressure gets too much.

3 We are all Celtic Cubs, and if the title was missing from 'September 1913', we could read this poem as a scathing attack on New Ireland, avaricious, selfish and materialistic. But Yeats wrote this poem primarily in response to the 1913 lock-out and the failure to fund the Hugh Lane Gallery with its collection of wonderful modern art. The anger spits off the page as he graphically describes these self-centred people concerned with outward appearances only. The phrase 'fumble in a greasy till' shows their dependence on money. Equally depressing is their attitude to religion which does not sustain them, but 'dries the marrow from the bone'. O'Leary, the Irish Fenian poet, is what an Irishman should be, someone who thought of his country, not himself. The refrain 'It's with O'Leary in the grave' drives this message home, as Yeats gets angrier ('Was it for this?') at the inability of the contemporary Irish to understand the bigger picture. Bitterly he resigns himself to the fact that his contemporaries just don't understand and he warns them not to judge these heroes by their own standards, 'But let them be ... They're with O'Leary in the grave'.

4 'Easter, 1916' is, I admit, a difficult poem, but it is worth the struggle. I particularly liked the fact that Yeats was big enough to admit he was wrong. The people he had condemned in the previous poem were capable of great sacrifices and indeed 'A terrible beauty' was born. Even Major MacBride who had married Maud Gonne, the love of Yeats's life, 'A drunken vainglorious lout', was included in 'the song'. The structure of the poem is very clever, four verses, two with twenty-four lines, two with sixteen lines, commemorating the date of the rebellion, the twenty-fourth of April 1916. Yeats admires the revolutionary spirit and their dream for independence for Ireland. But his choice of 'the stone' as a symbol of this spirit warns of danger. Sacrifice can turn a heart to stone. When is enough enough? 'O when may it suffice?' We see this every day in current political struggles. The poem ends with a litany, a list of holy names, of the dead: they are 'changed' and will be remembered 'wherever green is worn'.

5. My personal favourite is 'Sailing to Byzantium'. Yeats wrote some of his best poetry in his final years, as he raged against old age and death. He writes from an unusual perspective, looking back as he embarks on a journey. He realises he has to go because 'That is no country for old men'. The alliteration shows a fertile land teeming with passionate young life. 'Fish, flesh, or fowl, commend all summer long/Whatever is begotten, born, and dies'. Pitiful images describe old age, 'A tattered coat upon a stick', something that is only used to scare birds. Again, as in our first poem, Yeats longs to escape. He decides that he will not have a body that is natural because then it is subject to age. Instead, he chooses one that is an 'artifice'. But even in Paradise there is a problem. The emperor is 'drowsy' to whom Yeats, in his new form of a golden bird, sings. His heart really wishes to be with 'the young/In one another's arms'. I thought it was very interesting how a man could write so openly about growing old. It has very modern echoes when we see the acres of media space devoted to actually preventing ageing!

6. Before reading this article, you probably had a stereotypical image of Yeats as a serious young man staring sternly out through old-fashioned glasses. Who would have guessed the spirit and passion that lay beneath the stern exterior? Truly Yeats is a poet who sings to us 'Of what is past, or passing, or to come' and we are wide awake to listen.

(approx. 880 words)

Grade: A1
P = 15/15
C = 15/15
L = 15/15
M = 5/5
Total = 50/50

• Poetry Focus •

EXAMINER'S COMMENT

The candidate fulfilled the task eloquently and displayed a robust personal engagement with the poetry. The answer ranged widely to discuss Yeats's subject matter, what was interesting about the writing and the most enjoyable poems. Excellent use of accurate quotation throughout. A very impressive response.

SAMPLE LEAVING CERT QUESTIONS ON YEATS'S POETRY (45–50 MINUTES)

1. Give your personal estimation of the poetry of W.B. Yeats. Support your answer with reference to the poems on your course.

2. Consider the versions of Ireland that emerge from Yeats's poems. Do these versions form a consistent picture or not? Support your answer with close reference to the poems.

3. If you were asked to give a public reading of some of Yeats's poems, which ones would you choose? Give reasons for your choices, supporting them by reference to the poems by Yeats that you have studied.

SAMPLE ESSAY PLAN (Q1)

Give your personal estimation of the poetry of W.B. Yeats. Support your answer with reference to the poems on your course.

- *Intro*: A personal response is required; mention both content and style in the response. Public and personal poems are interesting and thought provoking.
- *Point 1*: 'September 1913' – public poem, accusatory. Note the changing refrain, litany, rhetorical questions, bitter tone, nostalgic view of Irish history.
- *Point 2*: 'Easter, 1916' – another public poem, an attempt to answer questions about the Rising. All had changed. Yeats admits he was wrong.
- *Point 3*: 'The Wild Swans at Coole' – autumnal retrospection as he realises how his life had changed in 19 years. Laments loss of youth, passion and love.
- *Point 4*: 'Sailing to Byzantium' – theme of ageing, use of contrast to convey theme.

	Declamatory opening, uncertainty a sign of his humanity.
Conclusion:	Yeats – ideal past contrasted with unsatisfactory present, attitude to Irish patriotism, escape, ageing. Raises questions rather than providing answers.

EXERCISE

Develop one of the above points into a paragraph.

POINT 4 – SAMPLE PARAGRAPH

I find the poem 'Sailing to Byzantium' very intriguing. Here was a man who hated the weaknesses brought on by old age: 'An aged man is but a paltry thing'. Yet with passion and fire, he defies time: 'Once out of nature I shall never take/My bodily form from any natural thing'. The rhythmic phrasing of threes conveys the natural harmony of youth and fertility: 'Fish, flesh, or fowl'. This is the world of which Yeats wants to be a part, 'The young in one another's arms'. But that is not life. He presents us with the contrasting truth as he states, 'That is no country for old men'. Again, contrast is used as the beauty of 'artifice', 'the gold mosaic of a wall' is lined up against the brute reality of the soul 'fastened to a dying animal'. Through his clever contrasts, the poet explores the dilemma of ageing, which will come to us all, even though at seventeen it seems very remote to me. I was also interested in Yeats's discovery of a flaw in Paradise. Now Yeats is immortal as his soul has taken the bodily form of a golden bird, 'such a form as Grecian goldsmiths make/Of hammered gold and gold enamelling'. However, the audience for his songs/poems, the Emperor, is 'drowsy'. He is not paying attention. Yeats is now raising the question: Is Paradise, 'artifice', all that it is supposed to be? Who will listen as Yeats sings of the great truths, 'Of what is past, or passing, or to come'? All great poets raise questions about life and existence for us to consider. Yeats is no exception.

EXAMINER'S COMMENT

As part of a full essay answer, this is a competent A grade paragraph which offers a personal response firmly rooted in the text. The paragraph centres on the use of contrast used by Yeats to explore ageing, and both style and content are examined effectively. Very well supported by suitable quotes.

• Poetry Focus •

Last Words

'He had this marvellous gift for beating the scrap metal of the day-to-day life into a ringing bell.'
Seamus Heaney

'Yeats's poetry is simple and eloquent to the heart.'
Robert Louis Stevenson

'I have spent my life saying the same thing in different ways.'
W.B. Yeats, writing to his wife

Glossary of Common Literary Terms

alliteration: the use of the same letter at the beginning of each word or stressed syllable in a line of verse, e.g. 'boilers bursting'.

assonance: the use of the same vowel sound in a group of words, e.g. 'bleared, smeared with toil'.

aubade: a celebratory morning song, sometimes lamenting the parting of lovers.

blank verse: unrhymed iambic pentameter, e.g. 'These waters, rolling from their mountain-springs'.

conceit: an elaborate image or far-fetched comparison, e.g. 'This flea is you and I, and this/Our marriage bed'.

couplet: two successive lines of verse, usually rhymed and of the same metre, e.g. 'So long as men can breathe or eyes can see,/So long lives this, and this gives life to thee'.

elegy: a mournful poem, usually for the dead, e.g. 'Sleep in a world your final sleep has woken'.

emotive language: language designed to arouse an emotional response in the reader, e.g. 'For this that all that blood was shed?'

epiphany: a moment of insight or understanding, e.g. 'Somebody loves us all'.

free verse: unrhymed and unmetred poetry, often used by modern poets, e.g. 'but the words are shadows and you cannot hear me./You walk away and I cannot follow'.

imagery: descriptive language or word-pictures, especially appealing to the senses, e.g. 'He was speckled with barnacles,/fine rosettes of lime'.

irony: when one thing is said and the opposite is meant, e.g. 'For men were born to pray and save'.

lyric: short musical poem expressing feeling.

metaphor: image that compares two things without using the words 'like' or 'as', e.g. 'I am gall, I am heartburn'.

onomatopoeia: the sound of the word imitates or echoes the sound being described, e.g. 'The murmurous haunt of flies on summer eves'.

paradox: a statement that on the surface appears self-contradictory, e.g. 'I shall have written him one/poem maybe as cold/ And passionate as the dawn'.

persona: the speaker or voice in the poem. This is not always the poet, e.g. 'I know that I shall meet my fate/Somewhere among the clouds above'.

personification: where the characteristics of an animate or living being are given to something inanimate, e.g. 'The yellow fog that rubs its back upon the window panes'.

rhyme: identical sound of words, usually at the end of lines of verse, e.g. 'I get down on my knees and do what must be done/And kiss Achilles' hand, the killer of my son'.

rhythm: the beat or movement of words, the arrangement of stressed and unstressed, short and long syllables in a line of poetry, e.g. 'I will arise and go now, and go to Innisfree'.

sestina: a six-stanza, six-line poem with the same six end words occurring throughout. The final stanza contains these six words. '*Time to plant tears,* says the almanac:/The grandmother sings to the marvellous stove/and the child draws another inscrutable house'.

sibilance: the whispering, hissing 's' sound, e.g. 'Singest of summer in full-throated ease'.

sonnet: a fourteen-line poem. The Petrarchan or Italian sonnet is divided into eight lines (octave) which present a problem or situation. The remaining six lines (sestet) resolve the problem or present another view of the situation. The Shakespearean sonnet is divided into three quatrains and concludes with a rhyming couplet, either summing up what preceded or reversing it.

symbol: a word or phrase representing something other than itself, e.g. 'A tattered coat upon a stick'.

theme: the central idea or message in a poem.

tone: the type of voice or attitude used by the poet towards his or her subject, e.g. 'O but it is dirty'.

villanelle: a five-stanza poem of three lines each, with a concluding quatrain, using only two end rhyming words throughout, e.g. 'I am just going outside and may be some time,/At the heart of the ridiculous, the sublime'.